CURRICULUM DEVELOPMENT
A Guide to Practice

Fifth Edition

Jon Wiles
University of South Florida at St. Petersburg
Joseph Bondi
University of South Florida at Tampa

Merrill
an imprint of Prentice Hall
Upper Saddle River, New Jersey   *Columbus, Ohio*

Library of Congress Cataloging-in-Publication Data

Wiles, Jon.

  Curriculum development : a guide to practice / Jon Wiles, Joseph Bondi.—5th ed.
    p.   cm.
  Includes bibliographical references and indexes.
  ISBN 0-13-262098-7
    1. Curriculum planning—United States. 2. Education—United States—Curricula.
  Bondi, Joseph. II. Title.
  LB2806.15.W55   1998
  375'.001—dc21   97-16967
                                                                           CIP

Editor: Debra A. Stollenwerk
Production Editor: Mary Harlan
Design Coordinator: Karrie M. Converse
Text Designer: Ed Horcharik
Cover Designer: Brian Deep
Production Manager: Laura Messerly
Electronic Text Management: Marilyn Wilson Phelps, Matthew Williams, Karen L. Bretz, Tracey
    B. Ward
Copy Editor: Colleen Brosnan
Illustrations: Tracey B. Ward
Director of Marketing: Kevin Flanagan
Marketing Manager: Suzanne Stanton
Advertising/Marketing Coordinator: Julie Shough

This book was set in Aldine by Prentice Hall and was printed and bound by R. R. Donnelley &
Sons Company. The cover was printed by R. R. Donnelley & Sons Company.

© 1998, 1993 by Prentice-Hall, Inc.
Simon & Schuster/A Viacom Company
Upper Saddle River, New Jersey 07458

Earlier editions © 1989 by Macmillan Publishing Company; 1984, 1979 by Merrill Publishing
Company.

Printed in the United States of America

10 9 8 7 6 5 4

ISBN: 0-13-262098-7

Prentice-Hall International (UK) Limited, *London*
Prentice-Hall of Australia Pty. Limited, *Sydney*
Prentice-Hall of Canada, Inc., *Toronto*
Prentice-Hall Hispanoamericana, S. A., *Mexico*
Prentice-Hall of India Private Limited, *New Delhi*
Prentice-Hall of Japan, Inc., *Tokyo*
Simon & Schuster Asia Pte. Ltd., *Singapore*
Editora Prentice-Hall do Brasil, Ltda., *Rio de Janeiro*

PREFACE

As this century concludes, and educators anticipate the twenty-first century, change is imminent. The coming decades will present planners with a bewildering variety of choices, and the decisions they make will affect the lives of millions of schoolchildren. These choices and decisions that confront education as we transition to the next century will challenge and probably enhance the role of curriculum workers.

Imagine, for a moment, someone in the late 1890s trying to predict the transformations that would take place in the twentieth century. Students writing on slates would shift to using laptop computers. Teachers lecturing from handwritten notes would be supplanted by children exploring the marvels of the information superhighway. Jobs dependant on manual labor would be supplanted by robotic assembly lines. Watching birds fly would progress to space travel. Women would achieve a more egalitarian role in our society, and minorities would attain full citizenship status. Everything imaginable would incorporate electronics.

In all probability, the sort of changes that we have experienced in our lives will continue at the same dizzying pace. Can our schools, already dated and out-of-step, continue to be the mechanism for the transmission of culture and the preparation for citizenship? Looking just around the corner, the privatization of education, technology in the workplace, and the diversity of the new population present significant challenges to our ability to plan and provide leadership. Education will be redefined by technology, only the form remains to be determined. These promise to be very exciting years, and the field of curriculum should be on the cutting edge of redefining how we guide our children into the future.

New to This Edition

The fifth edition of *Curriculum Development: A Guide to Practice* contains many changes while retaining what has made the book so well received during the previous editions. You will find, for instance, a complete reworking of the chapters addressing instruction—elementary, middle, and secondary—as well as the chapter on future directions. The impact of technology on today's curriculum is discussed in detail in Chapters 9 and 10. Learning activities, references, suggested readings, figures, and tables have all been updated.

Our text ends in the same way it began, with a focus on the philosophical aspects of curriculum work. The substantive arguments among early curriculum theorists remain unanswered after nearly one hundred years, and we feel that those working into the next century will have to address those ideas that seek to guide education in America. The starting point for providing such leadership is, of course, clarity on the part of the leader about the purposes and practices of education. It is our belief, as authors, that this book can serve as a reliable resource for both practitioners and leaders-in-training well into the twenty-first century.

Acknowledgments

We are grateful, as always, to our reviewers, who suggested changes and exchanged ideas during the formative revision of this edition:

- ☐ Rodney M. Borstad, Northern Illinois University
- ☐ Leigh Chiarelott, Bowling Green State University
- ☐ Monroe Johnson, Ohio University
- ☐ Sid T. Womack, Arkansas Tech University

We are thankful, too, for the editorial guidance of Debbie Stollenwerk and the staff at Prentice Hall. Finally, we wish to thank our wives, Margaret Wiles and Patsy Bondi, who as classroom teachers always provide a realistic sounding board for our ideas.

J. W. W.
J. C. B.

Jon Wiles

Joseph Bondi

ABOUT THE AUTHORS

Jon Wiles is a professor of education at the University of South Florida at St. Petersburg, and Joseph Bondi is a professor of education at the University of South Florida at Tampa. Both have served in various educational roles—as teachers, school and college administrators, and researchers. Their consulting firm of Wiles, Bondi, and Associates has conducted practice in forty states and ten foreign countries.

In addition to *Curriculum Development: A Guide to Practice,* Fifth Edition, Jon Wiles and Joseph Bondi have coauthored a number of other education books, including *Curriculum Planning: A New Approach* (1974), *Supervision: A Guide to Practice,* Fourth Edition (1996), *The Essential Middle School,* Second Edition (1993), *Practical Politics for School Administrators* (1981), *Principles of School Administration* (1983), and *The School Board Primer* (1985).

Both received their doctoral degrees from the University of Florida and reside in Tampa, Florida.

BRIEF CONTENTS

CONTENTS

Chapter 9
Secondary School Programs and Issues   319

PART IV
CURRICULUM PROSPECTIVES   345

Chapter 10
Curriculum Design Alternatives   347

PART I

CURRICULUM PERSPECTIVES

chapter 1

CURRICULUM IN EDUCATION

To those not in professional education, the term *curriculum* is usually associated with a textbook, guide, or course of study to be mastered in school. To professional educators, however, the term is usually more broadly defined. It may include a set of global intentions, perhaps a formal plan or organizational structure, and any one of a number of delivery mediums. Above all, a curriculum developer is concerned with the purpose of the design, and clarification of that purpose is always an essential prerequisite to sound program development. The element of choice is present in every curriculum decision, and those choices reflect values.

Curriculum development is a process whereby the choices of designing a learning experience for students are made and then activated through a set of coordinated activities. Curriculum development, for the professional, is a logical process that begins with clear goals and proceeds in an "if-then" manner until finished. In other words, the process of curriculum development is deductive in nature, resulting in finer and finer actions to accomplish the intended purpose of the curriculum.

Curriculum development usually begins with a set of questions that initially reveal value preferences and then later undergird planning efforts and program evaluation. When formalized, these value preferences are referred to as *educational philosophies* or *learning theories.* Examples of such questions might be, "What learner outcome do we wish to promote?" or "How do students actually learn?" To begin curriculum work without such clarification and structure is to invite an incomplete or inconsistent product.

For the curriculum development process to be logical, boundaries for inclusion or exclusion must be established. These boundaries are usually determined through a process of developing goals, objectives, or desired outcomes that provide both structure and direction to efforts. Sometimes, however, forces external to education introduce variables that cannot be predicted or controlled, thus introducing an illogical element into the curriculum development process. In the United States, political, economic, and social forces disrupt and redirect curriculum development efforts. Because of such influences, being consistent is a major concern of workers in the field.

The assessment of curricula is always subjective since the plan always reflects preferences and values. However, curriculum development as a process is neutral and can be judged by its efficiency. The critical question for curriculum developers is, "Does the program developed serve the intentions?" You will find that, even though considerable controversy surrounds the purposes of various curricula, the process of curriculum development is fairly standard and has long been widely accepted.

A traditional way of thinking about curriculum development is to use a model or an analogy. Like an architect who cannot design a home until certain information about style (ranch, colonial, modern) and function (number of bedrooms, special rooms) is known, curriculum planners can't design a gifted program or a new social studies program until they know the purpose and the intended audience. Over time, the field of curriculum has focused on a cyclical model to guide the process of development: analysis, design, implementation, and evaluation. If followed, this model provides a rational and deductive way of creating school programs from inception to assessment. We shall return to the model later in this chapter.

Given these observations, curriculum development activities in a school setting can be both purposeful and process-oriented. A generic theme in all curriculum development efforts in schools is the improvement of learning for students. A point of origin for understanding how this process works, or doesn't work, is the history of American education and the area of professional focus known as *curriculum development.*

THE EVOLUTION OF SCHOOLING

A sense of history is very important for persons entering into teaching or curriculum leadership. The American education system is unique in the modern world; without the historical perspective, many of our contemporary conditions might seem odd or illogical. This perspective may also prove valuable in keeping the curriculum focused on long-term goals as opposed to events of the moment.

Although all of the events and names important to the history of American education can't be included within the scope of this text, we have identified certain core ideas, events, and figures that we believe have been most influential in shaping today's schools. This history begins only twenty-seven years after the landing on Plymouth Rock, when the settlers established a regulatory act to govern their first "grammar" school (1635).

Early European settlers came to America to escape religious persecution, and they pursued their religious beliefs with vigor. Martin Luther had taught that the

Bible must be read to ward off the work of the devil, and so the first known regulation, the Old Deluder Satan Act (1647), established schools for that purpose.[1]

A second purpose for education in America, established quite early, was to develop a "literate citizen" capable of participating in acts of governance for the common good. Benjamin Franklin, for instance, spoke often of the "rise of the common man" and the need for strong citizen participation. The concept of a "participatory democracy" rationalized many early schools in America.

Finally, a third idea about schools in the colonies was that schools were useful to promote the common good and to bring about desired changes in society. Following the War of 1812, for instance, schools were expected to teach about our national identity and emerging beliefs.

As civilization spread in the colonial areas and beyond, forming schools went hand-in-hand with the development of communities. Usually, such schools were of minimal duration (several years at most), were taught in a one-room schoolhouse erected by the community, and focused on basic literacy skills. Quite early, these "American" schools took on characteristics that were unlike European schools of that era.

Horace Mann (1796–1859) is forever linked to early education efforts in this nation and is often called the "Father of the American Public School." Mann, a legislator and United States Congressman from Massachusetts, was instrumental in passing early laws governing education in his home state. He helped establish the first teacher training institution in 1839 and later served as the first Commissioner of Education in Massachusetts. He advocated schooling that was universal, free, and nonsectarian. After a visit to Prussia in 1843, Mann returned to the United States to establish a "graded school ladder" concept and helped gain support for the first tax-supported elementary schools in 1850.

As early as 1779, Thomas Jefferson was advocating free schools for the children of colonists. This proposal was in stark contrast to the prevailing European practice in which "dual tracks" of free and private education were maintained. A Free Public School Society was formed around 1800 in New York City and educated over 600,000 pupils in its fifty-year history.

Indicative of the early social functions of education in America was the provision of the Northwest Ordinance (1787) that made it mandatory for all townships in new states to set aside land for schools as a precondition for becoming a recognized community.

Paralleling the establishment of this popular education system in the elementary grades was an unrelated system of higher education dating from the establishment of Harvard College in 1636. The higher education system, unlike the public elementary system, was private and exclusive. The conception of education at this level was focused solely on producing learned men and leaders for the emerging nation. This distinction between the two systems is very important to understand because, even as we enter the twenty-first century, various philosophies compete in American society to define education. The roots of these differences were present from the beginning of our nation.

Private education in the early colonies produced judges, legislators, and persons in other leadership roles. Upon finishing the elementary years, these students would secure a tutor or attend an academy to prepare for college. This private "bridge" to leadership roles in American society existed for most of the eighteenth and nineteenth centuries. Eventually, laws to support secondary schools with taxes (1821) and the establishment of public land-grant colleges and universities (1862) began to break this private schooling domination. Public taxation for secondary schools became universal in the United States following the historic Kalamazoo Case, an 1872 Michigan Supreme Court case.

Thus, after two centuries, a solid educational system consisting of both public and private elements had been established in America and was being supported by citizens. With the exception of the turmoil surrounding the Civil War, the development of schools was an ever-expanding process leading to the establishment of this nation's strongest institution. The purpose of the American school was clearly literacy and knowledge acquisition, but with signs of some social utility mixed in.

The final stage for completing the universal school ladder in America came during the 1890s when a number of national committees met to organize and coordinate both the subjects taught and the various organization of levels of schooling. By far, the best-known of these committees was the prestigious Committee of Ten, headed by President Charles Eliot of Harvard University. Working in 1892 and 1893, this committee sought to coordinate the secondary education programs of the states by establishing college entrance requirements. The committee recommended a standard set of high school courses, and a parallel committee established a "unit" measure for each course taken. Thereafter, students were awarded unit credits (Carnegie units) for each course with a set number required for graduation and college entrance.

Thus, by the end of the nineteenth century, students could attend tax-supported free public schools for up to twelve years and study a highly standardized curriculum at the secondary level despite the fact that education is a "state right" according to the United States Constitution (a residual right by omission). As the twentieth century began, a modern form of education was in place.

Anyone vaguely familiar with today's schools knows that the schools are not alike, despite various graduation requirements and college entrance requirements. In fact, during the twentieth century, numerous attempts have been made to alter the curriculum of the public schools, and most of these attempts reflect the early value differences in our nation concerning education. The roots of the differences of opinion, or philosophies, can be found by reviewing the past.

In the late eighteenth century and early nineteenth century, new ideas about children and learning were emerging in Europe. The traditional wisdom of that era viewed children as incomplete adults who needed to be shaped into preferred forms. Several European educators challenged those traditional views and became early advocates for working with the young in different ways.

Jean-Jacques Rousseau (1712–1778) was one of the earliest writers to see children as unfolding and malleable. Writing in his book *Emile* (1762), Rousseau argued that children were innately good (not evil) and called for a controlled environment in which positive growth could occur naturally. Rousseau believed that learning was most successful when education began with the student's interests.

Another early child advocate was Johann Pestalozzi (1746–1827) who advocated a "learning by doing" approach to education. In his book *Leonard and Gertrude* (1781), Pestalozzi described the behavior of children at his school in Yverdon, Switzerland, an early laboratory school. This educator is known for addressing the growth of the whole child in learning: the head, the heart, and the hand.

A third widely read European of this era, Friedrich Froebel (1782–1852) has been credited with establishing the early kindergarten *(Kleinkinderschaftig)* and having an important impact on later American education. Froebel, who had studied with Pestalozzi, spoke of the natural development in children and developed "readiness" materials to help each child move along in his or her early growth.

Finally, the German educator Johann Herbart (1776–1841) provided an influence on the thoughts of American educators, but with a different philosophical orientation. Unlike Rousseau, Pestalozzi, and Froebel, Herbart believed that schools should be highly structured and should prepare future citizens of the social-political community by shaping their minds. He felt that teachers could "build" the minds of children from the outside, using subject matter as building blocks and delivered through systematic lesson plans. Education for Herbart was a social mission rather than a matter of individual growth in pupils, and his methodology stressed concentration and mental immersion to accomplish the mission.

The effect of these European ideas was to suggest that education might be more than recitation and the "pounding in" of predetermined subject matter. Instead of focusing on what the teacher taught, each of these Europeans looked at the child and the methodology as critical. In doing so, their ideas introduced the concept of choice in educational decision making and launched some of the earliest debates about the what, who, and how of planning for learning.

Also affecting the first curriculum debates in this nation was Charles Darwin (1809–1882), the naturalist, who drew together the works of many others to suggest his theory of natural evolution in living things. As the official naturalist on the *Beagle* during its scientific expedition (1831–1836), Darwin documented that different surroundings tend to produce different outcomes in the growth of plants and animals *(On the Origin of Species,* 1859). Although educators did not directly apply Darwin's theory to education, his ideas were certainly in the minds of many educators who first began to explore the possibility that environment influenced learning.

At a centennial celebration in Philadelphia in 1876, many of the ideas just mentioned were showcased for American educators and soon took root in their writings. From that time on, more than one conception of education existed in the United States, and modern educational theory competed with traditional beliefs about education.

On the traditional side during this period of early diversity, knowledge became the focus of educators. Francis Parker, for example, began a unification process in 1883 to define subject areas. An early survey of teaching practices by Joseph Mayer Rice (1892) found the public school curriculum to be "meandering" and disorganized. In that same year, Eliot's Committee of Ten began advocating five common content areas (his "windows on the soul") to serve as college entrance prerequisites for all students regardless of their home state. These notions of a "general educa-tion" quickly shaped all public schooling and were based on a "like students and sin-gle purpose" rationale. Traditionalists saw all children progressing through a fixed, sequential curriculum with progress marked by a ladder of grade levels.

In sharp contrast to these traditionalists' view of education, new or progres-sive educators at the turn of the century were building on the European ideas of the previous century. These educators saw each child as being unique and sought to broaden the purpose of education to include both social and personal development. John Dewey (1859–1952) is usually credited with bridging this gap from the old definition of education to the broader definition of education in America.

Dewey built on those earlier European thoughts to advocate a new and very active definition on education for children. Seeing the mind as something to be developed (not filled and not shaped), Dewey suggested taking old principles of learning and demonstrating practical applications as defined by the experiences of the learner. The goal of education, according to Dewey, was to both organize and activate knowledge. But, said Dewey, the learner rather than the teacher is the source of such organization. Each individual, he proposed, must find ideas that work in practical experience and see these ideas as truth.

Dewey's credibility as a writer and theorist came as he applied his theories at the University of Chicago Lab School (1896–1904). Here, children learned by doing. Dewey later advocated the need for citizens in a democracy to find the truths of participation during the school years by living in a democratic institution. His book *Democracy and Education* (1916) is a classic statement of this belief.

Dewey's influence around the beginning of the twentieth century is hard to overstate. Many of his students at the University of Chicago, like Harold Rugg *(The Child-Centered School,* 1928) and George Counts *(Dare the School Create a New Social Order,* 1932) became major advocates of the progressive ideas. The formation of the Progressive Education Association (PEA) in 1919 led to many publications and applications of Dewey's theme.

If a single year could be selected when the true differences of the approaches to education in America became evident, it would probably be 1918. In that year, another conception for secondary education was proposed, The Seven Cardinal Principles by the Commission on the Reorganization of Secondary Education, and the first text on curriculum was produced (Franklin Bobbitt, *The Curriculum,* 1918). The American way of educating was unfolding, and the field of curriculum was emerging as a subspecialty of professional education.

Decisions about whether the school should teach a body of knowledge, help develop the individual student, or promote social programs and priorities could not be made in a decentralized education system. In reality, American education pro-grams simply evolved during these formative years. The pattern of schooling that emerged from a historic model of scholarship was superimposed on a coarse and dynamic culture, which was then influenced by the advent of psychology and human development research; the result was a mixed bag at best.

The Commission on the Reorganization of Secondary Education was formed in 1913 and met for five years to resolve some of the problems. The committee debated the three conceptions (academic, personal, and social) and the emerging multitude of philosophies and learning theories. In 1918, this committee produced what stands as the definitive statement on the purpose of American education, The Seven Cardinal Principles. These directions for American educational planning are still referred to regularly by educational curriculum workers:

1. Health
2. Command of fundamental processes
3. Worthy home membership
4. Vocation
5. Citizenship
6. Worthy use of leisure time
7. Ethical character

Curriculum, as a specialized area of study in professional education, emerged from a growing need to study, order, arrange, and otherwise rationalize the changing forms of American education. To gather the many visions, clarify the intentions, organize schooling structures, implement programs, and assess the success of curricula in meeting goals required a new field of study.

As the twentieth century began, American education was in transition from a classical system practiced for centuries in Europe and in the United States to a more expedient form of schooling that served broader purposes. Among the accomplishments by 1900 were the following:

- ☐ Schooling was a state responsibility rather than a church role.
- ☐ Public education was seen as a social need, not a charity.
- ☐ Education was a right of citizens, not a privilege.
- ☐ Taxes could be used to support education through secondary levels.
- ☐ Education was compulsory for all children in all states.
- ☐ Control of education was established at the state level.
- ☐ Subjects were a constant in educational planning for learning.
- ☐ Human development was perceived as evolutionary.
- ☐ Schools could be used to promote social unity.
- ☐ Education could be used for social regeneration.

Among the realities for new curriculum theorists by the time of Bobbitt's first text was an awareness of humanistic thought, an emerging awareness of human development, and the beginning of mechanistic (behavioral) processes used to engineer curriculum development. These forces, and others, both broadened the horizons of early planners and presented those planners with a large number of choices in defining education. The unfolding of the field of curriculum, an area concerned with defining and developing educational programs, is best understood through a study of the definition and structure of the term.

DEFINING CURRICULUM

The word *curriculum* has been in existence since about 1820, although the first professional use of the word in America was about a century later. The Latin word *currere* means to run or to run the course. With time, the traditional definition of a school curriculum meant the course of study.

Most noneducators think of curriculum and curriculum development in terms of this traditional definition, equating the term with a course of study or a text—those items that establish the course. Some highly traditional educators think of curriculum in these terms as well, although to do so requires a very narrow definition of education:

> The curriculum should consist of permanent studies—the rules of grammar, reading, rhetoric and logic, and mathematics (for the elementary and secondary school), and the greatest books of the western world (beginning at the secondary level of schooling).[2]

> The curriculum must consist essentially of disciplined study in five great areas: (1) command of mother tongue and the systematic study of grammar, literature, and writing, (2) mathematics, (3) sciences, (4) history, (5) foreign languages.[3]

> The curriculum should consist entirely of knowledge which comes from the disciplines . . . Education should be conceived as a guided recapitulation of the process of inquiry which gave rise to the fruitful bodies of organized knowledge comprising the established disciplines.[4]

> The curriculum is a systematic group of courses or sequence of subjects required for graduation or certification in a major field of study.[5]

> The curriculum is such permanent subjects as grammar, reading, logic, rhetoric, mathematics, and the greatest books of the western world that embody essential knowledge.[6]

The definition of curriculum as a product, or as a completely contained experience, proved unsatisfactory to many educators involved in the development of school programs. Very early in this century, the enormous growth in knowledge meant that "knowing" could no longer be contained in print form only. With the dissemination of such knowledge through technical means, identifying the essential knowledge became difficult.

In addition, the composition of schools in this period changed considerably. The population of the secondary school grew from 200,000 students in the 1890s to nearly five million students by 1924. Schooling was no longer the preserve of a small elite who would attend college; it was now a universal experience. In some cases, skills of citizenship took precedence over classical knowledge acquisition, and new courses had to be devised for learners.

As new courses were added to the curriculum, and as the differences among individual learners became more obvious to teachers and administrators, the definition of the curriculum began to stretch. Specialists in the field began to differentiate among various kinds of curricula: planned and unplanned (the hidden curriculum) and technical and practical learnings. Bobbitt, for example, writing in 1924 stated:

The curriculum may be defined in two ways: (1) it is the range of experiences, both indirect and direct, concerned in unfolding the abilities of the individual, or (2) it is a series of consciously directed training experiences that the schools use for completing and perfecting the individual.[7]

Following this theme, Hollis Caswell and Doak Campbell in 1935 wrote of the socializing function of the schooling experience. The curriculum, they said, "is composed of all of the experiences children have under the guidance of the school."[8] Other writers have continued this same theme as seeing curriculum as an experience (process) rather than a product.

A sequence of potential experiences is developed by the school for the purpose of disciplining children and youth in group ways of thinking and acting. This set of experiences is referred to as the **curriculum.**[9]

The curriculum is now generally considered to be all of the experiences that learners have under the auspices of the school.[10]

Curriculum is all of the experiences that individual learners have in a program of education whose purpose is to achieve broad goals and related specific objectives, which is planned in terms of a framework of theory and research or past or present professional practices.[11]

By the mid-1950s, it became increasingly evident that schools had a tremendous influence on students' lives. Some of those influences were structured; others were due to the congregation of youth. It was recognized that students also had experiences not planned by the school. During this period, definitions were dominated by those aspects of the curriculum that were planned, as opposed to simply the content or general experiences of students.

The curriculum is all of the learning of students which is planned by and directed by the school to attain its educational goals.[12]

A curriculum is a plan for learning.[13]

We define curriculum as a plan for providing sets of learning opportunities to achieve broad goals and related specific objectives for an identifiable population served by a single school center.[14]

A curriculum [is] usually thought of as a course of study or plan for what is to be taught in an educational institution.[15]

Beginning in the 1960s and continuing in the 1990s, there has been concern for the performance of educational programs. This focus, often referred to as *accountability* in schools, has pushed the definition of the curriculum toward an emphasis on ends or outcomes:

Curriculum is concerned not with what students will do in the learning situation, but with what they will learn as a consequence of what they do. Curriculum is concerned with results.[16]

[Curriculum is] the planned and guided learning experiences and intended outcomes, formulated through systematic reconstruction of knowledge and experience, under the auspices of the school, for the learners' continuous and willful growth in personal-social competence.[17]

Finally, in the mid-1990s, the concept of an evolving and nonplanned set of experiences for children emerged under the label of "postmodern":

. . . a new sense of educational order will emerge as well as new relations between teachers and students, culminating in a new concept of curriculum. The linear, sequential, easily quantifiable ordering system dominating education today could give way to a more complex, pluralistic, unpredictable system or network. Such a complex network will, like life itself, always be in transition, in process.[18]

In closed societies, the elite's values are superimposed on the people. Education, as a practice of freedom, rejects the notion that knowledge is extended or transferred to students as if they were objects.[19]

As we move into the 21st Century, we find ourselves no longer constrained by modernist images of purpose and history. Elements of discontinuity, rapture, and difference (chaos) provide alternative sets of referents by which to understand modernity as well as to challenge and modify it. The term *post-modern* is a rejection of grand narratives and any form of totalizing thought. It embraces diversity and locality. It creates a world where individuals must make their way, where knowledge is consistently changing, and where meaning is no longer anchored in history.[20]

We see the curriculum as a desired goal or set of values, which can be activated through a development process culminating in experiences for students. The degree to which those experiences are a true representation of the envisioned goal or goals is a direct function of the effectiveness of the curriculum development efforts. The purpose of such a design is an option of the group engaged in such development.

Although the definition of curriculum has been altered in response to social forces and expectations for the school, the process of curriculum development has remained constant. Through analysis, design, implementation, and evaluation, curriculum developers set goals, plan experiences, select content, and assess outcomes of school programs. These constant processes have contributed to the emergence of structure in curriculum planning.

Emerging Structure in Curriculum Development

Definitions of curriculum and visions of the purpose of education have been expansive during the past century, but the structure of curriculum development has been a filling-in process. The principles that exist in the field of curriculum have evolved more from practice than from logic or enlightenment. In such instances, the theory of curriculum has followed the practice found in school environments.

The focus of most curricular principles is specific rather than global. As Daniel Tanner and Laurel Tanner have noted,

> In the absence of a holistic conception of curriculum, the focus is on piecemeal and mechanical functions . . . the main thrust in curriculum development and reform over the years has been directed at microcurricular problems to the neglect of macrocurricular problems.[21]

Principles of curriculum have evolved as core procedures rather than theoretical guidelines. The cause for this evolution of principles is a combination of the absence of systematic thinking about curriculum planning; the vulnerability of curriculum planning to social, political, and economic forces; and the constantly changing priorities of education in the United States.

Because of this situation, identification of curricular principles is difficult. Hilda Taba describes the almost unmanageable condition of curriculum approaches in this way:

> Decisions leading to change in curriculum organization have been made largely by pressure, by hunches, or in terms of expediency instead of being based on clear-cut theoretical considerations or tested knowledge. The scope of curriculum has been extended vastly without an adequate consideration of the consequence of this extension on sequence or cumulative learning. . . . The fact that these perplexities underlying curriculum change have not been studied adequately may account for the proliferation of approaches to curriculum making.[22]

Prior to the major curriculum reforms in the late 1950s and early 1960s, most curriculum development in school settings was oriented toward producing content packages. In developing courses of study, curriculum specialists sought to refine school programs by redesigning essential topic areas and updating older programs on a scheduled basis. This rather static role for curriculum practitioners in the field resulted in the evolution of both theoretical constructs for developing curriculum and operational procedures that changed little over time.

An early observation by Dewey that "the fundamental factors in the educational process are (1) the learner, (2) the society, and (3) organized subject matter"[23] set the stage for defining curriculum parameters. These themes were echoed in 1926 by Dewey's former student, Harold Rugg, who wrote, "There are, indeed, three critical factors in the educational process: the child, contemporary American society, and standing between them, the school."[24] Another student of Dewey's, Boyd Bode renewed this theme of three parts in 1931 when he observed, "The difference in curriculum stems from three points of view: (1) the standpoint of the subject matter specialists, (2) the standpoint of the practical man, and (3) the interests of the learner.[25]

By 1945, these three general concerns were finding acceptance in most curriculum literature. Taba, for instance, discussed the three sources of data in curriculum planning as (1) the study of society, (2) studies of learners, and (3) studies of subject matter content.[26] By the early 1960s, Taba had further refined the study of society to mean "cultural demands . . . a reflection of the changing social milieu of the school."[27]

Gaining acceptance as a fourth important planning base for curriculum in the mid-1950s and early 1960s was the study of learning itself. Studies from various schools of psychology and the advent of sophisticated technology in school settings raised new possibilities and choices for educators who were planning programs.

These four major areas of concern for curriculum planners, known as the foundations or "bases" of planning, remain today as the basis of most analysis, design, implementation, and evaluation of school programs. These vital areas of concern are addressed in the following chapter.

The importance of these planning bases as organizers for thinking about the development of educational programs is best summarized by Taba, a curriculum specialist concerned with the development aspects of curriculum:

> . . . semantics aside, these variations in the conception of the function of education are not idle or theoretical arguments. They have definite concrete implications for the shape of educational programs, especially the curriculum . . . If one believes that the chief function of education is to transmit the perennial truths, one cannot but strive toward a uniform curriculum and teaching. Efforts to develop thinking take a different shape depending on whether the major function of education is seen as fostering creative thinking and problem solving or as following the rational forms of thinking established in our classical tradition. As such, differences in these concepts naturally determine what are considered the "essentials" and what are the dispensable frills in education.[28]

Paralleling the conceptual mapping out of the field of curriculum concerns was the evolution of operational procedures. Early curriculum development focused on subject content, which was a mechanical and rather simple operational technique developed in the 1920s and which continued as the dominant operational concern until the early 1960s. Writing in the 1926 National Society for the Study of Education Yearbook, Rugg outlined the operational tasks of curriculum development as a three-step process: (1) determine the fundamental objectives, (2) select activities and other materials of instruction, and (3) discover the most effective organization and placement of this instruction.[29]

By 1950, the technique of "inventory, organize, and present" had reached refinement in Ralph Tyler's widely read four-step analysis:

1. What educational purposes shall the school seek to attain?
2. What educational experiences can be provided that are likely to attain those purposes?
3. How can these educational experiences be effectively organized?
4. How can we determine whether these purposes are being attained?[30]

By addressing the assessment of curriculum development, Tyler introduced the concept of the curriculum development cycle whereby evaluation led to a reconsideration of purpose. Such a cycle in schools illuminated the comprehensiveness of the planning activity and later gave birth to refinements such as systems analysis and taxonomies of learning. Tyler's four-step model also rekindled a fifty-year-old effort to develop manageable behavioral objectives in education.[31]

The ordering of the development procedure also encouraged a mechanistic approach to curriculum development. Such approaches, long practiced in schools, are thoroughly represented in curriculum literature through various definitions:

> Curriculum development . . . is basically a plan of structuring the environment to coordinate in an orderly manner the elements of time, space, materials, equipment and personnel.[32]

> The function of curriculum development is to research, design, and engineer the working relationships of the curricular elements that will be employed during the instructional phase in order to achieve desired outcomes.[33]

Perhaps the most refined version of Tyler's procedure for developing school curriculum was outlined by Taba in 1962. Seven major steps of curriculum development were identified:

1. Diagnosis of needs
2. Formulation of objectives
3. Selection of content
4. Organization of content
5. Selection of learning experiences
6. Organization of learning experiences
7. Determination of what to evaluate and means of doing it

Within each step, substeps were provided, which identified criteria for action. For example, in the selection of learning experiences, it is important that the curriculum developer consider the following:

1. Validity and significance of content
2. Consistency with social reality
3. Balance of breadth and depth of experiences
4. Provision for a wide range of objectives
5. Learnability-adaptability of the experience to life of student
6. Appropriateness to needs and interests of learners.[34]

More modern lists of these steps differ from Taba's in that they see curriculum as a more comprehensive process, which may or may not be tied to a content product. In the following example, for instance, Kathryn Feyereisen presents curriculum development as a problem-solving action chain:[35]

1. Identification of the problem
2. Diagnosis of the problem
3. Search for alternative solutions
4. Selection of the best solution
5. Ratification of the solution by the organization
6. Authorization of the solution

7. Use of the solution on a trial basis
8. Preparation for adoption of the solution
9. Adoption of the solution
10. Direction and guidance of staff
11. Evaluation of effectiveness

The broader focus of the Feyereisen description reflects a growing concern in curriculum development with planning for change in school environments from a macroperspective. Curriculum development is increasingly a process with systemic concerns.

Other examples of the basic structure of the curriculum cycle could be provided at this point, but it should be clear that a regular review process developed and was widely practiced in American schools between 1920 and 1960. It is certain that this process reflected the historical dominance of subject matter content as the focus of curriculum renewal:

> Certainly, a review of the plans made and implemented today and yesterday leaves no doubt that the dominant assumption of past curriculum planning has been the goal of subject matter mastery through a subject curriculum, almost inextricably tied to a closed school and graded school ladder, to a marking system that rewards successful achievement of fixed content and penalizes unsuccessful achievement, to an instructional organization based on fixed classes in the subjects and a timetable for them.[36]

Progress in the so-called substantive dimension of curriculum development continues today. Since the early 1970s, curriculum specialists have employed systems thinking in school planning efforts. Such comprehensive planning efforts have allowed curriculum leaders to engineer program improvement in new and efficient ways. The process of curriculum development, from the inception of an idea to the final assessment of the reconstruction effort, is becoming a highly skilled area of curriculum leadership.

In sharp contrast, the visionary or theoretical dimension of curriculum work has progressed little in half a century. Despite an increased knowledge base, growing understanding of human development, sophistication in the use of technology, and an emerging focus on teaching and learning, curriculum models remain primitive and traditional. It has been observed that if Rip Van Winkle woke up in America after a long sleep, he would at least recognize schools. As we approach the twenty-first century, theoretical dimensions of curriculum development remain suppressed by a dependence on economic sponsorship, political conservatism, and the failure of educators to gain consensus for any significant change in the schooling process.

FOUNDATIONS OF CURRICULUM PLANNING

In the evolution of curriculum as a professional focus in education, four major planning areas have dominated thinking about schools:

1. Social forces in society
2. The treatment of knowledge

3. Human growth and development
4. Learning as a process

These areas, called the *foundations of curriculum,* organize information for planners and help us to see patterns in the "who, what, when, and why" of public education.

Social Forces

As outlined in our preface, we see the United States entering a major period of transformation in the 1990s. Changes in the composition of our population, dramatic changes in the power of our economy, new technologies, and an emerging world order all suggest changes for schools. In the lifetime of our grandparents, America transitioned from an agrarian society to an industrial society. Work became mechanized, the population became urban and mobile, and the role of an individual in society was redefined. Today, with the transformation to a post-industrial society dominated by technology and global interdependence, the nation is once again redefining itself.

In advanced countries, the relationship between education and such change is dynamic and interdependent. To the degree that education programs all children for a society that no longer exists, education is dysfunctional to that society. By the same token, if a changing society insists that schooling retain traditional forms in the face of massive changes, it may well doom itself to obsolescence and decline. As we progress into the twenty-first century, curriculum planners seek to understand the true nature of social changes so that they can program these changes into the schooling process. Looking at how communication affects the changing social structure of America illustrates one such social force.

At the beginning of the twentieth century, communication was fairly primitive by today's standards. There was a great dependence, of course, on the printed page. The telegraph existed, the telephone was in the infant stages of development, and motion pictures were a promising medium. Mass communication, however, was both scarce and inefficient. Any communication, such as the result of a presidential election, took considerable time to disseminate. Within a fifty-year period, three mass communication devices appeared that altered this pattern: (1) radio, (2) television, and (3) the computer.

Radio was the first communication medium to broaden the scope of the organized knowledge that had previously been in the domain of schools. Large amounts of information could be distributed quickly and by mid-century could be broadcast to other countries.

> The effect of radio on expansion of nonrelated and nonapplied knowledge is analogous to the distribution of seed by a grass spreader, creating in effect a "carpet of knowledge" by cultivating a lawn so thick that single blades became indistinguishable. Regarding the interrelationships between segments of knowledge, the nuances and vagaries of the unusual become entwined with the simplicity and ordinariness of the mundane. Perspectives of knowledge are clouded and often obfuscated entirely by their lack of definition. Conjecture becomes fact.[37]

Television added another means by which we gained information and was even more influential in one respect. Beaming into 97 percent of all homes an average of six-and-one-half hours daily by 1970, this medium influenced the values and standards of American society. In *Crisis in the Classroom,* Charles Silberman observed:

> Television has taken over the mythic role in our culture; soap operas, situation comedies, Westerns, melodramas, et al., are folk stories or myths that convey or reinforce the values of the society . . . The trouble is that television does not enable its audience to see things the way they really are. On the contrary, while more current and realistic than schools, television nonetheless presents a partial and, in important ways, distorted view of contemporary society.[38]

By the late 1970s, concern for controlling the impact of television, particularly as a medium affecting the thoughts and perceptions of children, was intense. Congressional hearings, campaigns by parent-teacher organizations, and criticism by members of the television industry were common.[39] A line from a widely acclaimed movie, *Network,* summarized the impact of television as a communication medium:

> This tube can make or break presidents, popes, prime ministers. This tube is the most awesome goddamned force in the whole godless world. And woe is us if it ever falls into the hands of the wrong people.[40]

Most recently in the late 1990s, manufacturers are presenting a "lock-out chip" to parents as one option in trying to control youths' viewing of television.

A third communication innovation of the twentieth century that has had a major effect on both society and schools is the computer. The initial impact of the computer was more subtle than that of radio or television because of its mystique and inaccessibility. The final implications of computer usage are much more powerful than either radio or television.

> Fifty years ago the comical product of the "madcap" scientists' nocturnal devisements, today computer science is as much a part of our lives as our favorite breakfast cereal, and with every day that passes encroaches ever so more fitfully into the domain of human life, human decisions, and human behavior.
>
> Partly akin to the television in its mechanical wizardry, whereas the television indoctrinates, the computer coerces us into action through its assumed infallibility in making decisions and plotting paths of action necessary to our living in comfort. While the computer habituates the pinnacle of man's intellectual genius, it is likewise the jailer who holds the key to our intellectual freedom. With his piece-by-piece orientation to information and knowledge application, man is, quite simply, presented with an unchallengeable opponent in the computer. The variance in speed in processing knowledge posits man in the impossible position of receiving computation as *fait accompli* from the computerized savant. In creating the computer, man has performed the heretofore-thought-impossible task of devising a being superior to himself in intellectual capacity, a being who can theoretically "outthink" all men combined, a being who in fact is a god.[41]

In terms of data processing and the generation of cross-referenced knowledge systems delivered at lightning speed and multiple forms, the computer age has presented a momentous challenge to society and school planners. In one decade, we have grown accustomed to satellite-transmitted instantaneous relays, home videocams, direct-dial networked telecommunication (cell phones), through-the-wall cable transmission, and facsimile capacities. The advanced world and segments of the Third World are awash in technology that is significantly impacting our conceptions of school.

Only one century ago, schooling was almost exclusively a knowledge-focused activity. Students and teachers interacted to master essentials such as Virgil's *Aeneid* and Xenophon's *Anabasis,* orthography, and Latin prose. In the late 1990s, social changes and technological access have called this kind of curriculum and learning into question. Steven Wozniak, co-founder of Apple Computer, states the case in the following manner:

> It's healthy to learn basic concepts such as arithmetic and logic, but there is just no point in having to solve the problems over and over again every day. It's a waste of time. . . . machines can do that stuff and leave us to think about more important things . . . personal computers are going to free people from the mundane things . . . they will allow people's minds to work at a higher level.[42]

Today, because of communication capability advances—radical advances in a very short period of time—some fundamental issues about schooling have been revived. If, for instance, knowledge is being generated, disseminated, and delivered at a pace beyond our capacity to absorb it, what is the point in organizing schools around the mastery of essential data? If there is too much to be known today, what essential data knowledge should all of our citizens possess? Or, if radio, television, and personal computers can serve as the disseminators of fundamental information about the society in which we live, at a cost a fraction of that of the schooling process, what should be the new role of the formal educating medium?

In the United States, the changing social patterns and their implications for schooling are perhaps even more challenging than technology. A complex web of family-work-government programs and mobility have altered the type of student seen in public schools and the role of the school for that pupil. Beginning in the 1960s when Great Society programs rewarded single-parent family patterns, America has seen the emergence of a new, nonnuclear family, which may combine persons with different names and origins into a loose economic network, dependent on constant economic and social support from agencies. Such new families move often and reconstitute themselves often, which disrupts school continuity. They can require large sums to accommodate special needs.

This new society has as one of its major characteristics a shrinking population of children and a rapidly growing body of older citizens. Many children in the 1990s, one in nine, qualify for special education programs, and new trends such as children born with drug dependence make these already expensive students a challenging task for educators. These children of "new" families and the growing population of older citizens will make demands and expect services from public schools in the 1990s.

School planners who look ahead to the first decade of the twenty-first century, when children being born now will be school-age, can only guess at what additional change will occur in social institutions and structures. In the late 1990s, immediate trends include:

- [ ] Expanded social services to provide for growing needs of students in schools
- [ ] Longer school days and school years to accommodate child-care demands of working parents
- [ ] Better and more sophisticated information networks to monitor student mobility and school progress
- [ ] Increased communication between business and education to prepare a work force that will be suited to a service economy and post-industrial society.

Treatment of Knowledge

The kinds of social changes outlined in the previous section have had a major effect on the treatment of knowledge in curriculum planning. Not only has knowledge become more plentiful and more widely disseminated because of technology, but the shifting social currents in the United States have acted to redefine the utility of knowledge in everyday life. Since all knowledge contains value dimensions when applied, little knowledge is considered value-free in the 1990s. Increasingly, the public is interested in what is being taught in school and how that information is being conveyed to students.★ The curriculum planner in the 1990s must wrestle with the selection, organization, relevance, presentation, and evaluation of knowledge in schools.

Arno Bellack, writing forty years ago during the early curriculum reforms, outlined the planner's dilemma:

> In current debates about what should be taught in schools, the "conventional wisdom" long honored in pedagogical circles about the nature of knowledge and the role of knowledge in the curriculum is being called into question. The enemy of conventional wisdom, Professor Galbraith (the originator of that felicitous term) tells us, is the march of events. The fatal blow comes when conventional ideas fail to deal with new conditions and problems to which obsolescence has made them inapplicable. The march of events in the world at large that is placing new demands on the schools, and in the world of scholarship that is making new knowledge in great quantities, is forcing us to reexamine our ideas about the nature of knowledge and its place in the instructional program.[43]

The scope of information available to scholars, and to schoolchildren, was immense. Estimates of the rate at which organized knowledge doubled its volume ranged from every seven years in the mid-1960s to every two years by the mid-

---

★Note, for example, the controversy surrounding the 500th anniversary of the landing of Columbus in America.

1970s. Traditional curriculum tasks such as reviewing and updating the subject content became unmanageable.

Related to the problems of scope and volume of organized knowledge was one of organization. Cases of knowledge overload were plentiful, conjuring visions of a nation choking on the proliferation of its own wisdom:

> The American crisis, then, seems clearly to be related to an inability to act. It is not that we do not will action but that we are unable to act, unable to put existing knowledge to use. The machinery of our society no longer works or we no longer know how to make it work.[44]

Educational planners, in general, reacted to the glut of data that related to traditional school subjects by refocusing on the structure of information rather than on information itself. One of the best-known leaders of this reorganization movement was Jerome Bruner. Bruner rationalized that shift away from mastery of essential data to the study of representative data structures in this way:

> Teachers ask me about the "new curricula" as though they were some special magic potion. They are nothing of the sort. The new curricula are based on the fact that knowledge has an internal connectedness, a meaningfulness, and that for facts to be appreciated and understood and remembered, they must be fitted into that internal meaningful context.[45]

Another problem related to the organization of knowledge sources for the school curriculum was the advent of "new" fields of knowledge created from crossing standard disciplines of study. Knowledge in the sciences, such as biochemistry, and in the social sciences, such as demography, gave rise to new structures of organization. The incorporation and management of such new areas posed difficult problems for school planners owing to the compactness of traditional knowledge organizations.

With the dramatic increase in the volume of knowledge, and the corresponding questions of how to organize it meaningfully, came even more pressing inquiries about the purpose of knowledge in organized learning. Although challenges to the knowledge-based curriculum weren't novel, the regularity with which educators questioned the traditional motif of educating in public schools during this period was surprising. Defining education in a new way, Earl Kelley wrote:

> The only man who is educated is the man who has learned how to learn; the man who has learned how to adapt and change; the man who has realized that no knowledge is secure, that only the process of seeking knowledge gives the basis for security.[46]

Futurist Alvin Toffler, in assessing the onrush of the knowledge explosion as it related to the role of schooling, observed:

> Instead of assuming that every subject taught today is taught for a reason, we should begin from the reverse premise: nothing should be included in the required curriculum unless it can be strongly justified in terms of the future. If this means scrapping a substantial part of the formal curriculum, so be it.[47]

By the early 1990s, the delivery of knowledge direct-to-the-learner was increasing dramatically. Bypassing the traditional schooling format were new inter-active video networks and a host of personal computers with sophisticated software capability. Most schools in the United States possessed computer capability by 1990. However, the average district had an uneven pattern of hardware and soft-ware programs, and the computer became a disruptive element in some cases. At home, many students learned music, art, languages, geography, and other topics of choice, thus breaking the monopoly of schools over knowledge and its delivery. In the coming decade in the United States, there will probably be a major demand for schools to provide more choice in learning within the school.

The reaction of educational planners to the problem of organization of knowledge was to place emphasis on the identification of goals and objectives of educating, which would serve as guidelines for content selection. This orientation placed knowledge in a new and different role in educational planning:

> The education received in school is not meant to perpetuate an academic discipline, prepare students for college, or train bricklayers. All these things may be accom-plished, but its chief mission is to produce graduates who are capable of becoming active, participating, contributing members of society. To achieve this goal the individ-ual must learn to live with himself and others and must have a system of values to guide him. Therefore, if this is the ultimate purpose of education, we must start by defining the needs of the individual, the nature and needs of society, and the system of values from which we can derive the objectives of the curriculum.
>
> The means should not determine the ends. For example, if the areas of knowl-edge are used to determine the objectives, they will in all probability prejudice the objectives. In addition, the inclusion of a variable such as knowledge areas would also predestine the content, curricular organization, scope, and sequence variables.[48]

Another consideration for educational planners that related to treatments of knowledge was the way in which individual learners reacted to information. In par-ticular, research efforts studying the effects of attitude, emotion, and feelings toward learning (affect), and the process of information manipulation, storage, and retrieval (cognition), linked reception and retention of learning with readiness and attitudes toward learning. The question of form of knowledge thus became a concern.

Mario Fantini, widely recognized advocate of change in urban educational environments, stated the relationship this way:

> Although educators have hinted at the relationship between affect and cognition, the functional linkage is seldom made. Too often, the school severely limits the relationship between the two with its definition of affect. It considers affect only in terms of play, interests, classroom climate, readiness, teacher-pupil interaction, motivation, and the like, all of which it can use to induce the child to accept prescribed academic content.
>
> Yet it is obvious that knowing something cognitively does not always result in behavior that follows on that knowing. This is because knowledge alone cannot influ-ence total behavior. Moreover, all kinds of knowledge are not equally influential. The missing ingredient in this equation seems to be knowledge that is related to the affec-tive or emotional world of the learner. What most often prompts action or behavior is

a feeling or emotion about something rather than knowledge per se. It may be that "knowing about" can prompt feeling, but it is feeling that generates behavior. Unless knowledge relates to feeling, it is unlikely to affect behavior appreciably.[49]

Closely related to the relationship of affect and knowledge were two other concerns of educational planners: language usage and the medium of delivery. When curriculum planners attempted to bring knowledge to the schools, they had to deal with school populations that represented many cultures. This situation meant that planners were confronted with both nonstandard English and a problem in communication. The "ebonics" controversy in 1997 illustrates this point.

> Communication is a funny business. There isn't as much of it going on as most people think. Many feel that it consists in saying things in the presence of others. Not so. It consists not in saying things but in having things heard. Beautiful English speeches delivered to monolingual Arabs are not beautiful speeches. You have to speak the language of the audience—of the whom in the who-says-what-to-whom communications diagram. Sometimes the language is lexical (Chinese, Japanese, Portuguese); sometimes it is regional or personal (125th Street-ese, Holden Caulfield-ese, anybodyese). It has little to do with words and much to do with understanding the audience. . . . [50]

In addition to language patterns and word usage, planners discovered the medium of delivery to have special effect on the interpretation and use of knowledge. Marshall McLuhan, in particular, opened the eyes of planners to the effects of electronic communication, describing information delivery systems in such terms as hot, cool, and slick. In its extreme form, according to McLuhan, the medium can be both the message and the massage.[51] How knowledge is delivered may be more important than what knowledge is delivered.

A final input that affected the planning of knowledge use in schools was the advent of serious forecasting of the future. As educators reviewed past use of knowledge and studied the present knowledge explosion, the wisdom of continuing with a content-dominated curriculum was questioned. After all, facts, by definition, were phenomena of the past and present rather than of the future. In some respects, traditional knowledge placed blinders on our ability to escape the pull of the present and open our minds to the real possibilities of the future. The call for creative, nonlinear thinking presented an interesting challenge.

Related to a futuristic treatment of knowledge was the concept of programming. In viewing school curriculums, it becomes clear that what we teach children programs their ability to meet the future. If education's image of the future is inaccurate, or if the knowledge given our students does not prepare them for the future, then the schools have betrayed those they teach.

In summary, the questions raised in assessing organized knowledge as a planning foundation are significant: What is to be taught? What should be the role of organized knowledge? What is the relative importance of knowledge bodies? What is the correct organization of information? What is the best form for bringing knowledge to students? All of these questions must be addressed by educational planners.

Human Growth and Development

A third foundational consideration important to educational planners has been the growing body of information related to human development. These data have been critical in such regular school activities as placement and retention, counseling, and planning curricular content and activities. Knowledge about human development has also provided the impetus for the development of a host of new school programs: early childhood education, special education, compensatory education, and middle school education. Perhaps most importantly, our understandings about patterns of growth and development have caused educators to perceive formal educational planning from the perspective of the individual student.

Contributions to our understanding of human development have been gradual throughout this century. As information about human development has accumulated, various schools of thought have emerged in an effort to organize the data. These interpretations of our knowledge about human growth provide the basis for the differences in educators' learning theories. Such differences can most clearly be understood in relation to several basic issues related to human development.

One issue revolves around the question of what constitutes normal development. Because of records kept over an extended time on the physical maturation of schoolchildren, educators are now fairly able to predict ranges of growth for chronological age. It appears, in general, that children in the United States are achieving physical maturation at an ever-earlier age. Such findings are attributed to better health and nutritional care during childhood.

Our knowledge of intellectual, social, and emotional development during the school-age years is considerably less precise. However, organized inquiry has developed significant studies that guide our present decision making about development-related factors in these areas.

In the area of intelligence, considerable documentation exists regarding student performance on intelligence-measuring devices such as the Stanford-Binet Scale. Little concrete evidence exists, however, to support hypotheses about intellect or intellectual capacity. What we currently operate with are models of how people are believed to develop and normal ranges of development in the capacity to think.

Without question, the dominant model in this area is one developed by Swiss educator Jean Piaget nearly sixty-five years ago. Piaget hypothesized four distinct but chronologically successive models of intelligence: (1) sensorimotor, (2) preoperational, (3) concretely operational, and (4) formal operational. Piaget's model of continual and progressive change in the structure of behavior and thought in children has assisted educators in preparing intellectual experiences in schools.

In the areas of social and emotional growth of students, even less precise data about human development exist. Classic studies such as Project Talent,[52] Growing Up in River City,[53] and the Coleman Report[54] provide long-term studies of particular populations. Data related to emotional development have been compiled by the National Institutes of Mental Health but are on abnormal populations. For educational planners, the question of what constitutes "normal" growth is largely unresolved in the late 1990s, particularly in areas such as creativity.[55]

Another issue relating to human development is whether such growth can be or should be controlled or accelerated. Primary research with infants and children by White and associates[56] suggests that development can indeed be accelerated through both experience and environment.[57] The work of behaviorist B. F. Skinner,[58] on the other hand, is conclusive in its demonstration that behavior can be shaped. These two options leave the curriculum developer with significant value decisions about both the anticipated outcome of an education and the more mechanical aspects of planning learning experiences.

Two final human development issues are indicative of the many planning considerations facing curriculum developers. First, we have the mind-boggling question of the ultimate human being that we might create, since human development is somewhat malleable. For instance, medical research in the 1980s and 1990s demonstrated an amazing capacity to change gene pools, transplant organs, and apply chemistry to alter behavior. Diet and direct stimulation seem capable of emphasizing one human behavior over another. Studies in mind control and extrasensory perception promise that "directing" human intelligence is within the domain of formal schooling.

Even more curious is our growing understanding of emotion and affective growth. Work with individuals of multiple personality may offer schools the possibility of directing emotions as well as moral development.[59]

Issues such as defining normal growth, promoting certain kinds of growth, and giving emphasis to certain types of cognitive and affective growth make the study of human development, or human engineering, a necessary foundation for curriculum planning.

Learning as a Process

New understandings of human development, new perspectives of the role of knowledge in learning, and new social values related to the schooling process have meant that a variety of learning approaches have become fashionable and acceptable in schools. Specifically, school planners must begin to incorporate the following planning data into their design of educational programs: (1) the biological basis of development can be altered, (2) physical maturation can be retarded or accelerated through diet and stimulation, (3) intellectual growth can be stimulated and directed, and (4) cultural influences on learning can be controlled or encouraged. These "new realities" suggest that schools can promote multiple types of learning in the classroom and, therefore, facilitate different types of development in students. The learning theory and the instructional approach selected by the curriculum planner are functions of the desired goals of student growth.

At the philosophical level, a topic to be treated more fully in the following chapter, educators differ considerably regarding the type of development that schools should promote. Three major approaches to learning have evolved: (1) a behavioral approach, (2) an approach incorporating drive theories, and (3) an environmental approach. These basic approaches to learning have numerous identifiable subtheories; an abbreviated form is presented here to indicate the range of learning theory that exists among school planners.

The **behavioral approach** is characterized by an external perspective of the learning process, viewing learning as a product of teacher behavior. Under this approach to learning, educational planners and teachers who deliver such plans study the student to ascertain existing patterns of behavior and then structure specific learning experiences to encourage desired patterns of behavior.

Armed with terms such as **conditioning** (repetitive response), **reinforcement** (strengthening behavior through supportive action), **extinction** (withdrawing reinforcement), and **transfer** (connecting behavior with response), the behavioral learning theorist seeks to shape the student to a predetermined form. Common school practices under this learning approach are fixed curriculums, didactic (question–answer) formats, and programmed progression through materials. Perhaps the most interesting and controversial use of this learning approach in schools today is the practice of behavior modification.

Behavior modification is a simple cause–effect programming of observable behavior. The procedure uses a four-step technique: (1) identifying the problem, (2) recording baseline data, (3) installing a system to alter behavior, and (4) evaluating the new condition. As an external system of behavior control, behavior modification is not concerned with the attitudes or motivations of students under such a system, but rather with the results of the modification system. According to this learning approach, behavior that is rewarded will continue; behavior that goes unrewarded will be extinguished.

A second learning theory is the **need-structured approach,** which is concerned with the needs and drives of students and seeks to use such natural motivational energy to promote learning. Teachers often analyze and use the interests and needs of students as instructional vehicles when following this approach.

Key terms used with the needs/drive approach are **readiness, identification, imitation,** and **modeling.** Taking a cue from Freudian psychology, this theory orders the curriculum to coordinate with developmental readiness. Students learn through pursuit of unfulfilled needs, often modeling behaviors of others or developing predictable identification patterns.

Drive theories rely heavily on findings of human growth and development in planning curricular activities. This set of theories is dependent on student growth in planning school experiences.

The **environmental approach** to learning is concerned with the restructuring of the learning environment or the students' perceptions so that they may be free to develop. Unlike the static definition of growth presented by the behavioral approach or the dependent theories of need-structured approaches, the environmental approach is dynamic in nature. It acknowledges human diversity, believes in human potential, and promotes both uniqueness and creativity in individuals.

The basis of the environmental approach is the belief that behavior is a function of perception and that human perceptions are the result of both experiences and understandings. When students have positive experiences that are self-enhancing, their perception and understanding of themselves and the world around them

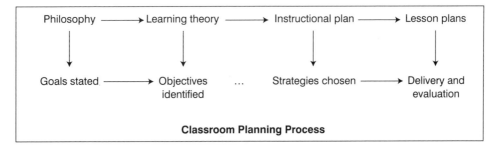

FIGURE 1.1   Classroom Planning as a Subset of Curriculum Planning

are altered. These new perceptions, in turn, allow for additional growth experiences. Student potential for development, under this learning approach, is limitless.

These three primary approaches to the structuring of learning in schools, which might be labeled *push, pull,* and *restructure,* are very different in their assumptions about people and possibilities for human development. They differ, for instance, in their beliefs about human potential. They differ in terms of their vantage point in describing learning (external versus internal). They differ in their beliefs about the source of academic motivation.

To select any one of these approaches to learning means that basic classroom considerations such as the design of learning spaces, the choice of materials, and the roles of participants will have a distinct form. The learning theory of the planner is crucial to decision making and projection. As such, learning as a process represents a strong fourth planning foundation (see Figure 1.1).

The area of educational foundations is highly complex. It is an effort to bring order to a rapidly changing world that has an increasing number of relevant variables. Throughout the treatment of foundations of curriculum planning, there is an element of choice: which input to select, which data to validate, which decisions to make.

Ultimately, the choices and decisions related to the selection, activation, and evaluation of educational designs are normative matters. Before educational planners can be effective and consistent in their work, they must understand their personal belief systems and formulate a philosophy of education that complements that system. The following chapter introduces some established philosophies of education and assists you in determining your priorities for schools.

ISSUES, IMPEDIMENTS, AND ROLES

Obviously, many choices face those who plan American educational programs, and from these choices come major issues reflecting bedrock values. The scope of our school programs, their purpose and organization, the focus of their delivery, and many other questions remain largely unanswered. Contrast the following list of questions compiled by Thomas Briggs in 1926 with those being asked today:

1. What are the desired ends of education?
2. What is the good life?
3. To what extent shall education modify the character and actions of future citizens?
4. For what ends are the schools responsible?
5. What subject areas are most vital in attaining these ends?
6. What should be the content of these subject arrangements?
7. How should the material be organized?
8. What is the responsibility of each level of schooling?
9. What is the relative importance of each course of study?
10. How much time should be allotted for each subject?
11. How long should education be continued at public expense?
12. What is the optimum length of the school day? School year?
13. What is the optimum work load for each pupil?
14. What are the most probable future needs of the pupil?[60]

Questions such as these, then and now, encourage debate, inquiry, and experimentation in schools. Curriculum, as a field of inquiry, has developed in an effort to study such issues and translate what is learned into viable school programs.

The answers to such questions would be made by appointed officials in a centralized or nationalized system of education, but the unique decentralization of the American education model presents abnormal impediments that include

- ☐ The absence of clear goals
- ☐ Unpredictable entry of power sources from outside
- ☐ A consistent dependence on "money" as the moving force
- ☐ Structural line and staff relationships in the district
- ☐ The absence of "systems" thinking in problem solving
- ☐ An operational orientation to the present rather than future
- ☐ Decentralized decision making and policy implementation
- ☐ The absence of evaluative feedback in policy renewal
- ☐ An incomplete linkage to vital research
- ☐ Inadequate training and understaffing of personnel
- ☐ Administrative turnover

At the school district level, where most practice is conducted, there are regular barriers to the improvement of school programs:

1. An inadequate theory of implementation, which includes too little time for teachers to plan for and learn new skills and practices
2. District tendencies toward faddism and quick-fix solutions
3. Lack of sustained central office support and follow-through
4. Underfunding of projects, or trying to do too much with too little support
5. Attempts to manage the projects from the central office instead of developing school leadership and capacity

6. Lack of technical assistance and other forms of intensive staff development
7. Lack of awareness of the limitations of teacher and school administrator knowledge about how to implement the project
8. The turnover of teachers in each school
9. Too many competing demands or overload
10. Failure to address the incompatibility between project requirements and existing organizational policies and structures
11. Failure to understand and take into account site-specific differences among schools
12. Failure to clarify and negotiate the role relationships and partnerships.[61]

The type of role assumed by the curriculum planner in making such decisions, under such conditions, is an issue itself. The extreme positions on this question of role are reflected in the following statements:

Curriculum planning lies at the heart of educational planning—dealing with the definition of educational ends and the engineering of means for achieving them.[62]

Curriculum theory should be a subordinate of total educational theory.[63]

Arguments about which of these role definitions is most suitable for curriculum workers are complex. The argument for an assisting technical role is that curriculum theory and practice have traditionally been far apart. So-called blue sky curriculum designs rarely achieve fruitful application in the real world of schools. If curriculum developers are to be useful, so the argument goes, they must meet the real needs of education. This can be done best by maintaining a tractive or static orientation, being specific in operations, and serving where needed.

Arguments, which hold that curriculum developers should provide leadership by being both dynamic and intellectual and by achieving a global orientation to education, are multiple. Bruce Joyce provides the strongest argument against the traditional posture:

In the past, educational planners have been technically weak (unable often to clarify ends or engineer means) and morally or technically unable to bring about a humanistic revolution in education . . . curriculum workers have defined themselves as helpers, not leaders, letting the community and teachers make decisions and then assisting in the implementation of those decisions.

By focusing on schools and teachers in schools, curriculum is being forced to operate within the parameters of the institution . . . by far the most paralyzing effect of the assumptive world in which the curriculum specialist lives is that it tends to filter out all ideas which might improve education but which fit awkwardly into the school pattern.[64]

Because of the traditional orientation, say those calling for an active role for the curriculum specialist, the field of curriculum has continued to speak the language of sequence, prerequisites, academic achievement, and mastery. Learning theories that do not fit the existing school program, or are not seen as feasible in terms of current teacher practices, are neglected.

The perception of a curriculum specialist as a thinker, designer, leader, and projectionist goes back to the writings of Dewey, Counts, and other progressives of the early twentieth century. Counts, for instance, observed that "the goals of education must be determined by philosophical and analytical concepts of the good life."[65]

Among those perceiving curriculum development as a dynamic operation, there is a great fear that the gravitational pull of bureaucracy in education has won out. With each consolidation of schools, with each new piece of legislation, with each new regulation, the school becomes more closed to change, more self-perpetuating, and more product-oriented. This trend is in direct conflict with the desire of some curriculum theorists to see education as a process. Louise Berman, for instance, calls for a process-oriented person who has opportunities in school to plan for the future—a planning that involves process skills and competencies. Such "communicating, loving, decision-making, knowing, organizing, creating, and valuing" persons will never evolve without strong curriculum leadership.[66]

Finally, it is worth noting that these differences in the perception of the role of the curriculum specialist reflect a differing time–image point of reference. Those seeing curriculum work as a support function are generally concerned with the here and now. Those who seek a more dynamic role for curriculum development are more concerned with what schools can become. These role expectations illuminate the great philosophical range among curriculum developers.

In most school districts, curriculum directors appear in a staff role on organizational charts that describe administrative relationships. This means that curriculum specialists have basic responsibilities without clear authority. Often, curricular decisions will affect other dimensions of school organization, such as legal, financial, and personnel. Curriculum workers must maintain lines of communication with all such offices and campaign for support of desired objectives. In many school districts, administrative policy and instructional activity are dictated by administrative concerns rather than by curriculum goals.

Related to the act of "borrowing" authority from administrators is a continual reliance on administrative action to implement curriculum change. Designing school structures, procuring materials and staff, informing the public, and activating programs are all beyond the immediate control of the curriculum specialist.

From the following list, note that some roles performed by curriculum personnel are active and change-oriented; others reinforce existing conditions in the schools:

expert	adviser	retriever
linker	manager	advocate
counselor	trainer	data collector
diagnoser	modeler	referrer
instructor	observer	confronter
demonstrator	evaluator	analyzer

We believe that the visionary aspects of curriculum development are essential to a rational process of improving school programs. We see curriculum development as a process of promoting desired change through purposeful activities, which produces a condition in which environmental variables are controlled and behavior is directional. When these things occur, quality programs can be designed, implemented, and evaluated by educational leaders.

Like the role of the curriculum specialist, the mission or end sought by those acting in a program development capacity is not always certain. The open nature of public schools, the diversity of value structures in the United States, the press of socioeconomic conditions, and the inability of educators to control change all contribute to a certain amount of murkiness in school planning.

To a degree greater than most educational planners like to admit, change occurs in school settings in spite of planning. James MacDonald has summarized the difficulty in this manner:

> The development of the curriculum in the American public schools has been primarily an accident. A description of what curriculum exists is essentially a political and/or ethical document rather than a scientific or technical one. It is a statement which indicates the outcomes of a very complex interaction of groups, pressures, and events which are most often sociopolitical in motivation and which result in decisions about what ought to be.[67]

The uneven and sometimes unpredictable flow of change in school environments is the result of increased public attention to education, media coverage, political activism, legal assessments of educational activity, and the discovery of education as a business market. Experienced school planners have found that all of these forces, and others, have led to a decrease in the control over change.

The absence of a systematic means of developing, reviewing, and selecting curricula on a national basis has contributed to the unclear mission of the curriculum worker. Despite strong convictions and development skills, the professional curriculum worker is only one of many forces vying for the control of change in the educational environment.

SUMMARY

A curriculum is a plan for learning. All such plans contain a vision of what should be, as well as a structure that translates those visions into experiences for learning. Curriculum development, then, is a process that organizes the learning act along the line of value preferences.

Because of the decentralized nature of American education, the role of curriculum workers in interpreting values and arranging learning experiences is extremely important. Considerable difference exists in curriculum definitions, which indicates varied perceptions of the responsibilities of school programming.

Although the question, "What will schools do?" is unanswered in the 1990s, the process by which curriculum is developed is highly defined. We see curriculum development as a deductive process following the historic cycle of analysis, design, implementation, and evaluation.

In the second half of the twentieth century, curriculum planners have been forced to assimilate and organize extensive data related to the development of school programs. Key issues about the purpose of school programs have led to the collection and ordering of such data in four areas: social forces, treatment of knowledge, human growth and development, and the process of learning. In the future, planners face an increasing number of choices about what schools can be.

SUGGESTED LEARNING ACTIVITIES

1. Develop a time line of major events that have influenced education and altered the definition of the term *curriculum*.
2. Identify some ways in which curriculum workers analyze, design, implement, and evaluate school programs.
3. After reading this chapter, write your own definition of curriculum. Which words suggest an active role? A passive role?
4. What major changes in the foundation areas have occurred in the past decade? What implications do they have for schools?
5. Looking ahead one decade, what additional changes can schools anticipate as they enter the twenty-first century?
6. How would you respond to the claim of postmodernism that history can no longer guide us in planning school curricula?

NOTES

1. The Old Deluder Satan Act, one of the first regulatory acts passed by the colonists in the 1640s.
2. Robert M. Hutchins, *The Higher Learning in America* (New Haven, CT: Yale University Press, 1936), p. 82.
3. Arthur Bestor, *The Restoration of Learning* (New York: Alfred A. Knopf, 1956) pp. 48–49.
4. Phillip H. Phenix, "The Disciplines as Curriculum Content," in A. Harry Passow, ed., *Curriculum Crossroads* (New York: Teachers College Press, 1962) p. 64.
5. Peter F. Oliva, *Developing the Curriculum* (New York: Longman, 1988) p. 6.
6. Colin Marsh and George Willis, *Curriculum Alternative Approaches: Ongoing Issues* (Upper Saddle River, NJ: Prentice Hall, 1995).
7. Franklin Bobbitt, *How to Make a Curriculum* (New York: Houghton Mifflin, 1924), p. 10.
8. Hollis L. Caswell and Doak S. Campbell, *Curriculum Development* (New York: American Book Company, 1935), p. 66.
9. B. Othanel Smith, William O. Stanley, and J. Harlen Shores, *Fundamentals of Curriculum Development* (New York: Harcourt Brace Jovanovich, 1957), p. 3.
10. Ronald Doll, *Curriculum Improvement,* 2nd ed. (Boston: Allyn and Bacon, 1970).
11. Ralph W. Tyler, "The Curriculum Then and Now," in *Proceedings of the 1956 Conference on Testing Problems* (Princeton, NJ: Educational Testing Service, 1957), p. 79.
12. Hilda Taba, *Curriculum Development: Theory and Practice* (New York: Harcourt Brace Jovanovich, 1962), p. 11.
13. J. Galen Saylor and William M. Alexander, *Curriculum Planning for Schools* (New York: Holt, Rinehart & Winston, 1974), p. 6.
14. Mauritz Johnson, "Appropriate Research Directions in Curriculum and Instruction," *Curriculum Theory Network* 6 (Winter 1970–71): 25.
15. John McNeil, *Curriculum: A Comprehensive Introduction,* 3rd ed. (New York: Macmillan, 1985).
16. Daniel Tanner and Laurel Tanner, *Curriculum Development: Theory into Practice,* 3rd ed. (New York: Macmillan, 1995), p. 67.
17. Tanner and Tanner, *Curriculum Development: Theory into Practice,* Preface.

18. William Doll, Jr., *A Post Modern Perspective on Curriculum* (New York: Teachers College Press, 1993) p. 3.

19. P. Friere, *Education for a Critical Consciousness* (New York: Seabury Press, 1973), p. 96.

20. S. Aronowitz and H. Giroux, *Postmodern Education* (Westport, CT: Greenwood Publishing Company, 1991).

21. Tanner and Tanner, *Curriculum Development: Theory Into Practice,* 3rd ed., p. 68.

22. Taba, *Curriculum Development: Theory and Practice,* p. 9.

23. John Dewey, *The Child and the Curriculum* (Chicago: University of Chicago Press, 1902), p. 4.

24. Harold Rugg, *Curriculum-Making: Past and Present,* 26th Yearbook, Part I, National Society for the Study of Education (Chicago: University of Chicago Press, 1926), p. 22.

25. Boyd H. Bode, "Education at the Crossroads," *Progressive Education* 8 (1931): 543–44.

26. Hilda Taba, "General Techniques of Curriculum Planning," *American Education in the Postwar Period,* 44th Yearbook, Part I, National Society for the Study of Education (Chicago: University of Chicago Press, 1945), p. 58.

27. Taba, *Curriculum Development: Theory and Practice,* p. 10.

28. Taba, *Curriculum Development: Theory and Practice,* p. 30.

29. Rugg, *Curriculum-Making: Past and Present,* p. 22.

30. Ralph W. Tyler, *Basic Principles of Curriculum and Instruction* (Chicago: University of Chicago Press, 1949).

31. Robert F. Mager, *Goal Analysis* (Belmont, CA: Fearon Publishers, 1972).

32. Kathryn Feyereisen, A. John Fiorino, and Arlene T. Nowak, *Supervision and Curriculum Renewal: A Systems Approach* (New York: Appleton-Century-Crofts, 1970), p. 204.

33. A. Dean Hauenstein, *Curriculum Planning for Behavioral Development* (Worthington, OH: Charles A. Jones, 1975), p. 6.

34. Taba, *Curriculum Development: Theory and Practice,* p. 12.

35. Feyereisen et al., *Supervision and Curriculum Renewal,* p. 61.

36. William M. Alexander, "Curriculum Planning As It Should Be," address to Association for Supervision and Curriculum Development Conference, Chicago, October 29, 1971.

37. Jon Wiles and John Reed, "Quest: Education for a Technocratic Existence" (Unpublished manuscript, 1975), p. 58.

38. Charles Silberman, *Crisis in the Classroom* (New York: Random House, 1970), pp. 33–34.

39. For an unusual historical perspective of this problem, see *The National Elementary Principal* 56, No. 3 (January/February, 1977).

40. Paddy Chayefsky, *Network,* released by United Artists, 1977.

41. Wiles and Reed, "Quest," pp. 61–62.

42. Mike Malone, "Getting Personal," *Apple Magazine* 2, 1 (1981).

43. Arno A. Bellack, "Conceptions of Knowledge: Their Significance for Curriculum," in William Jenkins, ed., *The Nature of Knowledge: Implications for the Education of Teachers* (Milwaukee: University of Wisconsin—Milwaukee, 1962), p. 42.

44. Charles Reich, "The Greening of America," *New Yorker* (Sept. 26, 1970): 43–44.

45. Jerome S. Bruner, "Structures in Learning," *NEA Journal* 52 (March, 1963): 26.

46. Earl C. Kelley, *Education for What Is Real* (New York: Harper, 1947).

47. Alvin Toffler, *Future Shock* (New York: Random House, 1970).

48. Feyereisen et al., *Supervision and Curriculum Renewal,* p. 138.

49. Mario Fantini, "Reducing the Behavior Gap," *National Education Association Journal* 57 (January, 1968): 23–24.

50. John M. Culkin, "A Schoolman's Guide to Marshall McLuhan," *Saturday Review* 50, 11 (March 18, 1967): 71.

51. Marshall McLuhan and Quentin Fiore, *The Medium Is the Massage* (New York: Bantam Books, 1967).

52. John C. Flanagan, *The Identification, Development, and Utilization of Human Talents: The American High School Student,* Cooperative Research Project No. 635 (Pittsburgh, PA: University of Pittsburgh, 1964).

53. Robert J. Havighurst et al., *Growing Up in River City* (New York: J. Wiley & Sons, 1962).

54. Frederick Mosteller and Daniel P. Moynihan, eds., *On Equality of Educational Opportunity* (New York: Vintage Books, 1972).

55. Jon Wiles and Joseph Bondi, "The Care and Cultivation of Creativity," *Early Years* 12, 1 (August/September, 1981): 34–37, 46, 108.

56. Burton L. White, *Experience and Environment: Major Influences on the Development of the Young* (Englewood Cliffs, NJ: Prentice Hall, 1973).

57. "Baby Research Comes of Age," *Psychology Today* 21, 5 (May, 1987): 46–48.

58. B. F. Skinner, *Beyond Freedom and Dignity* (New York: Bantam/Vintage Books, 1972).

59. Lawrence Kohlberg and Rochelle Mayer, "Development as an Aim of Education," *Harvard Educational Review* 42 (November, 1972): 452–53.

60. Thomas H. Briggs, *Curriculum Problems* (New York: Macmillan, 1926).

61. Bruce Joyce, ed., "Changing School Culture Through Staff Development," *Association for Supervision and Curriculum Development 1990 Yearbook* (Alexandria, VA: ASCD, 1990), p. 7.

62. Bruce Joyce, "The Curriculum Worker of the Future," *The Curriculum: Retrospect and Prospect,* 71st Yearbook, Part I, National Society for the Study of Education (Chicago: University of Chicago Press, 1971), p. 307.

63. George Beauchamp, *Curriculum Theory* (Willamette, OR: Kagg Press, 1968).

64. Bruce Joyce, "The Curriculum Worker of the Future," p. 64.

65. Robert J. Schaefer, "Retrospect and Prospect," *The Curriculum: Retrospect and Prospect,* 71st Yearbook, National Society for the Study of Education (Chicago: University of Chicago Press, 1971), p. 10.

66. Louise Berman, *New Priorities in the Curriculum* (Columbus, OH: Charles Merrill, 1968).

67. James MacDonald, "Curriculum Development in Relation to Social and Intellectual Systems," *The Curriculum: Retrospect and Prospect,* 71st Yearbook, National Society for the Study of Education (Chicago: University of Chicago Press, 1971), p. 95.

BOOKS TO REVIEW

Aronowitz, S. and H. Giroux. *Education Still Under Siege.* Westport, CT: Greenwood Publishing Company, 1993.

Bobbitt, Franklin. *The Curriculum.* Boston: Houghton Mifflin, 1918.

Caswell, Hollis, and Doak S. Campbell. *Curriculum Development.* New York: American Book Company, 1935.

Dewey, John. *Democracy and Education.* New York: Macmillan, 1916.

Doll, Ronald. *Curriculum Improvement: Decision-Making and Process,* 9th ed. Needham Heights, MA: Allyn and Bacon, 1996.

Glickman, Carl. *Renewing America's Schools.* San Francisco: Jossey-Bass, 1993.

Jones, B., and R. Maloy. *Schools for an Information Age.* Westport, CT: Greenwood Publishing, 1996.

National Society for the Study of Education. *The Curriculum: Retrospect and Prospect.* Chicago: NSSE, 1971.

Sears, J. *Teaching and Thinking about Curriculum.* New York: Teachers College Press, 1990.

Taba, Hilda. *Curriculum Development: Theory and Practice.* New York: Harcourt Brace Jovanovich, 1962.

Tanner, Daniel. *History of School Curriculum.* New York: Macmillan, 1989.

Tanner, Laurel, ed. *Critical Issues in Curriculum.* Chicago: National Society for the Study of Education, 1988.

Toffler, Alvin. *Powershift: Knowledge, Wealth and Violence at the Eve of the 21st Century.* New York: Bantam Books, 1990.

chapter 2

THE ROLE OF PHILOSOPHY IN CURRICULUM PLANNING

At the heart of purposeful activity in curriculum development is an educational philosophy that assists in answering value-laden questions and making decisions from among the many choices. For John Dewey, America's most famous educator, a philosophy was a general theory of educating. One of Dewey's students, Boyd Bode, saw a philosophy as "a source of reflective consideration." Ralph Tyler, a leader in curriculum throughout much of this century, likened philosophy to "a screen for selecting educational objectives."

Philosophies can, therefore, serve curriculum leaders in many ways. They can help to

- [ ] Suggest purpose in education
- [ ] Clarify objectives and learning activities in school
- [ ] Define the roles of persons working in schools
- [ ] Guide the selection of learning strategies and tactics in the classroom

We believe that a philosophy is essential to any meaningful curriculum development effort.

In arriving at an educational philosophy, curriculum specialists are forced to consider value-laden choices. It is clear as we enter the twenty-first century that there are many ways to define and operate a school and that decisions made in defining the scope of curriculum will directly impact the substance and structure of educational programs. If curriculum specialists are aware of their own beliefs about education and learning, they will make better everyday decisions.

The need for curriculum workers to hold a philosophy of education has become increasingly obvious in the second half of the twentieth century as the rate of change in education has accelerated. Public education has witnessed wave after wave of innovation, reform, new themes, and other general signals of dissatisfaction with the status quo. Indicative of the seriousness of calls for reformation of public schools is the following statement issued by the President's Advisory Commission on Science:

> When school was short, and merely a supplement to the main activities of growing up, the form mattered little. But school has expanded to fill time that other activities once occupied, without substituting for them. . . . Every society must somehow solve the problem of transforming children into adults, for its very survival depends on that solution. In every society there is established some kind of institutional setting within which the transformation is to occur, in directions predicated by societal goals and values. . . . In our view, the institutional framework for maturation in the United States is in need of serious examination. The school system, as it now exists, offers an incomplete context for the accomplishment of many important facets of maturation.[1]

Although it is certain that there is a desire for change in public education today, there is no strong mandate for the direction of such change in the United States. In the absence of centralized public planning and policy formation, local school boards rely on input from pressure groups, expert opinion, and various forces in the societal flow. Often, decisions about school programs are made in an isolated, piecemeal fashion, without serious consideration of the pattern of decision making. When goals are unclear, when there is no public consensus about what schools should accomplish, when there are value-laden decisions, or when curriculum specialists are unable to articulate positions on controversial issues clearly, schools slip into the all-too-common pattern of reactive thinking and action.

The absence of direction often results in a curriculum that includes nearly everything but which accomplishes little. Given the public nature of American education, the dynamic nature of public school decision-making forums, and the dependence of school boards and superintendents on curriculum specialists for direction, the beliefs and values of the curriculum leader must be clear.

THE SEARCH FOR A PHILOSOPHICAL ATTITUDE

Although there has been a steady interest in educational philosophies for over a century in America, the use of such an orientation in program planning has been severely limited in the United States public education system. With the exception of the "progressive schools" of the 1930s, the "alternative" schools of the early 1970s, and the magnet and charter schools of the 1990s, few American education programs have emerged that reflect strong philosophical understanding and commitment. As Robert M. McClure has noted:

> With depressing few exceptions, curriculum design until the 1950s was a process of layering society's new knowledge on top of a hodgepodge accumulation of old knowl-

edge and arranging for feeding it, in prescribed time units, to students who may or may not have found it relevant to their own lives.[2]

The dependence of school leaders on public acquiescence for the development of school programs explains, in large part, the absence of philosophic consistency and the standardization of school programs over time. Without public demand for or approval of change, often interpreted in the public forum as no opposition, elected school leaders have failed to press for more distinct school programs.

Equally, the mandate of public education to serve all learners has acted to restrict the specification of educational ends and the development of tailored programs. The role of the schools as the assimilator of diverse cultures, from the turn of the century until the mid-1960s, contributed to the general nature of public school education.

Another factor in the absence of educational specificity in programs has been the lack of strong curriculum leadership at state and local levels. With the exception of university-based theorists, few curriculum specialists have had the understanding of philosophy, the clarity of vision, and the technical skills to direct school programs toward consistently meaningful activity. Although this condition is rapidly improving because of the greatly increased number of persons trained in curriculum development, the presence of a highly skilled curriculum leader often separates the successful school district from the mediocre school district.

The development of a clear and consistent set of beliefs about the purpose of education requires considerable thought, for there is a great amount of information to consider and strong arguments for the many philosophical positions which have developed. Perhaps the most important is Galen Saylor and William M. Alexander's observation that schooling is always a "moral enterprise":

> A society establishes and supports schools for certain purposes; it seeks to achieve certain ends or attain desired outcomes. Efforts of adults to direct the experiences of young people in a formal institution such as the school constitute preferences for certain human ends and values.
>
> Schooling is a moral venture, one that necessitates choosing values among innumerable possibilities. These choices constitute the starting point in curriculum planning.[3]

To illustrate the diversity of beliefs about the purpose of formal education and approaches to educating, consider the two following statements by Robert Hutchins and A. S. Neill. These statements are representative of two established educational philosophies: *perennialism* and *existentialism*. First, Hutchins:

> The ideal education is not an ad hoc education, not an education directed to immediate needs; it is not a specialized education, or a preprofessional education; it is not a utilitarian education. It is an education calculated to develop the mind.
>
> I have old-fashioned prejudices in favor of the three R's and the liberal arts, in favor of trying to understand the greatest works that the human race has produced. I believe that these are permanent necessities, the intellectual tools that are needed to understand the ideas and ideals of our world.[4]

Now, Neill:

> Well, we set out to make a school in which we should allow children to be themselves. In order to do this, we had to renounce all discipline, all direction, all suggestion, all moral training. . . . All it required was what we had—a complete belief in the child as a good, not evil being. For almost forty years, this belief in the goodness of the child has never wavered; it rather has become a final faith. My view is that a child is innately wise and realistic. If left to himself without adult suggestions of any kind, he will develop as far as he is capable of developing.[5]

Such differences of opinion about the purpose and means of educating are extreme, but they illustrate the range of choices to be made by curriculum planners. These statements also indicate the trends of education that various philosophies favor. The perennialists who favor a highly controlled curriculum, much structure, strict discipline, and uniform treatment for students can easily identify with trends such as back-to-the-basics and accountability. The existentialists who see a nonschool environment for personal growth, an environment with highly individualized activities and low degrees of formal structure, can identify with alternative programs, student rights movements, and other nonstandard choices.

Critical Questions to Be Answered

Each curriculum planner must face and answer some difficult questions about the purpose and organization of schooling. The answers to such questions are critical to school planning and establish the criteria for future decision making and action. As Saylor and Alexander state the condition, it is one of defining responsibility:

> In selecting the basic goals which the school should seek to serve from among the sum total of ends for which people strive the curriculum planner faces the major issue: In the total process of human development what parts or aspects should the school accept responsibility for guiding?[6]

Daniel Tanner and Laurel Tanner observe that three major ends for schooling have been suggested repeatedly in the past:

> Throughout the twentieth century educational opinion and practice have been sharply divided as to whether the dominant source and influence for curriculum development should be the body of organized scholarship (the specialties and divisions of academic knowledge), the learner (the immature developing being), or society (contemporary adult life). . . . [7]

The decision of the curriculum leader to relate to the knowledge bases of the past, the social concerns of the present, or the future needs of society is critical. Among other things, this decision will determine whether the role of the curriculum specialist is to restructure or only to refine the existing system of education.

Most often, curriculum development in schools is a mechanical, static function because the content base is accepted as the main criterion for curriculum work:

In the absence of reflective consideration of what constitutes the good man leading the good life in the good society, the curriculum tends to be regarded as a mechanical means of developing the necessary skills of young people in conformance with the pervading demands of the larger social scene. Under such circumstances, the school does not need to bring into question the existing social situation, nor does it need to enable pupils to examine through reflective thinking possible alternative solutions to social problems. Instead, the school is merely expected to do the bidding of whatever powers and forces are most dominant in the larger society at any given time.[8]

If, however, the curriculum planner accepts the needs of learners as a criterion for planning school programs, such as in the early childhood and middle school programs of the 1970s or special education "inclusion" of the 1990s, the purpose of the formal education program is altered. The same is true if social reform or improving the society is chosen as the purpose of schools. In accepting an alteration of the traditional criterion for developing school programs, curriculum developers "cross over" into an advocacy role for change as they attempt to restructure the existing curriculum. The effectiveness of such a position in curriculum work is often determined by the clarity of the new objectives to be achieved.

A number of primary questions override the value choices of all major educational philosophies: What is the purpose of education? What kind of citizens and what kind of society do we want? What methods of instruction or classroom organization must we provide to produce these desired ends?

McNeil poses eight questions that are useful in developing the philosophical assumptions needed to screen educational objectives:

1. Is the purpose of school to change, adapt to, or accept the social order?
2. What can a school do better than any other agency or institution?
3. What objectives should be common to all?
4. Should objectives stress cooperation or competition?
5. Should objectives deal with controversial issues, or only those things for which there is established knowledge?
6. Should attitudes be taught? Fundamental skills? Problem-solving strategies?
7. Should teachers emphasize subject matter or try to create behavior outside of school?
8. Should objectives be based on the needs of the local community? Society in general? Expressed needs of students?[9]

The Struggle to Be a Decisive Leader

Few educators would deny the importance of a philosophy in directing activity, but few school districts or teachers relish discussions on the topic. Even well-known educators have confessed a dislike for such discourse:

It is well to rid oneself of this business of "aims of education." Discussions on this subject are among the dullest and most fruitless of human pursuits.[10]

> A sense of distasteful weariness overtakes me whenever I hear someone discussing educational goals and philosophy.[11]

In the past, part of the problem with discussing educational philosophies in earnest has been the pervasiveness of the subject-dominated curriculum in American schools. This problem has been further compounded by "expert opinion" on the topic by college professors who are products of the system and, therefore, possess monumental conflict of interest in rendering an opinion. In school districts where inquiry into the purpose of educating has been quickly followed by retrenchment of the subject-matter curriculum, there has been little payoff in conducting philosophical discussions. But, where inquiry into educational purpose is honest, open, and leads to meaningful change, philosophical discussions are among the most exciting endeavors.

Charles Silberman, in his book *Crisis in the Classroom,* expressed the meaning of philosophical understandings for the learning programs of the school:

> What educators must realize, moreover, is that how they teach and how they act may be more important than what they teach. The way we do things, that is to say, shapes values more directly and more effectively than the way we talk about them. Certainly administrative procedures like automatic promotion, homogeneous grouping, racial segregation, or selective admission to higher education affect "citizenship education" more profoundly than does the social studies curriculum. And children are taught a host of lessons about values, ethics, morality, character, and conduct every day of the week, less by the conduct of the curriculum than by the way schools are organized, the ways teachers and parents behave, the way they talk to children and each other, the kinds of behavior they approve or reward and the kinds they disapprove and punish. These lessons are far more powerful than verbalizations that accompany them and that they frequently controvert.[12]

Two major benefits can be derived from an exploration of philosophical attitudes. First, major problem areas and inconsistencies in the school program can be identified:

> Many contemporary educational principles and practices are something of a hodge-podge rooted in premises about the nature of man and his relationship with his physical-social environment that frequently are incompatible with one another.[13]

Second, areas of common ground among those responsible for educational leadership can be discovered. Common values that overlap individual beliefs form the most fertile ground for curricular collaboration and the development of successful projects and programs.

Before curriculum specialists can work with parents, teachers, administrators, and other educators to explore educational values, they must complete an examination of their own attitudes. During this process, the curriculum worker is seeking to identify a value structure that can organize and relate the many aspects of planning.

To clarify the values and beliefs that will tie together curriculum organization, instructional procedures, learning roles, materials selection, and other components of school planning, curriculum leaders must identify themes that seem true to them. Although this process may be time consuming, the investment is necessary.

Curriculum leaders, in order to be both decisive and effective in their roles, must combat the urge to ignore the value implications of the job or reduce all arguments to "thoughtful uncertainty."

DETERMINANTS OF AN EDUCATIONAL PHILOSOPHY

Major philosophies of life and education have traditionally been defined by three criteria: What is good? What is true? What is real? Individual perceptions of goodness, truth, and reality differ considerably, and an analysis of these questions reveals unique patterns of response. When such responses are categorized and labeled, they become formal philosophies.

In the language of philosophy, the study of goodness is referred to as *axiology,* truth as *epistemology,* and reality as *ontology.* Axiological questions deal primarily with values; in a school context, philosophical arguments are concerned with the ultimate source of values to be taught. Questions of an epistemological nature in a school context are directed toward the mediums of learning or the best means of seeking truth. Ontological questions, in search of reality, are most often concerned with the substance of learning, or content of study. Thus, the standard philosophic inquiries concerning goodness, truth, and reality are translated into questions concerning the source, medium, and form of learning in a school environment.

These queries are not simple, for there are many ways to select ideas, translate them into instructional patterns, and package them into curriculum programs. Those possibilities are forever increasing as our knowledge of the world becomes more sophisticated. Essential questions arise, questions that must be answered prior to planning learning experiences for students. Why do schools exist? What should be taught? What is the role of the teacher and the student? How does the school deal with change?

FIVE EDUCATIONAL PHILOSOPHIES

There are many kinds of educational philosophies, but for the sake of simplicity, it is possible to extract five distinct ones. These five philosophies are (1) perennialism, (2) idealism, (3) realism, (4) experimentalism, and (5) existentialism. Collectively, these philosophies represent a broad spectrum of thought about what schools should be and do. Educators holding these philosophies would create very different schools for students to attend and in which they would learn. In the following sections, each of these standard philosophies is discussed in terms of its posture on axiological, epistemological, and ontological questions.

The five standard philosophies are compared in Table 2.1 in terms of attitudes on significant questions.

Perennialism

The most conservative, traditional, or inflexible of the five philosophies is *perennialism,* a philosophy drawing heavily from classical definitions of education. Perennialists believe that education, like human nature, is a constant. Because the distin-

TABLE 2.1 Five Major Educational Philosophies

	Perennialism	Idealism	Realism	Experimentalism	Existentialism
Reality Ontology	A world of reason and God	A world of the mind	A world of things	A world of experience	A world of existing
Truth (Knowledge) Epistemology	Reason and revelation	Consistency of ideas	Correspondence and sensation (as we see it)	What works What is	Personal, subjective choice
Goodness Axiology	Rationality	Imitation of ideal self, person to be emulated	Laws of nature	The public test	Freedom
Teaching Reality	Disciplinary subjects and doctrine	Subject of the mind—literary, philosophical, religious	Subjects of physical world—math, science	Subject matter of social experiences—social studies	Subject matter of choice—art, ethics, philosophy
Teaching Truth	Discipline of the mind via drill	Teaching ideas via lecture, discussion	Teaching for mastery, of information—demonstrate, recite	Problem-solving, project method	Arousing personal responses—questioning
Teaching Goodness (Values)	Disciplining behavior (to reason)	Imitating heroes and other exemplars	Training in rules of conduct	Making group decisions in light of consequences	Awakening self to responsibility
Why Schools Exist	To reveal reason and God's will	To sharpen the mind and intellectual processes	To reveal the order of the world and universe	To discover and expand the society we live in to share experiences	To aid children in knowing themselves and their place in society
What Should Be Taught	External truths	Wisdom of the ages	Laws of physical reality	Group inquiry into social problems and social sciences, method and subject together	Unregimented topic areas
Role of the Teacher	Interprets, tells	Reports, person to be emulated	Displays, imparts knowledge	Aids, consultant	Questions, assists student in personal journey
Role of the Student	Passive reception	Receives, memorizes	Manipulates, passive participation	Active participation, contributes	Determines own rules
School's Attitude Toward Change	Truth is eternal, no real change	Truth to be preserved, anti-change	Always coming toward perfection, orderly change	Change is ever-present, a process	Change is necessary at all times

guishing characteristic of humans is the ability to reason, education should focus on developing rationality. Education, for the perennialist, is a preparation for life, and students should be taught the world's permanencies through structured study.

For the perennialist, reality is a world of reason. Such truths are revealed to us through study and sometimes through divine acts. Goodness is to be found in rationality itself. Perennialists favor a curriculum of subjects and doctrine, taught through highly disciplined drill and behavior control. Schools for the perennialist exist primarily to reveal reason by teaching eternal truths. The teacher interprets and tells. The student is a passive recipient. Because truth is eternal, all change in the immediate school environment is largely superficial.

Idealism

Idealism is a philosophy that espouses the refined wisdom of men and women. Reality is seen as a world within a person's mind. Truth is to be found in the consistency of ideas. Goodness is an ideal state, something to strive to attain.

Idealists favor schools that teach subjects of the mind, such as are found in most public school classrooms. Teachers, for the idealist, would be models of ideal behavior.

For idealists, the schools' function is to sharpen intellectual processes, to present the wisdom of the ages, and to present models of behavior that are exemplary. Students in such schools would have a somewhat passive role, receiving and memorizing the reporting of the teacher. Change in the school program would generally be considered an intrusion on the orderly process of educating.

Realism

For the *realist,* the world is as it is, and the job of schools is to teach students about the world. Goodness, for the realist, is found in the laws of nature and the order of the physical world. Truth is the simple correspondences of observation.

The realist favors a school dominated by subjects of the here-and-now world, such as math and science. Students would be taught factual information for mastery. The teacher would impart knowledge of this reality to students or display such reality for observation and study. Classrooms would be highly ordered and disciplined, like nature, and the students would be passive participants in the study of things. Changes in school would be perceived as a natural evolution toward a perfection of order.

Experimentalism

For the *experimentalist,* the world is an ever-changing place. Reality is what is actually experienced. Truth is what presently functions. Goodness is what is accepted by public test. Unlike the perennialist, idealist, and realist, the experimentalist openly accepts change and continually seeks to discover new ways to expand and improve society.

The experimentalist favors a school with heavy emphasis on social subjects and experiences. Learning would occur through a problem-solving or inquiry format. Teachers would aid learners or consult with learners who would be actively involved in discovering and experiencing the world in which they live. Such an education program's focus on value development would factor in group consequences.

Existentialism

The *existentialist* sees the world as one personal subjectivity, where goodness, truth, and reality are individually defined. Reality is a world of existing, truth subjectively chosen, and goodness a matter of freedom.

For existentialists, schools, if they existed at all, would be places that assisted students in knowing themselves and learning their place in society. If subject matter existed, it would be a matter of interpretation such as the arts, ethics, or philosophy. Teacher–student interaction would center around assisting students in their personal learning journeys. Change in school environments would be embraced as both a natural and necessary phenomenon. Nonschooling and individually determined curriculum would be a possibility.

PHILOSOPHY PREFERENCE ASSESSMENT

It should be noted that few educators hold a pure version of any of these philosophies because schools are complex places with many forces vying for prominence. These schools of thought have evolved as distinctive forms of philosophy following the examination of beliefs on pertinent issues. When an educator chooses not to adopt a single philosophy, or blends philosophies for experience, or selectively applies educational philosophies in practice, it is called an *eclectic* position. Most classrooms and public schools come closest to an eclectic stance, applying philosophic preferences as conditions demand.

Whatever the educator's philosophy or beliefs about schools—and each of the five philosophies presented here is a legitimate belief—it is critical that these values be clarified and understood in terms of their implications. To this end, you can participate in a self-assessment (see Figure 2.1) that has been developed to show preferences on value-laden educational questions.

What Is Your Philosophy?

The test question numbers from Figure 2.1 that relate to the five standard philosophies of education are as follows:

1. Perennialist:	6, 8, 10, 13, 15, 31, 34, 37
2. Idealist:	9, 11, 19, 21, 24, 27, 29, 33
3. Realist:	4, 7, 12, 20, 22, 23, 26, 28
4. Experimentalist:	2, 3, 14, 17, 25, 35, 39, 40
5. Existentialist:	1, 5, 16, 18, 30, 32, 36, 38

Scoring Steps
1. For each set (for example, the eight perennialist questions), add the value of the answers given. In a single set of numbers, the total should fall between 8 (all ones) and 40 (all fives).
2. Divide the total score for each set by 5 (example: 40 ÷ 5 = 8).
3. Plot the scores on the graph shown in Figure 2.2.

Directions: For each item below, respond according to the strength of your belief, scoring the item on a scale of 1 through 5. A one (1) indicates strong disagreement, a five (5) strong agreement. Use a separate sheet of paper.

1. Ideal teachers are constant questioners.
2. Schools exist for societal improvement.
3. Teaching should center around the inquiry technique.
4. Demonstration and recitation are essential components for learning.
5. Students should always be permitted to determine their own rules in the educational process.
6. Reality is spiritual and rational.
7. Curriculum should be based on the laws of natural science.
8. The teacher should be a strong authority figure in the classroom.
9. The student is a receiver of knowledge.
10. Ideal teachers interpret knowledge.
11. Lecture-discussion is the most effective teaching technique.
12. Institutions should seek avenues toward self-improvement through an orderly process.
13. Schools are obligated to teach moral truths.
14. School programs should focus on social problems and issues.
15. Institutions exist to preserve and strengthen spiritual and social values.
16. Subjective opinion reveals truth.
17. Teachers are seen as facilitators of learning.
18. Schools should be educational "smorgasbords."
19. Memorization is the key to process skills.
20. Reality consists of objects.
21. Schools exist to foster the intellectual process.
22. Schools foster an orderly means for change.
23. There are essential skills everyone must learn.
24. Teaching by subject area is the most effective approach.
25. Students should play an active part in program design and evaluation.
26. A functioning member of society follows rules of conduct.
27. Reality is rational.
28. Schools should reflect the society they serve.
29. The teacher should set an example for the students.
30. The most effective learning does not take place in a highly structured, strictly disciplined environment.
31. The curriculum should be based on unchanging spiritual truths.
32. The most effective learning is nonstructured.
33. Truth is a constant expressed through ideas.
34. Drill and factual knowledge are important components of any learning environment.
35. Societal consensus determines morality.
36. Knowledge is gained primarily through the senses.
37. There are essential pieces of knowledge that everyone should know.
38. The school exists to facilitate self-awareness.
39. Change is an ever-present process.
40. Truths are best taught through the inquiry process.

FIGURE 2.1 Philosophy Preference Assessment

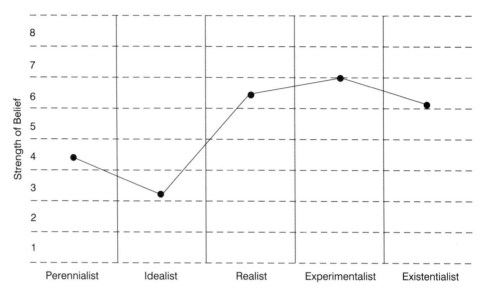

FIGURE 2.2   Composite Graph for Philosophy Preference Assessment

Interpretation of Scoring.   Having scored and plotted your responses on the grid provided, you now have a profile distinctive to your own beliefs about schools. It can be noted that some patterns are common and, therefore, subject to interpretation. The pattern already on the grid (Figure 2.2), for instance, is a composite response by over 5000 students, both graduate and undergraduate, at five universities.

Pattern 1.   If your profile on the response grid is basically flat, reflecting approximately the same score for each set of questions, an inability to discriminate in terms of preference is indicated. See Figure 2.3.

Pattern 2.   If your pattern is generally a slanting line across the grid, you show a strong structured or nonstructured orientation in your reported beliefs about schools. See Figure 2.4.

Pattern 3.   If your pattern appears as a bimodal or trimodal distribution (two or three peaks), it indicates indecisiveness on crucial issues and suggests the need for

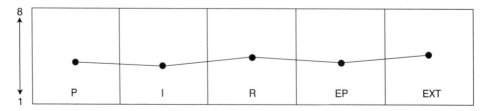

FIGURE 2.3   Pattern 1

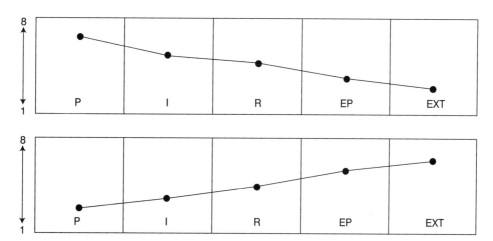

FIGURE 2.4   Pattern 2

further clarification. The closer the peaks (adjacent sets), the less contradiction in the responses. See Figure 2.5.

Pattern 4.   If the pattern appears U-shaped, as in either of the graphs in Figure 2.6, a significant amount of value inconsistency is indicated. Such a response would suggest strong beliefs in very different and divergent systems.

Pattern 5.   Finally, a pattern that is simply a flowing curve without sharp peaks and valleys may suggest either an eclectic philosophy or a person only beginning to study his or her own philosophy. See Figure 2.7.

PHILOSOPHIES AS FOUND IN SCHOOLS

During this century, schools in America have evolved from highly standardized content-focused institutions to more flexible and diverse forms of education. Our understandings of human development and the learning process and the pressures on our rapidly changing society account for these alterations of the schooling form.

All schools are designed to promote an education, but the designs of school curriculums differ just as philosophies differ. Schools represent a blueprint, or plan, to promote learning; because the ends sought by planners differ, all schools are not

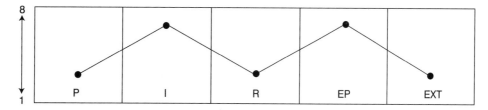

FIGURE 2.5   Pattern 3

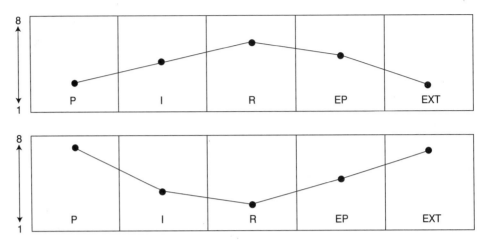

FIGURE 2.6   Pattern 4

alike. This section introduces the fifteen dimensions of school design, dimensions by which schools can be compared and contrasted. Each dimension has been prepared to illuminate the various philosophic continuums within schools. Although these continuums do not match our five philosophies precisely, you can begin to see a rough parallel between these philosophies and the various dimensions of the school setting. Questions for planners are highlighted for your consideration.

The intentions of schooling might be thought of as a continuum of choices. On one end of such a continuum is the belief that education is the process of shaping raw human talent into something definitive and useful to society. This classic view of education sees schools shaping and refining human thought and behavior through an increasingly controlled program of study. Such control, in the legitimate sense of the word, is accomplished by structuring the learning environment to facilitate highly predictable ends.

On the other end of that same choice continuum is the belief that human talents are best managed by allowing the natural capacities of individuals to develop through the removal of growth barriers. This definition of education would have schools acting to release the student from behaviors and perceptions that limit personal development. Thus, the institution of the school would formally seek the expansion of human potential in the process of learning by promoting flexibility in the learning environment.

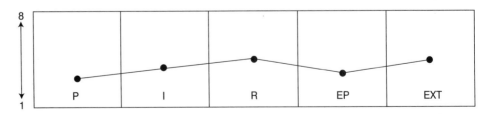

FIGURE 2.7   Pattern 5

Strong arguments can be made for either of these positions, as well as for the many intermediate stances on such a continuum. The crucial concept to be understood is that schools are institutions created by society to accomplish certain ends. Because there are many possible goals for the institution of the school, there are many legitimate forms of schooling. To the degree that the organization of the school corresponds with the objectives of the school, the school can effectively educate students.

The range of possible intentions for a school program, bordered on one end by a school seeking maximum control and on the other by a school promoting maximum freedom, can be translated into the universal variables of structure versus flexibility. These two variables—structure and flexibility—are used to facilitate the analysis of fifteen major dimensions of schooling. These fifteen dimensions can all be readily observed by a visitor to a school:

1. Community involvement
2. School buildings and grounds
3. Classroom spaces
4. Organization of knowledge
5. Uses of learning materials
6. Philosophy of education
7. Teaching strategies
8. Staffing patterns
9. Organization of students
10. Rules and regulations
11. Disciplinary measures
12. Reporting student progress
13. Administrative attitudes
14. Teacher roles
15. Student roles

Examining the school by such criteria, in a systematic manner, will help you see a school in its totality. The underlying beliefs about educating will become more obvious, and the program congruence or inconsistencies will be more visible. In short, you will be able to analyze the dimensions of a school setting in a selective and regular way and to understand the philosophic intent of the curriculum. The numbered rating scales in the following sections refer to this list.

The Learning Environment

It is clear that environments, both real and perceived, set a tone for learning. What people feel about the spaces that they occupy or in which they interact causes them to behave in certain ways. For instance, churches call for discreet behavior; stadiums elicit a different behavior.

Traditionally, schools have been solitary, sedate, and ordered environments. This atmosphere was the result of many forces: a narrow definition of formal education, a limited public access to knowledge, a didactic (telling–listening) format for learning.

In contrast, many innovative schools seem to be the organizational opposite of the traditional, structured school. They are often open, noisy, and sometimes seemingly chaotic activity centers. These changes in schools are the result of both a changing definition of education and a new understanding of the environmental conditions that enhance learning.

Three measures of the learning environments of schools are the relationship of the school and the surrounding community, the construction and use of buildings and grounds, and the organization of learning spaces within buildings. Within each of these three areas, selected dimensions have been identified that may help you to understand the learning environment of the school.

Community Involvement.   Individual schools differ according to the degree and type of interaction that they enjoy with the immediate community. Schools that perceive their role as shaping the behavior and thoughts of students into acceptable patterns normally seek to limit community access and involvement in the school program. By limiting community access, the school also limits community influence on the school program and thus ensures more predictable outcomes for students.

Conversely, schools intent on expanding student responses to the educational process generally encourage community access and involvement in school activities. By encouraging community access, the school encourages community influence, thus ensuring the divergent input characteristic of most communities.

Measures of community access and involvement with a school are plentiful. A simple measure readily available to the observer is to note how many and what kinds of nonschool personnel are in a school building on a given day. Perhaps a more analytic approach to the assessment of involvement, however, is to observe the school operation in terms of physical, legal, participatory, and intellectual access.

The descriptive continuums in Figure 2.8 suggest the potential range of alternatives present in schools.

Physical access.   In a physical sense, community involvement can be measured by the amount of quasi-school-related activity occurring in the school building. Activities such as school-sponsored visits to the building, community-sponsored functions in the building, parental participation in school-sponsored activities, and school programs being conducted in the community are indicative of interchange and involvement.

On the other hand, schools where the public is never invited to visit, where classes never leave the building, where the public is fenced out or locked out, held at the office when visiting, not welcome after school hours, or discouraged from mobility within the spaces of the school indicate limited access and involvement.

Legal access.   Legally, the community is allowed to become involved with the school at varying levels. In a tightly structured or closed school, legal access is normally restricted to setting limits and voting on school bonds. Increasing participation is measured by electing school officials and the chief administrative officer of the school district. Further access is indicated by school-building-level committees (such as a textbook selection committee) that allow community members to play an

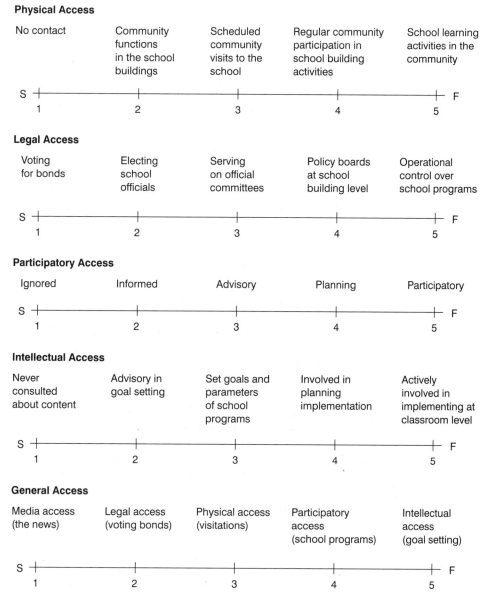

FIGURE 2.8   Types of Community Access to Schools

active role in policy formation. Not surprisingly, so-called community schools allow the ultimate access; parents and the community-at-large serve in governance roles over school operation and activity.

Participatory access.   In terms of participation in the daily operation of the school program, the community can be ignored, informed, included at an advisory level, or asked to participate wholly. Whether a school chooses to include the community in the type of school program that is being experienced by the students depends on whether such participation is seen as contributing to or detracting from the mission of the school.

Intellectual access.   Finally, there is an intellectual dimension to community involvement with the school that is indicated by access to goal setting, resource allocation, and program development. To the degree that the community is excluded from thinking about the substance of what is taught and the method of instruction, the school is characterized by limited intellectual access or high structures (S). If the school encourages programmatic and instructional participation from parents and members of the community, access or high flexibility (F) is evidenced.

There are great differences in the degree of access and community involvement with individual school buildings. As such, community involvement represents one salient dimension of the learning environment.

Questions.   What is the relationship of the school to the community? What rights do the tax-paying public have in school governance? How much autonomy should professionals have in operating public schools?

School Buildings and Grounds.   The physical nature of school buildings and school grounds may be subtle indicators of the school's perceived mission and, therefore, useful measures for a visitor or interested observer. Features such as access points, building warmth, traffic control inside the building, and space priorities may reflect the intended program of the school.

Architects have observed that buildings are a physical expression of content. A dull, drab, unexciting building may reflect a dull, drab, unexciting educational process. An exciting, stimulating, dynamic building may reflect an active, creative learning center. A building not only expresses its interior activity but may also reflect, and even control, the success of these functions. If school corridors, for example, are colorful, well lighted, and visually expansive, this excitement and stimulation direct the individual in such a space. It is for this reason that most new airports have extremely wide and brightly colored corridors. The environment "sets up" the participant dispositionally.

School buildings have changed a great deal during this century, and those changes in architecture and construction reflect more subtle changes in the programs of schools. A stereotypic evolution of school buildings in the United States would show a progression from a cellular lecture hall (many one-room school houses together) to an open and largely unstructured space, as illustrated in Figure 2.9.★

Although many of these changes might be explained by evolutions in architecture and cost-effectiveness demands, a primary force behind the diminishing structure in school buildings has been the dissemination of knowledge through other mediums. As the essential curriculum of the turn of the century gave way to

---

★In the 1990s, districts are opting to use site-constructed additions (portable) to expand capacity at school sites rather than construct totally new buildings. This modular strategy reflects an awareness of the ups and downs of school populations caused by mobility and birth rate.

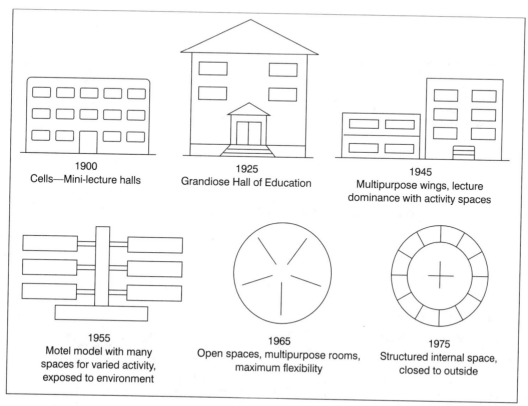

FIGURE 2.9   Evolution of School Buildings

a more broadly focused academic preparation, buildings were designed to incorporate diversity. Because spaces had multiple uses, the construction was necessarily flexible in design. With the advent of interactive computers and a universe of possible knowledge, the role of buildings is becoming less clear as this book is written. Storefronts may serve learning as well as traditional schools if "home schooling" and learning networks structure the curriculum.

Just because a school building is traditional or open-space in design, however, tells the visitor little about the current philosophy of the school. Many flexible programs are found in old "egg crate" buildings, and highly structured programs are sometimes found in modern open-space schools. Returning to our analytic tools—the degree of access, the warmth of the building, traffic control patterns inside the building, and space priorities—we can begin to know the real program in the building.

The descriptive continuums in Figure 2.10 suggest the potential range of alternatives present in schools.

Degree of access.   Many schools, because of genuine danger in the immediate neighborhood, limit the number of access points to the school building. Other schools deliberately limit public access as a means of controlling the environment and per-

Degree of Access

| Highly visible control of access exterior building | Access control visible interior only, high regimentation | Access control visible exterior only | Order visible but not excessive | Access not controlled exterior or interior |

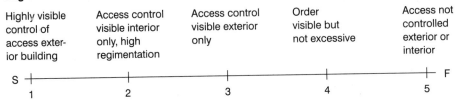

S   1   2   3   4   5   F

Building Warmth

| Spaces drab, overwhelming, repulsive, cold | Spaces ordered and monotonous | Spaces neutral, neither pleasant nor unpleasant | Spaces pleasant, light, clean, attractive | Spaces inviting, cheery, colorful |

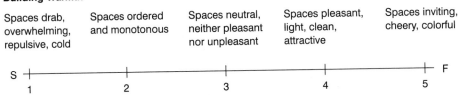

S   1   2   3   4   5   F

Traffic Control Patterns

| Movement in building highly controlled | Movement patterns structured by arrangement | Traffic patterns established | Traffic patterns not specified; options available to individuals | Movement patterns not discernible |

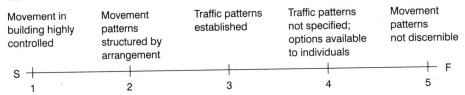

S   1   2   3   4   5   F

Space Priorities

| Space allocation grossly distorted | Space allocation highly disproportioned in building | Some priorities via space allocation obvious | Space equally allocated to various components, location key | No space priority observable by size or locale |

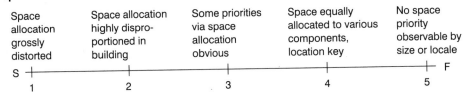

S   1   2   3   4   5   F

Grounds

| Grounds not in active use | Grounds used for informal activity | Grounds used for specific activity | Grounds use variable | Grounds used extensively for multiple activity |

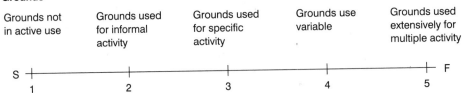

S   1   2   3   4   5   F

FIGURE 2.10 Alternative Uses of School Buildings and Grounds

sonnel in the building. Signs of extreme control in school buildings are a single entrance for all entering the building, constantly locked spaces such as bathrooms and auxiliary spaces, and purposeful physical barriers to movement, such as long unbroken counters in school offices.

Cues such as these tell visitors, students, and even teachers in the building that there are acceptable and unacceptable ways to enter the building and move in the building. Highly controlled access and mobility in school buildings indicate a belief that only certain types of movement in a building are conducive to successful education.

Building warmth.   Related to physical access is the concept of building warmth. The size of spaces, shape of spaces, scale of the environment (relationship between the size of the people and objects in the environment), coloration, and use of lighting all affect the warmth of a school building. Generally speaking, a combination of extreme space (large or small), extreme light (bright or dim), extreme coloration (too drab or too bright), repelling shapes (not geometrical or too geometrical), or disproportionate scale (too large or too small) can make occupants feel uncomfortable.

In the past, small classrooms with oversized furniture, drab coloration, and square walls have been used purposefully to control environment stimulation and direct attention to the teacher. Such a discomforting setting presupposed that teacher behavior was the significant action in the learning environment.

More recently, schools have used bright colors, curved walls, large expansive spaces, and acoustical treatments to encourage student mobility and mental freedom. Such an environment presupposes that education is an act that is highly individual and conducted through exploration. Control under such environmental conditions is often difficult.

Although a few school buildings are constructed to promote an identifiable pattern of instruction, the effect of environmental warmth is great on instructional procedure. Failure to consider this factor has led to many unsuccessful and inefficient teaching episodes.

Traffic control patterns.   Traffic control within a school building, made famous by Bel Kaufman's book *Up the Down Staircase,*[14] is also a reflection of the school's belief about the nature of education. Many schools go to great lengths to communicate order to inhabitants of the building. Adhesive strips dividing hallways into acceptable paths, turnstiles, fences, and children marching single file along walls are indicative of such structure in a building.

Buildings in which flexibility is encouraged will have curved sidewalks, doorless entrances to learning spaces, seating spaces where occupants can stop and rest enroute to their destinations, and multiple patterns of individual progression from point to point in the building.

Space priorities.   Finally, space usage and priorities reflect the learning environment in school buildings. Priorities are indicated by both the size of spaces in the building and the location of spaces in the building. In some schools, old and new, a significant portion of total available space is dominated by single-event spaces such as auditoriums, gymnasiums, swimming pools, and central office suites. In terms of construction costs and use, these spaces speak subtly of the priorities of the resident educators.

The number, kind, and quality of spaces can be a measure of the definition of educational priority in a school building.

A second, and perhaps more accurate, measure of space priority in a school building is the location of various areas. Studies of school buildings have indicated that teachers who have more seniority in a building have better resource bases than do the other teachers. How much space, for instance, does the English department have? Where is the fine arts complex located? What new additions have been made to the building, and which program do they serve?

Grounds.   Beyond the structural walls of the school building lie the school grounds. Sometimes, these spaces will reveal the attitude of the school toward learning. One interesting measure of the schoolyard is whether it is being used at all. Some schools located on ten-acre sites never plant a bush or add a piece of equipment to make the grounds useful to the school. Other schools, by contrast, use the grounds extensively and perceive them as an extension of the formal learning spaces.

Another question to be asked about the school grounds is whether they are generally used for student loitering, casual recreation, physical education, or comprehensive educational purposes. Equipment and student behavior will indicate which, if any, uses are made of this valuable resource.

There are great differences in how individual schools use their buildings and grounds. Thus, the use of these resources represents another relevant dimension of the school environment.

Questions.   In continuing to build traditional school buildings, do we force "function" to follow form? In this age of technology, could significant cost savings be realized by providing an alternative to school buildings?

Classroom Spaces.   Just as the school learning environment may be revealed in school dimensions such as community involvement and building use, the organization, movement, and ownership of physical space in the classroom are often indicative of the intentions of the school. In viewing these characteristics of the classroom, it is again obvious that not all schools are alike.

Classroom organization.   One way of viewing the classroom spaces is in terms of the organization for instructional effectiveness. A traditional pattern would be to arrange the room so that all vision and attention are on the teacher. Figure 2.11 shows that there is little opportunity for lateral communication. Activity is fixed by the arrangement of furniture. The conditions are perfect for teacher lecture but little else.

Another possibility in organization of classroom spaces is to create multipurpose spaces with the focus of attention generally in the center of the classroom (as shown in Figure 2.12). This style permits increased student involvement, mobility, and varied learning activities simultaneously. It does not focus attention solely on the teacher and cannot easily be controlled in terms of noise or lateral communication among students.

FIGURE 2.11 Traditional
Classroom Arrangement

The extreme degree of flexibility in organization of classroom spaces is, of course, to perceive the classroom as simply a place where learners meet to prepare for educational experiences both in the school building and in the community.

Classroom movement. Pupil movement within the classroom may be another subtle indicator of the structure or flexibility present in the learning environment (see

FIGURE 2.12 Classroom
with Multipurpose Spaces

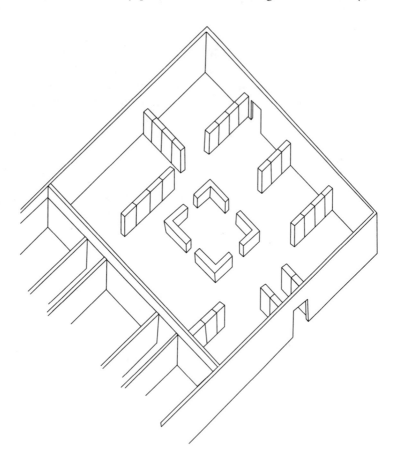

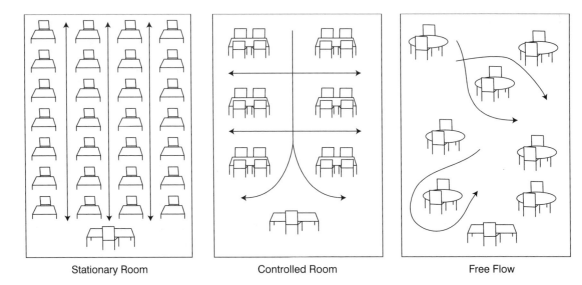

Stationary Room   Controlled Room   Free Flow

FIGURE 2.13   Patterns of Pupil Movement

Figure 2.13). Movement in some classrooms is totally dependent on the teacher. Students in such a classroom must request permission to talk, go to the washroom, or approach the teacher. Such structure usually minimizes noise and confusion but restricts activity to only verbal exchange. When movement occurs in such classrooms, it is generally to and from the teacher's desk.

In a less stationary classroom, movement is possible within controlled patterns monitored by the teacher. Movement is usually contextual, depending on the activity. During teacher talk, for instance, movement may not be allowed; at other times, students may be able to sharpen pencils, get supplies, or leave the room for water without complete dependence on teacher approval.

Pupil movement is sometimes left to the complete discretion of the student. Even during a lesson or a teacher explanation, a student may leave to use the washroom. In open-space buildings with high degrees of program flexibility, students are often seen moving unsupervised from one learning area to the next. Parents who have attended more structured, traditional programs often view such movement as questionable because it is believed that the teacher must be in direct contact with students for learning to occur. Yet, self-directed, unsupervised movement is an integral part of any open, activity-centered curriculum.

Classroom ownership.   A third consideration in viewing classroom spaces is what might be considered ownership, or territoriality, of the area. In most classrooms, this dimension can be seen by the spaces both the teacher and students occupy and by items that belong to those persons inhabiting the classroom.

At the most structured end of an ownership continuum in a classroom, the teacher has total access to any area or space in the room, and the student "owns" no space. In some classrooms, particularly in elementary schools, teacher ownership of space can extend even into the desks, pockets, and thoughts of students.

In somewhat less structured environments, student have zones where they can locate without being inspected or violating the teacher's territoriality. The average classroom is divided about two thirds for students and one third for the teacher (as illustrated in Figure 2.14).

The most flexible pattern of ownership is seen in the classroom with no overt symbols of territoriality. Either the teacher's desk is accessible for all purposes, or, in newer schools, the teacher has a private place somewhere else in the building. Furniture in such classrooms is uniform for students and teachers alike.

Another measure of ownership available to the observer is that of personal items on display in the room. In particular, the display of student work or student art is a useful indicator. When student work is displayed, for example, are samples drawn from the work of all students or simply a few? Are the samples on display uniform (everyone colors the same picture the same color) or diverse?

Other questions related to ownership would be concerned with the kind of teaching visuals on display (standard or tailored), the presence or absence of living objects, and any signs of reward for creative or divergent thinking. A highly structured classroom will generally be bland and uniform; a highly flexible room will be nearly chaotic in appearance.

There are great differences in school classrooms, and these differences reflect the intentions of the school in educating students. As such, classroom spaces represent another important dimension of the learning environment. The descriptive continuums in Figure 2.15 suggest the potential range of alternatives present in schools.

Questions.   How might teaching staffs use their limited spaces to better serve all learners? What does emerging research tell us about the organization of learning spaces?

Programs of Study

Schools differ to a great extent in how they organize and use knowledge and materials in the programs of study. In highly structured schools, knowledge is, for all practical purposes, the curriculum, and ordering knowledge represents the major activity of curriculum development. In highly flexible schools, by contrast, knowledge can be a simple medium through which processes are taught.

FIGURE 2.14   Division of the Average Classroom

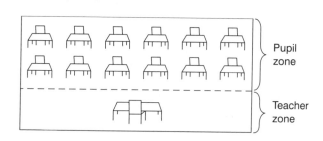

Classroom Organization

Uniform seating arrangement dominates room	Classroom furniture uniform but not symmetrical	Furniture arranged for each activity	Multipurpose spaces in room	Space outside classroom used for instruction

S +————————+————————+————————+————————+ F
 1   2   3   4   5

Classroom Movement

Movement totally restricted by teacher	Total teacher control with noted exception	Pupil movement contextual	Pupil has freedom of movement within limit	Pupil movement at pupil discretion

S +————————+————————+————————+————————+ F
 1   2   3   4   5

Classroom Ownership

Classroom space is dominated by teacher	Teacher dominates— some student zones	Classroom has areas of mutual free access	Territory only at symbolic level—open to all	All classroom spaces totally accessible to all persons

S +————————+————————+————————+————————+ F
 1   2   3   4   5

FIGURE 2.15   Differences in Classroom Spaces

Organization of Knowledge.   The organization of knowledge can best be understood by viewing it in several dimensions: the pattern of its presentation, the way in which it is constructed or ordered, its cognitive focus, and the time orientation of the context.

Presentation of knowledge.   In most schools, knowledge is presented as an essential body or set of interrelated data [as in Figure 2.16(a)]. In some schools, however, this essential knowledge is supplemented by other useful learnings, which may appear as unequal satellites around the main body of information [as in Figure 2.16(b)].

To the degree that student needs and interests are considered in planning the program of study, the satellites, or electives, are expanded and become a more important part of the program. In some schools, electives are equal in importance to essential knowledge areas and consume up to one half of school time [Figure 2.16(c)]. Once the school acknowledges the value of student-related content, it may find that it can teach the essential content in a form that accounts for student needs and interests [Figure 2.16(d)].

As the interrelatedness of essential subcourses is verified, cross-referencing of coursework may occur (interdisciplinary instruction). Finally, a maximum of flexibility in the ordering and use of knowledge may occur when a problem-oriented activity is the common denominator for organizing knowledge [Figure 2.16(e)].

Construction or ordering of knowledge.   Another distinguishing dimension of the organization of knowledge is how it is constructed or ordered. Most programs of study employ one of three standard curriculum designs: (1) the building blocks design, (2) branching design, or (3) spiral design. It is also possible, however, to order knowledge in school programs in terms of (4) task accomplishment or (5) simple learning processes. These five patterns of knowledge construction are symbolized in Figure 2.17.

The building blocks design takes a clearly defined body of knowledge and orders it into a pyramid-like arrangement. Students are taught foundational material that leads to more complex and specialized knowledge. Deviations from the prescribed order are not allowed because the end product of the learning design (mastery) is known in advance. Also, activities that do not contribute to this directed path are not allowed because of the efficiency of this model. Building blocks designs are the most structured of curriculum organizations.

Another common learning design found in schools is a branching pattern. Branching is a variation of the building blocks design but incorporates limited choice in the knowledge to be mastered. Branching designs recognize the value of foundational knowledge in learning but allow choice within prescribed areas beyond the common experience. Like the building blocks, branching prescribes the

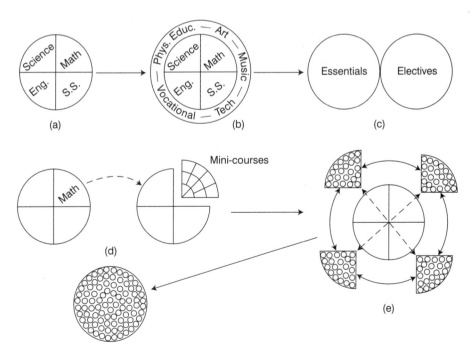

FIGURE 2.16   Patterns of Knowledge Presentation

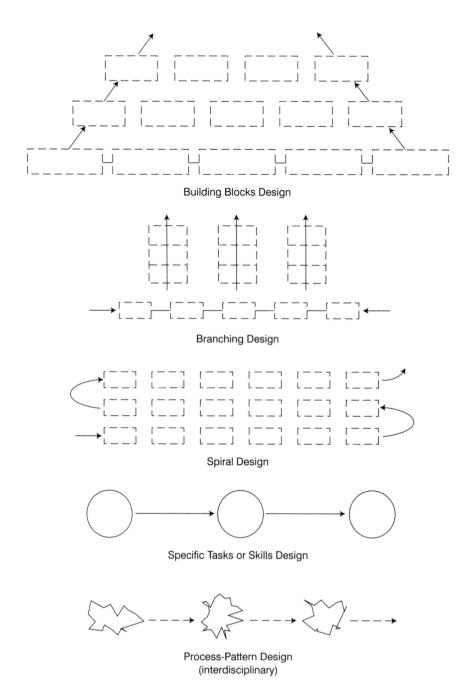

Building Blocks Design

Branching Design

Spiral Design

Specific Tasks or Skills Design

Process-Pattern Design
(interdisciplinary)

FIGURE 2.17 Patterns of Knowledge Construction

eventual outcomes of the learning program, although the prescription is multiple rather than uniform. The branching design allows for some variability in learning but only within tightly defined boundaries of acceptance.

A third organization of knowledge in programs of study is the spiral curriculum. In this design, knowledge areas are continually visited and revisited at higher levels of complexity. This design does have some flexibility, but it still controls what is taught and learned and even predetermines when it is to be received by the student.

A fourth possible organization of knowledge occurs when knowledge is organized to accomplish specified tasks. In specific tasks or skills designs, the purpose of the learning experience would be predetermined, but the student interaction with data in terms of both content and order of content would be flexible. Competency-based skill continuums are an example of this design.

A final organization of knowledge in a school program of studies might use knowledge as simply a medium for teaching processes. Thus, reading could be taught regardless of the particular material used by the student. Such a process pattern would feature great flexibility in terms of the knowledge used, its order in learning experiences, and the expected outcomes for its selection and use.

Cognitive focus.   Still another dimension of the treatment of knowledge is the cognitive focus of instruction. In addition to a focus on factual material, such as learning important dates in history, knowledge can also be organized for teaching generalizations. Sometimes conceptual treatments of information are related to the lives of students. Maximum flexibility in the treatment of knowledge is gained by focusing on the personal world of the students, drawing concepts and facts from their experiences.

Time orientation.   A final area related to knowledge in school settings is the time orientation of the instructional material. In some classrooms, all information is drawn from past experiences of humankind. In other rooms, information from the past is mixed with that from the present. Some classrooms will be strictly contemporary and deal only with the here-and-now. Beyond the present-oriented instructional space are those that mix current knowledge with projected knowledge and some that deal only in probabilities. With each step from the known (past) to the speculative (future) content, flexibility increases.

The descriptive continuums in Figure 2.18 suggest the potential range of alternatives found in schools.

Questions.   Why are schools unable to break away from the traditional content curriculum? Which format for organizing knowledge seems most applicable to life in the twenty-first century?

Uses of Learning Materials.   The ways in which learning materials are used or not used in classroom spaces vary tremendously from room to room. In some settings, no materials are visible to the observer except perhaps a single textbook. In other classroom spaces, the volume and variety of learning materials give the impression of clutter. Three measures of the use of learning materials are (1) the degree of

Presentation of Knowledge

Essential courses only	Essentials plus some satellite courses	Essentials and coequal elective courses	Cross-referenced courses	Integrated courses

S ├─────────┼─────────┼─────────┼─────────┤ F
1   2   3   4   5

Construction or Ordering of Knowledge

Building blocks	Branching	Spiral	Task focused	Process pattern

S ├─────────┼─────────┼─────────┼─────────┤ F
1   2   3   4   5

Cognitive Focus

Related facts	Series/set of facts	Conceptual organization	Concepts via world of the students	Concepts via personal life of individual

S ├─────────┼─────────┼─────────┼─────────┤ F
1   2   3   4   5

Time Orientation

Past only	Past and present	Present only	Present and future	Future only

S ├─────────┼─────────┼─────────┼─────────┤ F
1   2   3   4   5

FIGURE 2.18   Types of Knowledge Presentation

sensory stimulation present, (2) the diversity of learning mediums found, and (3) the location of usable learning materials. The descriptive continuums in Figure 2.19 suggest the potential range of alternatives found in schools.

Sensory stimulation.   On the most structured end of a continuum, the stimulation from learning materials can be fixed and absolute, as when all material is written or programmed. Sometimes, stimulation from learning materials is prescribed or controlled, as during lectures. A slightly more flexible version of stimulation is available when the materials are interpreted, such as during an animated film or game playing. Still greater stimulation occurs when the learner is in physical proximity to the materials and has a tactile experience. Finally, stimulation that immerses the learner in multisense experiencing represents the greatest degree of stimulation to the learner.

Diversity.   Another measure of the effect of learning materials is found in the diversity of mediums present. Although some classrooms have only textbooks, oth-

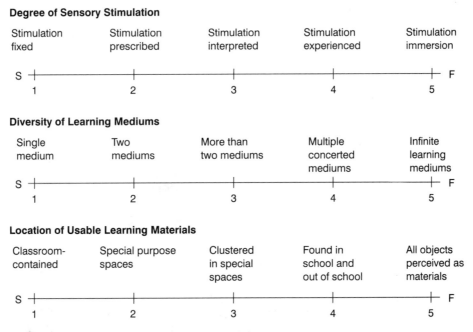

Degree of Sensory Stimulation

| Stimulation fixed | Stimulation prescribed | Stimulation interpreted | Stimulation experienced | Stimulation immersion |

S +————————+————————+————————+————————+ F
  1   2   3   4   5

Diversity of Learning Mediums

| Single medium | Two mediums | More than two mediums | Multiple concerted mediums | Infinite learning mediums |

S +————————+————————+————————+————————+ F
  1   2   3   4   5

Location of Usable Learning Materials

| Classroom-contained | Special purpose spaces | Clustered in special spaces | Found in school and out of school | All objects perceived as materials |

S +————————+————————+————————+————————+ F
  1   2   3   4   5

FIGURE 2.19   Types of Learning Materials

ers have printed matter, audiovisual aids, games, displays, and interactive materials. An important question is, "How many types of learning mediums are interacting with the learner at any moment?"

Location.   Finally, the location of usable learning materials is a variable in classroom settings. In some schools, all learning materials are contained in standard classrooms. Still others have special purpose spaces where students may interact with materials. A third, and more flexible, possibility is that the school possesses areas (Instructional Materials Centers) where learning materials are clustered. An even more flexible pattern would be to identify and select learning materials both in the school and outside the school. Maximum flexibility, of course, would perceive all objects as being possible learning materials for instruction.

Questions.   How might teachers be provided with a greater variety of learning resources? How might technology be applied to confront learner–materials interface?

Instructional Orientation

Three measures of instructional orientation are (1) philosophy of education, (2) teaching strategies, and (3) staffing patterns.

Philosophy of Education.   The descriptive continuums in Figure 2.20 suggest the potential range of alternatives found in schools.

Instructional Format

Teacher drills	Didactic format with closure	Free exchange with summation	Experience learning with individual summation	Nonstructured learning with no summation

S ├────────────┼────────────┼────────────┼────────────┤ F
  1   2   3   4   5

Acceptance of Diversity Among Students

Teacher enforces conformity	Teacher communicates expectations for conformity	Teacher tolerates limited diversity	Teacher accepts student diversity	Teacher encourages student diversity

S ├────────────┼────────────┼────────────┼────────────┤ F
  1   2   3   4   5

FIGURE 2.20   Types of Educational Philosophies

Instructional format.   In some classes, learning is absolutely structured. The teacher controls the flow of data, communication, and assessment. Such a condition is characterized by drill. Slightly more flexible is a pattern of didactic teaching whereby the teacher delivers information, controls the exchange of ideas, and enforces the correct conclusions through a question–answer session. A balance between complete structure and flexibility in the learning process is for the teacher to allow the free exchange of ideas in the classroom but to enforce a standardized summation of the process. Even more flexible would be a pattern in which students are allowed to experience a learning process and then draw their own conclusions about meaning. Most flexible is an instructional process that is not uniformly structured for all students, allows an exchange of ideas, and leaves the process open ended.

Acceptance of diversity.   Yet another measure of philosophy in the classroom is the acceptance of diversity among students. Sometimes, this is observable in norms relating to dress or speech enforced by the teacher. Sometimes, such a measure can be assessed by the appearance of the learning space. The key to this variable is whether students are made to act in standardized ways or whether differences are allowed. On the most extreme end of structure would be a classroom in which no individuality is allowed. In a classroom with maximum flexibility, diversity among students in appearance and behavior would be significant.

Questions.   What evidence exists to show that learners are diverse or unique? What is the essential difference between education and training?

Teaching Strategies.   Like the actions that suggest educational philosophies, the teaching strategies found in classrooms often give clues regarding the degree of structure in the learning program. Such strategies can often be inferred from teacher behaviors and organizational patterns. For instance, some teachers behave in ways that allow only a single learning interface with students, as in the case of the didactic method. Other times, teachers will provide multiple ways for students to interact and communicate during instruction.

Two behaviors that speak louder than words about the learning strategy employed in the classroom are the motivational techniques being used and the interactive distances between the teacher and student. By watching these phenomena, the observer can anticipate a pattern of structure or flexibility in other instructional areas.

The descriptive continuums in Figure 2.21 suggest the potential range of alternatives found in schools.

Motivational techniques. A range of motivational techniques is available to classroom teachers, and all are situationally legitimate. Some techniques, however, seek to control and structure learning; others encourage flexibility. Teachers using threats or fear as a motivator generally seek maximum structure in the classroom. Coercion, as a rule, arrests behavior and encourages conformity to previous patterns of behavior. Extrinsic rewards, immediate or deferred, also encourage structure by linking desired behavior with reward. Intrinsic rewards, whether immediate or deferred, have an opposite effect. Intrinsic rewards encourage student participation in the reward system and, thereby, a wider range of acceptable behaviors. If the motivational technique is observable, the overall learning strategy to constrict or expand student behavior is also understood.

Interactive distances. Another dimension of the learning strategy in a classroom setting is the interactive distance between the teacher and students. To the degree that it is important to have two-way communication in the classroom, and to the degree

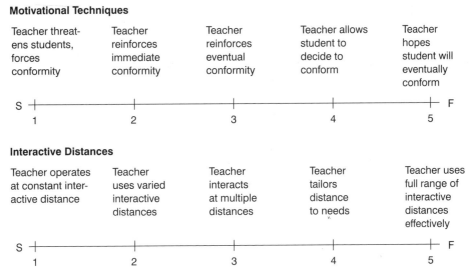

FIGURE 2.21 Types of Teaching Strategies

that the instructional strategy values multiple learning styles among students, the teacher will make adjustments for differences.

In his book *The Silent Language,* Edward Hall made observations about the appropriateness of certain distances between persons for certain activities.[15] Some distances (15 feet and beyond) were appropriate for broadcasting; other distances (6 inches or under) were reserved for intimate moments. In a classroom setting, it is possible to observe if the teacher makes adjustments in interactive distances during instruction or chooses to treat all situations alike.

Questions.   What are some combinations of teaching behavior that reflect motivational theory? What advantage can be gained by designing a classroom that allows for teacher mobility?

Staffing Patterns.   A final indicator of structure versus flexibility in schools, in terms of instruction, is found in the staffing patterns observed. Two staffing indicators are the role of teachers in staffing and the organization of teachers in the school building.

The descriptive continuums in Figure 2.22 suggest the potential range of alternatives found in schools.

Role of the teacher.   In some school buildings, all teachers are hired and assigned on the basis of subject-matter preparation. Such teachers are perceived as solitary artisans with the highly structured task of teaching a subject to students. In other schools, a teacher might be hired as a subject specialist but assigned to a team that is interdisciplinary in nature. A more flexible pattern would be to staff a school with teachers having two or more subject specialties. It might even be possible to have one teacher (as in the elementary grades) responsible for all subjects. Or, a teacher could be hired to teach students at a certain level, rather than subjects.

Role of the Teacher

Solitary subject specialist	Subject specialist on team	Subject specialist in multiple areas	Subject specialist all areas	Specialist in teaching at a level
S 1	2	3	4	5 F

Organization of Teachers

Teachers isolated in self-contained classrooms	Teacher and aide isolated	Teacher isolated except for planning	Two or more teachers work cooperatively	Teachers in active teams for instruction
S 1	2	3	4	5 F

FIGURE 2.22   Types of Staffing Patterns

Criteria for Organizing Students

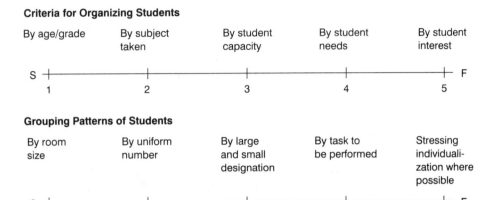

FIGURE 2.23   Ways of Organizing Students

Organization of teachers.   Another staffing pattern is the organization of teachers in the building. Are all teachers isolated in self-contained classrooms? Do the isolated teachers have instructional aides? Do the classroom teachers meet together to plan activities? Are their teaching units ever combined? Do the teachers teach in teams or other cooperative arrangements?

Questions.   What is the critical difference between deploying a single teacher versus organizing teachers into teaching teams? At what level of schooling would teaming be most appropriate?

Administrative Conditions

Organization of Students.   The way in which a school organizes students can give an observer some measure of the degree of structure in the school. Two differ-ent measures of student organization are the criteria for organization and the actual grouping patterns found in the school.

The descriptive continuums in Figure 2.23 suggest the potential range of alternatives found in schools.

Criteria for organization.   Most schools in the United States group students according to their age because most schools in the United States admit children into schools according to age. Schools use a more flexible criterion when students are organized by subject taught. Still greater flexibility is evidenced in schools that group students within grades and subjects according to capacity. Even greater organizational flexibil-ity is found in schools that group students by needs and by student interests.

Grouping patterns.   Besides criteria for grouping, the actual organization patterns of students can indicate the degree of structure or flexibility in the school. Perhaps the most structured situation exists when the size of the room determines the number of students present. A uniform number of students for all activities is also a highly structured condition. When a school begins to recognize that some activities should have large or small classes, a degree of flexibility is in evidence. The greatest flexibility in the organization of students is represented by the assignment of students on the basis of tasks to be accomplished and the individualization of instruction, whenever possible.

Questions.   What advantage is gained by organizing schools for professionalization (school-based management)? Given what is known about human development patterns, what grouping criteria seem most promising?

Rules and Regulations.   Within schools and within individual classrooms, rules and regulations vary. Perhaps the most structured situations are those in which an excessive number of regulations exist based on historical precedent. Slightly less structured is the school with numerous and absolute regulations. A more flexible condition is when there are a few rules that are formal and enforced. When there are few rules and the rules are negotiable, or when no formal or informal regulations are stated, maximum flexibility is indicated. The descriptive continuum in Figure 2.24 suggests the potential range of alternatives in schools.

Disciplinary Measures.   Discipline techniques used in schools to influence student behavior cover a wide range of actions. In some schools, all infractions are given the same treatment regardless of severity. In more flexible schools, there is a hierarchy of discipline measures to deal with differing discipline problems. Sometimes, the pattern found in schools will be to deal only with the severe or recurrent discipline problems. In schools where great flexibility is found, the pattern for discipline is sometimes unclear owing to the uneven application of discipline measures. In some schools, no discipline measures are observable.

The descriptive continuum in Figure 2.25 suggests the potential range of alternatives for discipline in schools.

Reporting Student Progress.   The reporting of student progress in the most structured schools and classrooms is a mechanical process whereby students are assessed in mathematical symbols such as 83 or upper quartile. A generalization of such preciseness is a system whereby student progress in learning is summarized by a symbol such as a B or U. Increased flexibility in reporting student progress is evidenced by narrative

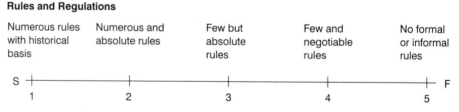

Rules and Regulations

Numerous rules with historical basis	Numerous and absolute rules	Few but absolute rules	Few and negotiable rules	No formal or informal rules
1	2	3	4	5

S +————————+————————+————————+————————+ F

FIGURE 2.24   Types of Rules and Regulations

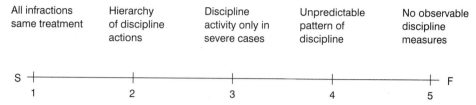

FIGURE 2.25   Types of Disciplinary Measures

descriptions that actually describe student work and by supplemental reporting by other interested parties, such as the student or the parent. Maximum flexibility in reporting student progress is found when such reporting is informal, verbal, and continuous.

The descriptive continuum in Figure 2.26 suggests the potential range of alternatives for reporting student progress found in schools.

Questions.   What is the purpose of any student control system? What adult behaviors are learned in school settings?

Roles of Participants

Administrative Attitudes.   Administrative style, more than any other single factor, determines the atmosphere of a school building. It is certain that how others in the school building perceive the administrator affects both teacher and student behavior. For this reason, clues about the structure or flexibility of a school or classroom can be gained by observing the administrator.

The descriptive continuums in Figure 2.27 suggest the potential range of alternatives for administrative behavior found in schools.

Decision-making role.   Administrators often assume one of five attitudes that characterize their pattern of interaction with others. At the most structured end is a warden, who rules by intimidation. Closely allied to this model is the benevolent dictator, who maintains absolute control while giving the impression of involvement. A more flexible posture for the administrator is to act as the program manager,

FIGURE 2.26   Ways of Reporting Student Progress

Decision-Making Role

Makes all decisions unilaterally	Makes all key decisions unilaterally	Shares decision making on specific items	Shares all decision making on all items	Abdicates all key decision making

S ├────────┼────────┼────────┼────────┤ F
1   2   3   4   5

Medium of Communication

Unknown to students	Communicates through an intermediary	Speaks through intercom or at assemblies	Visits classes for discussion	Holds individual conferences

S ├────────┼────────┼────────┼────────┤ F
1   2   3   4   5

FIGURE 2.27   Types of Administrative Interaction

reserving key decisions for the only person with the comprehensive viewpoint. Still more flexible is the collegial leader who shares all decision making with the teaching faculty. Finally, there is a leadership style that is nondirective or laissez faire.

Medium of communication.   A second interesting variable for studying administrative attitudes is the medium used to communicate with students. In some schools, the lead administrator is a phantom, known only by the presence of his or her portrait in the foyer. Such an administrator generally leaves communication with parents or students to an intermediary such as a vice-principal. Another impersonal medium is the intercom, which is often used to communicate to students. Slightly more personal is a live address at assemblies. Finally, some administrators communicate with students by coming into the classrooms and even sometimes by individual conferences.

Teacher Roles.   The role of a classroom teacher in a school can vary from being an instructor who teaches a prescribed set of facts to students to a multidimensional adult who interacts with students and others in the building. For the most part,

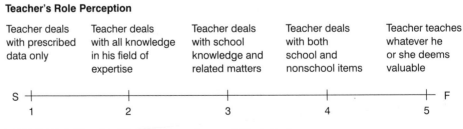

Teacher's Role Perception

Teacher deals with prescribed data only	Teacher deals with all knowledge in his field of expertise	Teacher deals with school knowledge and related matters	Teacher deals with both school and nonschool items	Teacher teaches whatever he or she deems valuable

S ├────────┼────────┼────────┼────────┤ F
1   2   3   4   5

FIGURE 2.28   Teachers' Perceptions of Their Roles

How Students Learn in Class

| They recite and copy from board | They listen, take notes, take tests | They listen, read, question, take tests | They work on things, read | They do things that interest them |

S ├────────────┼────────────┼────────────┼────────────┤ F
         1   2   3   4   5

FIGURE 2.29   Students' Perception of Their Roles

such perceptions are self-imposed. A key observation can be made from teacher responses to the question, "What do you teach?"

The descriptive continuum in Figure 2.28 suggests the potential range of responses to that question.

Student Roles.   Like teachers, students in schools hold a role perception of what they are and what they can do in a classroom setting. Sometimes such perceptions are self-imposed, but more often they are an accurate reflection of expected behavior for students. A question that usually receives a telling response for an observer in a school is, "How do students learn in this classroom?"

The descriptive continuum in Figure 2.29 suggests the potential range of responses to such a question.

Questions.   How might roles and relationships in school be altered to restructure education? What teacher and student roles seem appropriate for the twenty-first century?

SCHOOL ASSESSMENT

The value of viewing school components on a continuum, such as the degree of structure versus flexibility, is that program congruence or inconsistencies can be identified (see Figure 2.30). In schools in which the program intent (philosophy) is clear, the degree of structure or flexibility should be relatively constant. Said another way, if the fifteen dimensions were plotted across the five degrees of structure and flexibility, strong schools would have reasonably vertical columns. A zigzag pattern in such a school profile would indicate an inconsistency in the learning design.

SUMMARY

Educational philosophies are the heart of purposeful activity in curriculum development. Philosophies serve as value screens for decision making. Because educators today are confronted by multiple choices, it is vital that curriculum specialists understand their own values and beliefs about schooling.

Over the years, the American school has evolved from a highly structured and traditional institution to one that possesses considerable flexibility. The degree of structure or flexibility found in the learning design of a school is a reflection of the

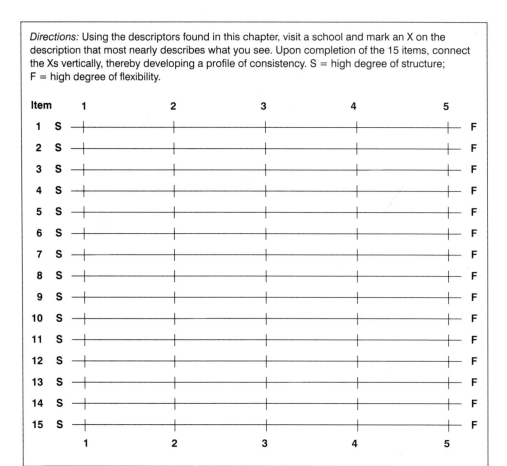

Directions: Using the descriptors found in this chapter, visit a school and mark an X on the description that most nearly describes what you see. Upon completion of the 15 items, connect the Xs vertically, thereby developing a profile of consistency. S = high degree of structure; F = high degree of flexibility.

FIGURE 2.30   School Assessment Worksheet

undergirding philosophy of education being practiced. Whatever the philosophy, consistency in the design is the key to effectiveness of the curriculum.

In this chapter, five major educational philosophies were presented, along with a philosophy assessment inventory to help you clarify your posture on key issues. We believe that to be a decisive leader, curriculum specialists must be aware of their own values and be able to assess accurately the value systems found in today's schools.

SUGGESTED LEARNING ACTIVITIES

1. Using the philosophy assessment inventory found in this chapter, analyze your beliefs about the roles of schools. If your profile does not correspond to what you think you believe, explain this discrepancy.

2. Using the scales found in this chapter, visit a school with which you are familiar and analyze its profile. What observations can you make about this type of analysis of a school?

3. Using Figure 2.9, describe the type of instructional program most likely to be implemented in the various structures. Where would you like to work? Why?

4. Describe how the following current concerns in public schools are philosophical in nature: schools of choice, cooperative learning, whole language reading, and middle schools.

NOTES

1. *Youth: Transition to Adulthood,* a report of the President's Advisory Commission on Science, 1973.

2. Robert M. McClure, "The Reforms of the Fifties and Sixties: A Historical Look at the Near Past," *The Curriculum: Retrospect and Prospect,* National Society for the Study of Education, (Washington, DC: NSSE, 1971), p. 51.

3. Galen Saylor and William M. Alexander, *Planning Curriculum for Schools* (New York: Holt, Rinehart & Winston, 1974), pp. 144–45.

4. Robert Hutchins, *On Education* (Santa Barbara, CA: Center for the Study of Democratic Institutions, 1963), p. 18.

5. A. S. Neill, *Summerhill* (New York: Hart, 1960), p. 4.

6. Saylor and Alexander, *Planning Curriculum for Schools,* p. 146.

7. Daniel Tanner and Laurel N. Tanner, *Curriculum Development: Theory into Practice,* 3rd ed. (New York: Macmillan, 1995), p. 82.

8. Tanner and Tanner, *Curriculum Development: Theory into Practice,* p. 64.

9. John D. McNeil, *Designing Curriculum: Self-Instructional Modules* (Boston: Little, Brown, 1976), pp. 91–92.

10. Martin Mayer, *The Schools* (New York: Harper & Row, 1961).

11. James B. Conant, as reported in Charles Silberman, *Crisis in the Classroom* (New York: Random House, 1970).

12. Charles E. Silberman, *Crisis in the Classroom* (New York: Random House, 1970), p. 9.

13. Morris L. Bigge, *Learning Theories for Teachers* (New York: Harper & Row, 1971), p. viii.

14. Bel Kaufman, *Up the Down Staircase* (Englewood Cliffs, NJ: Prentice Hall, 1965).

15. Edward Hall, *The Silent Language* (New York: Doubleday, 1959).

BOOKS TO REVIEW

Benne, K. *The Task of Post-Contemporary Education.* New York: Teachers College Press, 1990.

Berube, M. *American School Reform: 1883–1993.* Westport, CT: Greenwood Publishing Company, 1994.

Callahan, R. *Education and the Cult of Efficiency.* Chicago: University of Chicago Press, 1962.

Coleman, J. *Equality and Achievement in Education.* Boulder, CO: Westview Press, 1990.

Goodlad, J. *The Ecology of School Renewal.* Chicago: National Society for the Study of Education, 1987.

Knapp, L., and A. Glenn. *Restructuring Schools with Technology.* Needham Heights, MA: Allyn and Bacon, 1996.

chapter 3

BASIC TASKS OF CURRICULUM DEVELOPMENT

Curriculum development, at its best, is a comprehensive process that (1) facilitates an analysis of purpose, (2) designs a program or event, (3) implements a series of related activities, and (4) aids in the evaluation of this process. At its worst, curriculum development accomplishes none of these four activities. Clearly, there are basic tasks that distinguish quality curriculum work from accidental instructional change. It is also evident that modern curriculum development involves much more than the implementation of a new course of study or the updating of a guide to instruction.

Curriculum development proceeds in a deductive manner using an if–then logic (see Figure 3.1). The initial step in curriculum work is to clarify purpose. This involves first identifying a philosophy and then deducing appropriate goals and objectives. Once this framework for program development is established, an assessment of need is conducted to sharpen the focus in terms of the target—the learner. Finally, the curriculum itself is analyzed through a mapping-out process, and the instructional activities are ordered and aligned for maximum effect. What is desired by the curriculum worker is a near correspondence between the intention and the outcome of instruction.

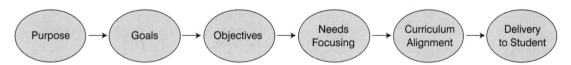

FIGURE 3.1   Tasks for Curriculum Development

ESTABLISHING THE PHILOSOPHY

A *philosophy*—the clarification of beliefs about the purpose, goals, and objectives of instruction—is the essential tapestry for all curriculum development efforts. School programs without this overarching backdrop either are disjointed, which makes them targets for social pressure, or operate in a state of programmatic contradiction. The development of a working philosophy of education is prerequisite to all other leadership efforts in school improvement.

The task of goal setting is a national function in most nations (see Figure 3.2 for sample national goals). In the United States, by contrast, it is a continuous process led by curriculum workers at various operational levels (state, district, school, classroom). Such developmental work is generally done in three ways:

1. Others can be asked to review existing statements of philosophy or related documents and restate them in terms of desired changes.
2. Others can be asked to transfer their own personal philosophy of living into a school context, setting goals for school from general life goals.
3. Others can be asked to look for patterns in current behavior in society that might suggest goals for schools.

Methods that can be used to help others achieve goal clarity and consistency include writing personal goal statements, assigning priorities to various items, surveying existing documents, and analyzing school programs. One widely practiced

Australia	1. Fulfilling lives and active citizenship 2. Joining the workforce 3. Overcoming disadvantage and achieving fairness in society
Taiwan (ROC)	The three principles: geography, history, and economy (the meaning of nation) Utilization of group life (operation of democracy) Productive labor (livelihood) Eight moral virtues: loyalty, kindness, love, faith, righteousness, harmony, peace, fidelity
People's Republic of China (Red China)	1. Develop good moral character 2. Develop love of motherland 3. Literacy and intellect 4. Healthy bodies 5. Interest in aesthetics

FIGURE 3.2   Sample Statements of Purpose for National Education Systems

Source: From national documents from respective state education departments. See also C. Postlethwaite, *Encyclopedia of Comparative Education and National Systems of Education,* Oxford, Pergamon Press, 1988.

Students
1. WE BELIEVE that students are individuals with unique characteristics and interests.
2. WE BELIEVE that students should have an equal opportunity to learn, based on their needs, interests, and abilities.

Learning
1. WE BELIEVE that students learn best when content is relevant to their own lives.
2. WE BELIEVE that students learn best in an environment that is pleasant and one in which the democratic process is modeled.

Teaching
1. WE BELIEVE that the role of the teacher in the classroom is primarily that of a facilitator of learning.
2. WE BELIEVE that student learning may be affected more by what teachers do than by what they say.

Grouping
1. WE BELIEVE that a more effective program of instruction can be provided for students if they are grouped according to maturation level and similar interest.
2. WE BELIEVE that a high school should include those students who are mature enough to participate in a program that is more specialized than the middle school and those students beyond the age of 18 who have a need to complete the requirements for a high school diploma.

The Educational Program
1. WE BELIEVE that all special programs should incorporate specific educational objectives that complement the total school program.
2. WE BELIEVE that evaluating and changing programs to more effectively meet the needs and interests of students should be a continuous process.

FIGURE 3.3   Example of Belief Statements

method of clarifying philosophic positions is to have persons develop belief statements. These statements rest on a simple premise: each time that a person acts, there is a rationale for action. Without a formalization of such rationales, it is impossible to coordinate or manage individual activities.

Belief statements can be organized in numerous ways, and the correct way for any individual district depends on the planning format. Figure 3.3 lists examples of belief statements organized around students, learning, teaching roles, grouping of students, and educational programs in general. The generic philosophy from which these are drawn is that the school exists to meet the needs and interests of students.

After identifying a philosophy and stating it in easy-to-understand belief statements, the school district or school is ready to develop goals that will serve to guide development. Such goals are drawn from the philosophic orientation of the district, the needs of the school population, and the unique characteristics of the community.

As curriculum specialists clarify their own beliefs about the purpose of education and assist others in finding their value systems, the odds for meaningful curriculum development increase. Shared values can form the bond of commitment to change. The time spent in assessing group philosophies has significant payoff in areas such as continuity in school programs and articulation among school levels, development of relationships and roles among school faculties, selection of learning activities and materials, evaluation of school programs, and redesign of basic curriculum offerings.

Most important, however, is the connection of philosophy to leadership and decision making in education. To be decisive leaders and consistent decision makers, curriculum specialists must know their values and those of the persons around them.

FORMULATING GOALS

Educational goals are statements of the intended outcomes of education. The **scope** of the entire educational program can be found in the goals espoused by a school. Goals are also the basic building blocks of educational planning.

Goals may be stated at various levels of specificity. Many school goals are purposefully broad so that a majority of the public can support the intentions of the school. Sometimes, there is an attempt to state the goals in terms of student behaviors that the school seeks to promote (see Figure 3.4). Over the years, commissions have attempted to define American education by developing formal goals.

Perhaps the most familiar goals were defined by the Commission on Reorganization of Secondary Education in 1918. Those goals were (1) health, (2) command of fundamental processes, (3) worthy home membership, (4) vocation, (5) citizenship, (6) worthy use of leisure time, and (7) ethical character. These became widely known as the Seven Cardinal Principles of Secondary Education.

A second attempt at defining the purposes of secondary education was expressed in 1938 by the Educational Policies Commission of the National Education Association and the American Association of School Administrators. The group developed a number of goals under the headings of (1) self-realization, (2) human relationships, (3) economic efficiency, and (4) civic responsibility.

The Association for Supervision and Curriculum Development, a national organization of curriculum specialists, has identified a set of valued learning outcomes "that reflected the 'holistic' nature of individuals." Hundreds of organizations, including state departments of education and regional research and development centers, were requested to share their goals with the group. The group identified ten major goals for youth:[1]

1. Self-conceptualizing (self-esteem)
2. Understanding others
3. Basic skills
4. Interest and capability for continuous learning
5. Responsible member of society
6. Mental and physical health
7. Creativity
8. Informed participation in the economic world of production and consumption

Academic Goals

Achievement
Maintain or improve test scores
Reduce failures and parental notices
Reduce retentions and dropouts
Produce better grade point averages
Increase honor roll (based on grades)
Institute new honor rolls in nonacademic areas
    (based on nonacademic achievement)
Meet needs of high achievers

Responsibility
Arrive on time
Decrease vandalism cases
Decrease discipline counts
Admit to wrongdoing
Take care of academic areas

Respect for Others
Decrease sarcasm and put-downs
Increase sensitivity to need of others
Increase their role in helping others (peer
    learning)

Behaviors

Exhibits Healthy Habits
Monitoring self
Exhibit smoking and drug awareness
Exhibit awareness of physical growth
Walk for health
Participation in intramural sports

Higher Self-Esteem
Increase openness to new experiences
Eliminate self-abusive behaviors
Increase ability to self-reveal
Exhibit school pride

Attendance and Participation
Increase daily attendance count
Increase club memberships
Decrease make-up work

Stress and Misbehavior
Decrease visits to counselor
Decrease outbursts in class
Decrease aggressive behaviors
(Teachers) distribute homework more evenly

Organized
Bring materials to class
Complete homework frequently
Maintain personal calendar
Bring gym clothes
Manage time wisely
Ask questions to clarify responsibilities

Problem-Solver
Possess analysis skills
Solve word problems
Apply subjects to "real world"
Possess creative thinking skills
Learn in hands-on manner

Love of Knowledge
Belong to an academic club
Read designated books
Meet with adult tutor/mentor
Develop a personal library
Exhibit awareness of state, national, and
    world events

Attitudinal Goals

Positive Attitude
Exhibit enthusiasm about learning
Participate in school activities
Volunteer/join school service clubs

Mannerly and Courteous
Exhibit ability to introduce self to adults
Dress neatly and appear well groomed
Know etiquette

FIGURE 3.4   Goals for Students in Terms of Behaviors

Source: Authors' work with Kellogg Foundation Model Middle School, Ishpeming, Michigan. Our
thanks to Principal Ed Sansom for his contribution to this set of ideas.

9. Use of accumulated knowledge to understand the world
10. Coping with change

In the late 1980s and early 1990s, numerous prestigious commissions, such as America 2000, have suggested additional goals and directions for public education. Among the most widely circulated and discussed recommendations were

☐ *Time for Results, The Governors' 1991 Report on Education* (Chicago: National Governors' Association Center for Policy Research and Analysis, 1991.)
☐ *A Nation Prepared: Teachers for the 21st Century* (New York: Carnegie Forum on Education and Economy, 1986).
☐ *Turning Points* (New York: The Carnegie Commission, 1990).
☐ *What Works: Research about Teaching and Learning* (Washington DC: U.S. Department of Education, 1986).

Although these commissions have made their reports, their findings should not be considered final. The United States has pondered both the ends and the means necessary to implement public education goals; this process will continue well into the twenty-first century.

In the following sections, we consider the steps and procedures involved in clarifying goals and objectives. The focus of this discussion is the school and classroom level.

Classifying Goals and Objectives

Educational goals inherently reflect the philosophical preferences of the writer of the goals. Objectives, too, have a philosophical underpinning and form the fabric of instructional development at the school and classroom level.

Goals for educational planning generally occur at three levels (see Table 3.1). Level I goals are broad and philosophical in nature. For example, "The environment of the school must be conducive to teaching and learning—safety for all is a primary concern."

Level II goals are more specific than Level I and are often used to define or give form to such aspirations. For example, the following indicators might be used to define an orderly and safe environment:

Indicators
1. The school climate reflects an atmosphere of respect, trust, high morale, cohesiveness, and caring.
2. Expectations for student behavior are clearly stated in a student handbook.
3. A variety of classroom management skills are used to create a businesslike, orderly, and comfortable classroom environment, conducive to learning.
4. Discipline within the school is enforced in a fair and consistent manner.
5. Parents are informed of disciplinary action as it refers to their child.
6. Positive reinforcement of expected behavior is observable throughout the school.

TABLE 3.1 The Relationships Between Levels I, II, and III Learning Objectives

Level of Objectives	Type	Origin	Features
Level I	Broad goals or purposes	Formulated at district level by councils or school board	Seldom revised
Level II	General but more specific than Level I	Formulated at school or department level	Contains an outline of process to accomplish Level I objectives
Level III	Behaviorally stated	Formulated by teams of teachers or single teacher	Describe expected outcome, evidence for assessing outcome, and level of performance

7. Student work is attractively displayed throughout the school.
8. The physical plant is
   a. clean
   b. aesthetically pleasing
   c. safe
   d. well maintained
9. School improvement needs are assessed annually, the needs are prioritized, and the principal is resourceful in getting the tasks accomplished.
10. The principal is involved in prioritizing countrywide maintenance requests.

Finally, Level III objectives are specific to the classroom level and are stated in terms of student behavioral outcomes. These objectives structure learning activities and tell the teacher if the intention of the curriculum has been met.

Behavioral objectives are statements describing what learners are doing when they are learning. Teachers need to describe the desired behaviors well enough to preclude misinterpretation.

An acceptable objective lets students know what is expected of them. It also enables teachers to measure the effectiveness of their own work.

Behaviorally stated objectives contain three essential elements:

1. The terminal behavior must be identified by name. An observable action must be named indicating that learning has taken place.
2. The important conditions under which the behavior is expected to occur should be described.
3. The criteria of acceptable performance should be specified.

A simple method of developing a complete behavioral objective is to apply the A, B, C, D rule. A stands for the audience, B for the behavior, C for the condition, and *D* for the degree of completion. A behavioral objective containing all of these elements will be a complete objective. For example:

A. The student will (the audience)
B. successfully complete the multiplication problems (behavior)
C. during the class period (condition)
D. getting 80% correct (degree)

The advocacy of behavioral objectives by those seeking to clarify educational purpose has met resistance from those who believe describing learner outcomes in this fashion is simplistic and reduces education to training.

In the rush to write clear, precise statements, teachers often chose simple objectives that required little thinking on the part of their students. Those teachers actually were writing objectives in the lowest levels of cognitive behavior. Through **in-service training,** teachers can master the skill of writing objectives requiring higher forms of thinking on the part of their students. In addition, teachers should write objectives leading to affective and psychomotor behaviors.

Using Objectives to Order Learning

Anyone familiar with program development in schools knows that there is regularly a discrepancy between the intentions of the curriculum and what the teacher actually delivers to students. This "disorder" is a result of not refining goals and objectives, not specifying what the teacher is to do with the student, or not defining what the student is to do after having been taught. A wonderful tool for "ordering" the curriculum are the three taxonomies of learning: (1) the **cognitive domain,** (2) the **affective domain,** and (3) the **psychomotor domain** (see Figures 3.5, 3.6, and 3.7).

Each of these hierarchies of learning was developed to assist planners in "targeting" the level of learning desired and to direct the complexity of the teaching act and the materials encountered by the student. **Cognition,** the mental processing of information, is conceived by Bloom as a six-tier model from the most simple processing (knowledge) to the most complex (evaluation). Krathwohl's Affective Domain, a five-level model, addresses the degree of "feeling" experienced by the student about the material encountered. Harrow's Psychomotor Behaviors suggest an order of physical response to learning situations.

When planning learning, the curriculum worker should ask, "What is specifically intended for the learner?" and then write an appropriate objective to guide the teacher in the classroom. For instance, if we teach the student about the Civil War, what is our intention? Do we want them to know about it (Bloom's first tier) or be able to analyze the activities (Bloom's fourth tier)? A corresponding degree of feeling would accompany the learning experience. Seen in this way, planning a curriculum at the instructional level might be thought of as a matrix as shown in Figure 3.8. At point *A,* the junction of cognitive 2 and affective 2, the student should comprehend the material and respond to it.

	Comprehension (ability to comprehend what is being communicated and make use of the idea without relating it to other ideas or material or seeing fullest meaning)	Application (ability to use ideas, principles, theories in new particular and concentrated situations)	Analysis (ability to break down a communication into constituent parts in order to make organization of the whole clear)	Synthesis (ability to put together parts and elements into a unified organization or whole)	Evaluation (ability to judge the value of ideas, procedures, methods, using appropriate criteria)
Knowledge (ability to recall; to bring to mind the appropriate material)	Requires knowledge	Requires knowledge	Requires knowledge	Requires knowledge	Requires knowledge
Comprehension		Requires comprehension	Requires comprehension	Requires comprehension	Requires comprehension
Application			Requires application	Requires application	Requires application
Analysis				Requires analysis	Requires analysis
Synthesis					Requires synthesis

FIGURE 3.5   The Taxonomy of Educational Objectives: Cognitive Domain

Source: Adapted from *Taxonomy of Educational Objectives: The Classification of Educational Goals. Handbook I: Cognitive Domain* edited by Benjamin S. Bloom et al. Copyright © 1956 by Longman, Inc.

Receiving	Responding	Valuing	Organization	Characterization
(attending; becomes aware of an idea, process, or thing; is willing to notice a particular phenomenon)	(makes response at first with compliance, later willingly and with satisfaction)	(accepts worth of a thing, idea or a behavior; prefers it; consistent in responding; develops a commitment to it)	(organizes values; determines interrelationships; adapts behavior to value system)	(generalizes certain values into controlling tendencies; emphasis on internal consistency; later integrates these into a total philosophy of life or world view)
	Begins with attending	Requires a response	Requires development of values	Requires organization of values
		Begins with attending	Requires a response	Requires development of values
			Begins with attending	Requires a response
				Begins with attending

FIGURE 3.6 The Taxonomy of Educational Objectives: Affective Domain

Source: Adapted from *Taxonomy of Educational Objectives: The Classification of Educational Goals. Handbook II: Affective Domain* edited by David R. Krathwohl et al. Copyright © 1964 by Longman, Inc.

Reflex Movements	Fundamental Movements	Perceptual Abilities	Physical Abilities	Skilled Movements	Expressive Movements
(actions without conscious volition in response to stimuli)	(formed by combining reflex movement, e.g., walking)	(interpreting the environment and making adjustments, e.g., dodging ball)	(use of organic vigor, e.g., lifting weights)	(efficiency in performing complex movements, e.g., dancing)	(communication through body movement, e.g., facial expression)
	Begins with movement	Begins with movement	Begins with movement	Begins with movement	Begins with movement

FIGURE 3.7 Levels of Psychomotor Behavior

Source: Adapted from Table 5, pp. 104–106, in *A Taxonomy of the Psychomotor Domain: A Guide for Developing Behavior Objectives*, Anita J. Harrow (New York: Longman Publishing Group), Copyright © 1972 by Anita J. Harrow. Reprinted by permission of the author.

FIGURE 3.8 Curriculum
Planning Matrix

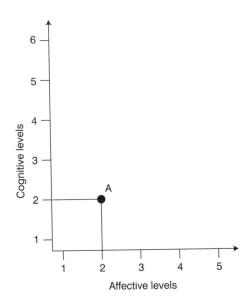

SPECIFYING BEHAVIORAL OBJECTIVES

Following the development of goals and general descriptors of direction, long-range planning requires the specification of objectives that will guide the creation of school programs. *Objectives* are written operational statements that describe the desired outcome of an educational program. Without such objectives, the translation of general goals into programs is likely to be haphazard.

The objectives developed by a school district should be derived from existing goal statements. If objectives are developed that do not directly relate to a goal area, they may suggest goals that need to be addressed by the district. The major purpose of identifying objectives, from a planning perspective, is so that the population to be served, timing, and expected outcomes can be managed and evaluated.

Many school districts become bogged down in an attempt to translate goals into objectives because of the behavioral aspect of stating objectives. In general, objectives attempt to communicate to a specific group the expected outcomes of some unit of instruction. They identify both the capability learned and the performance that the capability makes possible. The process can become mechanical and sometimes threatens individualized programs when the objectives are stated in behavioral terms. If the emphasis of the school program is on experiencing rather than on being able to exhibit behaviors, such specificity may be altogether inappropriate for curriculum planning.

The advantages of using **behavioral objectives** are that they

□   Help identify the specific behaviors to be changed
□   Increase interschool and intraschool communication
□   Direct instructional activities in the classroom
□   Provide a meaningful basis for evaluation

Disadvantages that can occur when using behavioral objectives are that they

☐   Sometimes are simplistic; human behavior is more than the sum of the parts
☐   Disregard the interrelatedness of human activity
☐   Limit choice frequently; remove or prohibit alternatives
☐   Limit concomitant learning in the classroom

In terms of working through understandings about a desired educational program, it is believed that general or conceptual descriptors can serve as planning objectives. School districts may, however, wish to pursue instructional objectives that are behaviorally stated, and many guides are available to assist such a task. Examples of planning objectives in the area of science are shown below:

Have scientific observation and description skills
a.   Observe and identify phenomena, objects, and their properties
b.   Observe and identify changes in physical and biological objects
c.   Order a series of observations

Have scientific hypothesis formation skills
a.   Distinguish among hypothesis, prediction, inference, and opinion
b.   Formulate a simple hypothesis and give explanations for various phenomena on the basis of known information and observations

Understand the content and concepts of advanced science
a.   Understand concepts about the life of man
b.   Understand the concepts relating to physical science
c.   Understand the concepts relating to ecology

ASSESSING NEEDS: FOCUSING FOR RESULTS

Once the basic framework of the curriculum plan is in place, a substantial amount of focusing is necessary to increase efficiency and meet intentions. In many school districts, a failure to assess the true needs of the learners results in a dysfunctional curriculum. The needs assessment technique represents a comprehensive inquiry into the educational status of a district or school. The major intent of the process is to determine if the real intentions are being met through the existing instructional form. Such inquiry often leads to adjustments in goals, instructional technique, and expectations for students.

The actual data gathered in a needs assessment is determined locally. Figure 3.9 shows a typical outline of areas that may be reviewed. Needs assessments are characteristically conducted locally by school or district staffs, as opposed to **accreditation** visits and surveys that usually use outside experts to make observations about the condition of the program. The emphasis in the needs assessment is not so much a matter of what exists, but rather how those conditions affect the program.

I. General Information
   a. Location of school district
   b. Demographic characteristics of immediate area
   c. Natural resources of region
   d. Commercial–industrial data
   e. Income levels of area residents
   f. Special socio-economic considerations
II. General Population Characteristics
   a. Population growth patterns
   b. Age, race of population
   c. Educational levels of population
   d. Projected population
III. School Population Characteristics (Ages 3–19)
   a. School enrollment by grade level
   b. Birthrate trends in school district
   c. In-migration, out-migration patterns
   d. Race/sex/religious composition of school district
   e. Years of school completed by persons over 25 years of age
   f. Studies of school dropouts
IV. Programs and Course Offerings in District
   a. Organization of school programs
   b. Programs' concept and rationale
   c. Course offerings
   d. Special program needs
V. Professional Staff
   a. Training and experience
   b. Awareness of trends and developments
   c. Attitudes toward change
VI. Instructional Patterns and Strategies
   a. Philosophical focus of instructional program
   b. Observational and perceptual instructional data
   c. Assessment of instructional strategies in use
   d. Instructional materials in use
   e. Decision-making and planning processes
   f. Grouping for instruction
   g. Classroom management techniques
   h. Grading and placement of pupils
   i. Student independence
   j. Evaluation of instructional effectiveness
VII. Student Data
   a. Student experiences
   b. Student self-esteem
   c. Student achievement
VIII. Facilities
   a. Assessment of existing facilities and sites
   b. Special facilities
   c. Utilization of facilities
   d. Projected facility needs
IX. Summary of Data

FIGURE 3.9 The Basic Needs Assessment Framework

The first steps of a needs assessment are to decide what data are needed for decision making and to develop a strategy for data gathering. A typical needs assessment in a school district will use citizens' groups or study teams comprised of a mixture of persons from the school community. Sometimes, natural resources that might affect local school operation should be included. Information should also be included about local commerce and industry, which may indicate the tax support for schools in the area as well as the relative wealth of the parents of schoolchildren.

Special social or economic conditions in an area should also be noted. For instance, if a nearby military base is served by the district, or if there is a seasonal migrant population, it is important to acknowledge these variables.

General data about the community, regardless of location, are available in public libraries in standard census reports. Current information dating from the last census data can generally be gained from the local chamber of commerce.

General Information

It is important in any needs assessment that the meaning of educating in a public school be put in perspective. Each of the 13,000 school districts in the United States has unique variables that are reflected in schools. Failure to know and understand such variables often leads to school plans that are either inappropriate for community standards or impossible to implement, given community resources. Any needs assessment should begin with an accurate but brief description of the school setting. The size of the district, its population, the governance pattern (elected or appointed officials), and its resource capacity are information items critical to school planning.

General Population Characteristics

In gathering information about the people who live in the area served by the school district, an attempt should be made to understand the educational and cultural levels of the community, general attitudes about schools, and expectations for education in the area.

Some of the most important information to be gathered about the people who are served by the school district is their cultural heritage and set of traditions in the community. In areas where populations are stable, both in terms of turnover and composition, there is usually minimal social or cultural change. Because schools tend to reflect the communities that they serve, a comparable stability should be present in school data. In communities that have experienced considerable growth or turnover of population, however, school planning data tend to be more varied and expectations for change in the schools increased.

Along with information about population changes, data about economic development in the community often indicate anticipated population changes that will affect schools. The closing of key industries, declining farm populations, closing of military bases, or seasonal industries can signal new patterns for school districts. Out-migration of urban population, regional economic prosperity, or the development of new industries based on natural resources can also affect school planning.

In looking at the composition of the population to be served, a number of variables are important indicators for school planners. Birthrate projections, population stability patterns, racial and economic composition, and special social and cultural characteristics such as languages spoken or national origin of parents all have planning implications for school leaders.

Another influential variable to include in a formal needs assessment is the educational level of parents and persons in the community over twenty-five years of age. Data about the educational achievement in the community often indicate the amount of belief in, and support for, education.

School Population Characteristics

Among the most stable and useful data available to school planners are the birthrate trends in the district and the school enrollment patterns by grade level. Because of the rise in births in the late 1980s, school populations showed an increase at the elementary levels in the early 1990s and the intermediate grades in the late 1990s. Using such data, planners can determine how many classrooms and teachers will be needed, as well as programs for special students (one in nine students in 1990 was categorized as special). Birthrate information is available through county health department records.

The racial, ethnic, religious, and sexual composition of a school district is also important to school planners. The population in the United States is increasingly mobile due to changes in family structure and the economy. As a result, primary characteristics of communities can change rapidly, and the educational organization may need to make adjustments. When such change goes unnoticed, obsolescence is often a major problem.

Perhaps the most important data about school population come from our study of dropouts. Most school districts in the United States have an alarming number of students who terminate their formal education prematurely. The school and the communities should be particularly concerned about any student who walks out the door, never to return, by personal choice. Not only can such an exodus indicate a deficiency in school programming, but such dropouts have severe implications for the community, which must absorb them. In Florida, for example, 80 percent of all persons incarcerated are school dropouts, and the cost for each person in prison is five times the cost of attending a public school.

Students who quit school prior to graduation are usually faced with employment difficulties, limited job opportunities, low earning power, lessened opportunities for promotions, and emotional stress from related cultural and social pressures. To accept a high dropout rate as a normal event* in the schooling process is a shortsighted position for an agency charged with the task of preparing the young to become citizens. Table 3.2 illustrates how one school monitors dropout numbers.

---

*In some states the high school dropout rate is close to 40 percent but is reported by the schools to be 10 percent (per year). *Source:* National Center for Educative Statistics, Washington, DC.

TABLE 3.2 Sample
Dropout Grid

Year	Number of Dropouts	Total Number of Students	Dropout (percentage)
1990–91	34	258	13
1991–92	38	253	15
1992–93	44	239	18
1993–94	30	234	13
1994–95	48	277	17
	Total 194	Total 1,261	Average 15

Programs and Course Offerings in the District

The general scope and depth of an educational program can be best identified by reviewing the number and types of courses and special activities offered by individual schools. Of importance in understanding the programs of a school district are the organization of school programs, the rationale for such organization, the breadth and scope of course offerings, and the degree to which special education needs are met.

Many school districts conceptualize schooling according to levels of attainment and reference programs such as primary school, elementary school, middle school, and high school. In such an organization, students advance through the program by grades rather than by age, maturation, achievement, readiness, or interest.

In such programs, content and skill development are dominant organizers; there is little consideration for individual differences, and curriculum planning focuses on the sequencing of experiences. Such programs are usually organized in quantitative units, with teachers, students, classrooms, and textbooks assigned by a predetermined formula. Supplemental activities, enrichment experiences, and student services are added to the core program as resources allow.

Regardless of the avowed purpose of schooling and the primary organization of the educational program, the heart of the assessment process should address the course offerings and experiences that the students have. Most school districts in the United States, because of history and state and local requirements, arrange school into subject areas. Nearly all schools provide a core of activities that includes mathematics, science, English, and social studies. Most districts also provide supplemental programs in physical education, art, music, and vocational arts. Beyond such basic programs, courses and experiences are offered that reflect the capacity of the district to address individual differences. Often, the degree to which a school district tailors such offerings indicates how aware school leaders are of the needs of students.

In recent years, owing to research and legislation, school districts in the United States have become sensitive to the needs of special groups of students found in the school. A list of all such special students would be lengthy, but addressing programs to serve special education, **career education,** and adult education can illuminate course offerings outside the general curriculum.

Every community has children and youth with special educational needs that cannot be met within the operation of the general program of instruction. There are many definitions of students with special needs in existence; most include those children with emotional, physical, communicative, or intellectual deviations that interfere with school adjustment or prevent full attainment of academic achievement. Included in such a broad classification are children who are intellectually gifted, mentally retarded, physically handicapped, speech handicapped, behaviorally disordered, multihandicapped, homebound, autistic, hospitalized, and visually or hearing impaired. School districts vary in how they serve these special learners. Legislation at the national level (Public Law 94-142) has set strong guidelines for special education programs, which affect about one child in eight.

Career and vocational education is fast becoming a major curriculum component of many school districts in the nation. The impetus for this trend comes from many sources, but career and vocational education still represents the major alternative for secondary school students who choose a noncollege preparatory program.

Student interest in vocational programs is generally high among all types of students. The mandate for school districts to provide quality vocational experiences is heightened when it is recognized that the majority of all students graduating from secondary schools do not go on as full-time students in post-secondary institutions.

A valuable resource for those assessing student vocational interests is the *Directory of Occupational Titles,*[2] produced by the United States Department of Labor. This directory identifies over 21,000 job titles that may be of interest to students. Using instruments such as the Ohio Vocational Interest Survey, areas in which vocational experiences might be developed can be identified. Questionnaires that seek to pinpoint students' plans following graduation can also provide school leaders with rough indicators of need.

A third type of special education program provided by some school districts is adult education. A program for adults will depend on their level of educational attainment, the skills and knowledge needed by adults in the community, and whether interests are occupational or for personal development. School districts can effectively use adult education programs to increase community involvement as well as to build bridges to parents of schoolchildren.

For adults in the community who have less than a high school education, offerings may be geared to meet basic education needs. Such programs often lead to completion of a high school equivalency test. Other adults may be interested in education for job opportunities. Still other adults in the community may participate in education for personal improvement. Popular items are such topics as family-oriented courses, household mechanics, child development courses, and record keeping.

Schools providing educational experiences for adults in the community can use questionnaires and other devices to assess needs and interests effectively. The following list is illustrative of the types of offerings regularly requested by adult learners:

Job-Oriented Courses	**Personal Development Courses**
a. Typing	a. Reading improvement
b. Bookkeeping	b. Arts/crafts
c. Shorthand	c. Horticulture
d. Office machines	d. Slimnastics

e. Income tax
f. Electric wiring
g. Brick masonry
h. Cosmetology
i. Sales clerking
j. Carpentry

e. Self-projection
f. Home improvement
g. Photography
h. Interior decorating
i. Leisure activities
j. Basic sewing

Professional Staff

A thorough needs assessment also reviews the professional staff in the school district. Among primary concerns are the training and experience of teachers, supervisors, and administrators, the balance among the various teaching positions, and anticipated staff needs. Also subject to analysis is the staff's awareness of recent trends and developments in the field, as well as their attitudes toward change.

A review of staff training often will indicate a dominance of age, race, or sex among school faculties. These patterns are important in terms of the goals of the district and the specific programs being promoted in the buildings. Such an assessment will sometimes reveal an excessive number of graduates from a single university or a pattern of inbreeding among teachers. The latter situation is sometimes unavoidable in remote regions; however, a diversity among teaching backgrounds is desirable in terms of the experiences that teachers bring to the classroom.

A districtwide assessment of allocated teaching positions will often reveal overstaffing in particular subject areas at the expense of other equally important areas. Such a districtwide review will also indicate trends in staffing that can assist planners in projecting future staffing needs.

An analysis of faculty familiarity with new trends and developments in subject areas and new innovative concepts is important if the district anticipates new programs. Such a review can often pinpoint **staff development** needs that can be addressed in in-service sessions.

Finally, school districts can find extremely useful the analysis of professional staff attitudes toward change in general and toward specific curriculum alterations in particular. Such attitudes are the result of many factors, and experience has shown that age and experience of teachers are poor predictors of readiness to change.

Data for Instructional Planning: Instructional Patterns and Strategies

By far, the most important segment of a needs assessment in schools is the part that focuses on instructional patterns and strategies. Such teacher behaviors should reflect uniformly the intentions of the district to deliver quality programs to students. The types of instruction found in classrooms should result from an understanding of the goals of the district; an assessment of strategies and techniques can occur only following a clarification of the district philosophy.

In some districts, the predominant goal of instruction is to have all students master the essential data that will distinguish them as educated persons. Other school districts place greatest emphasis on the needs, interests, and abilities of students. A key distinction in these two extreme positions is the role of the student in the learning process. Because needs assessments tend to use subjective perceptual data about schools, they are most useful in districts favoring a student-centered curriculum.

Two major techniques can be used to assess instructional patterns and strategies: (1) the observation technique and (2) the administration of projective instruments. The projective approach is by far the most common method of reviewing instruction in the needs assessments.

The projective data technique, commonly referred to as the *opinionnaire,* requires the administration of instruments to teachers and, in some cases, students and parents. This perceptual survey is based on findings of phenomenological psychology, which holds that people behave in terms of personal meanings that exist for them at a given moment. In short, behavior is based on perception because we behave and react to that which we believe to be real. A personal perception may or may not be supported by facts, but such perceptions serve as facts to each of us.

Projective instruments possess several distinct advantages. First, they are quick to administer and tally. Second, they are easily managed and are less time consuming than interviews or quantitative measures. Most important, however, is that such perceptual techniques allow all teachers in the district to participate in the data-gathering stage. Such involvement is critical if programmatic responses to such findings are to be credible and supported.

Data for Instructional Planning: Student Data

In school districts where there is an attempt to serve the individual needs of learners, as opposed to giving all students the same academic treatment, it is important to gather student data. Data relating to student experiences are valuable for preplanning input, and information about student feelings and achievement can assist school planners in making adjustments to the existing curriculum.

In reviewing student experiences, a number of variables are useful indicators of both the breadth and depth of the student's world. A questionnaire that assesses student travel, recreational, aesthetic, and cultural backgrounds can provide teachers with invaluable points of reference for instruction. Examples of such questions at the elementary level might be the following:

- ☐ Have you ever seen an ocean?
- ☐ Have you ever flown on an airplane?
- ☐ Have you ever been to a band concert?
- ☐ Have you ever been in a public library?
- ☐ Have you ever visited a foreign country?

Questionnaires that deal with assessments of experiences, at the secondary as well as the elementary level, give teachers insights into students' backgrounds and levels of sophistication. When tallied as a percentage, the general level of experience for entire schools can be developed. Another equally valuable assessment device that may provide the same type of experience is a projection technique that asks students how to spend extra money or to plan trips.

Information about student attitudes, particularly those relating to self-esteem, can assist school planners in personalizing the instructional program. Beyond learning of student interest, motivation, and attitudes toward learning itself, such assessments often give clear portraits of student confidence in the instructional setting. Research over the past twenty years has shown consistently that individuals who feel capable, significant, successful, and worthy tend to have positive school experiences. In contrast, students who have low self-esteem rarely experience success in school settings.[3]

Measures of self-esteem, an individual's personal judgment of his or her worthiness, are plentiful. Two measures used regularly in needs assessments are the *When Do I Smile?* instrument (grades K–3) and the *Coopersmith Self-Esteem Inventory* (grades 4–12). *When Do I Smile?* is a twenty-eight item instrument that can be administered to nonreaders. Students respond by marking faces that are happy, blank, or sad. By this means, school planners can gain insight into attitudes about school, peers, and general self.

The *Coopersmith Self-Esteem Inventory,* a fifty-item instrument, assesses student attitudes about themselves, their lives at home, and school life. Students respond to statements such as "I can make up my mind without too much trouble" or "I'm pretty happy" and choose either a "like me" or "unlike me" response. Such instruments can tell school planners a great deal about student confidence, support from home, and attitudes toward the existing curriculum.

Assessments of student achievement can be either broad or narrow in focus. The measure of this essential category is really a reflection of the school district's definition of education. When an educational program is perceived as primarily the mastery of skills and cognitive data, standardized **achievement tests** can be used exclusively to determine progress. When education is defined more broadly, measures of achievement become personal and more affective in nature.

Standardized achievement testing is carried out in most school districts in the United States on a scheduled basis. Tests such as the California Achievement Test can provide computer-scored analyses in areas such as math, language arts, and reading. Such standardized tests give school districts an assessment of relative progress in terms of validated national norms. Achievement tests compare a student's progress with what is considered to be normal progress for students in the nation of approximately the same age or grade level, or both. These tests do not address a student's ability to perform.

It is useful for school planners to know if students in a district or particular school are achieving above or below grade level, for such information might suggest the retention or elimination of a specific curriculum program. More important, however, are general trends revealed by such tests. A continuing decline in reading scores, for instance, may pinpoint a level of schooling where curriculum review is needed. In Table 3.4, students in a district are displayed according to whether they are achieving above or below grade level in reading according to three commonly used standardized tests: (1) *Gates McGinitie* (lower elementary), (2) *Iowa Test of Basic Skills* (middle grades), and (3) *Test of Academic Progress* (secondary grades).

☐ Indicates Below Grade Placement

Grade Level	Number of Students by Grade							
	2	3	4	5	6	8	11	Total
14.0–14.9								
13.0–13.9							6	6
12.0–12.9							6	6
11.0–11.9						1	8	9
10.0–10.9						5	16	21
9.0–9.9						6	21	27
8.0–8.9					1	14	16	31
7.0–7.9				1	7	9	9	26
6.0–6.9				2	16	29	7	54
5.0–5.9		3	7	9	29	27		75
4.0–4.9		5	27	25	43	13		113
3.0–3.9	3	14	28	55	26	2		128
2.0–2.9	16	40	30	21	9			116
1.0–1.9	75	41	3	11	0			130
0.0–0.9								
Total	94	103	95	124	131	106	89	742

TABLE 3.4 Summary of Reading Achievement in One School District

In school districts where education is defined in terms of comprehensive criteria, assessments of student achievement are generally multiple. Sometimes, such assessments have multiple dimensions, such as achievement in knowledge use, skill acquisition, and personal development. Sometimes, such assessments are criterion-referenced, matching student achievement against goals rather than norms. Almost always, the evidence of student achievement is multidimensional, supplementing standardized tests with samples of student work, teacher observations, and other such measures of growth.

Data for Instructional Planning: Facilities

A final area considered by most needs assessments is that of the educational facilities used by the district to accomplish its program goals. Ideally, such facilities should be designed on the basis of program concepts.

An in-depth study of facilities seeks to answer the following critical questions:

□   What is the overall pattern of facilities in the district?
□   How adequate is each plant and site for educational use?
□   How are the facilities currently being used?
□   What is the net operating capacity of each facility?

Assessments of facilities and sites attempt to analyze the adequacy and capacity ratings of all plants and grounds for maximum benefit to the educational program. A basic principle of most such studies is that flexible, multiuse facilities are more beneficial than those that limit programs to a single instructional pattern. A facility (school building) is considered adequate and modern if it provides for

□   A variety of grouping patterns
□   The use of educational mediums, guidance
□   Health and food services
□   Special interest instruction (music, art, home economics, s   e, horti-culture, and so on)
□   Large group assembly
□   Administrative functions

One commonly used criterion for assessing school facilities is the *Linn-McCormick Rating Form for School Facilities,* developed by the Institute of Field Studies, Teachers College, Columbia University. The Linn-McCormick scale uses a point system that systematically evaluates school buildings from classroom through custodial facilities. Facilities are then rated on a scale from excellent to poor. Such a scale does not consider the financial capability of the district to provide such facilities.

For educational planning, the value of such a building-by-building analysis is that it allows school planners to see facilities in terms of the desired educational program. School plants can be compared and priorities for new building programs identified. If additional school sites are projected, lead time is available for survey and acquisition. Remodeling, where needed, can be scheduled.

In the assessment of facilities, an important phase is the identification and analysis of special facilities. In most school districts, special facilities are perceived as supplemental to regular instructional spaces and, thus, are a luxury. School districts must choose among a host of special rooms and spaces such as gymnasiums, art rooms, teacher offices, and so forth. Additionally, many schools have had to plan rooms specifically for students with physical handicaps or other special needs. The decision on which kinds of special rooms and spaces to have should be based on school planning rather than convenience or familiarity.

When school facilities are assessed, considerable attention should be directed to the use of these facilities. Detailed study can often lead to more efficient use of existing buildings and sites. Such study also will often reveal multiuse potential in spaces where only a single use is presently in effect, for example, the "cafetorium."

The assessment of school facilities and sites, including special areas and use patterns, should assist school planners in developing long-range facilities planning. Such planning can eliminate an undesirable pattern of building schools and acquiring sites after housing needs are in a critical state. Under such conditions, educational facilities are rarely adequate or appropriate to the needs of the instructional program.

ALIGNING THE CURRICULUM: THE CURRICULUM MAP

Once the scope of the curriculum has been determined by an operational philosophy, complete with goals and carefully selected objectives for learning, the curriculum must be **sequenced** or **aligned.** Over the past decades, we have spent a great deal of time working with schools on curriculum mapping since it is a prerequisite to meaningful interdisciplinary teaching and is useful in gaining efficiency from the curriculum in the form of test results. A typical mapping form is found in Figure 3.10.

Curriculum mapping, whether carried out on a district level or at the classroom level, is most effective when the materials and experiences encountered by the student are presented in a meaningful pattern. Not only does the teacher have to deal with the mundane task of pacing the coverage of the curriculum, but, even more importantly, the teacher must also give appropriate emphasis to the information being addressed. In curriculum mapping, the content, skills, and objectives are laid out and arranged in an optimal order. Where appropriate, these teaching acts are keyed to test items or other expectations. It is extremely important to identify

Grade Level _____			Subject _____	
Grading Period _____			Teacher _____	
Content	Concepts	General Skills	Specific Skills/ Objectives	Texts/Materials

FIGURE 3.10   Curriculum Mapping Format

the concepts or "big ideas" that guide all subsequent definition. Too often, teachers cover material without thinking about *why* they are teaching it to students.

There are two major benefits in this mapping process, which connects goals and objectives to programs. First, by viewing the intentions for students in totality, school planners can often identify redundancy in both the scope (breadth) and the sequence (order) of the general curriculum. Second, such an overview can help planners see commonality among parts of the curriculum. Understanding the interrelatedness of the curriculum can have payoffs in both instructional coordination and in a maximum use of district resources.

Once objectives have been generated for each desired goal and placed in a format that allows a review of the total blueprint for educating students in the district, it is necessary to identify program concepts that will give form to instruction. Program concepts are, in essence, sets of instructional and organizational strategies that are philosophically based.

The program concept phase of curriculum development is perhaps the most difficult step in building school programs. Although the need is to develop programs that are compatible with the district philosophy, there is always a tendency to return to what is familiar to us. Hence, the conceptual objectives often end up being translated into school programs with standard characteristics such as a textbook-dominated, six-period day. At this stage, the educational philosophy adopted before specific objectives were developed can assist in answering the question of which is the best teaching method to achieve the desired ends.

Schools and school districts differ tremendously in how they interact with students to accomplish desired goals and objectives. Generally speaking, however, schools vary according to how much structure they demand in the instructional program (see Chapter 2). Structure, as opposed to flexibility in instructional organization, is a reflection of the anticipated conciseness of the desired outcomes. School districts that desire highly predictable outcomes for all students who experience their program should not encourage instructional flexibility, for each variable encourages diversity of outcome.

In schools where there is a philosophy focusing on the student as an individual, there is a wider choice for instructional patterns. The program concept, when translated into instructional arrangements, indicates to school planners how desired outcomes should be approached. In the example in Figure 3.11, a school district identifies seven concepts that are felt to reinforce their desire to develop a program focused on the individual child.

There is a planning flow from philosophy to goals to objectives. Within this sequence of if–then logic, there should be consistency; if we believe this, then our objectives should be thus and so.

PROVIDING THE LEADERSHIP FOR CURRICULUM DEVELOPMENT

Role of the Curriculum Worker/Leader

The term *curriculum worker* applies to most educator-teachers, central office administrators, or principals. *Curriculum leader* refers to anyone in a school district who is

FIGURE 3.11 Concepts for Child-Focused Program

Philosophy Statement

We desire in each school, kindergarten through adult education, a program that will focus on the individual student to provide learning experiences in the affective, cognitive, and psychomotor areas.

Program Concepts

1. A program of individual instruction will be implemented.
2. A basic diagnostic-prescriptive approach to teaching will be used.
3. A variety of materials, both commercial and teacher-made, will be used.
4. A flexible schedule will be implemented.
5. Instructional assistance will perform teaching, planning, and clerical tasks.
6. Instructional leaders (teachers) will serve as facilitators of program planning and implementation
7. A facility that provides as much flexibility in programming as possible will be promoted.

primarily responsible for one or more of the following: planning, coordinating, or managing curriculum activity. Curriculum leaders may be any one or a combination of the following: teachers chairing departments or committees, supervisors, or school administrators.[4]

There is a growing emphasis on curriculum development at the school or district level. The identification of curriculum leaders who can facilitate curriculum development is essential to the success of any change process. Many competencies have been compiled for the curriculum leader. Because the success of a curriculum leader depends on good human relations, the following competencies have been identified that will help the curriculum leader coordinate the activities of an educational staff related to curriculum planning and development. The curriculum leader should be able to do the following:

- ☐ Produce and implement a year-long plan focused upon curriculum planning and the development of problems involving staff, parents, students, and support personnel, indicate their specific assignments and responsibilities, and provide a schedule of steps toward completion.
- ☐ Coordinate programming for instructional development at a variety of levels and areas (locally as well as regionally).
- ☐ Define, with staff, common problems and help staff with the solution of these problems.
- ☐ Develop, with staff, behavioral objectives, that will be measurable and compatible with the content area.
- ☐ Schedule periodic interdepartmental meetings within a school or a school system to define common curricular problems and to seek solutions.

- ☐ Help and encourage teachers to be innovative and to accept different methods as long as they produce the desired outcomes.
- ☐ Develop a program for continuous curriculum development.
- ☐ Accept the individual differences of adults in conducting workshops for the development of curriculum.
- ☐ Be a primary resource person.
- ☐ Help determine integration of subject areas into total overall curriculum.
- ☐ Evaluate the current educational trends and know the philosophical basis for these trends.
- ☐ Recognize the dangers to educational development inherent in each of these trends.
- ☐ Assist the group to pursue various possible solutions to a problem.
- ☐ Summarize various solutions clearly and concisely.
- ☐ Assist the group in coming to decisions based on the alternative choices.
- ☐ Follow through on a course of action decided.
- ☐ Evaluate the effects that course of action may have on those affected by the program change.
- ☐ Disseminate information on current innovations to staff members directly involved in a specific area of **innovation.**
- ☐ Promote and encourage the direct involvement and participation of teachers in planning, implementing, and evaluating curricular innovations and adjustments.
- ☐ Describe the various points of view and the proper relationships of different subject areas to each other.
- ☐ Coordinate curriculum planning and development for the local district, K–12.
- ☐ Open channels of communication within professional staff that will allow crossing grade levels, ability levels, and individual discipline structures.
- ☐ Develop an attitude of commitment to local, district, state, and national curriculum development and improvement programs.
- ☐ Determine the needs of the community and of individual pupils in planning and developing programs at all levels of instruction to fulfill these needs.
- ☐ Plan budgetary allocations to ensure that curriculum plans can be inaugurated.
- ☐ Improve personal ability to communicate positively and influentially with many different personalities.
- ☐ Offer, by example, personal philosophy of education.
- ☐ Provide vision for long-range planning.
- ☐ Seek help and cooperation from staff members in setting up programs of curriculum development or improvement, or both.
- ☐ Use research on child development and learning in selecting and sequencing concepts for curriculum development.
- ☐ Communicate progress, plans, and problems between staff members and curriculum-making bodies.
- ☐ Speak competently before faculty and critically appraise their efforts.
- ☐ Understand both elementary and secondary education (with a strong background in one of the levels).

☐   Establish a personal philosophy or a frame of reference (from which to operate; act in a manner consistent with such a philosophy or frame of reference).

SUMMARY

Curriculum development is a process of development that creates educational experiences to meet the intentions of planners. The basic tasks of curriculum work have been clearly defined during this century. Using an if–then logic, curriculum development identifies purpose, sets goals and objectives, aligns curriculum content, focuses on critical needs of learners, and delivers a program. This process is more difficult in the United States because of the decentralization of control.

Much of the difficulty in schools today stems from the lack of definition at the school and classroom level. Seeing the teacher (instruction) as an extension of curriculum calls for curriculum planners to use taxonomies and behavioral objectives to focus instructional activities. The curriculum mapping process and a needs assessment can further adjust the curriculum to the specific target of the design.

Leading curriculum development efforts call for a cluster of skills. You are encouraged to assess their abilities against the provided list.

SUGGESTED LEARNING ACTIVITIES

1. Develop an outline of events that would lead a school or district from no clear philosophy to a state of logical internal consistency in program development.
2. Develop a list of "quality indicators" that a district might want to review in conducting a needs assessment.

3. Using the list of skills for a curriculum worker found at the conclusion of this chapter, rank the ten most important skills for a school-level curriculum specialist.

NOTES

1. Report to the Executive Committee of the Association for Supervision and Curriculum Development, Research and Working Group, 1982.
2. *A Directory of Occupational Titles,* 3rd ed. (Washington, DC: United States Department of Labor, Bureau of Employment Security, 1965).
3. G. Brookover, *Self-Concept* (Alexandria, VA: Association for Supervision and Curriculum Development, 1981), pp. 13–14.

4. Working group on "The Role, Function, and Preparation of the Curriculum Worker," in *Curriculum Leaders: Improving Their Influence* (Alexandria, VA: Association for Supervision and Curriculum Development, 1976), p. 16.

BOOKS TO REVIEW

Bean, J. *Affect in the Curriculum.* New York: Teachers College Press, 1990.

Centron, M., and M. Gayle. *Educational Renaissance: Our Schools at the Turn of the Twenty-First Century.* New York: St. Martins Press, 1991.

Heinich, R., M. Molenda, J. D. Russell, and S. E. Smaldino. *Instructional Media and Technologies in Learning,* 5th ed. Upper Saddle River, NJ: Prentice Hall, 1996.

Joyce, B., and J. Wolf. *The Self-Reviewing School.* Alexandria, VA: Association for Supervision and Curriculum Development, 1993.

Longstreet, W., and H. Shane. *Curriculum for the New Millennium.* Needham Heights, MA: Allyn and Bacon, 1993.

Mager, Robert. *Preparing Instructional Objectives.* Palo Alto, CA: Fearon Press, 1962.

McNeil, John, and Jon Wiles. *The Essentials of Teaching.* New York: Macmillan, 1990.

Siskin. L. *Realms of Knowledge: Academic Departments in Secondary Schools.* Bristol, PA: Falmer Press, 1994.

PART II

CURRICULUM PROCEDURES

chapter 4

INSTRUCTIONAL CONSIDERATIONS IN CURRICULUM DEVELOPMENT

Instruction in schools is always a subset of curriculum planning. The substance, methodology, and assessment of classroom teaching can only be understood or rationalized by the purpose or objectives of the curriculum. A teacher who is ignorant of the curriculum intent or who acts as a "free agent" in selecting instructional objectives is usually dysfunctional to the educational process. By the same token, the classroom teacher is always the final filter in curriculum work. The architectural work of the teacher in selecting activities and methods gives meaning to the planned curriculum. It can be said that careful selection of learning objectives and a purposeful organization of the classroom are a necessity for directional learning in schools.

Instructional concerns at the classroom level require the curriculum planner to move beyond the kind of theoretical frameworks described in the previous chapter to a more practical level of planning how the teacher will interact with the student. The determination of these conditions will go a long way toward ensuring that the curriculum planned is the curriculum experienced by the student. Daily decisions about teaching variables such as content, materials, grouping, pacing, and student evaluation will cause certain aspects of the curriculum to be emphasized to the exclusion of other areas. This relationship between curriculum and instruction calls for the teacher to understand how the classroom influences curricular outcomes.

In previous chapters, we have seen how value orientations, foundational decision-making data, and curriculum development tasks can "shape" the school program. In this chapter, the reader will learn that similar processes of planning occur at the classroom level and that our body of knowledge about how teaching and learning occur is quite large. Teachers, too, are curriculum developers, and they must exercise their ability to influence classroom learning to the best of their professional knowledge. It is this skill of knowing how things work in the classroom that separates the true professional from the novice teacher.

Just as curriculum development goes through a cycle of analysis, design, implementation, and evaluation, classroom teachers must consider the what, why, how, and when dimensions of their work. If learning in school can be defined as having the student learn what the teacher intends in the form that the teacher desires, careful planning must occur prior to teaching. Figure 4.1 is presented as a way of thinking about this planning process.

CURRICULUM PLANNING PROCESS

Initially, the teacher must arrive at an understanding of the nature of the teaching task. This includes an identification of teaching objectives and a review of any mandated student outcomes in the curriculum. With this understanding, a general plan for content coverage would emerge, with "time" being the most important variable.

In the second phase, the teacher matches these curricular expectations with the capacities of the students to be taught. Are the students capable of such learning? Do they have the prerequisite knowledge base to proceed? Is there any problem with student motivation or the relevance of this curriculum to their lives? Following such a review, the teacher may want to alter or reassess the purpose of the proposed teaching.

In a third phase, the teacher becomes a designer of the instructional process. Important in the 1990s is the growing body of professional knowledge about students and learning in general and the methods and acts of teaching in particular. A major section of this chapter addresses such information. Based on these choices, the teacher selects techniques and plans activities believed to be effective for these purposes.

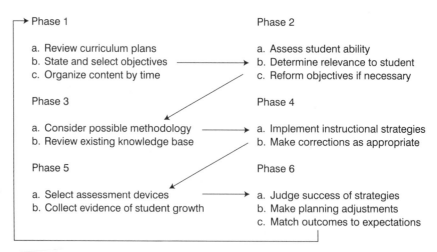

FIGURE 4.1   An Instructional Paradigm

A fourth phase finds the teacher actually delivering the curriculum in the classroom. In this process, the teacher makes minute-by-minute adjustments in how he or she is acting, according to student responses. Time, space, media, and materials are woven together into a unique tapestry according to how well the plan is working.

In the fifth phase, the teacher assesses the degree to which he or she has been successful in delivering the curriculum in its intended form. Measuring devices, both formal and informal, are applied. The expectation is that student behavior will change in some manner because of the teaching/learning experience.

In the final phase—redesign—the teacher weighs the appropriateness of both the curriculum and the instructional delivery and makes adjustments for future episodes.

Phase 1 Defined

Curriculum plans can be in numerous forms, including content outlines (frameworks), syllabi, textbooks, and guides. These curriculum documents project for the teacher an overarching plan for achievement of some end. Teachers should request and study these aids prior to teaching so that they can determine the overall objective of the curriculum (the *intent*) as well as the part that their subject or grade level plays in the education of the student. Too often in the less effective schools and districts, each teacher is an island, shut off from other teachers by the classroom door.

If such direction is not available, the teacher should use whatever resources are available to determine the task. During the initial analysis, questions concerning how much *(scope)* is to be learned, the suggested order of learning (the *sequence)* and perhaps even the value of the various areas *(balance)* should be determined. Teachers should try to determine what previous learning the student has experienced, as well as what he or she will be expected to know at higher levels of learning. Areas in which there is a lack of continuity *(no curriculum articulation)* should be noted.

Having conducted this review, with or without extensive guides, the teacher must then determine how much can be done *(time analysis)* given the task. Almost always, time will be a critical factor, and the teacher will have to determine which content is most important. An easy way to do this is to construct a "map" of the curriculum (see Chapter 3). Using the grading period as an easy organizer (four 9-week or six 6-week periods), divide the content by time estimation. For example, a 12-chapter text divided into 9-week chunks would mean covering three chapters per grading period. Having divided the material, the teacher then outlines the content, the learning skills, and perhaps life skills *(relevance)*. From this content analysis, the teacher then tries to determine the reason *(concept)* that organizes the teaching. If, for example, we are teaching American literature by studying the works of Hemingway, Faulkner, or Clemens, what are we really teaching? Identifying the concept (the criteria for selection) will allow the teacher greater control of time by adding or deleting content during delivery.

Phase 2 Defined

A rule of thumb in teaching is that, for every year in school, there is a year of range in performance. A third-grade teacher, for example, may have a three-year reading range in her class. Teachers may also experience increasing range in social matura-tion, knowledge background, and other skills development. In the second phase, teachers should seek whatever information is available (see the needs assessment section of Chapter 3) to determine whom they are teaching. An early determina-tion should be made on whether students are capable (have the knowledge, skills, background, intelligence, or maturation) to master the planned curriculum.

The teacher must also look ahead to the question of student motivation by thinking about the relevance of the planned teaching. Students often ask why they must study a subject (Treaty of Ghent, pi, periodic tables) and this question directly addresses the question of relevance. Each teacher will put a "spin" on information depending on whether it is presented as history, something useful now, or some-thing that the student will need in the future.

In some cases, the classroom teacher, as the last quality control agent in cur-riculum development, will adjust the plan to fit his or her students. As long as the adjustment is a matter of means, not ends, this is appropriate. Who else knows the students as well as the teacher? From this vantage point, teaching is an art form, and the adjustments are those of an artist. This phase is completed as the teacher brings the objectives into their final form.

Phase 3 Defined

In this phase, the teacher is fully into design work and operating out of an "if–then" mindset. "If my task is to teach this material but my students are poor readers, then I must. . . . " The possibilities for applied methodology are many. Figure 4.2 pre-sents eighteen common methods that may be appropriate for accomplishing some curricular task. The instructional design, and selection of method, occurs only after an analysis of conditions.

If there is anything that separates teachers of the past from teachers of today, it is their knowledge base about the teaching/learning act. Certainly, teachers have prac-ticed the kind of analysis outlined here for a century, but modern teachers add another dimension in phase 3. For the past twenty-five years, research has been accumulating about what makes a teacher effective in presenting the curriculum to the student. This knowledge base is now large, and we will present a sample of that information in the next section. Unfortunately, many teachers don't know how to teach under varied conditions, and learning by trial-and-error is a long, often painful practice. However, if a teacher knows where to find information on the best way to proceed, he or she will instantly be more effective and be following a more professional model.

After determining the best procedure, the teacher can then select the most appropriate strategies and order them for effect. In combination, this series of teacher behaviors will become a teaching style that will facilitate understanding and learning on the part of the student. A teacher with many strategies and skills, as well as an understanding of how they fit together under certain circumstances for maximum effect, will be a superior teacher.

Phase 4 Defined

In this phase, the teacher is actually delivering instruction in the classroom under live conditions. As the teacher delivers the lesson, all of the planning pays off in a more predictable set of events, hopefully leading to a mastery of the planned or intended objectives.

Along the way, the teacher will have to make adjustments for variables such as time (too much or too little), equipment and materials (the projector wasn't delivered), student behaviors, and some 3500 other variables found in any classroom. The key to success under such complex conditions is organization—organization resulting from an understanding of purpose and a thorough, realistic plan for accomplishing the objective of the lessons. Corrections in mid-course due to unanticipated events or conditions are both the prerogative and the "stuff" of successful teaching.

1. *Comparative Analysis.* A thought process, structured by the teacher, that employs the description, classification, and analysis of more than one system, group, or the like in order to ascertain and evaluate similarities and differences.

2. *Conference.* A one-to-one interaction between teacher and learner where the individual's needs and problems can be dealt with. Diagnosis, evaluation, and prescription may all be involved.

3. *Demonstration.* An activity in which the teacher or another person uses examples, experiments, or other actual performance, or a combination of these, to illustrate a principle or show others how to do something.

4. *Diagnosis.* The continuous determination of the nature of learning difficulties and deficiencies, used in teaching as a basis for the selection, day by day or moment by moment, of appropriate content and methods of instruction.

5. *Direct Observation.* Guided observation provided for the purpose of improving the study, understanding, and evaluation of that which is observed.

6. *Discussion.* An activity in which pupils, under teacher or pupil direction, or both, exchange points of view concerning a topic, question, or problem to arrive at a decision or conclusion.

7. *Drill.* An orderly, repetitive learning activity intended to help develop or fix a specific skill or aspect of knowledge.

8. *Experimentation.* An activity involving a planned procedure accompanied by either the control of conditions or a controlled variation of conditions, or both, together with observation of results for the purpose of discovering relationships and evaluating the reasonableness of a specific hypothesis.

9. *Field Experience.* Educational work experience, sometimes fully paid, acquired by pupils in a practical service situation.

10. *Field Trip.* An educational trip to places where pupils can study the content of instruction directly in its functional setting, for example, factory, newspaper office, or fire department.

FIGURE 4.2   Eighteen Common Methods Used by Teachers

11. *Group Work.* A process in which members of the class work cooperatively rather than individually to formulate and work toward common objectives under the guidance of one or more leaders.

12. *Laboratory Experience.* Learning activities carried on by pupils in a laboratory designed for individual or group study of a particular subject-matter area, involving the practical application of theory through observation, experimentation, and research, or, in the case of foreign language instruction, involving learning through demonstration, drill, and practice. This applies also to the study of art and music, although such activity in this instance may be referred to as a studio experience.

13. *Lecture.* An activity in which the teacher gives an oral presentation of facts or principles, the class frequently being responsible for notetaking. This activity usually involves little or no pupil participation by questioning or discussion.

14. *Manipulative and Tactile Activity.* Activity by which pupils use the movement of various muscles and the sense of touch to develop manipulative or perceptual skills, or both.

15. *Modeling and Imitation.* An activity frequently used for instruction in speech, in which the pupils listen to and observe a model as a basis upon which to practice and improve their performance.

16. *Problem Solving.* A thought process structured by the teacher and employed by the pupils for clearly defining a problem, forming hypothetical solutions, and possibly testing the hypothesis.

17. *Programmed Instruction.* Instruction using a workbook together with either a mechanical or electronic device, or both, which has been programmed by (a) providing instruction in small steps, (b) asking one or more questions about each step in the instruction and providing instant feedback if the answer is right or wrong.

18. *Computer-Assisted Instruction.* Software programs provide students with practice in key skill areas or are used to search for further information about selected topics.

FIGURE 4.2 *(Continued)*

Phase 5 Defined

Many teachers fail to understand the importance of **feedback** about their teaching. In a later section of this chapter, we will present several examples of self-monitoring by the teacher in the classroom. However, from a curriculum perspective, feedback is very important. Since most curricula are sequential learning and often dependent on previous learning, we must know if the teacher was successful.

In highly organized schools and districts, the teacher will be provided with specific learning objectives (behavioral) that indicate what the student should be able to do because of their experience in the classroom. In some states, **competency** testing is conducted periodically to ensure that learning is occurring. Whether these structures are in place or not, teaching is improved if the classroom teacher builds evaluation into his or her lesson plans.

In phase 1, the teacher asked, "What am I really teaching to these students?" A second important question might be, "What will I see in my students when I am done?" Teaching isn't about talking; it is about learning. After the teacher finishes, hopefully, their students will have knowledge, skills, and attitudes that they didn't possess prior to the teaching act.

A sign of a highly competent teacher is that there is an evidence trail that documents and monitors student learning. Although tests are the most common evidence, teachers have moved more recently to **portfolios** and other forms of true or "authentic" assessment. Even nonobtrusive measures, such as the number of library books checked out after a topic is taught, can be effective feedback for the teacher. In the best schools and districts, these "proofs" of student learning are passed on from year to year in a traveling folder for each student.

Phase 6 Defined

Finally, each teacher as a curriculum worker will be a judge of his or her own teaching. The behavior of the desired teacher is one who is reflective or analytical about his or her work. Even a twenty-year veteran of the classroom should seek to refine his or her delivery to the highest level of competence. When appropriate, planning adjustments should be made, and professional development opportunities (in-service learning or staff development activities) should be perceived as the means by which teaching is upgraded on a continuing basis.

In phase 6, the teacher compares expectations of the curriculum with the results of the teaching. Where there is a discrepancy, the cycle begins anew.

PROFESSIONAL KNOWLEDGE BASE IN TEACHING

For over thirty years, since the advent of computer technology, serious inquiry about the effects of teaching has been ongoing. Early hypotheses about what makes a teacher effective were studied using both a statistical approach (correlation of cause and effect) as well as an anthropological approach (grounded) using trained observers. Early findings in many areas of inquiry have been reexamined (meta-analyses and syntheses) as the powers of the computer have become stronger. In the 1990s, a significant body of knowledge exists to guide teachers, and this knowledge base possessed by new teachers makes them distinctive in comparison to teachers without such knowledge. No longer do new teachers have to learn to teach by trial-and-error methodology. Research can provide that new teacher with a "best bet" perspective on practice.

In the following section, we present a number of well-researched areas that continue to draw teacher interest. At the conclusion of this section, some research-prescribed changes in instruction are proposed for your study and reaction.

CONTEXT OF SCHOOLING

Social Influences

Schooling is a social experience and, all things being equal, the higher the social-economic status of the student (SES), the greater his or her educational achievement. In fact, the standard deviation of student achievement is, in most cases, dependent on socioeconomic factors.[1] The effects of socio-economic factors on schooling success have been studied heavily for over thirty years.[2]

The social components that detract from, or contribute to, a child's success in school include social status, language abilities, level of parent education, and parental involvement in a child's schooling. Improvement in any of these conditions will generally improve school performance. Even the size of the school attended affects attendance, with children from low SES generally benefiting from smaller schools.[3]

Special conditions in the society have a greater impact on the achievement of low-performing students. A cut in budget, for instance, has a greater impact on special programs. Reconstitution of the family through divorce or abandonment usually means greater family mobility and less parental attention.

Especially important today are two problems—cocaine and homelessness—that affect many young children. It is estimated that 23 million Americans (roughly 10 percent) have tried cocaine and that five to six million are addicted. A euphoric drug that reaches the brain pleasure center in five to seven seconds, cocaine is passed through the placenta to the fetus in pregnant women with each use.[4] About 11 percent of all babies in the United States are drug exposed; 70 percent of these have been cocaine exposed. Cocaine exposure causes disabling effects on organ development, resulting in visual, speech, and motor retardation and abnormal social and "attachment" development.[5]

Another example of a current social influence in schools is the new wave of homeless children in America. Estimated at between 300,000 and two million, homeless children present a special challenge to a society that counts on an educated population. Approximately 17 percent of these children do not attend school at all.[6] The homeless child is protected by the McKinny Act (1987), and the cost of ensuring educational opportunity for such children is about $25 million annually. However, a child who is attending school but has no home is more concerned with Maslow's lowest needs—shelter, nutrition, and safety—than with educational excellence.

In summary, it has been shown that "advantaged" children perform in a different way than do "disadvantaged" children in school settings. This accident of circumstances affects the ability of these children to learn in a school setting. Studies of intervention with parents[7] and facilitating school group experiences[8] show that schools can make a difference in the lives of such children.

Readiness

Closely related to social and economic background is the readiness of students to benefit from schooling. How students perceive their social environment accounts for such important schooling factors as feelings of self-worth, peer acceptance, motivation, and attribution of academic success. Without appropriate support and preparation, a student can enter school without the necessary skills and never catch up to their peers.

In the Havighurst study cited in the last section, 500 nine-year-olds were divided into four socio-economic groupings and studied over time. The unstable families in the study had a disproportionate number of maladjusted children who had identifiable school problems. For example, the most disadvantaged group had 4.5 times as many absences and 4.9 times as many instances of tardiness as the least disadvantaged group. The former group had no higher than a C+ average in their studies.

The in-depth study of this group of disadvantaged students indicated three problem patterns: poor learning ability and aggressiveness toward others, withdrawn and shy behavior, and a lack of motivation. These children also lacked achievement drive, models of success, parental and peer expectation, and intrinsic pleasure in learning. Recognizing the scope of the problem and the importance of early childhood learning, the federal government in the mid-1960s moved to intervene in the lives of low SES students or students lacking readiness to learn. These programs of compensation are discussed in the next section.

Any number of specific learning difficulties can prevent a child from having a successful start in school. Among the most common neurodevelopmental dysfunctions are

- ☐ **Attention** Concentration disrupted by daydreaming and lack of school focus
- ☐ **Memory** Inability to make specific mental placement of information
- ☐ **Language** Manipulation of spoken and written words
- ☐ **Visual/spatial** Interpretation of symbols and sound/sight relationships
- ☐ **Sequencing** Ordering and arranging ideas, information, or events
- ☐ **Motor** Difficulties in hand/eye coordination or body movements

One of the responses in the early 1990s to this wide range of possible difficulties affecting readiness in students is the "full-service school" which provides services such as health and nutritional support, basic medical services, family support, parent counseling, and even adult education. These schools attempt to help students by filling in the gaps in their backgrounds that might be preventing their full participation in the learning experience.

Newer research concerning school readiness is providing interesting insights about the variables that contribute to success. In one study, it was documented that our dependence on verbal performances in the early years may be giving educators a false view of student capacity. Often, verbal calculations (recitation, reading out loud) reflect linguistic knowledge rather than true ability.[9] In a second series of studies of children, it was found that those who were started in school too early (so-called "summer children") were retained more frequently, referred for psychological help more often, had overall poorer academic performance, and had less social acceptance. In one study in Montgomery County, Ohio, a higher suicide rate was found in those summer children who began schooling at a younger age.

Compensatory Programs

Compensatory programs (comp ed)—programs that compensate—seek to remedy deficiencies in a disadvantaged student's background by providing specific curricula designed to make up for what is lacking. These programs have been heavily funded by the federal government since the passage of the Elementary and Secondary Education Act (ESEA) of 1965.

Perhaps the best-known compensatory program is *Head Start.* This program for preschoolers, ages two to three, uses the criteria of family income and physical disabilities (10 percent of the children chosen must be physically challenged) to select children who are likely to be disadvantaged by school age. Heavily researched in the 1970s and 1980s, Head Start has been found to promote industry, initiative, dependability, social control, better reading and math skills, and a greater likelihood of promotion.[10] A 1985 follow-up of Head Starters found that those attending were more likely to graduate from high school and less likely to be placed in special education.[11] Some nutritional gains were found as well.[12]

Research findings concerning Head Start have been challenged, and some evidence exists that the gains of Head Starters evaporate with time. Nearly everyone believes that Head Start provides a "higher platform" for children starting school, and, recently, the Council on Economic Development recommended an investment of $5000 for each three- and four-year-old. In return, it was calculated, society would get a $7 return for each dollar invested in terms of fewer expenditures on remedial education, welfare, and criminal justice.[13]

Because educators noted a subsequent drop in achievement of Head Starters when the program ended, a second program, *Follow Through,* was begun and is still found in schools. This program also found that fewer participants were held back a grade or dropped out, and they were less likely to have a special education designation than might have been anticipated without intervention.

A third compensatory program found in most public school systems is *Title One,* a program providing extra educational services to low-income and low-achieving students. At a cost of over $5 billion, Title One has now served over five million students in forty-five states.

Title One uses five basic designs including in-class, pull-out (the student leaves the class for instruction), add-on (the student attends an extra class), replacement (the student goes to a Title One class instead of the regular class), and schoolwide (all students in the school receive the same treatment). To date, using reading gains as the indicator, the pull-out design works best (but also is most disruptive to the regular program). Ranging up to the sixth grade, Title One appears more effective with younger pupils.* The cost of individual programs has not been correlated with student achievement gains[14] Extending the Title One program into grades seven and eight is forecast for the late 1990s.

Yet another type of compensating program deals with language. Programs of English as a Second Language (ESL) and English for Speakers of Other Languages (ESOL) are found throughout the United States. The basis of most programming is the U.S. Supreme Court ruling in *Lau v. Nichols* (1974) that affirmed the respon-

---

*In 1996, Title One began serving students according to their income level rather than their achievement level.

sibility of schools to take action so that non-English-speaking students have equal access to educational opportunity.

Among the major findings to date are that young children have higher proficiency levels in languages prior to puberty,[15] that speaking, per se, does not cause language acquisition,[16] and that children who know one language well will be able to learn a second one better.[17] Of all programs studied, the *immersion* model that places children in the English-speaking room early scored worst in achievement, whereas extended instruction in a native language through grade 6 showed the most achievement gains. The worst-case scenario, quite common in public schools, is to place a non-English-speaking student over age 12, with poor language skills in his or her native language, in a regular classroom.[18]

Language will be especially important in the future. According to demographers, by the year 2020, 46 percent of all people in the United States will be a "minority," and many will have a language other than English as a native tongue. The ratio will be higher, of course, among the school-age population.[19]

Parents and Guardians

From a contextual vantage point, what goes on at home before and during the early school years is very important to school success. In fact, some researchers believe that parents and the home have at least as much influence on student learning and behavior as do the teacher and the school.[20] If this is true, curriculum workers should help teachers learn how to gain parental support for learning.

Six types of at-home behavior have been suggested as important for student success at school:

1. **Task structure**   Children participating in activities at home.
2. **Authority structure**   Home responsibilities, participation, and decision making.
3. **Reward structure**   Parents recognize student growth and advancement.
4. **Grouping**   Parents influence peer relations.
5. **Standards**   Clear and realistic expectations for behavior.
6. **Time structure**   Parents insist on time management for schoolwork.[21]

Studies reveal a great deal about what kind of parental involvement helps students achieve in school. It comes as no surprise that children with higher socio-economic status have parents who are more involved in school.[22] Parents from a higher socio-economic level, however, more often criticize the teacher and school.[23] Surprisingly, it is not the amount of parental participation at school (volunteer work) that influences students success,[24] but rather the goal setting and planning that a parent does with his or her child. Overall, research supports the notion that parental involvement is associated with academic achievement, better attendance, reduced dropouts, decreased delinquency, and fewer pregnancies while in school. Most importantly, parental support is crucial regardless of the economic, racial, or cultural background of the family.

One of the major problems in studying family support is the changing nature of the American family. As late as 1960, only 5 percent of all children in America were born out of wedlock. The average in the early 1990s is about 22 percent of all children born to single mothers, with the figure ranging upward to 60 percent for some ethnic groups. Many educators have been quick to note that the decline in achievement test scores has occurred in the same period as the decline in the two-parent family.[25]

The number of single-parent families in the United States is increasing ten times faster than the number of two-parent families, and females head up nine out of ten of these newer, single-parent homes.[26] It has been estimated that in the 1990s one half of all American public school children will spend time in a single-parent home.[27]

For the 15 million children in single-parent homes, it makes little difference if the cause of the condition is divorce, separation, death of a parent, or a single mother's choice. There are, however, some startling statistics that accompany this status that directly affect schooling. For example, 60 percent of these single mothers will have more than one child; 50 to 90 percent of these families will fall below the poverty level earning less than half the income of a two-parent family; the single parent will be more likely to be employed outside the home; the parent will have less time to attend to the child's intellectual and emotional needs; the child's sense of security will be diminished; the child's chances of abuse and neglect are increased in such a household (2.5 million cases were reported in 1997).[28]

In school, children of single parents were found to exhibit a number of personality differences including low self-esteem, low achievement motivation, poor peer relations, and high anxiety. These children also were more likely to be rebellious, act out, become juvenile delinquents, and use drugs and alcohol at school.[29] More troubling for teachers are the findings of a National Association of Elementary School Principals study of 18,000 children from single-parent families. In this study, it was documented that such children are more likely to be low achievers, earning half the A's and B's of the children from two-parent families and with a solid 38 percent getting mostly D's and F's in school.[30]

Researchers have found that parental separation tends to have more effect on boys than girls,[31] that death of a parent is less detrimental than separation, and that problems at school caused by a divorce tend to decrease after the initial year.[32] Giftedness in children does not shield the child from such problems.[33]

There is hope that school intervention can help overcome these conditions caused by our changing society. Numerous studies have found that when communication is established with the parent about the role that he or she can play, student school performance is improved. The seventeen-year study by Dr. James Comer of Yale University serves as a benchmark in documenting the positive effects of parent involvement.[34] It is noteworthy, however, that the variable that is most critical appears to be family income.

Classrooms

It has been estimated that students spend about seven hours per day in schools, and many of these 1260 hours per year are in a classroom. It is vital, then, that teachers understand the impact of this contextual variable on learning. The physical setting of a classroom affects the psychology, emotion, and physiology of learning, and it can cause both physical and mental dysfunction.

Physical space, seating patterns, light, color, noise, and temperature all combine to orient the child to the learning experience. One of the most interesting things about schools is how little space that they allocate to each student. Most school classrooms are about 30 × 30 feet or 900 square feet. When divided by 30 students, each student has approximately 6 × 5 feet of space. After subtracting space taken up by desks, hat racks, learning centers, and so forth, each student's personal space shrinks to about 3 × 3 or 9 square feet. What is interesting about this allocation is that it is a "short duration" space—like a phone booth. By contrast, prison cells and fallout shelters are spacious. Surely, being contained in such an area for long durations is counterproductive.

High density classrooms have been shown through research to encourage aggression[35] and to increase noninvolvement by students.[36] Room organization can be an important tool in shaping student attitudes toward school.[37] It appears that personal space in a classroom, rather than the pupil—teacher ratio, is a critical variable for student achievement.[38]

Seating patterns appear very important to different kinds of learning. Although some studies support straight rows and others support circles (tables), one study determined that people sitting at a 72 × 36-inch table had different communication patterns according to location. Those at right angles to each other communicated with each other twice as often as those seated side by side, and those seated side by side talked three times as often as those seated across the table from each other. No conversations were recorded by those at the far ends.[39]

Not only does distance affect communication,[40] but we have noted in numerous schools that the pattern of furniture is important. A cafeteria, for instance, with tables arranged in a herringbone pattern will feel less institutional than will one with tables arranged in rows.

Choice of seating affects learning as well. Problem children will choose to sit in only the back and sides of a classroom, whereas nonproblem children will use the full space. Teachers, unconsciously, teach to the front and middle of the classroom[41] and to the side of their handedness (right-handed teachers look right; left-handed teachers, left). Younger children are found to be more "on-task" when the gender of seating is mixed. Older children are more on-task when there is a segregation of gender.[42]

The look of the room also draws a response from student learners. One researcher reports that students in rooms created purposefully ugly (as opposed to beautiful or average) worked faster and reported irritability and fatigue. Specifically, light, color, noise, and temperature can induce fitfulness or calmness in students.[43]

Light seems to have a most important impact on student learning. Light that is too bright or too dim can have a negative emotional response on learning. Visual fatigue is accelerated when the amount of light alternates frequently from one level to another. Further, students exposed to ultraviolet light (UV) are found to have better attendance and better academic performance.[44] Sodium bulb lights seem to have the opposite effects on learning. It is prescribed that agitated and tense students should be placed in softly lit areas, whereas unresponsive students should be located in brightly lit areas.[45]

The color of a learning space seems significant in relation to learning. Color has been shown to have a physiological effect on the level of blood pressure, respiratory rate, task confusion, and reaction time. Bright, warm colors produce activity, whereas cooler colors produce thought and contemplation.[46] For this reason, it is prescribed that elementary rooms be painted yellow, peach, or pink (activity colors) and secondary rooms be in shades of blue or green. Teachers can use bulletin boards to establish a "color set" for learning.

Noise definitely impacts learning in the classroom, with sounds above 70 dB producing accelerated heartrate, elevated blood pressure, and even higher cholesterol rates. Since the ear is a second route to the brain, noise affects thinking. One study documented a 19 percent increase in energy expended in a noisy classroom as contrasted with a quiet classroom.[47]

Finally, temperature and humidity affect learning. The ideal temperature for learning is probably between 68 to 74 degrees Fahrenheit, but younger children require cooler rooms because of their higher metabolism rate. Adults have been shown to operate efficiently at 80 degrees. A temperature that is too high can produce stress, cause people to work more slowly, and increase the frequency of mistakes.

The effect of humidity on learning and health is surprising. Humidity that is too low causes negative physical reactions. In one study, classrooms with humidity ranges from 22 to 26 percent had 13 percent more illness than those at 27 to 33 percent humidity.[48]

Organizing for Learning

In addition to the physical environment of a school, any number of organizational factors influence classroom instruction. Items such as disciplining, failing or retaining a student, awarding marks for achievement, and using testing for placement are standard practice in most school districts. Yet, these factors are not often supported by professional study and may even be detrimental to learning. In this section, we look at four such areas.

Management and Discipline

The notion of a teacher managing a classroom or disciplining unruly students seems simple enough. *Discipline* can be defined as "methods used by teachers to bring about student conduct orderly enough for productive learning." However, a word-by-word breakdown of the preceding definition shows key action words such as *methods, orderly,* and *productive*. A clear definition of learning must precede a definition of discipline.

Several large patterns emerge from studies on discipline. First, effective and ineffective teachers tend to respond to student misbehavior about the same way, but effective teachers are better at preventing disruption in the first place.[49] Another finding is that classroom climate, or how formal groups interact, is directly related to teacher behavior.[50] Another key difference between discipline programs and styles is how much the teacher chooses to involve the student in the process of control.

The many variables of discipline include commitment, teacher expectation, rules, classroom climate, principal involvement, community roles, and authority invoked. By far the most widely used discipline program is *assertive discipline,* now used by over 400,000 teachers. A meta-analysis of all studies on this approach found "no significant difference" when compared to any other or no program.[51] Few quality studies were available, according to the researchers.

Finally, literature on discipline indicates certain techniques effective at certain ages. Preschoolers tend to react to physical controls. Lower elementary students respond to materialistic consequences. Upper elementary students are sensitive to social rules and norms. Early middle schoolers respond to peer pressure, whereas upper middle schoolers begin to use inner direction and individual responsibility for control. With high school students, freedom seems to be an effective variable in building a program.[52]

Retention

One of the most common practices in American education is *grade retention.* The underlying principle of "failing" or "flunking" a child, or "holding a child back," seems to be that low achievement at grade level is more traumatic than being placed with younger age students. Studies show that about 5 to 7 percent of all public school students are retained annually[53] and that some 16 percent of all students will be retained twice by the sixth grade.[54] The annual cost of retaining 2.4 million children has been estimated to be $10 billion.[55]

The practice of retention dates from the 1840s when the Prussians adopted the first age-grade system. It continues today because parents, administrators, and teachers believe it works. Nearly 800 studies of retention have been conducted with few supporting the practice. Major reviews of these studies have found no evidence to support the practice of retention.[56]

Studies show that the students who are retained come from a certain background; the most common pattern is a disadvantaged student, a minority, or a male. In 1992, for example, 40 percent of all fourteen-year-old males were overaged for grade compared to 20 percent of all females.[57] Students who are younger, have a perceived behavior problem, and live in the South are more likely to be retained.[58] Students tend to be retained at certain grade levels (traditional transition levels), and the practice has been reinforced in the past decade by competency testing laws. In one New York study, the best predictor of who might be retained was the school lunch program (children enrolled in the free lunch program were also from lower income homes).[59]

The effects of retention have been widely documented and suggest a highly undesirable byproduct. Dropouts are five times more likely to have repeated a grade, and students who are retained twice have virtually no chance of high school graduation.[60] A 1988 Texas study estimated that repeaters were 2.7 times more likely to quit than comparable students who were promoted to the next grade.[61]

Other negative byproducts of retention that have been documented include poor school adjustment, low self-esteem, low attendance, more behavioral problems, and less popularity. Although advocates of retention believe that the social costs are minimal, one study found that students reported the prospect of repeating even more stressful than being caught stealing or "wetting in class." In that study, 88 percent of the students ranked retention as the third most stressful event after losing a parent and going blind.[62] One 1989 study found the majority of students believed that retention was "punishment for being bad in class."[63]

A major California study documented that the anticipated academic benefit from retention was nonexistent. Even when intervention programs are attempted, there is no significant difference after three years in any subject or skill area. In the words of the researcher, "When low-achieving students are retained, they remain low achievers—when promoted they continue to be low achievers."[64]

It is possible that statistics on overagedness are somewhat misleading since they include students "placed" in a grade when entering school. In the last decade, the United States has experienced massive immigration from underdeveloped countries, and many students from those countries were placed in a grade below their modal grade level.

There remains a widespread belief that early intervention can make a difference, and programs to help retainees account for about 7 percent of school expenditures (including summer school programs). Short-run gains have been documented,[65] but no long-term successes have. Ironically, the best candidates for early intervention and retention are those who are academically able, making progress, but immature.

Prescriptions for the many students in this category, as an alternative to retention, include compensatory reading, transition (**nongraded** or multi-age) classes, tutoring, extended day classes, double promotions, and spreading the nine-month work over an eleven-month (summer) year.

Testing and Evaluation of Students

Schools spend a great deal of time assessing students by testing and sorting them according to their graded performances. Students take competency exams in most states to demonstrate progress through a prescribed curriculum and take S.A.T.'s to get into college. In classrooms throughout the country, teachers prepare report cards at regular intervals. How accurate are these tests and assessment activities? What should the supervisor know? Research in this area is extensive and raises many questions about practice.

Most school tests are treated as *norm-referenced* in that they are used to compare and contrast student progress against that of other students. In recent years, for example, American students have been compared unfavorably to students from other nations. Listen to former President George Bush:

> The ringing school bell sounds an alarm, a warning to all of us who care about the state of American education . . . every day brings new evidence of a crisis.[66]

The former president was referring to the scores on an International Assessment of Educational Progress that showed American students lagging behind the scores of students in other industrial nations. Although the newspapers played the story heavily, educators soon learned that the president hadn't done his home-work.[67] The use of the tests was political!

On standardized tests, supervisors need to understand that test makers, such as the Educational Testing Service, constantly renew their tests and, in fact, have some-thing of a "conflict of interest" in presenting a portrait of declining scores. Given the composition of the test takers and the sheer number of students taking these tests compared to twenty years ago, our standardized scores show remarkable health.

Educators need also to view state competency tests with a wariness, for they, too, are often presented politically rather than educationally in their reporting. In one recent study of the Florida state competency exam, for example, it was found that no correlation existed between passing or failing the state test and later acade-mic success in higher grades as measured by grade point average.[68]

Teacher-designed tests, too, have been found by research to be faulty in many ways. For example, it has been found that teachers use short-answer tests exten-sively, often omit directions and scoring criteria, sometimes use illegible tests, and have over 90 percent of all questions low-level.[69] In one study, it was found that the order in which the teacher read test papers determined the grade of students.[70] Another researcher estimated that about 84 percent of a student's grade is a mea-sure of competence and 16 percent is explained by the teacher's judging habits.[71]

If teachers use grades as a means of control, the reliability of testing and grad-ing declines further. Factors such as social class, gender, handwriting, physical attractiveness of the student, verbal patterns, and even the name of the student have been shown to distort the grading process.[72] Although all districts have grading policies, the teacher is the sole arbitrator in implementing that policy.[73]

INSTRUCTIONAL VARIABLES

A large number of instructional variables related to student learning have been studied and represent the foundations of a prescription for teaching. Each of the variables is, of course, influenced by the purpose of the teaching act. Among some of the best-evidenced areas are ability grouping, praise, questioning, memory and attention to learning, self-concept development, grouping, motivation and attribu-tion, thinking skill development, gender bias, and learning styles.

Ability Grouping

The practice of grouping students by ability is widespread in American education and developed from a set of beliefs about the purpose of schooling. The assump-tion that the learner has fixed and measurable abilities that must be assessed and then matched with appropriate teaching suggests a mechanical model of education in which learning is "engineered." In contrast is a view of learning that sees stu-dents as growing, though at different rates and perhaps in different ways. Here, the task of schooling is to facilitate and document progress in learning. David Elkind refers to these two assumptions as *psychometric* versus *developmental* philosophies of education, and the two are shown in comparison in Figure 4.3.[74] Most arguments for ability grouping are made from a psychometric perspective.

Developmental Philosophy	Psychometric Philosophy
Learner has developing mental ability	Learner has measurable abilities
Differences found in rate of growth	Differences reflect amount of ability
Task to match curricula to student rate of development	Task to match student with others of like ability
Learning a creative activity	Learning set by principles that are independent of content
Aim of education to facilitate learning	Aim of education to promote measured achievement . . . to maximize acquisition of knowledge and skills
Assessment by documenting work accomplished	Assessment by testing and comparing to like students

FIGURE 4.3   Contrasting Views of Development

Source: David Elkind, "Developmentally Appropriate Practice: Philosophical and Practical Implications," *Phi Delta Kappan* (October 1989): 113–16.

The origin of **ability grouping** (or **tracking**) in the United States is a system created in the Boston Public Schools in 1908 to "fit" education to the student. Over 1500 studies have analyzed this practice since then. Of these studies, the vast majority advise against this practice.

If the operational hypothesis is that students in various ability groups learn more (academic gain) than would normally be expected in mixed ability groups, then there is almost no support for the practice. Although various studies (Kulik,[75] Nevi et al.,[76] Jaeger,[76] Wolff,[77] Hill,[78] and Kerchhoff[79] reveal greater gains among high ability students when ability grouped, such studies cannot attribute the gain to grouping alone. For instance, other studies attribute such "relative gains" to smaller classes,[80] different teacher expectations, use of different teaching strategies and communication patterns by the teacher, and even the removal of "high student" influence from the comparison classrooms. One major study of tracking by Robert Slavin documented that grouping the upper two thirds of the students together, as opposed to the more traditional upper, middle, and lower thirds can be done without a loss of achievement.[81]

Besides indicating that teacher behavior, not grouping per se, is a critical variable in higher achievement when students are grouped, there is also evidence of significant teacher bias. One study, for instance, found Asian and Hispanic students with comparable profiles grouped differently.[82] Studies of Hispanic children and their performance in public and private settings also raise serious questions about teacher expectation and treatment.[83]

What appears in study after study is that teachers make judgments about student ability on factors other than ability (appearance, clothes, ethnicity) and that once such judgments are made, students tend to remain in that ability group for the rest of their school careers.[84] Once grouped, students experience discrimination in grading patterns,[85] and there is some research to suggest that girls, economically disadvantaged children, and minorities are further discriminated against at the secondary level.[86]

Although numerous adverse byproducts of ability grouping, such as lowered self-concept and retardation of academic motivation, are regularly reported among low ability groups, it is interesting to note that research shows that not all high ability students benefit from the practice. There is a relationship in learning between self-cognition, behavior, and achievement, and some high ability students lose confidence under grouping conditions.[87] This phenomena is referred to in the literature as the "big fish, small pond" syndrome.

It should be noted that most students of ability grouping are concerned with low ability students, and the existence of high mixed populations available for study (for example, gifted mixed with low) are rare. Sample variables to contend with are sex, SES, school characteristics, student ability, self-concept, academic effort, teacher grading patterns, and the subject.

Teacher Expectation

Teachers regularly make inferences about future student behaviors, and teachers treat students differently based on these expectations. Such teacher behavior affects and influences student academic performance.

Studies on teacher expectation date from 1938, and the most widely known publication on the subject is Rosenthal and Jackson's classic *Pygmalion in the Classroom*.[88] In this study, researchers sought to influence teacher expectancies positively by providing them with test scores that were said to be predictive of learning growth spurts. In reality, the scores were no different between the experimental and control populations; the difference was in the mind of the teacher. In the lower grades, students whom teachers thought should spurt ahead did, creating a self-fulfilling prophecy. Although the methodology of this study has subsequently been questioned, the study did seem to demonstrate that a teacher's favorable expectation can be responsible for student academic gains.

Some researchers have suggested that the difference in school success between advantaged and disadvantaged students may quite simply be rooted in their teachers' expectations for achievement. A study by G. Farkas et al., for instance, stated,

> Teacher judgments of student work habits, behavior in class, and appearance have a causal effect on the rewards teachers used and join with other factors to almost completely account for the grade differentials observed for gender, ethnicity, and poverty groups.[89]

It has been documented that once a teacher decides a student is of "low ability," the teacher will wait less time for answers to questions, provide more answers for the student when questioning, reward incorrect answers by the low student, give more criticism of the student after the answer, provide less praise for the low student, and seat the low ability student farther from the teacher.[90] It is interesting to note that research shows that teacher prediction of student performance is usually quite correct.[91] Further, students of all ages know that the teacher judges them and that treatment is differential according to expectations.

More recently, teacher expectation has been linked to teaching styles. It was found that

> Since teaching often reflects the teachers' personal thinking style, the teacher inadvertently rewards students whose style (learning style) corresponds to the teachers' teaching style . . . at the expense of those whose styles differ. Thus, the teacher labels as "slow" or "stupid" those students who learn well but in ways different from the teacher.[92]

Student behaviors in the classroom, particularly language patterns, influence teacher expectation. Nonstandard English, for example, has been shown to alter the way a teacher thinks of a student.[93] Some educators suggest that the impact of speech is even greater than a writing sample or photograph.

Finally, and most disturbing, is the evidence that teacher expectation can even alter the measurable I.Q. of a student.[94] This finding documented the fact that teachers who reached "expectation induction" early altered their teaching behaviors accordingly and either increased or retarded student intellectual growth as measured by such testing.

Use of Praise

Behaviorists tell teachers that if a pleasant consequence follows a behavior *(reinforcement)*, the behavior is more likely to occur in the future.[95] Many teachers believe that the use of praise or criticism *(negative reinforcement)* can alter student behavior. The research on praise supports this notion, but only under certain conditions. Researchers have determined that praise in classrooms is infrequent, often noncontingent, and global rather than specific. Further, in many classrooms, praise is determined more by the student's need for praise than by the quality of student conduct.

Researchers identified early that praise occurs infrequently; perhaps only once or twice a day for most pupils.[96] A 1974 study estimated the frequency at 6 percent of the time. These researchers also determined that "high expectation" students received more praise than "low expectation" students.[97]

Regardless of the frequency, response to praise varies with the student and, in particular, according to variables such as grouping, socio-economic level, ability level, age, personality, gender, and learning style.[98] For some students, being praised may promote feelings of embarrassment or being manipulated,[99] whereas other students may see praise as the way in which the teacher establishes superiority or creates dependence.[100] In one study of second graders, praise actually lowered student confidence and reduced participation.[101] Another study showed praise lowering self-esteem. In general, the older the student, the more likely false praise is perceived as a putdown.[102]

It has been learned that students can actually elicit praise from the teacher, even at the preschool level, through training in certain behaviors. Teachers have been found to praise only the students who regularly smile and participate in class discussions.

In short, the effect of praise or criticism is influenced by the students themselves. The key to understanding the effect of praising is how the person receiving the praise interprets that teacher behavior. Praise that is insincere or nondirective is ineffective. Also, it has been found that such general praise is often accompanied by negative affect in nonverbal expression. In a similar fashion, praise perceived by the student as "evaluative" is often rejected as counterproductive. By contrast, some higher ability students see teacher criticism as an indication that they are intelligent.[103]

Effective praise should be specific to the task, sincerely expressed, delivered in private when possible, credible and relevant (see Figure 4.4). The teacher should deliver criticism from close proximity, speak softly, and use eye contact or touch to reinforce the meaning.

Questions

Questions asked in a classroom are often the intellectual link between the thoughts of teachers and students. As such, this teaching variable has been heavily researched since 1970. It is generally accepted that teachers ask many more questions than students; 50,000 questions per year for the teacher versus ten questions per year for the average student. The nature of these questions tell more about the cognitive processes of the questioner than those of the listener.[104]

Studies of questions asked reveal that some 20 percent are procedural and another 60 percent are factual; the remainder may be higher level in nature.[105] Continuous procedural questions were found to promote listlessness among the listeners.[106] There is a correspondence between the cognitive level of the teacher question and the student response.[107]

Three studies of the relationship between higher level questions and achievement have failed to establish a causal relationship.[108,109,110] This is probably due to the nature of the achievement assessed rather than to an absence of effectiveness in questioning. In general, direct questions *(didactic)* bring short and direct answers; open-ended questions employing more "wait time" on the part of the teacher elicit longer and more complex answers by the student.[111]

By far, the greatest number of teacher questions are didactic in nature. These short and direct questions can be used for the following reasons with effect to

- ☐ Stimulate student participation
- ☐ Initiate a review of materials previously covered
- ☐ Initiate discussion of a topic or issue
- ☐ Involve students in logical thinking
- ☐ Diagnose student knowledge and thinking ability
- ☐ Determine the extent to which objectives have been mastered
- ☐ Encourage student participation in class discussion

Memory and Attention

Studies of students' memory and attention in the classroom have been ongoing since the 1920s in the United States. Quite simply, *memory* can be defined as the

1. You're on the right track.
2. You're doing a super job.
3. You did a lot of work today.
4. Now you've figured it out.
5. Now you have the hang of it.
6. That's exactly right.
7. That's absolutely correct.
8. That's the way.
9. You're really going to town.
10. You are really something.
11. You're doing just fine.
12. Now you have it.
13. Nice going.
14. That's coming along nicely.
15. That's great.
16. You did it that time.
17. You really outdid yourself.
18. Right on.
19. Great work.
20. Fantastic.
21. Terrific.
22. Good for you.
23. Good work.
24. Excellent.
25. Super job.
26. Good job.
27. That is the best you've ever done.
28. Good going.
29. Way to wrap it up.
30. That's a neat idea.
31. That's really nice.
32. Wow, that's incredible!
33. Keep up the good work.
34. Good thinking.
35. Super!
36. How did you ever think of that?
37. That's awesome.
38. You make it look so easy.
39. I've never seen anyone do it better.
40. You're doing much better today.
41. Way to go.
42. That's superb.
43. You're getting better every day.
44. Wonderful.
45. I knew you could do it.
46. You're doing beautifully.
47. You're really working hard today.
48. That's the way to do it.
49. Keep on trying.
50. That's it.
51. Nothing can stop you now.
52. You've got it made.
53. You're very good at that.
54. You're learning fast.
55. You're really on top of things.
56. I'm very proud of you.
57. You certainly did well today.
58. You've just about gotten it.
59. That's really good.
60. I'm happy to see you working like that.
61. I'm proud of the way you worked today.
62. You can be proud of yourself.
63. Great effort today.
64. That's the right way to do it.
65. You're really learning a lot.
66. You're impressive.
67. That's better than ever.
68. That's quite an improvement.
69. You made my day.
70. You're really concentrating.
71. I've noticed the improvement in your work.
72. That's marvelous.
73. Beautiful.
74. Perfect.
75. That's not half bad.
76. That's just fine.
77. You've got your brain in gear today.
78. That's it.
79. You figured that out quickly.
80. You remembered.
81. You're really improving.
82. I think you've got it now.
83. Well, look at you go!
84. You've got that down pat.
85. That's perfection.
86. Tremendous.
87. Outstanding.
88. I couldn't have done it better myself.
89. That's what I call a fine job.
90. You did that very well.
91. You're getting better and better.
92. Congratulations.
93. That was first-class work.
94. You're unreal.
95. How did you think of that?
96. That's sensational.
97. That's the best ever.
98. Good remembering.
99. You haven't missed a thing.
100. You make teaching a pleasure.
101. You make my job so much fun.
102. You got everything right.
103. You've mastered that.
104. You've been practicing.
105. That's very nice.
106. You sure fooled me.
107. Your behavior has really improved.
108. One more time and you'll have it.
109. You're doing much better.

FIGURE 4.4 109 Ways to Praise

ability to focus the mind,[112] and some students do this better than others. In general, the primary elements affecting retention of information seem to be prior knowledge and the instructional methods employed by the teacher.

The development of memory is thought to occur in the sixth or seventh postnatal month, at which time ideas or objects can first be associated with other items in the long-term memory. Memory is increased when the individual relates the item or information to his or her personal knowledge base. When students are unable to correlate subject matter or other school learnings with their knowledge or experience, inattentiveness arises.

Memory plays an important role in deciding what is processed by the brain. Recent studies support the notion of a cooperative process in which the behavior of large groups of neurons within a tangible circuitry mediate the processing of information and the retrieval of memories.[113] The problem of localizing the neuronal substrates of learning and memory has been the greatest barrier to progress in this area and remains fundamental to all work on the biological basis of memory.

Most memories originate as sensory impressions. Tracing *engrams,* defined by Dorland's *Medical Dictionary* as traces allegedly left in the nervous system by an experience, researchers can record and even replay memory tracks. That is, sensory experiences are transformed into memory engrams, and, as we grow, we become something of a "pattern recognition device."[114] Research is currently ongoing concerning how these "patterns" can be focused and enhanced for school learning.

There are two ways that researchers have attempted to learn about student attentiveness and mental activity. One, the *behavioral approach,* observes student engagement and speaks to teachers of concepts such as academic learning time (ALT). In a major study of twenty-five second-grade classes and twenty-one fifth-grade classes, it was found that the time on task was associated with achievement.[115]

The second way, the *cognitive approach,* focuses on the mental processes used by the student to determine the degree of attentiveness. The perspective sees teachers increasing student attentiveness and learning by facilitating learning through questions, relating learning to previous student knowledge, and teaching thinking skills associated with school success. It has been shown that students who use certain cognitive strategies do, in fact, increase their attentiveness.[116]

Studies of learners reveal that some students don't grasp information easily and can't maintain academic attention. Overall, brighter students are more attentive and slower students more passive. It is believed that certain teacher behaviors trigger this latter condition in slower students.[117] It also has been found that girls tend to be more attentive than boys[118] and are less likely to become inattentive because they employ superior planning processes.[119] As academic difficulty increases in a classroom, attention decreases correspondingly; however, students who are verbally fluent tend to have better attention and memory regardless of difficulty.[120] Any positive academic feedback from the teacher will increase student attention to task.[121]

Attribution

In the search for qualities that determine school success, researchers have looked at variables such as the student, the teacher, the parent, the home and school environment, and the methodology of instruction.[122] In the early 1970s, researchers began to identify a possible cause of low motivation in school[123]; students with low motivation rarely attributed success to themselves.[124] By contrast, successful students were more likely to attribute school success to internal and controllable factors such as effective study techniques.

Research has documented that low achievers often have "learned helplessness" and that this condition is most prevalent in girls and upper level students.[125] Such learners believe that effort is unrelated to outcomes and, therefore, futile. Training students to attribute outcomes to controllable causes and to interpret failure as a natural stage in learning has shown promise.[126,127] Specifically, such training involves appropriate praise, minimizing criticism, and giving effort feedback to students.

Thinking Skill Development

During the 1980s, researchers have investigated the manner in which thinking occurs in students. Four areas have evolved with which every supervisor should be familiar in order to lead teachers in planning instruction. Those areas include metacognition, semantic mapping, scaffolding, and scheme theory.

Metacognition refers to the student's awareness of his or her mental processes. Such awareness is critical to planning and setting goals, assessing content, and monitoring for understanding. Teachers can help students in metacognition development by modeling, "thinking out loud," rehearsing for coming tasks, employing anxiety reduction techniques, using directional questioning, and using games as analogies.[128]

Research has found that most students are not aware of their own thinking as they approach tasks,[129] and younger children, in particular, do not recognize major blocks to understanding in their own thinking.[130] It appears that all children, regardless of ability level, can benefit from such training. Metacognition training has been shown to aid in memory development.[131]

Another area under investigation is **semantic mapping,** a technique designed to help students tap into their prior knowledge base and expand that knowledge base through vocabulary development. In this thinking skill, students give their associations (concepts) for the topic to be studied. The procedure gives the students "anchor points" and bridges what is known to what is to be learned. As a generic thinking skill, it is effective in all subject areas and uses all of the elements of learning including reading, writing, speaking, and listening.

A third kind of thinking skill that has been researched and found effective with elementary and middle school students is **scaffolding.**[132] Originally an extension of a theory of *proximal development* which seeks the difference between actual and potential development of a student,[133] the term now refers to techniques that structure learning. Outlines and question stems are used to transfer thinking to form a framework, or "scaffold," for further learning. This approach to learning requires constant teacher monitoring of student progress.

Finally, researchers have developed an understanding of how old information structures new learning under the label of **schema theory.** According to schema theory, the organized, structured, and abstract bodies of information *(schemata)* that we all possess through personal experience "structure" new learning. Said another way, the way in which new information is perceived and interpreted is predetermined by existing understandings which may, or may not, be accurate. This research indicates that it is very important for teachers to learn what their students know prior to placing new knowledge *(schema)* on old knowledge *(schemata)*.[134]

Collectively, these four new areas of inquiry suggest that teachers must first learn how learning occurs before improving instruction. Although the areas cited are new and lacking in longitudinal studies, they promise to provide more relevant and useful knowledge in the years immediately ahead.

Self-Concept

The idea that the self-concept of a student *(self-esteem)* is a critical variable for school success has been around since the 1940s. Self-concept is thought to be related to attitudes toward school and teachers, basic responsibility for learning, motivation, participation, and personal and social adjustment, to name a few items known to affect school success. The topic has been researched with mixed results.[135]

It is generally recognized that personality factors contribute something beyond intellectual abilities in the performance of academic tasks. Students who feel secure and confident generally experience a positive schooling experience. These feelings of confidence and well-being are generally higher in boys than in girls,[136] are somewhat subject or content specific, and have been found to be valid predictors of academic success as measured by college attendance.[137] Grades, not surprisingly, are reinforcers for academic self-concept, and high self-concept is correlated with attribution.

Recent studies have indicated the role of self-concept in linking cognition and affect; how students feel about themselves has a direct relationship to classroom experience which, if successful, increases feelings of academic self-worth.[138]

Self-concept has been shown to be multifaceted, hierarchal, and somewhat differentiated with age.[139] There is a sharp but natural drop in the academic self-concept of students during puberty,[140] but it rises again in grades nine to twelve.

Gender Bias

The research on gender bias tells us that girls appear to be better students than boys, are more well-behaved, and receive higher grades. They even score better on achievement tests than boys do in the elementary grades. However, with each year in school, the achievement of girls drops; by the time that they take the Scholastic Aptitude Test in high school, the average girl will score fifty-seven points lower than will the average boy.[141] Why?

Research has looked at the possibility that girls are treated with an inclination or preference that somehow interferes with an impartial judgment due to sex classification. For instance, it has been shown that teachers direct more cognitive questions and statements to girls in reading classes but direct such questions to more boys in math classes.[142] Such treatment may lead to feelings of lowered academic self-concept.[143,144]

Clearly, in the past, there has been extensive documentation that women and men are portrayed differently in books, magazines, and other media. In 1972, the National Council of Teachers of English concluded that an overwhelming number of books found in schools depicted women and girls in a demeaning fashion.[145] Another study by Women on Words and Images entitled "Dick and Jane as Victims: Sex Stereotyping in Children's Books," looked at 2,760 books and found none that portrayed men and women as equals.[146] Since children seem to read stories about same-sex characters, girls were seen as being programmed for inferiority.

Attitudes of administrators show great discrepancy between the attitudes of men and women concerning gender bias and content of school materials. Also, practices such as lining students up by their gender, grouping students competitively by gender, and greeting classes each day by gender ("hello, boys and girls") are prevalent in the 1990s.

Although the results of gender bias appear verifiable, causation has not been proved. Among current theories of why, for instance, girls decline in mathematics are

- ☐ They mature early, and boys catch up.
- ☐ Male teachers dominate the subject in the upper grades and treat girls differently.
- ☐ Girls evidence maturity in the middle grades by affiliation whereas boys evidence maturity by independence, resulting in a more confident learner.
- ☐ The hormone testosterone in males activates a part of the brain associated with mathematical logic. This latter biological theory seems supported by the fact that women who excel in math generally have elevated levels of testosterone.[147]

Small Learning Groups

Teachers have a number of choices in grouping students, including whole-class instruction and subgrouping instruction. The latter category can be ability groups or mixed-ability groups. In addition, teachers can pair students in a number of patterns, or they can allow them to work independently. Some of the general purposes for grouping are shown in Figure 4.5. Research has looked at most of these combinations, and the findings are interesting.

Whole-group instruction through lecture has shown superior achievement under certain conditions. The "drill and practice" methodology of Mastery Learning and "time on task" studies[148] reveal that when the teacher is introducing new materials, covering material in a sequence, or asking students to master material verbatim, whole-class instruction is effective.

If the objective of instruction is not so direct or requires cognitive or affective input from students, small-group instruction may be appropriate. Small-group arrangements seem to be of two varieties: giving and receiving help, and cooperative learning. Giving and receiving help *(tutoring)* is usually either cross-age or of a peer design.

Research has shown consistently that when grouping is of the cross-age tutorial pattern, both the tutor and the tutee benefit. When tutoring is done by peers,

Purpose	Choice
1. To give students necessary information 2. To demonstrate a skill or technique 3. To practice listening and note taking	Whole-group lecture
1. To share ideas, knowledge, and experiences 2. To make applications to real-life conditions 3. To check student understandings 4. To reveal student interests	Whole-group discussion
1. To conduct planning 2. To share ideas or perceptions 3. To carry out specific learning tasks 4. To allow student leadership	Small-group work/projects
1. To allow students to work at their own pace 2. To allow practice in managing time 3. To allow students to pursue their own interests 4. To employ a learning modality that fits students	Individual work

FIGURE 4.5   Grouping Students Purposefully

good things happen also. In one study of four hundred students at the University of Kansas (Classwide Peer Tutoring Program), students in peer formation scored significantly higher than in regular whole-class arrangements.[149] In another study of 118 pairs of students who were asked to discuss academic motivation problems, opinions became alike, indicating the potential for increases in academic attitude under peer arrangements.[150]

In cooperative learning designs, small groups of students work together, and their grade is based on common, or group, performance. Such cooperative groups can be same ability or mixed ability in design, depending on the objective of the lesson. **Cooperative learning** has received more attention in the educational journals of the 1990s than any other form of classroom instruction.[151]

Most studies and meta-analyses of cooperative learning have documented positive results in areas as diverse as standardized achievement test scores, improving race relations, improving attendance, and **mainstreaming** special education students.[152] Not all reviews have been positive, however, stating that cooperative learning is effective only under certain circumstances.

Among the positive findings have been higher achievement and increased retention of learning,[153] more on-task learning,[154] greater achievement motivation,[155] and higher self-esteem among students engaged in cooperative learning.[156] The largest number of supportive studies for achievement has been in the form of cooperative learning known as "Teams-Games-Tournament."[157]

Critics of the highly publicized research on cooperative learning are many, and their reservations are diverse. J. Stallings, for instance, states that the cause of achievement under the TGT pattern is more like rewards and incentives than the act of cooperating.[158] Some critics have noted that the measures of the success of cooperative learning have been low-level thinking skills.[159] Most studies have been conducted in grades 7 through 9, and the greatest successes in cooperative behaviors have been recorded in rural rather than urban communities.[160]

Perhaps the most damning observations of cooperative learning research have come from A. Chambers who observes that "students low in prior achievement who work in successful teams can benefit academically, but students low in prior achievement who work in unsuccessful teams are at a disadvantage academically."[161] This concern is amplified by another researcher who states that "high achieving students tended to either dominate in the group or choose to work alone, and some poorer students manifested passive behaviors in the cooperative small group setting . . . low achieving students were relatively passive in cooperative learning small groups in comparison with their high achieving peers."[162] Noted researcher Thomas Good adds, "if teachers did not address this problem, passive students were content to allow other students to do the work."[163] Finally, G. Hooper concludes, "The benefits expressed by the less able students in heterogeneous groups are made at the expense of their more able counterparts."[164]

Learning Styles/Teaching Styles

Educators have possessed an interest in styles of teaching and learning for a long while. In the 1920s, for instance, Carl Jung identified different behavior types and found that there are two ways of perceiving the world: through sensation and intuition. He also hypothesized that people made decisions in two ways: logical and emotional. This early work has formed the framework for many of today's learning-style inventories.[165,166,167]

The basic excitement over this research is the premise that if a teaching style and a learning style could be "matched," higher achievement would occur. Not only would such a match help to explain why some students "bond" with some teachers, but also why the many types of methodology (mastery learning, individualized instruction, cooperative learning, computer-assisted learning, and so on) are appropriate for only some students.

Research on teaching styles and learning styles has tended to follow specific systems. Some researchers feel that an eclectic teaching style (many approaches) would best fit all students.[168] Another study found that adolescent learners and girls favored more direct teaching styles.[169] Still a third study using the Hanson and Silver instrument found that 60 percent of the average students favored a "sensing," or

Context	1. Lower the school entry age and stress life skills and language at an early age.
	2. Develop a K-8 compensatory education package to reinforce early gains throughout the formative years.
	3. Conduct instruction in the student's first language until that language is mastered, no matter how long such language is required.
	4. Increase efforts to involve and train parents, especially single parents, in the education of their children.
Environment	5. Place fewer students in each classroom, or make classrooms larger, for the purpose of increasing personal space and instructional flexibility.
	6. Ensure that no classroom or learning space has sodium vapor or blinking lights.
	7. Code room color to learning task when possible.
Organization	8. Invest staff development in classroom management (offense) rather than discipline techniques (defense). Make discipline programs age-appropriate.
	9. Do not retain children (grade failure) except in the case of bright but immature kindergarten pupils.
	10. Put achievement test scores and teacher grades in perspective; they should be seen as general indicators subject to gross distortions.
Instruction	11. If ability grouping is used, combine middle and upper students and be aware of the danger of high placement for some students.
	12. Continue to make teachers aware of teacher bias in "expectation" and grouping.
	13. Accelerate exploration of matching teaching styles with learning styles.
	14. Tailor the use of praise in school to patterns appropriate for the groups being taught.
	15. Understand that questioning is the link between teacher thoughts and student thoughts and that questions structure the level of thinking in a classroom.
Staff Development Areas	16. Accelerate study of attribution theory as a means of increasing academic motivation in all students.
	17. Help students gain control of learning by teaching thinking skills and modeling ways of approaching learning.
	18. Review self-concept programs for both appropriateness and results.
	19. Recognize that gender bias is a two-way street. Follow carefully the medical research on gender performance that is currently unfolding.
	20. Note the limitations on small-group and cooperative learning programs and the increasing criticism of social dynamics in some cooperative learning programs.

FIGURE 4.6   Twenty Suggestions from Research for Instructional Improvement

affective, approach to learning whereas 60 percent of the bright and gifted students preferred an "intuitive" teaching style.

Research on teaching and learning styles continues today, but without the objectivity necessary to document causal relationships through controlled research.

A summary of the research areas presented is offered as a twenty-point suggestion for designers of instruction in Figure 4.6.

Having reviewed some of the more heavily researched areas influencing the effectiveness of the classroom teacher, you may well conclude that a curriculum developer is a student of learning. Possessing knowledge about the various studies on teaching enables the curriculum developer to improve learning experiences for students. Clearly, because of the vast amount of material, some important ideas are sometimes hidden in the volumes of data:

- ☐ A teacher's effectiveness is defined by the purpose of the curriculum.
- ☐ Many patterns of effectiveness exist in teaching.
- ☐ Seeing a pattern of need and prescribing a pattern of teaching based on reasonable evidence is the curriculum developer's task.

PLANNING CONSIDERATIONS

Knowing about teaching and learning in the classroom is not enough. Teachers must be able to activate this knowledge through their daily actions.

Education is a tool for learning. Since there are many purposes for educating, formal learning can have many forms. The curriculum planner uses the development act to structure and focus learning experiences for students. The teacher implements the curriculum using a teaching style to provide emphasis to directional learning.

In developing instructional experiences, there are some general indicators of a good curriculum that might be considered:

1. A good curriculum provides experiences that are rich and varied and designed for culturally diverse students.
   a. Content is in tune with social and cultural realities of the times.
   b. Subject matter has meaning for the learner and an importance that the student accepts and understands.
   c. Classroom activities are arranged to provide a balanced program of learning opportunities.
2. A good curriculum is flexibly organized to serve the educational objectives of the school.
   a. Grouping practices do not discriminate against students because of their sex, race, or socio-economic status.
   b. Both formal and informal grouping methods are used to promote individualization of instruction.
   c. Variable time allotments and schedules are provided for individual and group activities.
3. A good curriculum uses resources that are appropriate to the needs and interests of learners.

     a. Resources are selected that are relevant to the goal-seeking activities involved.

     b. Materials are used that are free from biases of sexism and racism.

     c. Students are provided with necessary skills for sorting out messages provided by mass media.

4. A good curriculum includes appropriate teaching strategies to carry out learning objectives.

     a. Teaching strategies take into consideration characteristics of learners.

     b. Cooperative teaching and planning are encouraged so teachers can share learning resources and special talents.

     c. Classroom practices give attention to the maturity and learning problems of each student.

Instructional Skill Areas

Any number of characteristics can contribute to the quality of a teacher's performance including the teacher's personality, knowledge of the subject matter, philosophical and psychological understandings, and pedagogy (the principles and practices of teaching). To be effective, the teacher must be able to organize and execute teaching strategies so that the intended goals are reached. In most cases, good teaching is a direct result of good decision making by the teacher. The best teachers can transform the complexities of the classroom into a conceptual system that allows the interpretation of events and the anticipation (and direction) of classroom activities.

Beyond an understanding of the purposes of the curriculum, and the teacher's personality, is a set of skills and practices that can be called *pedagogy.* The pedagogical knowledge allows the teacher to do the following:

- ☐ Set up the classroom for instruction, establish routines, and organize student groups for a variety of learning activities and purposes.
- ☐ Conduct lessons in an efficient manner, asking appropriate questions, establishing an effective pace, avoiding disciplinary problems, and managing various forms of misbehavior.
- ☐ Adapt subject matter so that it can be understood in the intended form; making it appropriate to student needs and background, coordinating content with concepts, skills, attitudes at a desired level, and using media and methods effectively.
- ☐ Encourage active learning through interactive teaching; develop adequate self-concepts in students, and teach critical thinking skills.

Selection of Instructional Experiences

Selection of instructional experiences has always been a problem in curriculum development. Today's schools have inherited responsibilities for instruction that go well beyond the basic instruction provided by schools fifty years ago. There is more for students to learn than there is time available in school. Because of the back-to-the-basics movement in recent years, there is less time available for those learning experiences not classified as basic instruction, yet the needs of society have made the school assume more of the responsibilities formerly assumed by other institutions. How to reconcile the push for more time for basics and more time for the personal development of children is a major problem facing the modern curriculum leader.

At the classroom level, the push and pull of pressure groups becomes even more critical. Here, the teacher is often faced with a school board mandate to provide a certain number of minutes of reading per day for every child. This is often accompanied by a push for so many class periods a week of mathematics. Many school districts have requirements that certain subjects be taught in certain years in a prescribed manner. Curriculum planners must realize that the classroom teacher must ultimately carry out the instructional program and must have some flexibility in selecting curriculum experiences.

Providing Balance in the Instructional Program

In the past, most curriculum experiences were grouped as *curricular* or *extracurricular.* Furthermore, they were almost universally grouped or described within subject fields. The broadening of the definition of *curriculum* today has diminished somewhat the distinction between curricular and extracurricular experiences.

Within a school program, all learning experiences can be classified under the following headings:

- ☐ The personal development of the individual
- ☐ Skills for continued learning
- ☐ Education for social competence

The previous classification can serve as the basis for planning a school program and provides direction for instruction at the classroom level. Clear attention can be given to each of the three phases of the school program while still recognizing that the three phases are related.

Using such a classification system, curriculum planners can develop a plan that will provide a great variety of rich learning opportunities in each area. The **personal development** phase would include exploratory and enrichment experiences in a broad range of human activities. There can be activities leading to better self-understanding, health and physical activities appropriate to levels of maturity, and various school services involving the learner's family and home. The skills for the **continued learning** phase can include diagnosis of learning needs, with cognitive learning experiences structured so that students can master critical skills and progress in an individualized manner. The **social competence** phase might include courses of study in the sciences and mathematics, social studies, humanities, languages and literature, and the vocational fields.

Although such a classification system would be primarily a check on the scope of the school program, it might also provide teachers with a way to determine balance in the **curriculum guides.** Classroom instructors would also use different means of organizing for instruction as they provide learning experiences in the different phases of the curriculum. For instance, there might be more organized group instruction in the social competence phase than in the personal development phase. Group sizes could also vary with respect to the particular phase of the curriculum.

Relevancy of Subject Matter

Content should be relevant and significant. To be relevant and significant, content must constantly be examined to see that it reflects not only recent scientific knowledge, but also the social and cultural realities of the times.

In the advanced technological age in which we are living, subject matter in school curriculums may become obsolete before it reaches the printed or audiovisual form. Publishers and other producers of school materials are not only faced with the growing body of knowledge itself, but also with the growing complexity of that knowledge. The minimum level of understanding of mathematics and science that an ordinary person must develop to live comfortably in a technical society has increased dramatically in recent years. What is "basic" today was not even imagined fifty years ago.

Similar problems exist in social studies and language arts. What social studies text can keep up with the changes in government experienced in recent years? What literature book can compete with television for the attention of schoolchildren? Certainly, there will be a need for texts that deal with fundamental concepts underlying each of the disciplines. Distinguishing what is fundamental or basic knowledge is not an easy task for curriculum planners. The more fundamental a concept, the greater will be the breadth of application, for the concept is fundamental because it has a broad and powerful applicability. In those districts and states where there is mandated mastery of certain "fundamentals," students run the risk of being exposed to information that will have very little applicability outside the classroom.

If content is to be useful, it must be in tune with the social and cultural realities of the times. American education tends to be overly responsive to immediate social pressures, as evidenced by the emphasis on science and mathematics during the Sputnik era and the current back-to-the-basics movement. Although public education must be responsive to society, taking cues for the demands of an immediate situation sometimes leads to an imbalance of curriculum experiences that poorly prepares students for the future.

Selecting the curriculum experiences that are critical in developing a future generation that can exist in an ever-shrinking world means that the curriculum planner must be aware of all of the changes taking place. Independence has changed to interdependence in today's world. Our curriculum can no longer perpetuate the degree of provincialism and ethnocentrism it had in the past. Understanding our own diverse society is important, but we must also have comparative materials and experiences to understand other cultures as well as our own.

Educating a Diverse Population

In selecting curriculum experiences today, teachers must acknowledge the changing composition of the public school student body and address the needs of **cultural diversity** among students. In our largest population states such as California, New York, Florida, and Texas, we are approaching a time when no single ethnic group will form a majority of the population. The various ethnic groups, which include Latinos, African Americans, Asians, and Native Americans, bring special concerns and needs to the classroom.

The Association for Supervision and Curriculum Development Commission on Multicultural Education has suggested all educational content and processes be examined for evidence of realistic treatment of **cultural pluralism.** They offer the following recommendations:[170]

- Examine text materials for evidence of racism, classism, sexism, and realistic treatment of cultural pluralism in American society.
- Develop new curricula for all levels of schooling—curricula that enhance and promote cultural diversity.
- Provide opportunities to learn about and interact with a variety of ethnic groups and cultural experiences.
- Include the study of concepts from the humanistic and behavioral sciences, which are applicable for understanding human behavior.
- Organize curricula around universal human concerns, which transcend usual subject-matter disciplines; bring multicultural perspectives to bear in the study of such issues.
- Broaden the kinds of inquiry used in the school to incorporate and facilitate the learning of more humanistic modes of inquiry.
- Create school environments that radiate cultural diversity.
- Maximize the school as a multicultural setting, with the idea of utilizing the positive contributions of all groups to accomplish common tasks and not just to reduce deficiencies for the deprived.
- Recognize and utilize bilingualism as a positive contribution to the communication process and include bilingual programs of instruction of monolingual children.
- Examine rules, norms, and procedures of students and staff with the purpose of facilitating the development of learning strategies and techniques that do not penalize and stigmatize diversity, but rather encourage and prize it.
- Institute a system of shared governance in the schools, in which all groups can enter equally in the learning and practice of democratic procedures.
- Organize time, space, personnel, and resources to facilitate the maximum probability and flexibility of alternative experiences for all youngsters.
- Institute staffing patterns (involving both instructional and noninstructional positions) that reflect our culturally pluralistic and multiracial society.
- Design preservice and in-service programs to improve staff ability to successfully implement multicultural education.

PLANNING FOR CLASSROOM INSTRUCTION

Teachers must possess a way of thinking about learning to be effective instructors. Those who have not conceptualized an approach to teaching and learning often present unclear patterns to students and fail to achieve their intended outcomes.

Preparing to teach might be thought of as a series of questions that a teacher must ask and then the activation of those ideas through a lesson plan (see Figure 4.7).

Questions for Teachers
1. **What am I expected to teach?**   Upon arrival in the classroom, the teacher will be confronted with a textbook, perhaps a syllabus or guide, and other assorted learning materials. In better schools and districts, there will be evidence of solid curriculum work: objectives for each course, curriculum maps, cross-referenced resources for finding materials for specific purposes, and a content supervisor who can provide the teacher with assistance when needed. Since teaching is the delivery of a curriculum plan, an absence of such directives is cause for alarm.

1. Is the room prepared? Is furniture arranged to promote desired learning? Is the environment conducive to what I intend to teach?
2. Do I have a plan for getting students into the room and settled in their seats?
3. Have I thought of a "motivational opener" to make the transition from the last class they attended to this one?
4. Can I give the students a preview (advanced organizers) of what we'll be doing during the period so they'll know what to expect?
5. Have I estimated the time required for each activity this period?
6. Are the major concepts for this lesson covered by my planned activities?
7. Are the essential facts I want taught in the materials to be used?
8. Have I planned for the appropriate level of affect desired?
9. Have I planned to allow each student to participate at an appropriate level of learning?
10. Are the necessary and appropriate materials present in the room?
11. Do I have a plan for discussion? Have I clarified what kind of discussion will contribute to the lesson objectives?
12. Have I planned for relevance? Do I have some real-life examples?
13. Have I considered handout procedures and steps for collecting homework?
14. How will I involve special students in this lesson?
15. What is my plan for grouping? What directions will I give?
16. Do I have a plan for possible deviant behavior today?
17. Do I want to emphasize a certain format/standards for today's homework or assignment?
18. What kind of test questions would I ask about today's material? Do I want to share these expectations with students?
19. What kind of a technique will I use for closure of today's class?
20. What is my procedure for dismissal of the class?

FIGURE 4.7   Twenty Questions Before Teaching

2. **To whom am I teaching this material?**   Since nearly all learning is *associative* (based on previous knowledge), it is vital that the teacher know the backgrounds and needs of the students being taught. Some of this information is cumulative and will be found in a continuing school record. Other data can be obtained by soliciting information from the student using a needs assessment or less formal vehicles such as topical essays.

3. **What is the expected outcome or product of my teaching?**   Although many responses are possible in any teaching episode, it is the teaching "pattern" that elicits the student response. Teachers can arrange their desks to be near to or far from students, ask questions that are broad or specific, and provide a level of cognitive focus that "directs" student thinking. If the outcome of this teaching is known in advance (the *curriculum plan*), instructional choices will increase the probability of a successful and productive experience.

4. **How can classroom learning best be organized to reach that outcome?**   The way in which content is arranged will have a major impact on the form of student learning. In the following five common structures, the teacher uses curriculum form to "color" instruction:

   a. *Content structures*   Learning is organized as a linear series of knowledge, and the student masters that knowledge in a sequential order. Sometimes that knowledge "branches" out for specialization or enrichment.

   b. *Spiral structures*   A set or ideas or concepts serve as the big organizers, and these ideas are revisited at intervals using increasingly sophisticated examples or content.

   c. *Conceptual structures*   This method may use a "themes" approach, in which content is organized to support a series of interlocking ideas.

   d. *Minicourse format*   Content or knowledge is presented to the learner in "chunks" rather than as a series. Student interest is renewed on a periodic basis with the introduction of a new **minicourse.**

   e. *Interdisciplinary structures*   In this design, concepts, content, and skills from two or more subject areas are intertwined around life problems or student interest areas.

      The effect of these five learning designs is to make the material more or less specific (or general), relevant, applied (or theoretical), and accessible.

5. **What can I do to get students to learn in this manner?**   The teacher as instructional leader has the ability to orchestrate a large number of variables into a pattern by making decisions and emphasizing some things over others. Together, these choices form the basis of a lesson plan in which all of these things are coordinated. The who, what, why, and how of teaching lead to a directed classroom experience.

The Lesson Plan

The lesson plan serves the teacher, and others, by summarizing major concerns and by projecting teacher activities. In most plans, some common elements help us think about how the teacher delivers the curriculum (see Figure 4.8).

Teacher name _____

Subject/Course _____

  1. Unit _____

  2. Instructional objective(s) _____

      _____

  3. Rationale _____

  4. Primary content _____

      _____

  5. Instructional procedures

     a. Design _____

     b. Activities _____

        _____

        _____

  6. Evaluation procedures _____

      _____

  7. Materials and aids_____

      _____

FIGURE 4.8   Sample Lesson Plan Format

- **The unit of study**   The pertinent sections of a larger plan (taken from syllabi or district guides) that are to be addressed by the lesson.
- **Instructional objectives**   Subgoals that shape and define the lesson by describing student outcomes resulting from the teaching lesson.
- **Rationale**   States the purpose of the lesson in relation to some criteria.
- **Content**   Describes the selection and organization of instructional materials in terms of instructional objectives.
- **Materials and media**   Identifies the "tools" that the teacher will use to complete the lesson and its objectives.
- **Evaluation processes**   Describes what the teacher should look for in terms of students behaviors and organized by instructional objectives.

Choosing Instructional Strategies

In addition to the curriculum organization or design, the teacher can also employ strategies to shape student learning (see Figure 4.9). If learning is an active, constructive, and purposeful process dependent on the mental activities of the student, the teacher can influence these behaviors by what he or she does. Like a zoom lens, the teacher can cause the student to learn with a broad or narrow focus simply by selecting an appropriate strategy. Following are five such teaching strategies:

1. Identify and separate the contributing elements constituting a given teaching–learning situation.

2. Conceptualize the relationships between those interacting elements.

3. Select and plan appropriate instructional strategies.

4. Develop and sharpen suitable skills in order to translate the selected strategies into practice.

5. Acquire reliable and meaningful feedback in the form of empirical and objective data.

6. Evaluate the effectiveness of the selected strategies.

7. Modify and revise strategies for future improvement.

FIGURE 4.9   Developing Instructional Strategies

☐ **Linking new information to prior knowledge**   In activating relevant prior knowledge on the part of the student, the teacher is assuming that all learning occurs in the context of prior learnings. This important learning principle might include asking questions to learn about students' experiences, checking students' vocabulary through a form of *semantic mapping,* or coaching students' inquiries in an area to be studied.

☐ **Restructuring the student background**   Sometimes students possess misinformation from previous learnings that will interfere with the lesson of the day. The teacher, upon knowing this, may work with the student to restructure understanding. If the student is complacent, believing that he or she knows all there is to be known, the teacher may have to create *cognitive dissonance* or provide the student with knowledge that doesn't fit into his or her previous understanding. By **restructuring,** the student is "stretched" to new learning.

☐ **Teaching students how to learn**   Sometimes teachers will guide the student in a certain way of thinking or doing in order to accomplish the teaching lesson. For instance, the teacher may provide the student with a large organizer for information or a way of thinking about information **(metacognition).** The teacher may also show the student how to do something **(modeling).** A third example is that the teacher may direct the student how to receive, order, and store information by giving the student a platform (scaffolding) for learning.

☐ **Making learning purposeful**   A fourth set of teaching strategies works on student disposition toward learning or attitude formation. Students can be provided an experience that builds curiosity or interest for learning. Groups can be used to help students develop attitudes or new understandings. For students who are reluctant learners or who have developed a habit of not participating, the teacher can help connect the student behavior to the outcome **(attribution training).**

☐ **Organizing knowledge**   Finally, in arranging content, the teacher can suggest order and relationships for the student. Advanced organizers or verbal roadmaps can help the student see patterns. Guides and outlines (conventional, array, radial) aid the student in certain kinds of orientations to learning. The use of mental images (such as cartoons) may provide meaning for knowledge. The way in which the teacher responds to student questions can also highlight certain learning.

In summary, these five families of teaching strategies, like the five curriculum content designs, will influence the way in which the student interprets or construes meaning from the same body of knowledge. The teacher, like an orchestra leader, waves a magic wand as he or she selects strategies in planning.

Selecting Methods and Media

Another way in which the teacher gives meaning to curriculum is the format of delivery. Some methods, for instance, are solely teacher controlled whereas others may be interactive or even student directed. Media may be graphic, visual, auditory, or even "virtual," and each of these possibilities will have an effect on learning.

Methods and media can act to reduce monotony and boredom in learning. They can also be used by the teacher to adjust the curriculum to the diversified needs of the students being taught. In some instances, teachers use varied methods and media to allow student access to the teaching experience. Finally, these "tools" allow students to understand the application of ideas and information in ways which would be impossible in the conventional classroom setting. By making these choices and establishing a "pattern" in their use, the teacher becomes a designer and final filter in curriculum development.

Structured or teacher-controlled methods may include lecture, didactic questioning, the exclusive use of textbooks or workbooks, drill and review techniques, and learning activity packages. More interactive methods include active question-and-answer sessions, films, movies and video tapes, the use of guest speakers, debates, and small-group discussions and inquiry. Some methods become almost self-directed by the student, such as project learning, **independent study,** and interactive computer learning. It is important for the teacher to make such choices and understand that some allow more student influence of instruction than do others.

Going further, the teacher makes media decisions (anything that carries information), and these media will share and focus student learnings. If it is true that learning is restricted by what the learner perceives, then each medium can be seen as a learning tool to increase student perception. Some of the common uses of media are to visualize concepts, rate instruction to personal experience, gain closure on certain thoughts or ideas, help students participate in the learning experience, alter attitudes or feelings toward information, have a vicarious experience, individualize the rate of learning, or filter information through a preferred medium (learning style) of learning.

Media have changed dramatically in the last decade and more so in this century. Originally nonprojected (chalkboard, lapboard, flipchart, posters), media soon became projected (overhead, movies, television) and auditory (phonograph, radio, cassette tapes). This was followed by multimedia systems (dissolve units, computer-assisted instruction). More recently, media have exploded through computer applications (videodisc, distance learning, electronic bulletin boards) and the telephone (coaxial cable and teleconferencing). Many of these media can be used to add an "affective punch" to learning. Through such use, the teacher may highlight the important from the mundane. Once again, the purpose of the teaching will define the selection of methods and media.

Making Instructional Choices

As explained in the previous sections, the teacher is constantly making choices in planning and in teaching that affect the curriculum experienced by the learners. Examples of such choices and their implications can be drawn from three sample areas: grouping, discipline, and testing.

Teachers must decide prior to teaching how to group their students in order to gain a desired outcome. Students can be grouped as a whole or in subgroups. The whole-class model may be useful in orienting, motivating, setting directions, solving common problems, or giving common information. Whole-class patterns are usually justified on the basis of economy of time or when an instructional sequence must be followed.

Subgroups may be organized by like qualities or by a mix of qualities. Ability grouping in school, a widespread practice, exists because it is believed that students learn best when grouped with other students of like ability. Research, generally speaking, does not support this belief as we learned earlier in this chapter. Mixing students (cooperative learning) is believed to have many favorable byproducts, such as attitude formation and increased participation.

Teachers can also group students in smaller groups, such as in tutoring, or even group them alone (independent study). Any of these choices and decisions by the teacher will have a significant impact on what is learned in the classroom.

Discipline procedures, like grouping, will "shape" classroom learning. The various discipline policies in schools and classrooms contribute to an academic atmosphere by emphasizing certain important variables such as attendance, promptness, and work habits. Approaches to discipline in the classroom run the philosophic gamut from perennial to existential. Behavior modification, for example, is quite structured and will narrow the leading field. *Assertive discipline,* a widely used set of strategies, will introduce a group dynamic into the learning environment. *Reality therapy,* yet another widely known program, allows the student to be an active participant in the decision-making process concerning discipline. Advocates of the Carl Rogers approach are still more permissive and see all discipline activity in the classroom as a learning experience.

Teacher choices of discipline techniques and practices should be selected for their correspondence with other teacher methods and techniques.

Finally, a third example of teacher choice in instructional design is that of test construction. Tests can be used for diagnosing, for readiness and placement, and for determining competency. All tests are either **criterion-referenced** (achievement of a known at some level of mastery) or **norm-referenced** (comparing performance against some expected level).

Teachers can give multiple-choice tests, essay tests, fill-in tests, short-answer tests, matching tests, true-false tests, or even have the students create a portfolio of their work. The important consideration is that the test used by the teacher should be appropriate to and supportive of the instructional goals of teaching and the intended outcomes of the curriculum.

An overall condition of consistency and purposefulness is the desired state in effective teaching practice.

ANALYZING INSTRUCTIONAL PERFORMANCE

Instructional supervision is not normally considered a function of those responsible for curriculum development, but we believe that it should be. The truth is that any curriculum program is only as good as the instructor who delivers it. By any logic, the classroom teacher is a part of the curriculum and, therefore, should be a concern of curriculum planners. Until recently, educational research has not been very helpful to educational practitioners. Other than a general checklist of teacher competencies, a leader was armed with little else to judge the effectiveness of a particular teacher. Since about 1960, however, systems and instruments have been developed to help us look at classroom instruction in a more systematic way.

The concept of systematic observation is certainly one of the more widely publicized of these recent innovations. By its very nature and basic construct, an observational system represents an effective means for providing objective empirical data describing specific teacher and student variables that are found to interact in a given teaching–learning situation. Data of this kind have been found to be quite helpful in helping teachers analyze and improve their individual teaching effectiveness.

Currently, several manageable observational systems are available for teacher use. Each is specifically designed to assess a different and particular dimension of the classroom situation and can be used by the teacher for self-assessment as well.

Originally developed by Ned Flanders, interaction analysis is designed to assess the verbal dimension of the teacher–pupil interaction in the classroom.[171]

Flanders developed a category system that takes into account the verbal interaction between teachers and pupils in the classroom. The system enables an observer to determine whether the teacher controls students in such a way that increases or decreases freedom of action. Through the use of observers or by using audio- or videotape equipment, a teacher can review the results of a teaching lesson. Every three seconds, an observer writes down the category number of the interaction that he or she has just observed. The numbers are recorded in sequence in a column. Whether the observer is using a live classroom or tape recording for his or her observations, it is best for the observer to spend ten to fifteen minutes getting oriented to the situation before categorizing. The observer stops classifying whenever the classroom activity is inappropriate, for instance, when there is a silent reading, when various groups are working in the classroom, or when children are working in their workbooks.

A modification of the Flanders system of ten categories is a system developed by John Hough.[172] That system provides three more categories of behavior than the Flanders system. In the thirteen-category system, teacher statements are classified as either indirect or direct. This classification gives central attention to the amount of freedom that a teacher gives to the student. In a given situation, the teacher can choose to be indirect—that is, maximizing freedom of a student to respond—or the teacher can be direct—that is, minimizing the freedom of a student to respond. Teacher response is classified under the first nine categories.

Student talk is classified under three categories, and a fourth category provides for silence or confusion where neither a student nor the teacher can be heard. All categories are mutually exclusive, yet totally inclusive of all verbal interaction occurring in the classroom. Figure 4.10 describes the categories in the thirteen-category modification of the Flanders System of Interaction Analysis.

Verbal Patterns of Teachers in the Classroom

Using the Flanders system and other modifications of that system, teachers and supervisors can begin to isolate the essential elements of effective teaching by analyzing and categorizing the verbal behavioral patterns of teachers and students.

Four classroom patterns that particularly affect pupil learning are thrown into sharp relief when verbal patterns are identified and revealed by these techniques.

The first pattern can be labeled *excessive teacher-talk.* This occurs when teachers talk two thirds or more of the time in the classroom. Obviously, if teachers are talking that much, there is very little time for students to get in the act. In classrooms where teachers talk at least two thirds of the time, pity the curriculum approaches that emphasize extensive student participation in learning. Yet the two thirds' percentage of teacher talk is found in many classrooms today. Teachers can become aware of and able to control the amount of time that they spend talking in the classroom through the use of feedback from interaction analysis. This finding alone makes interaction analysis an effective teaching and supervisory tool.

A second verbal pattern is *recitation.* Arno Bellack, a pioneer in describing verbal behavior of teachers and pupils, has noted that despite differences in ability or background, teachers acted very much like one another. They talked between two thirds and three quarters of the time. The majority of their activity was asking and reacting to questions that called for factual answers from students. Bellack and others presented an elaborate description of the verbal behavior of teachers and students during a study of fifteen New York City area high school social studies classrooms. They summarized the results of their analysis in a set of descriptive "rules of the language game of teaching." Among their observations were the following:

- ☐ The teacher–pupil ratio of activity in lines of typescript is three to one. Therefore, teachers are considerably more active in amount of verbal activity.
- ☐ The pedagogical roles of the classroom are clearly delineated for pupils and teachers. Teachers are responsible for structuring the lesson and soliciting responses. The primary task of the pupil is to respond to the teacher's solicitations.
- ☐ In most cases, structuring accounts for about ten lines spoken; soliciting, responding, and reacting each account for twenty to thirty percent of the lines.
- ☐ The basic verbal interchange in the classroom is the solicitation-response. Classes differ in the rate at which verbal interchanges take place.

Category Number	Description of Verbal Behavior
INDIRECT TEACHER	1. *Accepts Feeling:* Accepts and clarifies the feeling tone of students in a friendly manner. Student feelings may be of a positive or negative nature. Predicting and recalling student feelings are also included. 2. *Praises or Encourages:* Praises or encourages student action, behavior recitation, comments, ideas, etc. Jokes that release tension not at the expense of another individual. Teacher nodding head or saying "uh-huh" or "go on" are included. 3. *Accepts or Uses Ideas of Student:* Clarifying, building on, developing, and accepting the action, behavior, and ideas of the student. 4. *Asks Questions:* Asking a question about the content (subject matter) or procedure with the intent that the student should answer. 5. *Answers Student Questions (Student-Initiated Teacher Talk):* Giving direct answers to student questions regarding content or procedures.
DIRECT TALK	6. *Lecture (Teacher-Initiated Teacher Talk):* Giving facts, information, or opinions about content or procedure. Teacher expressing his or her own ideas. Asking rhetorical questions (not intended to be answered). 7. *Gives Directions:* Directions, commands, or orders to which the student is expected to comply. 8. *Corrective Feedback:* Telling a student that his answer is wrong when the correctness of his answer can be established by means other than opinions (i.e., empirical validation, definition, or custom). 9. *Criticizes Student(s) or Justifies Authority:* Statements intended to change student behavior from a nonacceptable to an acceptable pattern; scolding someone; stating why the teacher is doing what he is doing so as to gain or maintain control; rejecting or criticizing a student's opinion or judgment.
STUDENT TALK	10. *Teacher-Initiated Student Talk:* Talk by students in response to requests or narrow teacher questions. The teacher initiates the contact or solicits student's statements. 11. *Student Questions:* Student questions concerning content or procedure that are directed to the teacher. 12. *Student-Initiated Student Talk:* Talk by students in response to broad teacher questions which require judgment or opinion. Voluntary declarative statements offered by the student, but not called for by the teacher. 13. *Silence or Confusion:* Pauses, short periods of silence, and periods of confusion in which communication cannot be understood by an observer.

Indirect–Direct Ratio = Categories 1,2,3,4,5; Categories 6,7,8,9

Revised Indirect–Direct Ratio = Categories 1,2,3; Categories 7,8,9

Student–Teacher Ratio = Categories 10,11,12; Categories 1,2,3,4,5,6,7,8,9

FIGURE 4.10 Description of Categories for a Thirteen-Category Modification of the Flanders System of Interaction Analysis

☐ By far the largest proportion of the discourse involved empirical (factual) meanings. Most of the units studied were devoted to stating facts and explaining principles; much less of the discourse involved defining terms or expressing or justifying opinions. The core of the teaching sequence found in the classrooms studied was a teacher question, a pupil response, and, more often than not, a teacher's reaction to that response.[173]

A classroom in which recitation predominates suggests not only that a teacher is doing most of the work, but also that he or she is giving little attention to individual needs of students. Moreover, the educational assets of role recitation are only verbal memory and superficial judgment.

A third verbal pattern of teachers that affects student learning is *teacher acceptance of student ideas*. There is ample evidence that teachers who accept the ideas and feelings of students enhance learning in the classroom. A number of observational systems have been used to identify teacher acceptance. In a large-scale study, Flanders isolated junior high school teachers whose students learned the most and the least in social studies and mathematics. He found teachers of higher-achieving classes used five to six times as much acceptance and encouragement of student ideas as teachers in lower-achieving classes. Teachers in higher-achieving classes were also less directive and critical of student behavior.[174]

The fourth pattern of teachers that affects pupil learning uncovers a teacher's *flexibility*—or *inflexibility*. The teacher structures the game, asks the questions, evaluates the responses, and speaks the Truth while students respond to questions, keep their own questions to a minimum, are not allowed to structure the game, and depend on the teacher to decide whether or not they have spoken the Truth.

Marie Hughes, in a study of classroom behavior, found the most frequent teaching acts were controlling ones. Teachers in her study who were considered "good teachers" were those who were well organized and generally attentive. Control meant goal-setting and directing children to the precise thing to which they gave attention. Not only is content identified for pupils, but they are also held to a specific answer and process of working. The teacher wants one answer. As long as the question or statement that structures the class requires but one answer, the teacher is in absolute control.[175]

Classroom Questions

Questioning is probably the most ancient pedagogical method. The dialogues of Socrates and dialectics of Plato have been used throughout history as models for teachers. Unfortunately, most of the questions asked by teachers require little thinking on the part of students, as pointed out earlier in the section on recitation. A number of reports in recent years have confirmed the high frequency of questions asked by teachers that require little more than the recall of memorized material.[176]

The need for helping teachers analyze classroom questions and developing appropriate strategies of questioning indicates that systematic training in the use of questions should be made available to teachers. A number of systems of analyzing and controlling classroom questioning behavior has been presented in this chapter.

These and other systems should be used in helping to train teachers to stimulate productive thought processes in the classroom.

Nonverbal Communication in the Classroom

The importance of analyzing and controlling verbal behavior of teachers has been well documented. Another dimension of teaching that has drawn the attention of researchers is nonverbal communication. **Nonverbal communication** is often referred to as a silent language. Individuals send messages through a variety of conventional and nonconventional means. Facial expressions, bodily movements, and vocal tones all convey feelings to students. A student may be hearing a teacher verbally praise his or her work while the teacher's facial expression is communicating disapproval of that work. If a teacher fails to understand the nonverbal message being conveyed to pupils, he or she may not be able to comprehend their responses to him. In analyzing a classroom, then, it is just as important to examine how the teacher says what he or she has to say, how he or she behaves and expresses feelings, as what the teacher says, does, and feels. How teachers communicate their perceptions, feelings, and motivations can be identified with facial expressions, gestures, and vocal tones. Such expressions determine in large measure how pupils perceive those teachers.

In examining the significance of nonverbal communication, it is important to understand that teaching is a highly personal matter; prospective in-service teachers need to face themselves as well as to acquire pedagogical skills. Teachers need to become more aware of the connection between the messages that they communicate and the consequences that follow. Teachers also need to capitalize on the nonverbal cues expressed by students as keys to their clarity and understanding. Although nonverbal interaction in the classroom is less amenable to systematic objective inquiry than verbal interaction, the meanings that pupils give to a teacher's nonverbal message have significance for learning and teaching.

Through continued study of nonverbal behavior, teachers can sharpen, alter, and modify the nonverbal messages that they transmit to students. The advantage of adding nonverbal analysis in a study of teaching is that teachers can look at their behavior in two ways—what their behavior means to pupils and how their behavior is being interpreted by their pupils.

Classroom Management

Another aspect of teaching, and one that is becoming increasingly important in today's classrooms, is *classroom management*. The changing family structure and increased conflict found in all elements of our society have led to concern about a general breakdown of school discipline and the need for better classroom management. There are a number of techniques to help a teacher maintain an effective learning environment in the classroom.

Jacob Kounin has developed a system for analyzing classroom management that deals with transitions from one unit to another.[177] The following are examples:

- ☐ **Group alerting**   The teacher notifies pupils of an imminent change in activity, watches to see that pupils are finishing the previous activity, and initiates the new one only when all of the class members are ready. In contrast, *thrusting* is represented when teachers "burst" in on pupil activity with no apparent warning or awareness of anything but their own internal needs.
- ☐ **Stimulus boundedness**   Represented by behavior in which the teacher is apparently trapped by some stimulus as a moth by a flame. For example, a piece of paper on the floor leads to interruption of the ongoing activities of the classroom while the teacher berates the class members for the presence of the paper on the floor or tries to find out how it got there.
- ☐ **Overlappingness**   The teacher's ability to carry on two operations at once. For example, while the teacher is working with a reading group, a pupil comes to ask a question about arithmetic. The teacher keeps the reading group at work while helping the child with arithmetic.
- ☐ **Dangle**   When the teacher calls for the end of one activity, initiates another one, then returns to the previous activity. For example, "Now pupils, put away your arithmetic books and papers and get out your spelling books; we're going to have spelling." After the pupils have put away their arithmetic materials and gotten out their spelling materials the teacher asks, "Oh, by the way, did everybody get problem four right?"

    If the teacher never gets back to the new activity (which was spelling in the previous example), this is a *truncation*.
- ☐ **"With-itness"**   The teacher's demonstrated awareness of deviant behavior. It is scored both for timing and for target accuracy. *Timing* involves stopping the deviant behavior before it spreads, and *target accuracy* involves identifying the responsible pupil. For example, if whispering began in the back of the room and then spread, and at this point the teacher criticized one of the class members who joined in, this would be scored negatively both for timing and for target accuracy.

The Kounin examples illustrate the ways in which teachers can maintain the group and not hinder learning in the classroom. In analyzing classrooms, we must not ignore the techniques of group management that teachers must use daily. Teachers must be provided feedback of their own behavior if they are to improve instruction.

Evaluation of teaching performance has numerous meanings and connotations, ranging from a rating of grading to a gathering of information to assess the effects of program and teaching.

In this chapter, a number of different instruments and systems were identified that look at classroom instruction and provide teachers with feedback about teaching performance. The use of evaluation instruments involves appropriate procedures and techniques. The following guidelines should be used by professional personnel in using evaluation instruments:

- ☐ Evaluation instruments should be as objective as possible.
- ☐ Evaluation instruments should be relatively simple, understandable, and convenient to use.

□   Evaluation criteria should focus on performance.

□   All personnel should be familiar with the instruments used and procedures followed in evaluating effectiveness.

□   Personnel should be encouraged to make self-evaluations prior to formal evaluations by others.

Table 4.1 illustrates a former teacher assessment instrument from the practice field of schools.

SUMMARY

Instruction is a subset of curriculum, so planners must be concerned with teacher behavior in the classroom. Critical decisions made by the teacher establish a learning environment and structure lessons. Understanding the philosophy and goals of the lesson, and structuring the learning act with objectives and intended outcomes, will give guidance to the teacher in developing the actual learning plan.

Research tells us that there are many kinds of teaching and that any kind of teaching can be successful (lead to student achievement) if it is directional. Teaching acts should be consistent with the intentions of the directional. Teaching acts should also be consistent with the intentions of the curriculum plan, and teachers can emphasize, provide value, and highlight different types of student learning by their behavior. Being aware of the critical decisions that they are making is important to the teacher as well as the curriculum planner.

Traditional ways of assessing instruction are the method of selecting experiences, providing for instructional balance in the curriculum, ensuring relevancy in what is studied, and, most recently, providing for an educational diverse population of students.

Traditional concerns and problems of planning for instruction include how to individualize, grade arrangements, scheduling, and grouping combinations.

Selecting appropriate teaching strategies, from among the many possibilities, is a task for each teacher. Helping teachers analyze their own behaviors and make wise instructional choices provides a natural interface between curriculum and instruction. Various examples of areas that may be explored are provided for the reader's consideration.

SUGGESTED LEARNING ACTIVITIES

1. Prepare a checklist of the teaching skills that you think are most important. Try to identify instruments or systems available that would provide you with feedback on how those skills are being demonstrated in the classroom.

2. Develop an instructional plan in your own teaching field. Consider the differences it will make if the focus is on (a) content or (b) student interests.

3. Summarize the research on nongraded versus graded instruction.

TABLE 4.1 Teacher Assessment/Evaluation Instrument

I. **Dependability**: Punctual, reliable, fulfills duties.

II. **Human Relations Skills**
   A. *Helps Development of Positive Self-images in Learners.* Praises. Listens, making students feel important. Elaborates and builds on the contributions of students. Relates to students on an individual basis. Provides opportunities for successful experiences.
   B. *Works Effectively with Different Social/Ethnic Groups.* Relates well to students, parents, and staff from different ethnic and socio-economic backgrounds.
   C. *Demonstrates Skills in Various Kinds of Communications.* Enunciates clearly and correctly. Adjusts voice and tone to situation; large group, small group, and individuals. Listens accurately to pupils and staff. Recognizes nonverbal statements. Adjusts language and content to students' age level.
   D. *Helps Students Become Independent Learners.* Helps students identify personal goals. Facilitates individual exploration. Provides opportunities for diversity. Offers alternate paths to skill acquisition.
   E. *Facilitates Students' Social Interactions and Activities.* Helps in special activity: field trip, play, games, and PTA.
   F. *Works Effectively as a Team Member.* Gets along with staff. Assumes responsibility for tasks as a team member.

III. **Managing the Classroom**
   A. *Maintains a Safe Environment.* Follows safety regulations.
   B. *Maintains Physical Environment Conducive to Learning.* Arranges room with a variety of books, materials, and learning stations that produce a stimulating academic environment. Decorates room reflecting students' ages and interests. Maintains room lighting and temperature as comfortable as possible.
   C. *Maintains Socio-emotional Environment Conducive to Learning.* Uses students' mistakes as sources of new learning. Respects rights of individuals. Enthusiastic about class work. Sense of humor. Uses competition in a way that allows for the success of many. Provides opportunities for students to share experiences and feelings. Provides opportunities for cooperation.
   D. *Involves Students in the Management of the Classroom.* Delegates responsibility of housekeeping tasks to students. Involves students in decision making concerning the identification, implementation, and enforcement of classroom regulations. Matches management duties with students' needs as an opportunity for personal enhancement.
   E. *Manages Disruptive Behavior Appropriately.* Implements rules and procedures consistently. Standards of behavior are public and professionally justifiable. Attends to disruptive behavior in an individual and private manner. Maintains control.
   F. *Designs Procedures for Handling Routines in the Class.* Gets class started within five minutes of signal and finished on time. Establishes procedures for hall passes, lunch count, storage of materials. Keeps register accurately. Scores, reviews, and records grades properly.

IV. **Planning Instruction**
   A. *Selects appropriate learning goals and objectives.* Develops units and daily lesson plans that include appropriate learning objectives.
   B. *Demonstrates skills in organizing learners for instruction.* Organizes different-sized groups of students for various instructional purposes.
   C. *Selects appropriate teaching strategies.* Lecture discussion, lecture demonstration, lecture, inductive, individualization, group investigation, open classroom, simulations, programmed instruction

TABLE 4.1(*Continued*)

    D. *Skillful in selecting and preparing resource materials.* Selects and prepares resource materials for lessons. Utilizes a variety of printed and electronic media.

    E. *Involves students in design of the instructional plan.* Seeks students' suggestions in the designing of the instructional plan. Provides opportunity for student choices.

    F. *Demonstrates skill in evaluating the instructional plan.* Provides a rationale for instructional plans. Establishes critieria for attainment objectives. Evaluates effects of the instructional plan.

V. Implementing Instruction

    A. *Relates Instruction to the World of the Learner.* Relates learning objectives to students' perceptual world. Teaches at students' level in terms of language, examples, and activities. Deals with content in a problem-solving context. Provisions are made to learn by "doing" rather than listening only. Points out implications of material learned for students' career development.

    B. *Skillful in Use of Various Teaching Strategies.* Lecture discussion, lecture demonstration, lecture, inductive, individualization, group investigation, open classroom, simulations, programmed instruction.

    C. *Applies Group Dynamics Techniques.* Uses different group management and leadership styles when working with large groups, middle size groups, and small groups of students.

    D. *Skillful in the Individualization of Instruction.* Diagnoses individual levels of proficiency, prescribes appropriate activities, selects appropriate materials, manages learning procedures.

    E. *Skillful in the Use of A-V Equipment.* Operates overhead projector, opaque projector, tape recorder, movie projector, slide projector, ditto machine, and mimeograph.

    F. *Skillful in the Use of Multimedia Resources.* Incorporates printed and electronic media into learning activities.

    G. *Demonstrates Skills in Questioning and Responding.* Asks questions at various levels of cognitive taxonomy. Phrases and times questions appropriately. Elicits student participation through questions. Uses rapid-fire questions to move students into work. Uses questions as means of success for all learners. Builds new questions on students' answers. Challenges and probes through questions. Responds to answers by reinforcing or abstaining from judgment as the activity prescribes.

    H. *Demonstrates Skills in Value-Clarification Techniques.* Raises questions in the mind of the students to prod them gently to examine personal actions, values, and goals.

    I. *Evaluates and Modifies His/Her Own Performance.* Gathers self-evaluation data through VCR or audio tape playback, student oral and written feedback, supervisor feedback. Identifies areas of strength and weakness and formulates plan for improvement specifying criteria for accomplishment. Implements plan and evaluates and reports results.

VI. Knowledge of Subject Matter

    A. *Demonstrates Adequate General Academic Preparation.* Makes accurate statements and allusions to related fields of knowledge outside areas of specialization. Exhibits broad academic preparation.

    B. *Demonstrates Knowledge of Areas of Specialization.* Well-informed and skillful in field(s) of specialization.

VII. Assessing and Evaluating Students

    A. *Recognizes Individual Personalities/Learning Styles.* Designs and implements curriculum plans that provide for alternative learning styles and different cognitive and affective make-up.

    B. *Demonstrates Diagnostic Skills.* Skillful in the analysis of learning tasks. Determines student's level of proficiency in content area(s).

    C. *Skill in Selecting and Devising Formal Evaluation Instruments.* Writes tests utilizing variety of types of items. Appropriate to content area and student's level.

TABLE 4.1(*Continued*)

    D. *Skillful in Devising and Using Informal Evaluation Procedures.* Uses informal evaluation techniques to assess progression in learning such as interview, case study, analysis of student performance data.

    E. *Skillful in Providing Feedback to Students and Parents.* Devises formative evaluation events: teacher evaluated, learner/parent evaluated.

VIII. Professionalism

    A. *Seeks to Improve Own Professional Competence.* Reads professional journals. Attends professional meetings. Visits other programs and teachers. Seeks and utilizes professional feedback.

    B. *Is Accountable for Professional Actions.* Dependable. Fulfills responsibility of the professional teacher: planning, implementing, validating instruction, maintenance tasks, playground duties, and other tasks.

    C. *Demonstrates Skill in Professional Decision Making.* Possesses a rationale for professional action. Produces evidence to justify professional decisions. Evaluates the consequences of actions.

    D. *Demonstrates Awareness of Strengths and Weaknesses.* Identifies teaching roles and strategies most and least suited to own style. Identifies personal human interaction style and its effects in professional work. Identifies own value system and how it relates to teaching.

    E. *Behaves According to an Accepted Code of Professional Ethics.* Works to fulfill institutional goals. Bases public criticism of education on valid assumptions as established by careful evaluation of facts and hypotheses. Refrains from exploiting the institutional privileges of the teaching profession to promote partisan activities or political candidates. Directly uses information about students; refrains from unprofessional comments. Avoids exploiting the professional relationship with any student. Deals justly and considerately with each student.

    F. *Seeks to Improve the Profession.* Participates in professional organizations. Prepares plan for improvement of the profession to be implemented during first year of teaching.

Source: John McNeil and Jon Wiles. *The Essentials of Teaching.* Macmillan, 1990, pp. 120–22.

NOTES

1. P. Crone and M. Tashakkon, "Variance in Student Achievement in Effective and Ineffective Schools: Inconsistencies Across SES Categories" (Paper, American Educational Research Association, 1992).

2. Robert Havighurst, *Growing Up in River City* (New York: John Wiley and Sons, 1962).

3. A. Friedkin and P. Necochen, as cited in "Social Influences," in M. Aiken, ed., *The Encyclopedia of Educational Research,* 6th ed. (New York: Macmillan, 1992), pp. 562–67.

4. K. Howze and W. Howze, "Children of Cocaine: Treatment and Child Care" (Paper, National Association for the Education of Young Children, Annual Conference, 1989).

5. M. Poulson and P. Cole, "Children at Risk Due to Prenatal Substance Exposure" (Paper, Los Angeles Unified School District, December 1989).

6. J. Daniels, "Empowering Homeless Children Through School Counseling," *Elementary School Guidance and Counseling* 27 (December 1992): 105–111.

7. A. Shoho, "A Historical Comparison of Parental Involvement of Three Generations of Japanese Americans in the Education of Their Children" (AERA Paper, 1992).

8. D. D'Andrea, R. Daniels, and H. Morioka, *Building Strategies to Meet the Developmental Needs of Homeless Children* (Ann Arbor: University of Michigan Press, ERIC/CAPS, 1990).

9. N. Jordon, "Differential Calculations Abilities in Young Children from Middle and Low

Income Families," *Developmental Psychology* 26, 4 (1992): 644–53.

10. F. H. Palmer, "The Effects of Minimal Early Intervention on Subsequent I.Q. Score and Reading Achievement" (Final Report, Education Commission of the States, Denver, 1976).

11. A. Smith, "The Impact of Head Start on Children, Families, and Communities" (Final Report, U.S. Department of Health and Human Services, 1985).

12. R. Hubbell, *A Review of Head Start Research Since 1970* (Washington, DC: U.S. Department of Health and Human Services, 1985), pp. 14–18.

13. T. Toch, "Giving Kids a Leg Up: How to Best Help Kids Succeed in School," *U.S. News and World Report,* October 22, 1990, p. 63.

14. T. Fagan and C. Held, "Chapter One Program Improvement," *Phi Delta Kappan* 72 (1991): 562–64.

15. V. Collier, "How Long?: A Synthesis of Research on Academic Achievement in Second Language," *TESOL Quarterly* 23 (September 1988): 509–30.

16. K. Baker and A. deKanter, "1990 U.S. DOE Study," in J. Crawford, ed., *Bilingual Education: History, Politics, Theory* (Newark, NJ: Crane Publishing Co., 1991).

17. J. Crawford, *Bilingual Education: History, Politics, Theory, Practice* (Newark, NJ: Crane Publishing Company, 1991), pp. 210–19.

18. D. Larsen-Freeman, "Second Language Acquisition Research: Staking Out the Territory," *TESOL Quarterly* 25, 2 (1991): 215–60.

19. *Learning 94* (Springfield Corporation, 111 Bethlehem Pike, Springhouse, PA 19477).

20. G. Greenwood, "Research and Practice in Parent Involvement: Implications for Teacher Involvement," *The Elementary School Journal* 91, 3 (January 1993): 279–86.

21. J. Epstein, "Longitudinal Effects of Family-School Interaction on Student Outcomes," in A. Kerchhoff, ed., *Research in the Sociology of Education* (Greenwich, CT: Kingsman, 1989), pp. 171–89.

22. Baker and deKanter, "1990 U.S. DOE Study."

23. J. Epstein, "Longitudinal Effects of Family-School Interaction on Student Outcomes," *The Principal* 66 (1987): 6–9.

24. S. Scalover, "The Relationship Between Parent Involvement and Academic Achievement in High School Students (Ph.D. dissertation, Penn State University, 1988).

25. A. Milne et al., "Single Parents, Working Mothers, and the Educational Achievement of School Children," *Sociology of Education* 59, 3 (1986): 14–139.

26. H. Loucks, "Increasing Parent/Family Involvement," *NAESP Bulletin,* April 1992, pp. 39–42.

27. W. Shreeve, *Single Parents and Student Achievement: A National Tragedy* (Baltimore: HDA Research Report, 1985).

28. National Center for Education Statistics, Washington, DC, 1997.

29. C. Roy and D. Fuqua, "Social Support Systems and Academic Performance of Single-Parent Students," *School Counselor* 30, 3 (1983): 183–92.

30. National Center for Education Statistics, Washington, DC, 1997.

31. M. Shinn, "Father Absence and Children's Cognitive Development," *Psychological Bulletin (APA),* 1978, pp. 295–324.

32. E. Hetherington, *Cognitive Performance, School Behavior and Achievement of Children from One-Parent Households* (Washington, DC: National Institute of Education, 1981).

33. J. Gelbrich and E. Hare, "The Effects of Single-Parenthood on School Achievement in a Gifted Population," *Gifted Child Quarterly* 33, 3 (1989): 115–17.

34. National Center for Education Statistics, Washington, DC, 1997.

35. C. Hutt and M. Vaizey, "Differential Effects of Group Density on Social Behavior," *Nature,* 1966, pp. 1371–72.

36. S. Shapiro, "Preschool Ecology: A Study of Three Environmental Variables," *Reading Improvement,* 1975, pp. 236–41.

37. E. Phyfe-Perkins, *Applications of the Behavior-Person-Environment paradigm to the Analysis of Evolution of Early Childhood Programs* (Unpublished dissertation, University of Massachusetts, 1979.

38. Educational Research Service, *Class Size: A Critique of Recent Meta-Analyses* (Arlington, VA: 1980), as cited in *Florida Educational Research Council Bulletin* 27 (Fall 1995): 13.

39. J. Somer and K. Ross, "1958 Study of Hospital Cafeterias," in E. Hall, ed., *The Hidden Dimension* (Garden City, NY: Doubleday, 1966), p. 36.

40. E. Hall, *The Hidden Dimension* (Garden City, NY: Doubleday, 1966).

41. M. Dunkin and B. Biddle, *The Study of Teaching* (New York: Holt, Rinehart & Winston, 1974).

42. S. R. Neill, *Classroom Nonverbal Behavior* (New York: Routledge, 1991).

43. W. Hathaway, *A Study into the Effects of Light on Children of Elementary School Age—A Case of Daylight Robbery* (Edmonton: Alberta Department of Education, 1992, ERIC 343686), pp. 3–37.

44. F. Knirk, "Facility Requirements," *Educational Technology,* September 1992, pp. 26–32.

45. W. Hathaway, "A Study into the Effects of Light on Children of Elementary School Age," pp. 3–37.

46. N. Kwallek and C. Lewis, "Effects of Environmental Color on Males and Females," *Applied Ergonomics,* 1990, pp. 257–78.

47. E. Babey, "The Classrooms: Physical Environments That Enhance Teaching and Learning" (Paper presented at the American Association of Higher Education, Washington, DC, 1991).

48. F. Knirk, "Facility Requirements," pp. 26–32.

49. K. Cotton, "Schoolwide and Classroom Discipline," *School Improvement Research Series* V (1990): 1–12.

50. W. Goldstein, "Group Process and School Management," in M. Wittrock, ed., *Handbook of Research on Teaching* (New York: Macmillan, 1986), pp. 430–35.

51. E. Emmer and A. Ausikker, "School and Classroom Discipline Programs: How Well Do They Work?" in D. Moles, ed., *Student Discipline Strategies: Research and Practice* (Albany, NY: State University Press, 1990), pp. 89–104.

52. N. Sprinthall and K. Sprinthall, *Educational Psychology: A Developmental Approach* (New York: McGraw-Hill, 1990).

53. J. Shepard and S. Smith, "Synthesis of Research on Grade Retention" (Florida Dept. of Education, 1994), pp. 113–18.

54. I. Balow, *Retention in Grade: A Failed Procedure* (Riverside: California Education Research Cooperative, 1990).

55. National Center for Education Statistics, Washington, DC, 1977.

56. Shepard and Smith, "Synthesis of Research on Grade Retention," pp. 113–18.

57. *Phi Delta Kappan Research Bulletin* No. 15 (December 1995): 1.

58. N. Karweit, "Repeating a Grade: Time To Grow or Denial of Opportunity" (Pamphlet, Johns Hopkins University Press, May 1991).

59. Report of New York City Schools, 1996.

60. A. Thomas, "Alternative to Retention: If Flunking Hasn't Worked, What Does?" *Oregon School Study Council* 35, 6 (February 1992): 23–27.

61. N. Baenan, *Perspective After Five Years—Has Grade Retention Passed or Failed?* (Austin, TX: Austin Independent School District, 1988), pp. 1–51.

62. G. Yamomoto, "Survey of Preadolescent Fears" (Arizona State University Study, 1980).

63. Shepard and Smith, "Synthesis of Research on Grade Retention," pp. 113–18.

64. Balow, *Retention in Grade: A Failed Procedure.*

65. P. Peterson, "Direct Instruction Reconsidered," in P. L. Peterson, ed., *Research on Teaching: Concepts, Findings, Implications* (Berkeley, CA: McCutchan, 1987), pp. 11–27.

66. President George Bush, State of the Union Address, 1991.

67. R. Jaeger, "Weak Measurement Serving Presumptive Policy," *Phi Delta Kappan* 5 (October 1992): 116–26.

68. G. Bacoats, "The Relationship of the Florida State Student Assessment Test and the Grade Performance of Students in a Medium Sized School District in Florida" (Ph.D. dissertation, University of South Florida, 1992).

69. M. Fleming and R. Chambers, "Teacher-Made Tests: Windows on the Classroom," in W. Hathaway, ed., *New Directions for Testing and Measurement* (San Francisco: Jossey-Bass, 1983), pp. 29–38.

70. L. Hales and E. Tokar, "The Effects of Quality If Preceding Responses on the Grades Assigned to Subsequent Responses to an Essay Examination," *Journal of Educational Measurement* 12 (1975): 115–17.

71. P. Airaisian, "Classroom Assessment and Educational Improvement" (Paper, Conference on Classroom Assessment, Portland, OR, NWREL, 1984).

72. J. Hughes, "What's in a Grade?" (Paper presented at Speech Communication Association, Washington, DC, November 1983), pp. 1–19.

73. For a treatment of this policy question, see Betty Wallace, *The Poisoned Apple* (New York: St. Martin's Press, 1995).

74. David Elkind, "Developmentally Appropriate Practice: Philosophical and Practical Implications," *Phi Delta Kappan* 8 (October 1989): 113–16.

75. J. Kulik and C. Kulik, "Meta-Analysis: Findings on Grouping Programs," *Gifted Child Quarterly* 36, 2 (Spring 1992): 73– 76.

76. J. Nevi, V. Dar, D. Flemings, and A. Chankeer, as cited in *School Practices Series,* "Ability Grouping and Achievement Mathematics in the Middle School" (Tampa: Wiles, Bondi and Associates, 1990), pp. 3–4. Also, R. Jaeger, "Weak Measurement Serving Presumptive Policy," *Phi Delta Kappan* 7 (October 1992): 118–28.

77. C. Wolff, "Getting Our Students to Think Through Simulation," *Contemporary Education* 63 (1992): 219–20.

78. C. Hill, "Cooperative Learning and Ability Grouping: An Issue of Choice," *Gifted Child Quarterly* 36, 1 (1992): 11–16.

79. A. Kerchhoff, "Effects of Ability Grouping in British Secondary Schools," *American Sociological Review* 51 (December 1986): 642–58.

80. M. Hallinan, "The Effects of Ability Grouping in Secondary Schools, *Review of Educational Research* 60 (1990): 501–504.

81. R. Slavin, "Achievement Effects of Ability Grouping in Secondary Schools: A Best-Evidence Synthesis," *Review of Educational Research* 60 (1990): 471–99.

82. J. Oakes, "Detracking Schools—Early Lessons from Field," *Phi Delta Kappan* 72, 6 (February 1992): 448–54.

83. R. Valdiviesco, "Hispanics and Schools: A New Perspective," *Educational Horizons* 11 (1986): 190–96.

84. J. Oakes, *Keeping Track: How Schools Structure Inequality* (New Haven: Yale University Press, 1985), pp. 32–35.

85. Slavin, "Achievement Effects of Ability Grouping in Secondary Schools."

86. M. Hallinan, "The Effects of Ability Grouping in Secondary Schools."

87. H. Marsh, "Failure of High Ability High Schools to Deliver Academic Benefits Commensurate with Their Students' Ability Levels," *American Educational Research Journal* 28 (Summer 1991): 445–80.

88. R. Rosenthal and L. Jacobson, *Pygmalion in the Classroom* (New York: Holt, Rinehart & Winston, 1968).

89. G. Farkas et al., "Culture Resources and School Success: Gender, Ethnicity, and Poverty Groups within an Urban School District," *American Sociological Review* 55 (1990): 127–42.

90. C. Whelen and C. Teddlie, "Self-Fulfilling Prophecy and Attribution for Responsibility: Is There a Causal Link to Achievement?" (March 1989 ERIC Ed 323211).

91. T. Good, "Two Decades of Research on Teacher Expectation: Findings and Further Directions," *Journal of Teacher Education* 38 (1987): 32–48.

92. R. Sternberg, "Thinking Styles: Keys to Understanding Student Performance," *Phi Delta Kappan* 71 (1990): 366–71.

93. S. Pflaum, *The Development of Language on Literacy of Young Children* (Columbus, OH: Merrill, 1986), p. 19.

94. S. Rodenbush, "Magnitude of Teacher Expectancy on Pupil I.Q. as a Foundation of the Credibility of Teacher Induction," *Journal of Educational Psychology* 76 (1984): 85–97.

95. R. Tauber, "Criticisms and Deception: The Pitfalls of Praise," *NASSP Bulletin* 74, 528 (October 1990): 95–99.

96. N. Flanders, "Teacher Influence—Pupil Attitudes and Achievement (Washington, DC: H.E.W. Monograph 12, 1965).

97. M. Dunkin and B. Biddle, *The Study of Teaching* (New York: Holt, Rinehart & Winston, 1974).

98. J. Brophy, "Teacher Praise: A Functional Analysis," *Review of Educational Research* 51, 2 (1981): 5–32.

99. S. Henerey, "Sex and Locus of Control as Determinants of Children's Response to Peer Versus Adult Praise," *Journal of Educational Psychology* 67 (1979): 604–12.

100. T. Gordon, *Teacher Effectiveness Training* (New York: Wyden Press, 1974).

101. M. Rowe, "Wait Time and Reward as Instructional Variables," *Journal of Research on Science Teaching* 2 (1974): 81–97.

102. J. Brophy, "Teacher Praise: A Functional Analysis," pp. 5–32.

103. G. Morine-Dershimer, "Pupil Perception of Teacher Praise," *Elementary School Journal* 82, 5 (1982): 421–34.

104. C. Shiang, *The Effectiveness of Questioning on the Thinking Process* (San Francisco: American Educational Research Association, 1989, ERIC ED 013704), pp. 13–14.

105. M. Gall, "The Use of Questions in Teaching," *Review of Educational Research* 40 (1970): 707–20.

106. M. Mystrand and A. Gamoran, "Student Engagement: When Recitation Becomes Conversation" (Report, National Center on the Effectiveness of Secondary Schools, Madison, WI, February 1990), pp. 707–20.

107. J. J. Gallagher and M. J. Aschner, "A Preliminary Report: Analyses and Classroom Interaction," *Merrill Palmer Quarterly* 9 (1963): 183–94.

108. B. Winne, as cited in W. Carlson, "Questions in the Classroom: A Sociolinguistic Perspective," *Review of Educational Research* 61 (1991): 165.

109. J. Redfield and P. Rousseau, as cited in W. Carlson, "Questions in the Classroom: A Sociolinguistic Perspective," *Review of Educational Research* 61 (1991): 165.

110. H. Walberg, as cited in W. Carlson, "Questions in the Classroom: A Sociolinguistic Perspective," *Review of Educational Research* 61 (1991): 165.

111. D. Daines, *Teacher Oral Questions and Subsequent Verbal Behaviors of Teachers and Students* (Provo, UT: Brigham Young University, 1982).

112. J. Sylvester and L. Cho, as cited in M. Imal, "Properties of Attention During Reading Lessons," *Journal of Developmental Psychology* 84, 2 (June 1992): 160–72.

113. E. John, "Double-Labeled Metabolic Maps of Memory" *Science* 233 (1986): 1167–74.

114. D. Alkon, "Memory Storage and Neural Systems," *Scientific American*, 261 (1989): 42–50.

115. C. W. Fisher, "Teaching and Learning in the Elementary School: A Summary of the Beginning Teacher Evaluation Study" (Report VII-1, BTES Technical Report, 1978).

116. P. Peterson et al., "Student Attitudes and Their Reports of Cognitive Processes During Direct Instruction," *Journal of Educational Psychology* 4 (1982): 535–46.

117. H. Laharderne, "Attitudinal and Intellectual Correlates of Attention," *Journal of Educational Psychology* 59, 5 (1968): 321–23.

118. M. Imai, "Properties of Attention During Reading Lessons," *Journal of Educational Psychology* 84 (June 1992): 160–72.

119. A. Bardos, "Gender Differences on Planning, Attention, Simultaneous and Successive Cognitive Planning Tasks," *Journal of School Psychology* 3 (1992): 297–99.

120. R. Sylvester, "What Brain Research Says About Paying Attention, *Educational Leadership* 50, 4 (December 1992): 71–75.

121. T. Newby, "Strategies of First Year Teachers," *Journal of Educational Psychology* 83 (1991): 195–200.

122. W. Vispoel, "Success and Failure in Junior High School: A Critical Incident Approach to Understanding Student Attributional Beliefs," *American Educational Research Journal* 2, (1995): 377–412.

123. B. Weiner, *An Attributional Theory of Motivation and Emotion* (New York: Springer-Verlag, 1986), p. 8.

124. J. Lahti, in M. Wittrock, ed., *Handbook of Research on Teaching*, 3rd ed. (New York: Macmillan, 1986), p. 704.

125. C. Dweck, "The Role of Expectations and Attributions in the Alleviation of Learned Helplessness," *Journal of Personality and Social Psychology* 31 (1975): 674–85.

126. C. Dweck, "Motivational Processes Affecting Learning," *American Psychologist* 41 (1986): 1040–48.

127. S. Graham and V. Folkes, *Attribution Theory: Applications to Achievement, Mental Health, and Interpersonal Conflict* (Hillsdale, NJ: Lawrence Erlbaum and Associates, 1990).

128. D. Meichenbaum and J. Asarnow, "Cognitive Behavior Modification and Metacognition," in P. Kendall, ed., *Cognitive Behavior Interventions* (New York: Academic Press, 1979), pp. 137–211.

129. K. Baker and A. deKanter, "1990 U.S. DOE Study."

130. R. Garner, *Metacognition and Reading Comprehension* (Norwood: NJ: Ablex Publishing, 1987).

131. B. Moely et al., "How Do Teachers Teach Memory Skills?" *Educational Psychologist* 21 (1986): 55–71.

132. B. Rosenshine and J. Guenther, "Using Scaffolding for Teaching Higher Level Cognitive Strategies," in H. Walberg, *Teaching for Thinking* (Reston, VA: NAASP, 1992), pp. 35–48.

133. L. Vygotsky, *Mind in Society: The Development of Higher Psychological Processes* (Cambridge, MA: Harvard University Press, 1978), p. 8.

134. R. C. Anderson, "The Notion of Schemata and the Educational Enterprise," in *Schooling and the Acquisition of Knowledge* (Hillsdale, NJ: Lawrence Erlbaum and Associates, 1977).

135. D. Hamachek, "Self-Concept and School Achievement," *Journal of Counseling and Development* 73 (1995): 419–25.

136. K. Kelly and L. Jordon, "The Effects of Academic Achievement on Self-Concept: A Reproduction Study," *Journal of Educational Psychology* 84 (1992): 345–55.

137. M. Marsh, "Content Specificity of Relations Between Academic Achievement and Academic Self-Concept," *Journal of Educational Psychology* 84, 4 (1992): 3–51.

138. D. Cornell, "Achievement and Self-Concept: Minority Students in Elementary School Gifted Programs," *Journal of Education for the Gifted* 18 (1995): 189–209.

139. M. Marsh, "Age and Sex Effects in Multiple Dimensions of Self Concept: Preadolescence to Early Adulthood," *Journal of Education* 81 (1989): 417–30.

140. M. Rosenberg, *Conceiving of Self* (New York: Basic Books, 1979).

141. S. Gehshan, "College Admission Tests: Opportunity or Roadblocks," *AAUW,* June 1988, pp. 1–6.

142. A. Williams, "Class, Race, and Gender in American Education," *AAUW,* November 1989, p. 5.

143. J. Parsons et al., "Sex Differences in Attribution and Learned Helplessness," *Sex Roles* 8, 4 (1982): 421–32.

144. D. Stipek, "Sex Differences in Children's Attributions for Success and Failure on Math and Spelling Tests," *Sex Roles* 11, 11 & 12 (1984): 969–80.

145. Report of National Council of Teachers of English, 1972.

146. Report of National Council of Teachers of English, 1972.

147. "Hidden Threads of Illness," *Science Digest* (1997), pp. 6–7.

148. B. Rosenshine, "Synthesis of Research on Explicit Teaching," *Educational Leadership* 43 (April 1986): 65.

149. G. Greenwood, "Research and Practice in Parent Involvement: Implications for Teachers," *The Elementary School Journal* 91, 3 (January 1993): 279–86.

150. K. Berendt, "A Study of Friendship and Attitude Formation in Relation to Achievement Motivation," *Journal of Educational Psychology* 82, 4 (1990): 6–7.

151. R. Stevens, and R. Slavin, "The Cooperative Elementary School: Effects on Student Achievement, Attitudes, and Social Relations," *American Education Research Journal* 32 (1995): 321–51.

152. F. Newman and J. Thompson, *Effects of Cooperative Learning on Achievement in Secondary Schools: A Summary of Research* (Madison: University of Wisconsin-Madison, 1987), pp. 12–15.

153. D. Johnson and R. Johnson, *Cooperation in the Classroom* (Edina, MN: Interaction Book Co., 1990).

154. R. Larazowitz, "Academic Achievement and On-Task Behavior of High School Biology Students Instructed in Cooperative Small Investigation Groups," *Science Education* 72, 4 (1988) 475–87.

155. A. Kohn, "It's Hard to Get Left Out of a Pair," *Psychology Today*, October 1987, pp. 53–57.

156. R. Slavin, "Synthesis of Research on Cooperative Learning," *Educational Leadership* (May 1981): 655–60.

157. R. Slavin, "Synthesis of Research on Cooperative Learning," *Educational Leadership*, 48 (1992): 71–82.

158. J. Stallings, "Research on Early Childhood and Elementary Teaching Programs," *Handbook of Research on Teaching* (New York: Macmillan, 1986), pp. 746–50.

159. A. Kohn, "Group Grade Grubbing Versus Cooperative Learning," *Educational Leadership* 48 (1992): 83–88.

160. P. Okebukola, "The Influence of Preferred Learning Styles on Cooperative Learning in Science," *Science Education* 70 (1986): 509–76.

161. A. Chambers and B. Abrami, "The Relationship Between Student Team Learning Outcomes and

Achievement: Causal, Attributes, and Affect," *Journal of Educational Psychology* 83 (1991): 145.

162. C. Mulryan, "Student Passivity During Cooperative Small Groups in Mathematics," *Journal of Educational Psychology* 85 (1992): 6.

163. T. Good, "Using Work Groups in Mathematics Instruction," *Educational Leadership* 47, 4 (1990): 4.

164. G. Hooper, "The Effects of Interaction During Computer-Based Mathematics Instruction," *Journal of Educational Research* 85, 3 (1992): 180.

165. A. Gregorc, "Learning/Teaching Styles: Their Nature and Effects," *Student Learning Styles* (Reston, VA: NASSP), pp. 19–26.

166. B. McCarthy, "Using the 4MAT System to Bring Learning Styles to Schools," *Educational Leadership* 48, 2 (1990): 31–37.

167. J. Hansen and H. Silver, *The Learning Style Preference Inventory* (Moorestown, NJ: Hansen, Silver & Associates, 1978).

168. T. Gusky and S. Gates, "Synthesis of Research on Mastery Learning," *Educational Leadership* 43 (1986): 3–8.

169. T. Titus, "Adolescent Learning Styles," *Journal of Research and Development in Education* 23, 3 (Spring 1990): 165–70.

170. Association for Supervision and Curriculum Development Multicultural Education Commission, "Encouraging Multicultural Education," *Educational Leadership* 4 (January 1977): 291.

171. Ned Flanders, *Teacher Influence–Pupil Attitudes and Achievement* (Washington, DC: H.E.W. Research Monograph 12, 1965).

172. John Hough, *A Thirteen Category Modification of Flanders' System of Interaction Analysis* (Columbus: Ohio State University Monograph, 1965), pp. 11–15.

173. Arno Bellack, *The Language of the Classroom* (New York: Teachers College Press, 1966).

174. Joseph C. Bondi, Jr., "Verbal Patterns of Teachers in the Classroom," *National Elementary Principal* 50, 5 (April 1971): 90–91.

175. Marie Hughes, "What Is Teaching? One Viewpoint," *Educational Leadership* 19, 4 (January 1962): 37.

176. Ambrose A. Clegg, Jr., et al., "Teacher Strategies of Questioning for Eliciting Selected Cognitive Student Responses" (Report of the Tri-University Project, University of Washington, 1970), p. 1.

177. Jacob S. Kounin, *Discipline and Classroom Management* (New York: Holt, Rinehart and Winston, 1970).

BOOKS TO REVIEW

Bigge, M. *Learning Theories for Teachers*, 6th ed. New York: Harper and Row, 1985.

Bowers, C., and D. Flinders. *Responsive Teaching.* New York: Teachers College Press, 1990.

Buxton, T. *The Many Faces of Teaching.* Lanham, MD: University Press of America, 1987.

Gagné, R. *Instructional Technology—Foundations.* Hillsdale, NJ: LEA Publishers, 1987.

Grossman, P. *The Making of a Teacher.* New York: Teachers College Press, 1990.

Houston, R., ed. *Handbook of Research on Teacher Education.* New York: Macmillan, 1990.

Jackson, P. *The Practice of Teaching.* New York: Teachers College Press, 1986.

Jones, B., and A. Palinscar. *Strategy Teaching and Learning.* Alexandria, VA: Association for Supervision and Curriculum Development, 1987.

McNeil, J., and J. Wiles. *The Essentials of Teaching.* New York: Macmillan, 1990.

Wittrock, M., ed. *Handbook of Research on Teaching.* New York: Macmillan, 1986.

chapter 5

CURRICULUM MANAGEMENT PLANNING

Previous chapters have stated that curriculum development is a cycle—whether it is at the macro (state, district, school) or micro (classroom) level. Curriculum development begins with an analysis, proceeds to a design for learning, is implemented, and is assessed for results. This cycle, with its recurring tasks, is adaptable to any philosophy or starting point. Although philosophies are value laden, the development process is essentially value free.

The impurity of the work environment (distortions) often means that what is intended is not what is delivered to children in the classroom. The goal of the curriculum worker is to ensure that distortions are minimized and intentions are carried out to the degree possible. Failure to acknowledge this theory–practice gap, and to use sound management techniques to overcome it, results in many of the failures in today's curriculum work in schools.

We believe that the bridge between theory and practice is sound planning and management of change in schools. In our work in schools, we use a technique known as **Curriculum Management Planning,** which is covered later in this chapter. First, however, we begin with how schools traditionally improve their programs.

HOW DISTRICTS IMPROVE PROGRAMS

The methodology of school district reviews depends on both an understanding of curriculum development and the sophistication of the district in carrying out a review procedure. Sometimes, the district will review itself in terms of external criteria, such as when professional accreditation is sought. Sometimes, districts rely on expert opinion by having consultants survey the district. Finally, there are times when a district chooses to conduct an internal needs assessment. This occurs, often, after a change of leadership when the new leaders wish to have a status report. These three approaches are compared and contrasted in Table 5.1.

School districts can be differentiated by the degree to which they succeed in assessing themselves and projecting improved programs. Some districts, of course, never enter into such a cycle; for them, school programs are simply a historical accident. Others seemingly go through the motions but don't seem to get direction for all of their efforts. These districts have beautiful documents, but programs rarely change. Still a third pattern is those districts that plan well but are interrupted time and again by social forces. They are characterized by numerous false starts and some serious frustration with the lost investment of curriculum development. Finally, and happily, we can report that some school districts do it right and get the satisfying results of an ever-improving program. The next section focuses on what these more fortunate districts seem to do right.

COMPREHENSIVE PLANNING

As early as 1970, Kathryn Feyereisen[1] and others called for the application of systems concepts to curriculum work. These early systems analysts realized that, despite a

TABLE 5.1   Three Methods of Assessing School Conditions: Characteristics and Data

Characteristics		
(1) Accreditation	*(2) Survey*	*(3) Needs Assessment*
Organization orientation	Administrative orientation	Programmatic orientation
Concern with structure, organization	Concern with structure and management	Concern with clients and corresponding programs
Analysis of what actually exists (descriptive)	Analysis of what actually exists (descriptive)	Assessment of what should be in existence (prescriptive)
Scheduled	Self-contained	Ties to remediation
Comprehensive	Quasi-comprehensive	Focused on client needs
Validation emphasis	Judgmental	Objective with design
Data		
(1) Accreditation	*(2) Survey*	*(3) Needs Assessment*
Pupil-teacher ratio	Community background	School-community history
Number of library books	Administration and organization	Achievement patterns
Statement of purpose	Instructional patterns	Attitudes toward school
Quality of buildings	Finance	Motivation, self-concepts
Financial patterns	Extracurricular	Student interests
Pupil-personnel services		Teacher perception
Standards	Standards	Problems
External	External	Internal
Postevaluation	Postevaluation	Preevaluation

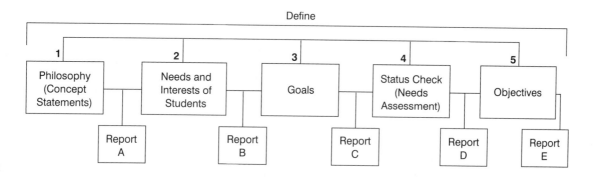

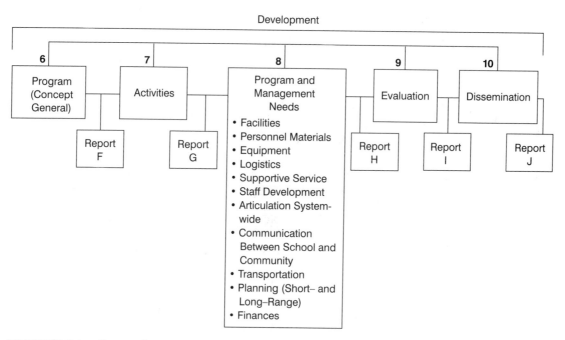

FIGURE 5.1   Comprehensive Management System
Source: Florida Department of Education, Tallahassee, FL.

rigorous process of curriculum review and honorable intentions by school leaders in assessing their programs, sometimes nothing happened. All of the regular methods of upgrading school programs could not guarantee results because they couldn't control or manage the many variables of curriculum change. These early advocates of a systems approach to curriculum development called for more comprehensive planning and an integration of the many functions involved in school improvement.

The nature of a comprehensive process is shown in Figure 5.1. Here, each of the deductive steps following the identification purpose is outlined for study. Note that actions to implement the desired change occur after the direction has been set, not vice versa.

In working with some of the better school districts in America, we have uncovered four premises that seem critical to successful and lasting curriculum improvement:

1. For lasting change to occur, the persons to be affected must be involved in planning the change.
2. In a bureaucratic environment (schools), change must be directed from the top level of leadership.
3. Good decisions are best made on the basis of data, and such data should be shared with all involved in planning.
4. Evaluation and expectation can drive change efforts forward.

The traditional failure patterns in curriculum development disappear in schools or school districts that develop a management plan for curriculum development that ensures these conditions. A review of the traditional cycle of development reveals some of the most common problems.

In the analysis stage, many districts fail to fully engage in a dissection of the current program. Reasons for this vary but include the following:

☐   The existing program has no design and therefore can't be analyzed.
☐   Leaders fear that analysis will reveal weakness or problems that will reflect on them in their leadership role.
☐   The analysis never gets beyond words (jargon), and true assessments aren't made.
☐   Leaders enhance the assessment because they feel it is expected.

If any of these conditions occurs in the analysis stage, subsequent curriculum development will fail because a deductive logic rests on its original premise.

In the design stage, there are numerous possible failures that will sabotage the process, including the following:

☐   The design is "blue sky" (unreal) in nature or follows a bandwagon (everyone else has it).
☐   The design is unachievable because of existing conditions (financial, academic).
☐   The design challenges bedrock values of those who must implement it.
☐   The design is couched in terms that are vague or wordy.

In the implementation stage, there are regular conditions that undermine successful efforts. These conditions include the following:

☐   The primary supporter of the design (such as the school board or superintendent) changes or leaves.
☐   The change is too complex, and the purpose is obscured.

- ☐ Time frames for changing are unrealistic, and the design is abandoned.
- ☐ Training to implement the design is not sufficient to carry the change.

Finally, in the traditional cycle, there is an evaluation step that assesses the completion of the effort. This step can break down if any of the following occurs:

- ☐ No baseline data were secured for a comparison to the completion.
- ☐ Evaluation is not in a form to be useful in redirecting efforts.
- ☐ Those involved in the process don't trust those evaluating the process or believe the reported outcomes.

"So much for curriculum development this school year. I hear you asking yourself, 'What about 1998, 1999, and the year 2000?'"
Source: Phi Delta Kappan. September 1981. Used by permission of Ford Button.

These common failure conditions are not meant to be all-inclusive, but they do illustrate some of the things that can go wrong. If such errors are commonplace, curriculum development is an unbelievable, frustrating, and even boring process. If these kinds of conditions can be controlled through management actions, the cycle of curriculum development becomes the most important function of school leadership.

In the following section, we introduce our own model of a curriculum management plan, developed over the past ten years in school districts, such as Denver, St. Louis, Miami, and Jacksonville.

CURRICULUM MANAGEMENT PLAN

A curriculum management plan (CMP) increases the odds that the curriculum cycle will successfully be completed by providing structure for (1) how changes are made and (2) the order of those changes. Such a plan also seeks to provide continuity across a district or school effort. When implemented, the CMP will minimize political interference and single-issue crises. Most importantly, the CMP provides a way in which the philosophy of education desired by planners can intersect the development process over a long period.

A curriculum management plan begins with an acknowledgment of power; that is, certain persons in each district or school have the power to make decisions, set or alter policy, allocate resources, and use procedures and regulations to provide emphasis to activities. Curriculum leaders must realize that without such top-down support, instructional improvement efforts will not regularly succeed.

In the Wiles-Bondi CMP model, such leaders form a management team that initiates action, communicates upward and downward for logistical purposes, and helps define political reality in districts or schools. It is this group that "allows" a process to be initiated, pursued, and completed. Figure 5.2 shows the relationship of this group to other groups in the CMP.

Analysis Stage

In the Wiles-Bondi Curriculum Management Plan, this "management team" plays a crucial role in the analysis stage of development. Many of the proposed changes in American education during the past thirty years have come from external

FIGURE 5.2   Committee Structure for Curriculum Management Plan (CMP)

Source: J. Wiles and J. Bondi, copyright © 1988. *Planning for Middle School Programs,* Wiles, Bondi & Associates (Tampa, FL: 1988), p. 12.

sources or have bypassed this influential group. In practice, as opposed to theory, this management team can facilitate or sabotage any change effort. Securing this team's endorsement, as a formal step in the development process, will eliminate problems of ownership down the road. Such an endorsement is best if in written form (Figure 5.3). The management team's endorsement is also a necessity for conducting a true needs assessment (Figures 5.4, 5.5, and 5.6), coordinating efforts across the district, and gaining true and accurate evaluation data. Without this group, the effort to improve curriculum will be external, lack coordination, and be destined to failure from an absence of internal support.

DADE COUNTY PUBLIC SCHOOLS

SCHOOL BOARD ADMINISTRATION BUILDING • 1450 NORTHEAST SECOND AVENUE • MIAMI, FLORIDA 33132

DR. JOSEPH A. FERNANDEZ
SUPERINTENDENT OF SCHOOLS

DADE COUNTY SCHOOL BOARD
DR. MICHAEL KROP, CHAIRMAN
MR. G. HOLMES BRADDOCK, VICE-CHAIRMAN
DR. ROSA CASTRO FEINBERG
MS. BETSY KAPLAN
MS. JANET R. McALILEY
MR. ROBERT RENICK
MR. WILLIAM H. TURNER

The Middle School Design Report was developed through a collaborative effort between staff of the Dade County Public Schools and members of the United Teachers of Dade (U.T.D.). This collaboration represents the continued effort of the district and union to work together for the betterment of education in Dade County's public schools.

The Design Report is to be considered a working blueprint that allows individual school communities maximum flexibility in developing programs and implementing the philosophies of the middle school.

The document is the result of the work of an ad hoc committee formed to provide a model for education to all middle schools in the district. The model recommends a shared philosophy; identified programs and components; and objectives, standards, and evaluative criteria for all middle schools.

The Dade County School Board has adopted a four-year plan to convert all its intermediate level schools to fully functioning middle schools by 1991-92. This four-year conversion process utilizes a Curriculum Management Plan (CMP) as a guide. The CMP focuses on using needs assessment, developing a clear set of goals, tying school needs to program needs, involving teachers, administrators, union, parents, and community, and providing an analysis of progress to the general public.

It is the hope of Dade County Public Schools that this type of long range planning and collaborative working arrangement will allow us to accomplish our goal of "National Excellence in Middle Grades Education."

Joseph A. Fernandez
Superintendent of Schools

FIGURE 5.3 Official Endorsement

A. *Pupil Performance*
   1. Standardized tests—teacher-made tests
   2. Pupil grades
   3. Dropout data
   4. Pupil attendance
   5. Observation of pupil performance
   6. Inventories—skill continuums
   7. Observations of teaching-learning situations in the classroom
   8. Degree of student attention and involvement

B. *Questionnaires—Polls of Opinions of Pupils, Teachers, Parents*
   1. Polls of parents regarding the success of certain school programs
   2. Group interviews with students, parents, teachers about the success of curriculum innovations
   3. Attitude surveys of students about certain programs
   4. Comparison of attitudes of pupils and teachers toward contrasting programs
   5. Systematic questionnaires, rating sheets, and interviews with small random samples of students

C. *Follow-up Studies of Learners*
   1. Success at the next grade level
   2. Continuation of schooling
   3. College success
   4. Success at work
   5. Application of skills learned, interests generated in school, for example, participation in lifetime sports, the arts

D. *Examination of Learning Materials*
   1. Examining learning materials to see if they are feasible and practical for use by teachers in the schools—accuracy and soundness of materials
   2. Determining if costs of materials are too great
   3. Checking materials to see if they are at the right level for students
   4. Determining whether teachers get special retraining in order to understand and use new materials
   5. Matching materials to students' interests, needs, and aspirations—relevancy of materials

FIGURE 5.4 Sources of Data about an Instructional Program

There are, of course, other groups to be consulted if the change process is to succeed, such as the teachers union, parents, political action groups, and so on. These groups are combined in the Wiles-Bondi CMP model into something known as the *coordinating committee*—a group of all-powerful individuals and organizations outside of the management team. This standing committee (as opposed to temporary or ad hoc) is a vehicle for involvement and dissemination. Involvement of the teachers union, for example, may gain access to classrooms, which revealed the pattern of instruction found in Figure 5.7.

FIGURE 5.5 Outline of Baseline and Projective Data to Be Gathered in Needs Assessment

Source: From *Making Middle Schools Work,* Fig. 2, p. 16, by J. Wiles and J. Bondi. Copyright © 1986, by Association for Supervision and Curriculum Development, Alexandria, VA.

Baseline Data (Where are we now?)
1. Existing Conditions
    a. Average daily attendance
    b. Absences per teacher per month
    c. Number of low socio-economic students
    d. Student mobility
    e. Corporal punishment patterns
    f. Grade distribution patterns
    g. Achievement analyses
    h. Teacher, student, parent attitudes toward present program
    i. Follow-up survey of junior high graduates
    j. Teacher training and certification patterns

2. Existing Resources
    a. Condition of facilities
    b. Analysis of instructional materials
    c. Community resources for education

Projective Data (Where do we want to go?)
1. Attitude Scales
    a. Parent attitudes and opinions
    b. Teacher attitudes and opinions
    c. Administrator attitudes and opinions
    d. Student instructional preference patterns

2. Program Definition
    a. Student self-concept ratings
    b. Teacher skills checklist
    c. Values surveys

In this stage, the primary task is to clarify purpose and goals. The following criteria can be applied to any set of goals as a measure of their usefulness to the organization:

☐ **Are the goals realistic?** If goals are attainable, they possess a quality that allows members of the organization to relate to them in daily work.

☐ **Are the goals specific?** Specific goals imply behaviors that need to be changed.

☐ **Are the goals related to performance?** Goals that are developed in an organizational context suggest patterns of interaction.

☐ **Are the goals suggestive of involvement?** To be effective, goals must be stated in a way that allows individuals in the organization to see themselves as being able to achieve the objective.

☐ **Are the goals observable?** Can people in the organization see the results of their efforts and monitor progress toward the desired condition?

After surfacing, stating, and reviewing goal statements, the next major step is to determine if these goals are realistic. A preliminary needs assessment, which

	Low	**High**
Enrollment range	670	1389
Average daily attendance (May 1984)	83%	95%
Absences per teacher per month	.36	1.27
Number of low socio-economic students (percentage)	11%	56%
Ratio of gifted students to other exceptional education students	1/104	179/63
Number of students moving in or out during year	33%	70%
Number of students experiencing corporal punishment	44	619
Number of students experiencing suspension	37	240
Number of students dropping out in academic year	0	22
Average score of students on CTBS total battery	36	80

Findings: These data confirm that a wide range of conditions and performance exists in the junior high schools of Orange County. The single greatest variable reflected in these data is variance in student population.

Implications: These statistics suggest that the quality of intermediate programs experienced in Orange County may depend upon the individual school. Efforts should be made to equalize programs and performance of the individual schools during the transition to middle schools.

FIGURE 5.6   Sample Baseline Summary of Existing Conditions in the Junior High Schools in District

Source: From *Making Middle Schools Work,* Fig. 5, p. 18, by J. Wiles and J. Bondi. Copyright © 1986, by Association for Supervision and Curriculum Development, Alexandria, VA.

views both hard data and perceptions of key groups, tells planners what actually exists and what aspirations are present.

Although many districts conduct this assessment informally using internal staff, we believe that such a step must be formal and open to the public. Failure to reveal true conditions at this point will deter setting attainable goals and will prevent a consensus of shared goals and beliefs. Using data (numbers) of decision making, as opposed to philosophical statements, will promote meaningful curriculum change. Use of the coordinating committee to monitor an assessment and interpret the reality will provide assurances to the public that there are no hidden agendas. We also recommend a standing evaluation committee, with at least some lay citizens, to provide continuous access to information from the coordinating committee.

Since most schools and districts in the late 1990s have access to computers, the process of massaging data is easier than in the past. Whether we are working with 500 pupils in a school or 50,000 pupils in a school district, the task is to gather data and look for patterns. Figures 5.8 and 5.9 show a typical questionnaire that asks teacher position and the summary response of those teachers. Here, 94 percent of the teachers felt that the school should have a child-centered focus—certainly a strong enough consensus for planners to proceed.

	Grade Level			
	6 (%)	7 (%)	8 (%)	Total (%)
Teaching Is Personal				
1. Student work is displayed prominently in the classroom.	37	25	12	25
2. Teacher/student-made bulletin boards rather than purchased displays are in use (not purchased displays); ideally, bulletin boards are activity-oriented.	56	43	37	45
3. There is a seating pattern other than straight rows.	12	25	0	12
4. Living objects (plants, animals) are found in classroom.	43	68	25	45
5. Teacher moves about room freely while instructing.	50	75	43	56
6. Teacher calls students by first name without difficulty.	56	56	50	54
7. Constructive student-to-student communication is allowed during class.	18	25	6	14
8. Teacher frequently uses specific praise and encouraging comments.	25	43	25	31
Teaching Is Individualized				
9. Multilevel texts or materials are in use for instruction.	50	25	6	27
10. Some students are doing independent research or study in the classroom.	0	18	12	10
11. Learning centers are present in the room.	12	6	6	8
12. Students are working together in small groups on assignments.	6	6	0	4
13. Supplemental learning materials are available in the classroom for student use.	75	81	62	72
14. Student work folders are used by teacher for work management.	18	37	18	25
15. Skill continuum cards are kept on individual students.	12	6	12	10
16. Instructional activity allows for creative or multiple outcomes over which the student has some choice.	18	6	0	8
Teaching Skills Are Utilized				
17. Conferences one-to-one with student in the classroom.	50	50	25	41
18. Diversifies instructional approach or method during observations.	12	31	6	16
19. Utilizes small groups to increase learning.	0	25	0	8
20. Groups and re-groups students for instructional purposes.	0	18	6	8
21. Teaches at varying level of difficulty around an idea or concept.	18	12	0	10
22. Stylized learning materials for the group.	0	6	6	4
23. Use real-life illustrations or examples during instruction.	25	25	25	25
24. References student interests or needs during instruction.	0	12	12	8
25. Maintains student discipline through nonpunitive behavior.	37	37	31	35
26. Uses student–teacher contracts for learning.	6	6	0	4
27. Works with other teachers across subject-matter lines.	0	6	6	4
28. Teaches general study skills while instructing.	18	12	12	14
29. Uses teacher-made interdisciplinary units during instruction.	0	0	6	2
30. Uses questioning techniques that encourage participation.	43	25	25	31

FIGURE 5.7 Middle School Instructional Checklist: Summary of Forty-Eight Classroom Visits in Eight Middle Schools

Please rate each of the following statements in terms of *their importance to you for the middle school.* Choose the answer that tells how you feel about each one and blacken the bubble below the letter of that choice on the separate computer answer sheet. *Use a Number 2 pencil only.* Use the following key to show your feelings.

A	B	C	D	E
Very Important	Important	Fairly Important	Not Very Important	Not Important at All

1. Specialized guidance and counseling services should be available.
2. Both teachers and counselors should be involved in guidance.
3. Emphasis should be on group guidance.
4. Emphasis should be on individual guidance.
5. Each student should have at least one teacher who knows him/her personally.
6. Each student should meet with that teacher individually.
7. Opportunities for social activities for students (dances, athletic games, boosters, etc.) should be provided.
8. Club activities should be scheduled during the day to provide opportunities for group work in areas of common interest.
9. School-wide opportunities should be provided to help students develop good attitudes and standards for themselves.
10. The middle school program should be more child-centered than subject-matter-centered.
11. The middle school program should be a unique program bridging the gap between the elementary schools and the secondary schools.
12. Provisions should be made for students to explore their individual interests through exploratory elective courses.
13. Provisions should be made for short-term exploratory/enrichment activities in addition to the regularly scheduled electives.
14. Behavior problems of students should be handled, when possible, by teachers and parents without the involvement of the administrators.
15. An alternative program to suspension should be provided for students having behavior problems (In-school Suspension Program).

FIGURE 5.8   A Sample Opinionnaire with Likert Scale Response

Source: From *Making Middle Schools Work,* Fig. 6, p. 19, by J. Wiles and J. Bondi. Copyright © 1986, by Association for Supervision and Curriculum Development, Alexandria, VA.

When a philosophy has been established (by consensus) and documented (by numbers), and when recommendations for change are presented to the board by a representative body of citizens and groups, and when the superintendent and his staff have been responsible for coordinating all such activities, then planners can advance to the design stage.

One of the key points of such a process is that it keeps political interference in schools to a minimum, thus overcoming one of the largest problems for school

```
EAST BATON ROUGE PARISH SCHOOL BOARD

SURVEY OF:   MIDDLE SCHOOL TEACHERS
GROUPING:    OVERALL TOTALS
```

Item	Resp	N	%		Item	Resp	N	%		Item	Resp	N	%
1.	A	497	71.10		2.	A	309	44.20		3.	A	77	11.00
	B	152	21.70			B	280	40.00			B	235	33.60
	C	42	6.00			C	89	12.70			C	283	40.50
	D	7	1.00			D	19	2.70			D	91	13.00
	E	1	.10			E	4	.50			E	12	1.70
	M		1.37			M		1.75			M		2.61
4.	A	292	41.80		5.	A	374	53.50		6.	A	189	27.00
	B	267	38.30			B	178	25.50			B	239	34.20
	C	119	17.00			C	106	15.10			C	184	26.30
	D	18	2.50			D	26	3.70			D	72	10.30
	E	1	.10			E	14	2.00			E	14	2.00
	M		1.91			M		1.75			M		2.26
7.	A	264	37.80		8.	A	243	34.80		9.	A	341	48.90
	B	264	37.80			B	272	38.90			B	245	35.10
	C	113	16.10			C	146	20.90			C	98	14.00
	D	42	6.00			D	26	3.70			D	9	1.20
	E	15	2.10			E	11	1.50			E	4	.50
	M		1.97			M		1.98			M		1.69
10.	A	136	19.50		11.	A	403	57.60		12.	A	290	41.50
	B	216	30.90			B	201	28.70			B	254	36.30
	C	240	34.40			C	85	12.10			C	112	16.00
	D	71	10.10			D	7	1.00			D	27	3.80
	E	34	4.80			E	3	.40			E	15	2.10
	M		2.50			M		1.58			M		1.89
13.	A	192	27.50		14.	A	166	23.30		15.	A	292	41.80
	B	275	39.50			B	225	32.30			B	189	27.10
	C	164	23.50			C	158	22.70			C	112	16.00
	D	43	6.10			D	82	11.70			D	49	7.00
	E	22	3.10			E	65	9.30			E	55	7.80
	M		2.18			M		2.50			M		2.12
16.	A	559	79.90		17.	A	284	40.60		18.	A	292	41.80
	B	108	15.40			B	212	30.30			B	281	40.20
	C	24	3.40			C	113	16.10			C	109	15.60
	D	1	.10			D	60	8.50			D	9	1.20
	E	7	1.00			E	30	4.20			E	7	1.00
	M		1.27			M		2.06			M		1.79
19.	A	369	52.80		20.	A	197	28.30		21.	A	262	37.50
	B	236	33.80			B	239	34.40			B	263	37.60
	C	74	10.50			C	196	28.20			C	134	19.10
	D	13	1.80			D	45	6.40			D	28	4.00
	E	6	.80			E	17	2.40			E	11	1.50
	M		1.64			M		2.20			M		1.94
22.	A	160	22.80		23.	A	494	70.60		24.	A	306	43.80
	B	249	35.60			B	161	23.00			B	267	38.20
	C	204	29.10			C	35	5.00			C	106	15.10
	D	57	8.10			D	5	.80			D	15	2.10
	E	29	4.10			E	3	.40			E	4	.50
	M		2.35			M		1.37			M		1.77
25.	A	267	38.10		26.	A	288	41.20		27.	A	353	50.50
	B	263	37.60			B	296	42.30			B	189	27.00
	C	133	19.00			C	101	14.40			C	101	14.40
	D	29	4.10			D	12	1.70			D	34	4.80
	E	7	1.00			E	2	.20			E	22	3.10
	M		1.92			M		1.78			M		1.83
28.	A	486	69.60		29.	A	474	68.30		30.	A	303	43.40
	B	163	23.30			B	171	24.60			B	195	27.90
	C	37	5.30			C	43	6.20			C	123	17.60
	D	9	1.20			D	2	.20			D	53	7.60
	E	3	.40			E	3	.40			E	23	3.20
	M		1.40			M		1.40			M		1.99
31.	A	221	31.70		32.	A	151	21.70		33.	A	196	28.00
	B	192	27.50			B	237	34.10			B	212	30.30
	C	141	20.20			C	181	26.00			C	165	23.60
	D	82	11.70			D	80	11.50			D	76	10.80
	E	60	8.60			E	45	6.10			E	50	7.10
	M		2.38			M		2.47			M		2.39
34.	A	267	38.40		35.	A	264	37.90		36.	A	363	52.20
	B	185	26.50			B	271	38.90			B	226	32.50
	C	134	19.30			C	128	18.40			C	84	12.00
	D	65	9.30			D	16	2.30			D	13	1.80
	E	43	6.10			E	16	2.30			E	9	1.20
	M		2.18			M		1.92			M		1.67

FIGURE 5.9 Sample Printout of Teacher Response

Source: Reprinted courtesy of East Baton Rouge School District.

177

planners in the late 1990s. If someone stands up at a parent-teacher association or school board meeting and objects to a book, a program, or a practice, and if the planners have done their homework, the intrusion can be countered if compelling data and hard facts are on hand.

In the Wiles-Bondi CMP model, the school board receives information from the coordinating committee in small bites rather than as a grand plan. Using semester or quarterly reports, the board is walked into change, much like a novice swimmer walks into the water. First, a philosophy is determined, then general goals and objectives are set, then the plan is endorsed by the public (evidenced by numbers) and decisions made. As time goes on, a track record of progress is established, making it increasingly difficult for a new player to change the game. This gradual unfolding process is crucial because school board composition can change each year and superintendents may last less than four years. Establishing this track record prevents a worst-case scenario where massive planning is undone by a change of players.

The needs assessment, because it is internal and seeks instructional direction, provides both macro and micro vantage points. This is in contrast to accreditation, which seeks endorsement, or surveys, which are often for consumption. Figure 5.10 outlines some of the problem areas that may be revealed by a comprehensive needs assessment. Figure 5.11, by contrast, reveals a larger pattern for planners. This display shows that the district is doing quite well until students reach the intermediate years, when achievement drops off sharply.

In the Wiles-Bondi model for curriculum management, a series of temporary committees (ad hoc) are used to process this information into school programs. Note that there is a Design Committee, a Program Development Committee, and a Staff Development Committee. All of these groups are used to involve people in the process of curriculum work and to eliminate distortion of the process.

Design Stage

The design stage of the Wiles-Bondi CMP model is carried out by a new, temporary committee whose job it is to define the goals for the school or district in broad strokes that establish a framework for subsequent curriculum work. This critical committee needs to be visionary, but it must work within the parameters of both the endorsed philosophy of the board and the realities of data gathered. We provide examples of this process for both a district and a school.

Curriculum Management Plan—District Example.   Our district example comes from the Dade County schools in Miami, Florida, where that district undertook the largest curriculum change effort ever in American education. Under our direction, fifty-two schools housing nearly 60,000 pupils will be converted to a middle school design over a five-year period (1987–1992).* The effort began with a

---

*Our thanks to Dr. Joseph DeChurch for his leadership in the preparation of these model documents shown in Figure 5.12 through 5.17.

1. **Improvement of Basic Academic Achievement**
   - ☐ Pupils perform below real ability
   - ☐ Students not prepared for grade level
   - ☐ Students consider curriculum irrelevant
   - ☐ Instructional materials are too difficult
   - ☐ Advanced course offerings not available in some subjects
   - ☐ Low standardized test scores
   - ☐ Students do poorly on daily work
   - ☐ Graduates seem unprepared for job market or higher education
   - ☐ High rate of student failure
   - ☐ Students cannot apply basic skills

2. **Continued Commitment to Reduction of Racial Isolation**
   - ☐ Student polarization along racial lines
   - ☐ Division among faculty along racial lines
   - ☐ Student-teacher antagonism along racial lines
   - ☐ Racially-motivated hostility in the community
   - ☐ Unequal status roles for minorities in curriculum materials
   - ☐ Transported students feel unwelcome
   - ☐ Racial groups establish certain areas of the school as their territory
   - ☐ School lacks unified approach to reducing racial isolation
   - ☐ Parents of transported students are not involved in the school
   - ☐ Avoidance of problem situation by school personnel

3. **Improvement in Staff Attendance and Continued Upgrading of Staff Performance**
   A. Attendance
      - ☐ Frequent staff absences
      - ☐ Habitual staff tardiness
      - ☐ Patterns of staff absences and tardiness

   B. Performance
      - ☐ Low expectations for student achievement and behavior
      - ☐ Apparent lack of productive teaching techniques and methods
      - ☐ Instruction not geared to student needs
      - ☐ Resistance to progressive change and professional growth
      - ☐ Learning experiences seem passive
      - ☐ Lack of positive learning environment
      - ☐ Poor classroom management
      - ☐ Lack of staff cooperative effort

FIGURE 5.10 Some Symptoms of School Problems

4. **Improvement in School Morale and Community Relations**
   A. School Morale
      - ☐ School administration viewed as cold and detached from student concerns
      - ☐ Administrator and staff feel isolated, lack of mutual support
      - ☐ Low status of some subject areas in teacher's view
      - ☐ Extensive vandalism
      - ☐ Negative student attitude toward learning
      - ☐ Students are uninvolved, unmotivated
      - ☐ Lack of harmonious staff relationships

   B. Community Relations
      - ☐ Inadequate efforts to involve students in community, or the opposite
      - ☐ Lack of parent interest
      - ☐ Lack of teacher involvement in the community served by the school
      - ☐ Principals and teachers do not try to involve parents and community in the school program
      - ☐ Lack of communication between school and community

5. **Student Attendance, Behavior, and Discipline**
   A. Attendance
      - ☐ Frequent truancy
      - ☐ Frequent tardiness
      - ☐ Frequent class cutting
      - ☐ High absentee rate
      - ☐ High dropout rate
      - ☐ High rate of student mobility

   B. Behavior and Discipline
      - ☐ Vandalism
      - ☐ Violence
      - ☐ Disruptive classroom behavior
      - ☐ Students' use of illegal drugs
      - ☐ Disruptive behavior on campus or playground
      - ☐ Frequent referrals of students to office for disciplinary action
      - ☐ Disruption caused by outsiders
      - ☐ Excessive noise level and confusion throughout the school
      - ☐ Disrespect for authority

FIGURE 5.10 *(Continued)*

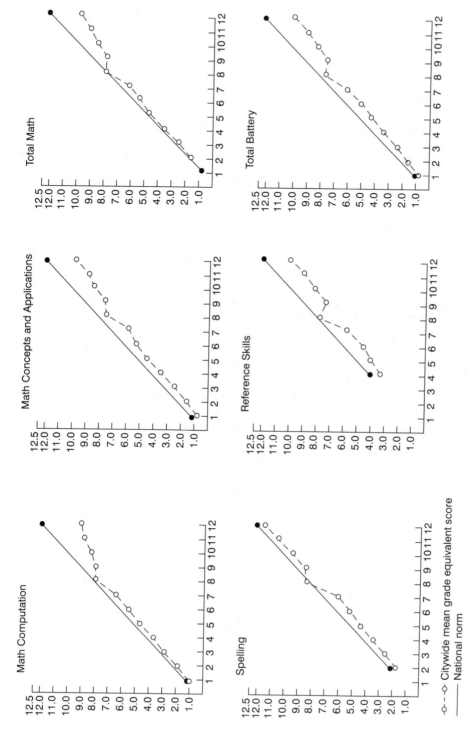

FIGURE 5.11 Graphs Showing the Relationship of Local District Achievement to National Norms by Grade Levels

Source: St. Louis School District One. Used by permission.

broad view of what students may need for life in the twenty-first century (Figure 5.12) and the role of the middle grades in meeting these needs.

Once these broad strokes were passed to the design committee, their task was to provide more definition. In Figure 5.13, an overview of the desired program is provided, followed by a definitional statement concerning the critical elements of the desired program (Figure 5.14). In Figure 5.15, the organizational schema of the new program is outlined, and in Figure 5.16 one area— exploratory programs—is given further definition. Figure 5.17 illustrates the kind of thinking skills that will be taught to students across all subject areas.

As the program design is given form by the design committee, certain tasks begin to emerge, which will be handled by the new program development committees or the staff development committee. A critical part of the Wiles-Bondi CMP model is that the function of the general program design (design committee) is separated from the specific development of programs (by the program development

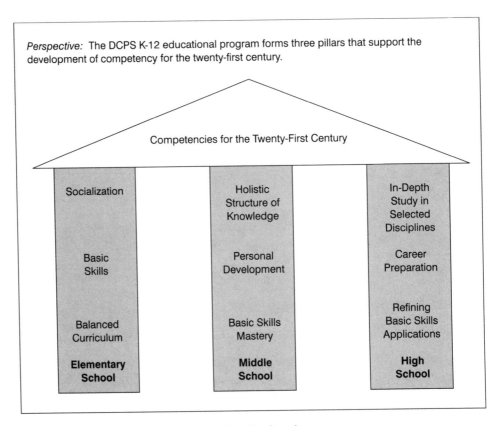

FIGURE 5.12   Generic Competencies Outlined
Source: Middle School Design Report, Dade County Public Schools, June 1989.

FIGURE 5.13 Overview of
Middle School Parameters

Source: Middle School Design Report,
Dade County Public Schools, June
1989.

I. **Philosophy**
    A. Child-centered
    B. Holistic knowledge structure is developed
    C. Thinking skills are priority goals
    D. Safety is essential
    E. Students' developmental needs are important

II. **Curriculum**
    A. Academic excellence/social competence
        1. Academic core
        2. Exploration and developmental programs
    B. Personal development
    C. Mastery of continuous learning skills

III. **Organization**
    A. Interdisciplinary teams
    B. Advisement program
    C. Block scheduling and flexible scheduling within blocks
    D. Team planning and shared decision making
    E. Exploratory and developmental experiences
        1. Elective classes
        2. Wheels and exploration credits
        3. Mini-courses
        4. Clubs, activities, interest groups, intramurals
    F. Integrated curriculum
    G. In-service education and professional development

IV. **Implementing Strategies** (delivery systems)
    A. Cooperative learning
    B. Interdisciplinary teaching
    C. Learning styles
    D. Student services and career planning systems
    E. Home–school partnerships and communications

committees). This "fading away" of one committee, and the assumption of more detailed work by another committee, prevents "special pleading" by members of the design group for their subject area. The program development committees must stay within the design parameters, and their work is reviewed by the coordinating committee against the criteria of compliance that the board adopted.

Curriculum Management Plan—School Example.   Our school example concerns a common move in the late 1980s—the establishment of state-mandated kindergarten programs. Such a program would come to the district from the state and be "fit" into an existing conception of early childhood programming. A sketch of one such program, its design, and some of the implications for management follows.

The Critical Elements Summarized

The middle grades education program has important functions different from the elementary and high school programs. Middle school students (transescents) have special needs that identify them as a unique group in the K–12 learning continuum. There are specific philosophical approaches, educational strategies, and school organizations that are effective during this period. Twelve critical elements are needed in the DCPS middle school.

1. The core of the middle school education program is based on the following beliefs:
   - Every child can learn
   - Middle school is a key time where students learn that the various disciplines and subjects are all related to humanity's search for understanding
   - Learners must feel physically and psychologically safe
   - Thinking skills instruction is a middle school responsibility
   - Every child's individual differences must be respected

2. To accomplish its mission, the middle school curriculum has three interwoven and connected threads. They are the pursuit of
   - Academic excellence as a way to achieve social competence in a complex, technological society
   - Self-understanding and personal development
   - Continuous-learning skills

3. The traditional academic core must be taught in a way that ensures that our students recognize
   - The relationships between such disciplines as math, language arts, science, and social studies and can transfer learning from one discipline to another
   - That their exploratory and developmental experiences are related to the academic core and are a way to broaden each individual's insights and potential for personal growth

4. The middle school curriculum contains a variety of exploratory experiences (into disciplines beyond the academic core), which will enable students to
   - Recognize, through exploratory experiences, that there are a multitude of routes to take to understanding and successful independence

FIGURE 5.14   Definitional Statement about Critical Elements of the Middle School Program

Plan for Establishing a Kindergarten

- □ **Population**   Approximately 300 students, ages 3 to 5, and 6-year-olds who do not have the readiness for the first grade.
- □ **Program concept**   The kindergarten program will be divided into two distinct components. An A.M. program will be provided, with a basic instructional format that will match the individualized and continuous progress concepts. The major focus of the A.M. program will be readiness for the more formal education program to follow; the specific objectives will be to develop social skills, motor skills, self-direction, self-esteem, and communication. During the P.M. program, a child-care service will be provided for those students who need the service because both parents

- Sample fields they may wish to pursue in greater depth in high school or beyond
- Develop a realistic overview of talents, aptitudes, and interests
- Begin to develop talents and special interests in a manner that provides balance and perspective

5. Thinking skills expand in scope and nature during the middle grade years. While problem-solving strategies need to be part of the K–12 learning continuum, formal instruction in critical and creative thinking skills is essential in the middle grades program.

6. Middle school students need someone to whom they can relate as an advisor and guide during the transescent period. Middle schools provide such advisors and ensure that advisors and advisees have time to work on the developmental issues of early adolescence.

7. Middle schools integrate academic knowledge and skills through use of interdisciplinary teaching teams. The structure of such teams may vary widely, but the essential elements are common planning time and teaching the same group of students.

8. The teachers of the academic core and the exploratory/developmental programs work together to foster transfer of learning from one discipline to another, enhance application of basic skills, and to help students develop a "big picture" on the scope and nature of our efforts to understand ourselves and the environment.

9. The exploratory program is provided in a variety of ways in addition to formal classes. These may include mini-courses, clubs, special activities, and interest group meetings built into the school day at regular intervals.

10. In-service education and methods for teachers to share insights and information are an important part of the middle school conversion.

11. Instructional delivery strategies used at the middle grades allow for the developmental traits of the students. Cooperative learning strategies, accommodation of different learning styles, recognition of attention span limitations, and understanding the transescents' preoccupation with personal development issues are all needed in the middle grade program.

12. The middle school must develop a closer relationship with the parents and community and serve as a guide to the student's departure from childhood and embarkation on the route to adulthood and citizenship.

FIGURE 5.14   *(Continued)*

Source: Middle School Design Report, Dade County Public Schools, June 1989.

work away from the home. The program will follow an action format that will have little structure. Focus will be primarily on socialization.

☐ **Areas of learning**   Socialization, school readiness, independence, motor skills, communication.

☐ **Program organization**   The student population will be divided into instructional units of thirty students each and will be comprised of students of varying ages, but with similar maturation characteristics. The formal program will be scheduled from 8:00 A.M. to 12:00 noon, with a breakfast and lunch program provided. Students who are eligible for the child-care program will remain at school until 3:00 P.M. The kindergarten program will operate five days a week, twelve months of the year when school is in session.

III. Organization of the Middle School
A middle school is organized so that students experience the integrated nature of our knowledge base and have opportunities to grow and expand.

The organization is flexible so that teachers have many options in meeting student needs and in implementing the mandated content and skills curriculum set forth by the school board and state board of education.

The following diagram illustrates the relationship between the parameters that are essential to middle school organization.

Team Planning	Advisement	Interdisciplinary Teams
Exploratory and Developmental Programs	Organizational Elements of the DCPS Middle School	Shared Decision Making
In-service	Integrated Curriculum	Block Schedules

FIGURE 5.15   Organization of the Middle School Program
Source: Middle School Design Report, Dade County Public Schools, June 1989.

- □ **Staff organization**   The staff will be organized to complement the instructional unit approach. For each unit, there will be one teacher and three instructional aides who will work as a team.
- □ **Staff requirement**   The kindergarten school staff will consist of one program coordinator, ten teachers, thirty instructional aides, one school nurse, and one secretary/bookkeeper.
- □ **Teaching strategies**   Some examples of teaching strategies to be used by the kindergarten staff are role playing, field trips, working with educational games, regular planned rest, rhythmical activities, positive reinforcement, creative expression, peer teaching, **exploration** of self, school, and community.
- □ **Facilities**   The kindergarten school will use the cafetorium and the auditorium located on the current high school site. Both buildings need remodeling in order to be adequate for an early childhood program. Floors and restrooms of the auditorium need remodeling; lighting, controlled air, and carpeting should be updated.

Using such a sketch of the program to be organized, management planners can then begin to translate the needs into the resources needed to implement such a plan. In Figure 5.18, for example, the financial implication of such a program for 300 students is calculated in rough form.

Implementation Stage

After clarifying the goals and objectives and setting the parameters of programs within an overarching structure, the next curriculum task is to coordinate the many efforts needed to implement such programs. In our opinion, this is where 90 percent of all curriculum work fails. In the future, curriculum specialists will need managerial skills to succeed in curriculum development. Under the Wiles-Bondi CMP model, efforts now shift into an implementation phase.

One of the first tasks for the planner is get the "big picture" in order. This requires that a time frame be established and that a natural order of development be decided on. All work from here on will be a refinement of basic concepts and programs into instructional prescriptions; the project can be envisioned as a basic distance-rate-time problem with resources determining the rate. If resources are inter-

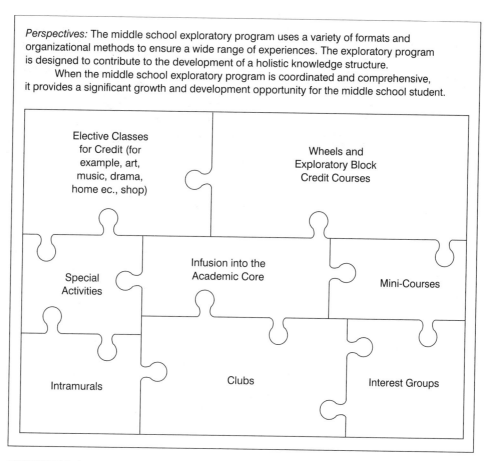

FIGURE 5.16 Middle School Exploratory Program

Source: Middle School Design Report, Dade County Public Schools, June 1989.

C. Teaching skills needed for continuous learning in school and in life are the joint responsibility of the entire educational staff.

The middle school seeks to instill mastery of the basic communication and mathematical skills taught in elementary school.

Due to the emergence of abstract thinking abilities during the transescence period, critical and creative thinking skills are infused through the curriculum and taught as specific skills.

Social cooperation skills and their application to problem solving are infused throughout the curriculum.

Perspective: Middle school students develop a unified set of skills that promote continuous learning, as the diagram illustrates.

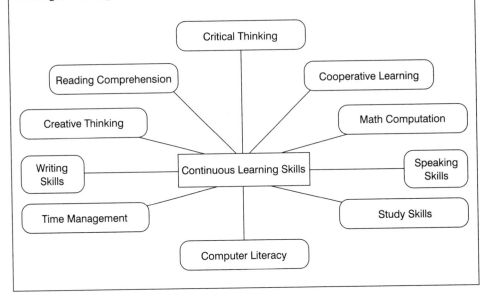

FIGURE 5.17   Thinking Skills Emphasized in the Middle School Program
Source: Middle School Design Report, Dade County Public Schools, June 1989.

rupted, for example, the project will simply take longer. Figure 5.19 shows the outline of steps in one such project.

The process of actually developing the curriculum under the Wiles-Bondi model falls to subject area subcommittees and special groups who are assigned to develop their area. Math and science, for example, would define their areas anew in terms of the parameters of the design report to the board. Standards would be formed to give further definition to the subject area (Figure 5.20). In areas that teach skills, the same process would occur (Figure 5.21). These standards would further establish purpose and guarantee that other areas could see the contribution of this part to the whole. Subsequent action plans in each area would help planners

| Item | Cost | |
	Start-up	Continuing
1. Personnel		
a. 10 Regular teachers		$300,000
b. 30 Instructional aides		300,000
c. 1 Program coordinator		25,000
d. 1 Secretary/bookkeeper		12,000
2. Fixed Charges		
Social Security and teacher retirement		
@ 15% of $637,000		95,500
3. Materials		
Continuous cost—10 teachers		
@ $1,000/teacher	20,000	10,000
4. Equipment		
Cots, chairs, tables, learning center		
equipment, playground equipment	30,000	4,000
5. Facilities		
Renovation of the cafeteria and auditorium		
on the present high school site	150,000	
6. Maintenance and Operation of Plant		
10 teachers @ $4,000/teacher		40,000
7. Staff Development		
a. Consultant honorarium and travel	3,000	15,000
b. Materials		800
Subtotal	$203,000	$802,350
Total Cost of Kindergarten School Program		$1,005,350

FIGURE 5.18   Cost of Proposed Kindergarten

understand the logistical needs of the area to meet its goals. The collection of all action plans would form the bulk of the implementation plan.

General administrative standards would also be established to envelope the program areas and service them. Among concerns would be areas such as grouping and use of time (Figure 5.22), facilities (Figure 5.23), and staff development (Figure 5.24). When "wedded" with the program standards and identified needs of specific areas, an overall calendar of activity and budget can be developed.

The calendar of events is a projection of what is going to occur, when it will occur, how much it will cost, and what is expected (in terms of the overall program intention) of this component. Calendars (Figure 5.25) and time lines (5.26) usually

Analysis Stage
1. Identify Denver Public Schools' philosophy
2. Identify board policy relative to middle schools
3. Superintendent (public) statement on middle schools
4. Outline time frame for implementation
5. Form centralized coordinating group
6. Delineate tasks and appoint subcommittees
7. Develop "definition" of Denver middle schools
8. Structure awareness/orientation campaign
   a. administrators
   b. teacher groups

Design Stage
9. Translate philosophy into goal statements
10. Project preliminary budget/resource base
11. Prioritize goal statements
12. Translate goal statements to objectives format
13. Block out 3–5 year plan for implementation
14. Establish management/information system to monitor progress of implementation (external audit)
15. Establish evaluation targets, time, responsibilities, resources; identify baseline data needed
16. Conduct needs assessment
17. Develop final management system (PERT)

Implementation or Management Stage
18. Provide advanced organizers (simple plan) to all interested persons
19. Provide each school with resource kits, glossaries, data bank from needs assessment (local planning/decision-making data)
20. Form teams in each school to serve as
    a. study group for mapping curriculum/skills
    b. planning group/house plan
    c. team/cooperative teaching unit
21. Provide preliminary staff development (demonstration teaching) in all schools on
    a. advisor/advisee program
    b. continuous progress curriculums
    c. team planning and teaching
22. Require school-by-school development plan including curriculum, staff development, evaluation, community involvement
23. Provide local budget supplement based on plan

Evaluation Stage
24. Conduct formative evaluation (external audit) every 6 weeks to monitor management outline
25. Conduct major review after 6 months—revise time line, goals, needs, and so on
26. Develop master evaluation plan (sum of all schools) for 3-year period

FIGURE 5.19   Comprehensive Plan of the Denver Public Schools

Source: Author's notes, Denver, Colorado.

Mathematics

The mathematics program provides for the sequential development of skills that enable students to comprehend our number system, to perform mathematical calculations, and to use mathematical thinking in solving problems.

_____ A skills profile card is maintained on each student.
_____ Diagnostic/prescriptive teaching techniques are used.
_____ Opportunities are provided to practice creative problem solving and computational skills in daily living situations.
_____ A variety of diagnostic test results are utilized to meet the needs of the students.
_____ Instruction is provided at different levels of achievement and understanding.
_____ Opportunities are provided to develop computer literacy.

Science

The science program reflects the character of science, encourages students to explore in order to increase scientific and technical knowledge, including computer literacy, and creates an awareness of the problems associated with science. The program ensures that each student can investigate and learn at his/her own level of understanding and guarantees that the scope of learning be broad enough to encompass contemporary issues of the scientific domain.

_____ The science program is exploratory in nature.
_____ The program is laboratory-centered.
_____ Scientific methods are utilized.
_____ Contemporary issues discussed in daily newspapers are emphasized.
_____ Scientific problems facing our community today, such as environmental problems, air pollution, and water pollution, are addressed.
_____ Instruction is provided at different levels of achievement and understanding.
_____ The range of topics studied by students includes the major areas of science.
_____ Computers and appropriate software are made available whenever possible.

FIGURE 5.20   Subject Area Standards

follow next which lead to products of activity. These products are chronicled in regular public board reports that tell everyone where the school or district is in its pursuit of this educational program.

Evaluation Stage

The CMP emphasizes evaluation from the beginning to support the curriculum development cycle. Evaluation is used in at least five ways:

1. To make explicit the rationale of the instructional program as a basis for deciding which aspects of the program should be evaluated for effectiveness and what types of data should be gathered

Curriculum Area: Computer Education

Purpose: The overall goal in the educational use of computers is to integrate computer literacy into all content areas of the middle school curriculum, thus providing an additional tool for interdisciplinary curriculum development. In addition, elective computer courses in application and programming provide for personal development and the reinforcement of essential skills.

Program Descriptors	Status		
	Yes	No	Action Plan to Achieve
1. Microcomputers, either permanently located in all classrooms or on mobile carts, are available for classroom use.			
2. Additional mobile computers will be available to move into classrooms when necessary or to develop a mini lab when desired.			
3. Each school will have at least two qualified full-time computer education teachers.			
4. Each school will have at least two complete computer labs containing a minimum of sixteen microcomputers and have a ratio of two students per computer. Each lab shall include necessary computer-system hardware, software, and peripheral equipment to meet current and future trends and developments. The complete computer lab will consist of necessary space, lighting, seating, air-cooling system, electrical system, and security, plus access to telecommunications.			
5. Daily lab schedules should include time set aside for independent student use.			
6. All students in grades 6 and 7 will be scheduled into one of the computer labs for a minimum of three hours a week in order to meet the state requirements for computer literacy.			
7. A minimum of two computers with needed peripherals will be located in the teachers' work area for teacher use (for grade recording, software review, word processing, and so on).			

Note: The Computer Literacy Program for the 6th and 7th grades should be interdisciplinary and taught through the team concept.

Both the media center and administrative offices need computerization. These noninstructional needs should be addressed by the appropriate middle school ad hoc committee.

Essential Skills: (Skills reinforced regardless of discipline or program spiral)

Reading	Writing	Problem solving	Thinking	Computation or calculation
Listening	Vocabulary	Decision making	Computer literacy	Motor

FIGURE 5.21 Mapping Worksheet with Standards in Skill Areas

The organization of the middle school is such that a smooth transition may be made from the self-contained classroom of the elementary school to the departmentalized high school. Provision is made to meet the unique social, academic, and personal needs of children as they emerge from childhood into adolescence. Flexibility in time utilization, and in the grouping of students and teachers, is provided to allow for balanced instruction.

1. Teacher grouping
   - ☐ Teachers are organized into interdisciplinary teams to provide instruction in the core subjects of reading, language arts, science, mathematics, and social studies.
   - ☐ The interdisciplinary team serves a common group of students.
   - ☐ The interdisciplinary team controls a block of time.
   - ☐ The members of the interdisciplinary team are assigned classrooms in close proximity to one another.
   - ☐ The members of the interdisciplinary team have a common planning period.
   - ☐ A member of the interdisciplinary team shall be designated as team leader.

2. Student grouping
   - ☐ The students are organized by trade levels.
   - ☐ Each grade level is divided into teams of approximately 90 to 135 students as is compatible with the interdisciplinary instructional team.
   - ☐ Provision is made for instruction at differing ability levels, at differing skills levels, and in different interest areas.

3. Time
   - ☐ Provision is made for a flexible daily time schedule.
   - ☐ A block of time equivalent to five 45-minute time segments (225 minutes) is assigned to the interdisciplinary team for academic instruction.
   - ☐ A 90-minute block of time is provided for exploration and physical education activities.

Proposed Middle School Student Schedule

25 min. A/A	225 min. Academic Block	25 min. Lunch	45 min. Enrich.	45 min. P.E.	25 min. Passing

The day schedule contains:
   7—45-minute periods
   1—25-minute A/A period (Advisory Activities)
   1—25-minute lunch period
   passing times (total of 25 minutes)

   Total student day of 6 hours 30 minutes

FIGURE 5.22 Proposed General Organization Standards

Source: From *Making Middle Schools Work,* Fig. 12, p. 26, by J. Wiles and J. Bondi. Copyright © 1986 by the Association for Supervision and Curriculum Development, Alexandria, VA.

Proposed Facilities Standards

The instructional program and the organizational pattern of the middle school dictate the facility requirements. The facilities should allow for varied instructional experiences, support the middle school concept, and meet the personnel and support-staff needs.

1. Essential considerations
    - ☐ Increased attractiveness by use of color schemes and graphics
    - ☐ Adequate instructional space and equipment for each curricular program
    - ☐ Clustered interdisciplinary team instruction rooms
    - ☐ Team planning/work/conference area
    - ☐ Flexible classroom space
    - ☐ Computer instruction area
    - ☐ Alternative education area
    - ☐ Clinic area
    - ☐ Closeable restroom stalls for boys and girls
    - ☐ Adequate area for physical education and recreational activities
    - ☐ Appropriate private shower and changing facilities for boys and girls
    - ☐ Appropriate exceptional education/student services

2. Desirable considerations
    - ☐ In-house television capability
    - ☐ Adequate acoustical treatment (ceiling tile, floor covering, and so on)

Note: Existing science facilities are clustered, which poses difficulties in the adjacent team room concept. It is suggested that the sixth-grade science program be taught in convenient classrooms, which are equipped with a water source, portable lab facility, storage, and student stations at tables. Seventh- and eighth-grade science classes should be taught in existing science rooms at the expense of being removed from the team area.

Any new facility or any major renovation of an existing facility should address the decentralization of science rooms.

FIGURE 5.23   Middle School Facility Needs

2. To collect data upon which judgments about effectiveness can be formulated
3. To analyze data and draw conclusions
4. To make decisions based on the data
5. To implement the decisions to improve the instructional program

These questions need to be asked prior to setting up an evaluation design to monitor curriculum development:

- ☐ What are the criteria for evaluating the program?
- ☐ What type of evaluation do we want to conduct?
- ☐ What constitutes good research?

Individual Professional Development Summary				
	From Personnel Records	Incentives	Source	Delivery
Sec. I Basic Certification Information		• Required for hiring and tenure		• Pre-service college courses
Sec. II Basic Required In-service 25 Growth and Development of Preadolescents 25 Middle School Philosophy and Curriculum 25 Fundamental and Specialized Instructional Strategies for Preadolescents 25 Counseling, Guidance, and Human Relations 25 Teaching of Basic Skills 25 Teaming and Team Teaching 25 ____ 25 ____ 25 ____	• 6 required 4-hr. courses (over 3 yrs. on release time) • Introduction courses to each of the 6 basic competency categories • 25 Professional Development points each (150 for teachers, 225 for administrators) 3 additional for Administrations	• Professional Development points awarded • **On paid contract time (release)** • Provided free of charge • Required by district for Middle School Specialist designation	• Needs assessment • Staff development committee	Location: on-site (e.g., teaming); area offices (e.g., philosophy); T.O.R.C. (e.g., basic skills); other central locations; Time: release time (partial day—sub provided) on rotating basis by content area, by grade release time (full in-service day—school closed) by school, by position.
Sec. III Renewal In-service 25 ____ 25 ____ 25 ____	• Allows in-depth in any of the 6 basic Competency Categories • Specialist designation requires 6 basic (150 points) + 3 add'l (75 pts.) • Minimum of 150 points (6 courses) every 3 yrs. for Specialist renewal • Fills in specific skills needed by individual (self & Principal assessment)	• P.O. points awarded • Required by district for Specialist designation and renewal • Provided free of charge • Release time or College credit • **Guarantees better choice of openings** • **State certification?**	• Needs assessment • Staff development committee • Individual skill assessment profile	Location: T.O.R.C.; other central locations Time: release time (see above) evenings (college credit)

FIGURE 5.24   Comprehensive Middle School Staff Development Design

Individual Professional Development Summary	Incentives	Source	Delivery
(Completion of Sections I–III provides District Middle School Specialist Designation)			
Sec. IV Supplemental In-service	• Additional courses as needed or desired • Recorded on I.S.P. check-list	• College credit (tuition paid if for state certification) or • Extra P.D.U. points or • Stipend w/minimum P.D. points	• Individual skill assessment profile • School improvement	Location: on-site (school based req., activity tailored to school; T.O.R.C.; area offices; colleges Time: evenings (w/stipend P.D.U. or college credit); staff meetings; team meetings.
Professional Self-Development	_____ _____ _____ _____	• Self-growth • Available, convenient, and free of charge	• Requests for service • Identified needs	Location: central location; I.S.S. Time: evenings, Saturdays, summer

Sec. V Program Development/Training/Consulting Experience
Program
  Development _____
  Contracts _____
Internal
  Presentations _____
External
  Presentations _____
	• Opportunity for release time to develop special programs/units
	• Release time for presentation
	• Preparation time
	• Presentation time (if after school)
	• Experience, pride, broadening of skills		

FIGURE 5.24 (*Continued*)

FIGURE 5.25 Middle School Staff Development and Meetings Schedule

Source: From *Making Middle Schools Work*, Fig. 21, p. 36, by J. Wiles and J. Bondi. Copyright © 1986 by the Association for Supervision and Curriculum Development, Alexandria, VA.

	Aug 22	26	27	Sep 5	6	12	13	19	20	26	27	Oct 10	11	17	18	24	25	31	Nov 1	7	8	14	15	21	22	Dec 5	6	7	8	10	12	13
Teachers																																
Leadership Group						1		2		3	1	4		5		6	3	7	8	5	9	6	10		7	5	6	7	8			
Principals									1						2						3						8					
Assistant Principals				1								2						3				4			3							
Management Team	1												2												3							
School Visits (as needed)						1				2									3				2				3					
School Board																																
Coordinating Committee																1												1				
Staff Development														1		1										2						
Grant																																
Evaluation Committee											1											2					3					
Program Consultants				1								2						3		2		4				5						
Public Relations Committee						1																	2									

197

Task	Time Line	Responsible Person(s)
23. Coordinating Committee meeting three	March 31, 1998	Paul Bell
24. Progress Report I to board a. Results of needs assessment b. Tasks completed c. Tasks pending d. Evaluation or progress of year one implementation	June, 1998	Joseph Fernandez Paul Bell J.L. DeChurch Wiles-Bondi
25. Summer training of staff. This will lead to middle school endorsement and internal certification.	June–August 1998	Kenneth Walker Karen Dreyfuss Margaret Petersen Wiles-Bondi
26. Clinical assistance-visitation to pilot schools	Ongoing 1997–2000	Wiles-Bondi District Staff Area Superintendents and Staff
27. Curriculum development, refinement of middle school subject areas	Spring, 1998–Ongoing	J.L. DeChurch
28. Development of middle school intra-mural program	Summer, 1998	District Staff
29. Piloting of intramural program	Fall, 1998	District Staff
30. Coordinating Committee meeting four	October, 1998	Paul Bell
31. Midpoint assessment/sharing of team implementation in second group of middle schools	November, 1998	Wiles-Bondi Team Leaders
32. Coordinating Committee meeting five	December, 1998	Paul Bell
34. Team Fair two	March 30, 1999	Wiles-Bondi Middle School Principals

FIGURE 5.26   Time Lines of Activity

These questions are addressed in the following section.

Criteria for Evaluating Instructional Programs.   The first consideration in the evaluation of instructional programs must be the purposes for which the instructional program is being planned. Whether these are the objectives stated for a particular lesson in a classroom or the general educational goals for a school or district, planning occurs on the basis of the purposes defined. As stated earlier, we believe that a good instructional program must adequately reflect the aims of the school or agency from which they come. At the school level, the faculty, students, and parents need to define comprehensive educational goals, and all curriculum opportunities offered at the school should be planned with reference to one or more of those goals.

A good instructional program must provide for continuity of learning experiences. Students should progress through a particular program on the basis of their achievement, not on the basis of how much time they have spent in the program. Instructional programs in a school that are planned over several years lend themselves to better vertical progress. Continuity of learning experiences within a program dictates that a relationship between disciplines be established. **Core,** or **interdisciplinary programs,** allow students to see purpose and meaning in their total instructional program.

All principles of learning need to be drawn upon in selecting an instructional program. Programs that rely solely on operant conditioning as a psychological base for teaching neglect the important theories of Combs, Piaget, and others. All of those associated in education understand the difficulty of putting psychological principles into practice. A careful analysis of new programs can reveal the psychological bases of those programs.

Programs selected should make maximum provision for the development of each learner. Any program selected should include a wide range of opportunities for individuals of varying abilities, interests, and needs. Each child is characterized by his or her own pattern of development. Youngsters are curious, explorative, and interested in many things. An instructional program must promote individual development in students rather than making them conform to a hypothetical standard.

An instructional program must provide for clear focus. Whether a program is organized around separate subjects such as history or science, or around related subjects such as social studies, it is important that whoever selects the program knows which dimensions to pursue, which relationships of facts and ideas should stand out, and which should be submerged. The problem for those who are reviewing programs is to decide which element of the program is the center of organization. Instructional programs may be organized around life problems, content topics, interests, or experiences. In selecting instructional programs, however, the organizing focus must also be examined to see which topics are emphasized, which details are relevant, and which relationships are significant.

A good instructional program should be well planned and must include a built-in process for evaluation. Steps need to be defined that would include a periodic assessment of the success of the program and a continuous process for reviewing and updating the program.

In the Wiles-Bondi CMP model, evaluation is built in from the beginning by establishing a standing committee to review and report on progress. As stated earlier, this committee includes several lay persons, which helps allay suspicions, and its purpose is to communicate all results. Assumed in the design of if–then logic is that if the program is built correctly, it will produce the results desired. If such results are not forthcoming, the program should be redesigned.

There are many types of evaluation; however, we find the following outline of evaluations, by D. L. Stufflebeam, to be a useful paradigm:

A. Focusing the Evaluation
1. Identify the major level(s) of decision making to be served, for example, local, state, or national.
2. For each level of decision making, project the decision situations to be served and describe each one in terms of its locus, focus, timing, and composition of alternatives.
3. Define criteria for each decision situation by specifying variables for measurement and standards for use in the judgment of alternatives.
4. Define policies within which the evaluation must operate.
B. Collection of Information
1. Specify the source of the information to be collected.
2. Specify the instruments and methods for collecting the needed information.
3. Specify the sampling procedure to be employed.
4. Specify the conditions and schedule for information collection.
C. Organization of Information
1. Specify a format for the information that is to be collected.
2. Specify a means for coding, organizing, storing, and retrieving information.
D. Analysis of Information
1. Specify the analytical procedures to be employed.
2. Specify a means for performing the analysis.
E. Reporting of Information
1. Define the audiences for the evaluation reports.
2. Specify means for providing information to the audiences.
3. Specify the format for evaluation reports and/or reporting sessions.
4. Schedule the reporting information.
F. Administration of the Evaluation
1. Summarize the evaluation schedule.
2. Define staff and resource requirements and plans for meeting these requirements.
3. Specify means for meeting policy requirements for conduct of the evaluation.
4. Evaluate the potential of the evaluation design for providing information that is valid, reliable, credible, timely, and pervasive.
5. Specify and schedule means for periodic updating of the evaluation design.
6. Provide a budget for the total evaluation program.[2]

Another useful resource for curriculum leaders responsible for designing evaluation systems is a classification outline developed by the Phi Delta Kappa National Study Committee on Evaluation. This outline presents four types of evaluation commonly found in schools that are broken down according to their objective, method, and relationship to the decision-making (DM) process:

1. Context Evaluation

   Objective: To define the operation context, to identify and assess needs in the context, and to identify and delineate problems underlying the needs.

   Method: By describing individually and in relevant perspectives the major subsystems of the context; by comparing actual and intended inputs and outputs of the subsystems; and by analyzing possible causes of discrepancies between actualities and intentions.

   Relation to DM Process: For deciding upon the setting to be served, the goals associated with meeting needs and the objectives associated with solving problems, that is, for planning needed changes.

2. Input Evaluation

   Objective: To identify and assess system capabilities, available input strategies, and designs for implementing strategies.

   Method: By describing and analyzing available human and material resources, solution strategies, and procedural designs for relevance, feasibility, and economy in the course of action to be taken.

   Relation to DM Process: For selecting sources of support, solution strategies, and procedural designs, that is, for programming change activities.

3. Process Evaluation

   Objective: To identify or predict, in process, defects in procedural design or its implementation, and to maintain a record of procedural events and activities.

   Method: By monitoring the activity's potential procedural barriers and remaining alert to unanticipated ones.

   Relation to DM Process: For implementing and refining the program design and procedure, that is, for effecting process control.

4. Product Evaluation

   Objective: To relate outcome information to objectives and to context, input, and process information.

   Method: By defining operationally and measuring criteria associated with the objectives, by comparing these measurements with predetermined standards or comparative bases, and by interpreting the outcome in terms of recorded input and process information.

   Relation to DM Process: For deciding to continue, terminate, modify, or refocus a change activity, and for linking the activity to other major phases of the change process, that is, for evolving change activities.[3]

When developing comprehensive programs, curriculum workers may wish to go beyond academic achievement as a goal for education. The authors see public education as no less than a program for future citizens; therefore, they recognize the need for physical, social, intellectual, and emotional growth of students while under the auspices of the school. Areas that are regularly assessed, and the instruments that are used are shown in Figure 5.27.

Informal measures of student development are sometimes created internally in a school or district to monitor changes in students as they respond to the new program. Over time, using a time series design, evidence of growth can be recorded and used to rationalize the program, make decisions, and reinforce the attitudes of teachers and parents. Figure 5.28 shows some of the categories that might be assessed in this way.

Assessing Educational Research.   Another task for curriculum workers that is related to school evaluation activities is to assess educational research. In some cases, such research will be conducted externally to the school district; in other cases, it will be in-house. The curriculum specialist should be able to identify good research and be able to assess research reports.

Good research possesses a number of characteristics that distinguish it from mediocre research. The following guidelines will assist the review of research efforts:

- ☐ The problem should be clearly stated, be limited, and have contemporary significance. In the proposal, the purpose, objectives, hypotheses, and specific questions should be presented concisely. Important terms should be defined.
- ☐ Previous and related studies should be reported, indicating their relationship to the present study.
- ☐ The variables, those which are controlled and those to be manipulated, should be identified.
- ☐ A description of procedures to be used should be clear enough to be replicated. Details such as the duration of the study and the treatments used should be spelled out in depth.

Instrument	Use	Author
Myers-Briggs Type Indicator	Team formation	Myers-Briggs
Teacher Preference Inventory	Teaching style	Canfield
Teacher Styles Inventory	Teaching style	Canfield
Curriculum Inventory Guide	Curriculum	R.S. Fox
Case Study Interview	Relationships	R. Havelock
Climate Questionnaire	Climate type	Litwin & Stringer
Community Power Interview	Leaders	Kimbrough
Organizational Climate Descriptor	Climate	Halpin-Croft
Group Cohesiveness Scale	Groups	S. Seashore
Community Attitude Scale	Community	Bosworth
Powerlessness Scale	Anomie	Neal and Seeman
Change Readiness Measure-C	Change	Duncan

FIGURE 5.27   Sample Assessment Instruments

Growth Areas for Consideration	**Measures of Development**
Aspects of Thinking	Achievement Tests in Subjects
Work Habits and Skills	Academic Aptitude Tests
Reading	Reading Tests
Content Mastery Measures	Social/Emotional Adjustment
Development of Social Interests	Health Assessments
Appreciations of New Areas	Home Conditions
Development of Social Sensitivity	Pupil Questionnaires
Social Adjustment	Behavior Ratings
Creativeness	Interest Indexes
Development of a Personal Philosophy	Writing Sample Inventories
Physical Health	Work Habit Measures
Mental Health	Teach-Behavior Assessments

FIGURE 5.28   Growth and Measures of Development

☐ The groups being studied should be defined in terms of significant characteristics.

☐ The report should note the school setting, describing things such as organization, scale of operations, and any special influences.

☐ The evaluation instruments should be applicable to the purpose of the study. Growth in self-concept, for instance, is not measured by standardized achievement tests in reading. Evidence of validity (Is this test the correct one?) and reliability (Does this test measure what it should?) should be given for all evaluation instruments used.

☐ Scoring of measures should be done by the most appropriate method whether it be means, medians, percentages, quartiles, rank, or whatever.

☐ Results or findings should be clearly stated in the report in a prominent location.

☐ Limitations on findings, and there usually are limitations, should be clearly stated.

In addition to understanding what goes into good research, the curriculum specialists may sometimes be asked to assess specific research reports that have application to the schools in which they work. The following questions will help in such an assessment:

☐ **Problem presentation**   Is the question being asked an important one? Will the question being asked add to further understanding? Will the question being asked aid in decision making? Is the problem explained well in light of limitations in the research area? Are the concepts presented reasonable and testable?

- □   **Methodology**   Are the hypotheses stated in a manner that will reveal expected differences? Can this research be replicated? Is the sampling adequate and representative? Is the study designed to show evidence of causation or correlation? Will the results be generalizable to other groups with similar characteristics?
- □   **Results**   Are the observational categories used relevant to the purpose of the study? Are the statistical treatments appropriate to the data presented? Are the reported differences statistically significant? (Significant at the 0.01 level of confidence, for instance, means that there is only 1 chance in 100 that differences as observed occurred by chance.) Are the results presented in a manner that makes them understandable?
- □   **Conclusions**   Are logical inferences drawn from the findings? Are inferences of any use to decision making? Are the limitations of the research identified?

Using such organizers as targeted data, evidence data, standards of excellence, and relevant data, evaluation decisions can help schools and districts measure the kinds of items that help them to assess real progress. What curriculum workers really need to know is if they are on-task and accomplishing what is intended.

If the evaluation stage in a CMP can tell the school board and other planners of their status, give general direction to planning, and answer the question, "Did we do what we wanted to do?" evaluation is a functional part of the curriculum cycle.

SUMMARY

Comprehensive school planning will mean seeing all areas of school operations as a system. All planning in a system must begin with a clear conception of purpose. The formalization of that purpose is important for the sake of continuity in program development. Assessing present conditions, usually through a needs assessment, provides planning data to support philosophic goals.

A curriculum management system (CMP) can be used to tie together the many activities needed to accomplish the planned change. Activation of this system depends on identifying responsible agents to carry out tasks and setting a time frame for the planned change. Various technical aids can assist the curriculum leader in managing the many variables.

The design phase of curriculum development proceeds deductively from goals previously identified and endorsed. Broad conceptualizations of the programs desired are projected, and plans for specific components of the program are developed. Placing these plans into one holistic understanding of the desired change leads to the management or implementation stage of the cycle.

Evaluation, a fourth step of the curriculum development cycle, is the critical stage for the 1980s and 1990s. **Accountability** by school leaders for their performance should encourage them to be both effective and efficient in developing quality school programs. Historic criteria for curriculum quality, plus sound educational research, will guide curriculum leaders in their evaluation of school programming.

SUGGESTED LEARNING ACTIVITIES

1. Develop a checklist for selecting new instructional programs in your school.
2. What sources of data would you use for a follow-up study of students leaving an elementary school? Middle school? High school?
3. You are chairing a committee to suggest an evaluation design for a new science program at your school. What things would you consider in the design?
4. What is the role of an accrediting agency? Which association of colleges and secondary schools represents your area?
5. You have been asked by your PTA to explain the accountability movement. Outline in detail what you would say.
6. Develop a program for the continuing evaluation of your school.
7. Describe the relationship between educational research and educational evaluation. Can you reduce this relationship to a model or outline?

NOTES

1. Kathryn Feyereisen, *Supervision and Curriculum Renewal* (New York: Appleton Century Croft, 1970), p. 138.
2. D. L. Stufflebeam, "Toward a Science of Educational Evaluation," *Education Technology* (July 30, 1968).
3. National Society for the Study of Education (Bloomington, IN: Phi Delta Kappa, 1978).

BOOKS TO REVIEW

Elmore, R., and S. Fuhrman. *The Governance of Curriculum.* Alexandria, VA: ASCD, 1994.

Geisert, P., and M. Futrell. *Teachers, Computers, and Curriculum.* Needham Heights, MA: Allyn and Bacon, 1995.

Glasser, W. *Quality School.* Port Chester, NY: National Professional Resources, 1990.

Hersey, P., et al. *Management and Organizational Behavior,* 7th ed., Upper Saddle River, NJ: Prentice Hall, 1996.

Joyce, B., et al. *The Self-Renewing School.* Alexandria, VA: ASCD, 1993.

Rossman, G. *Change and Effectiveness in Schools: A Cultural Perspective.* Albany, NY: SUNY Press, 1988.

chapter 6

LEADERSHIP AND CHANGE IN CURRICULUM DEVELOPMENT

Leadership is a critical element in any curriculum improvement effort. Without such leadership, goals and values will not be clarified, plans will not be developed and implemented, and individuals in the organization will not fully contribute to the improvement of instructional opportunities for students. Leadership is, in fact, the intangible driving force in educational change and one of the least understood concepts in professional education.

Over the years, considerable research has accumulated regarding leadership behavior. Part of the problem in using this body of knowledge is that it is so extensive that it often overwhelms the reader. Another difficulty is that it is very broad and contains many relevant peripheral elements. This chapter sorts out the essential elements from the peripheral and guides you to key concepts and ideas.

In today's literature, there are over 130 formal definitions of leadership![1] Some of those definitions are provided here for thought and discussion:

A leader is best when people barely know he exists. When our work is done his aim is fulfilled, they will say, "We did this ourselves." (Lao-Tzu, *The Way of Life,* Sixth Century, B.C.)

Love is held by a chain of obligation . . . but fear is maintained by the dread of punishment which never fails. . . . A wise prince must rely on what is in his power and not on what is in the power of others. (Niccolo Machiavelli, *The Prince,* A.D. 1500)

Leadership is the art of imposing one's will upon others in such a manner as to command their obedience, their respect, and their loyal cooperation. (*G-I Manual,* Staff College, United States Army, 1947)

Leadership is the ability to get a man to do what you want him to do, when you want it done, in a way you want it done, because he wants to do it. (Dwight Eisenhower, 1957)

Leadership is the human factor which binds a group together and motivates it toward a goal. (K. Davis, *Human Relations at Work*, 1962)

Leadership is the process of influencing the activities of an individual or group in efforts toward goal achievements in a given situation. (Paul Hersey and Kenneth Blanchard, *The Management of Organizational Behavior*, 1977)

In his major study, *Handbook of Leadership*, Ralph Stogdill identified seven families of definitions or conceptions of leadership; these also serve to illustrate the range of inquiry into the subject:[2]

1. **Leadership as the focus of group process**   The leader is the nucleus of social movement. By control of social processes (structure, goals, ideology, atmosphere), the leader becomes the primary agent for group change.
2. **Leadership as personality and its effects**   The leader processes the greatest number of desired traits. Using these, the leader exerts a degree of influence over those about him.
3. **Leadership as the art of inducing compliance**   The leader, through face-to-face control, causes the subordinate to behave in a desired manner.
4. **Leadership as the exercise of influence**   The leader establishes a relationship and uses this interpersonal influence to attain goals and enforce behavior beyond mechanical compliance.
5. **Leadership as a power relationship**   The leader is perceived as having the right to prescribe behavior patterns for others. Sources of power include referent power (liking), expert power, reward power, coercive power, and legitimate (authority) power.
6. **Leadership as the initiation of structure**   The leader originates and structures interaction as part of a process to solve problems.
7. **Leadership as goal achievement**   The leader is perceived as controlling the means of satisfying needs as the group moves toward definitive objectives.

The formal study of leadership has evolved through three distinct stages in the past century: (1) a traits, or "great man," approach, (2) a study of leadership in situations or environments, and (3) a study of leadership transactions or exchange. Each of these major avenues to understanding leadership as a concept is reviewed in the following.

Studies attempting to define leadership in terms of traits or characteristics of an individual were prevalent in the nineteenth and early twentieth centuries. A benchmark in such personality research was the 1933 list developed by H. L. Smith and L. M. Krueger.[3]

Personality Traits
Knowledge
Abundance of physical and nervous energy
Enthusiasm
Originality
Initiative
Imagination
Purpose
Persistence
Speed of decision

Social Traits
Tact
Sympathy
Faith in others and self
Prestige
Patience
Ascendance–submission

Physical Characteristics
Some advantage as to height, weight, and physical attractiveness

These so-called "great man" theories resulted from studies of leaders and were an extension of Aristotle's notion of a "born leader." Such studies were supported by the early work of psychology that focused on individual differences. In general, trait theories held that there were certain identifiable qualities that separated leaders from nonleaders and that these inherent traits were transferable from situation to situation.

Arguments for the trait theories tend to be circular since most of the leaders studied to identify traits were chosen because of the position that they already held. From an empirical viewpoint, the studies of traits were plagued by unreplicable conditions and a lack of control populations. Stogdill's 1948 review of some 124 studies organized around leadership traits was not able to substantiate a trait theory. Another study by F. H. Sanford (1952) concluded:

> From all of these studies of the leader, we conclude that: a) there are either no general leadership traits or, if they exist, they are not described in any of our familiar psychological or common sense terms, b) in a specific situation, leaders do have traits which set them apart from followers, but what traits set what leaders apart from what followers will vary from situation to situation.[4]

The work of Stogdill, Sanford, and others closed the door on a long-standing belief—a leader is born and leadership is limited to those possessing certain desirable traits. By the same token, inquiry during the first half of this century produced new avenues for further inquiry. Writing about leaders in 1948, Stogdill observed:

> The findings suggest that leadership is not a matter of passive status, or the mere possession of some combination of traits. It appears rather to be a working relationship among members of a group, in which the leader acquires status through active participation and demonstration of his capacity for carrying cooperative tasks through to completion.[5]

Stogdill later defined this *situational* factor in terms of needs and interests of the followers, objectives, and mental level, and so on.

A second avenue for the study of leadership revolved around the situation (environment) in which leadership is exerted. In general, it was hypothesized that a person does not become a leader because of the possession of certain traits, but rather because of the relationship of those traits to the characteristics, goals, or activities of the followers. Leadership must always be a group phenomenon.

Seeing a leader as a person who, owing to a situation, emerges to help a group attain certain goals, broadened the scope of leadership research and theory. For one thing, being a leader now appeared apart from exerting leadership. Such an active definition of leadership also helped to explain why leadership was sometimes lost—when the leader ceased the critical function of helping a group to attain its goals. From the social sciences came the contribution that leadership was actually a process of producing change.

Attempts to define leadership wholly in terms of situational factors met with the same general rejection as did the earlier trait theories. There were simply too many situations observable in which the leader with the correct set of skills or traits did not assume or maintain the leadership role. During the late 1960s, a third piece of the puzzle began to emerge with the development of transactional, or exchange theory. This third effort continues today.

Leadership exchange theory focuses on the methods by which leaders initially motivate groups to accept their influence, the processes that undergird prolonged exertion of such influence, and the ways in which the leader makes real contributions to group goals.[6] In short, exchange theory seeks to learn and explain how leaders work within their groups to establish and maintain influence. Leadership, by this definition, is an exchange or transaction that occurs (acceptance of influence) when needs are present (until satisfaction is achieved) between the leader and the follower. The following generalizations about leadership in school environments, in which multiple group needs are present, are offered by Kimball Wiles and John Lovell.

1. Leadership is a group role . . . he [the leader] is able to exert real leadership only through effective participation in groups.
2. Leadership, other things being equal, depends upon the frequency of interaction between the leader and the led.
3. Status position does not necessarily give leadership.
4. Leadership in any organization is widespread and diffused . . . if a person hopes to exert leadership for everybody, he is doomed to frustration and failure.
5. The norms of the group determine the leader.
6. Leadership qualities and followership qualities are interchangeable.
7. People who give evidence of a desire to control are rejected for leadership roles.
8. The feeling that people hold about a person is a factor in whether they will use his behavior as leadership.
9. Leadership shifts from situation to situation.[7]

In the 1990s, it is becoming clear that both the leadership message and the followership perception are critical ingredients for successful leadership practice. If a leader has the right skills for the right situation but cannot transact or send an appropriate message to the followers—and is therefore not perceived as a leader—leadership will not be successful. For this reason, seeing the pattern of leadership messages, or leadership style, is a very important skill in educational leadership training.

STYLES OF LEADERSHIP

The serious studies of leadership styles emerged from industry in the 1930s. A critical question for industrial leaders was how to match the organizational tasks of a bureaucracy with the human needs of the worker. Finding a compatible style of leadership to match organizational task requirements presented a research problem that is still being explored today.

The classic works in leadership styles categorized leaders into three groups: democratic, autocratic, and laissez-faire.[8] These styles were determined by a field observation approach, which viewed the relationship of the leader to those being led. Later approaches to the study of styles tended to conceptualize the style in terms of tasks. D. Cartwright and A. Zander, for instance, saw leaders as either helping a group attain a specific goal (change) or maintaining the group itself (maintenance).[9] D. Katz and R. Kahn continued this orientation by categorizing leadership according to function: introducing structural change, interpreting organizational structure, or using structure to keep an organization in motion.[10] By far, the most influential conception of leadership style, however, was provided by Douglas McGregor, who described leadership style in terms of the leader's view of the follower.[11]

McGregor presented two conflicting conceptions of managerial tasks. The conceptions were based on a number of assumptions about people in an organization (see Figure 6.1). A traditional view, which he labeled *Theory X,* saw leadership stemming from the position of the leader and viewed subordinates as unwilling partners in group or organizational tasks. Since the Theory X leader viewed followers as innately lazy or unreliable, a stern reform of leadership had to be employed to guarantee organizational achievement. McGregor contrasted this view of the role of leadership with another, *Theory Y,* which began with a different set of premises. Theory Y leaders assumed that leadership was given by the group to the leader and that people, who are basically self-directed and creative, will produce if properly motivated. McGregor's models of leadership saw the relationship between the leader and followers as involving four key variables:

1. The characteristics of the leader
2. The characteristics of the organization
3. The nature of the tasks to be performed
4. The social, economic, and political milieu

In a parallel model, Robert Blake and Jane Mouton devised a grid on which to plot leadership styles.[12] Using two poles—concern for people and concern for production—Blake and Mouton identified some eighty-one possible positions or combinations of these two directions. The value of the grid, as a model for understanding leadership, is to make the reader aware of many possible styles that might be

Theory X Assumptions	Theory Y Assumptions
People by Nature:	People by Nature:
1. Lack integrity	1. Have integrity
2. Are fundamentally lazy and desire to work as little as possible	2. Work hard toward objectives to which they are committed
3. Avoid responsibility	3. Assume responsibility within their commitments
4. Are not interested in achievement	4. Desire to achieve
5. Are incapable of directing their own behavior	5. Are capable of directing their own behavior
6. Are indifferent to organizational needs	6. Want their organization to succeed
7. Prefer to be directed by others	7. Are not passive and submissive
8. Avoid making decisions whenever possible	8. Will make decisions within their commitments
9. Are not very bright	9. Are not stupid

FIGURE 6.1   Organizational View of People

Source: From "The Human Side of Enterprise," by Douglas McGregor in *The Management Review* 46 (1957): 22–28, 88–92. Reprinted by permission.

employed to fit various situations (see Figure 6.2). Blake and Mouton characterized five primary styles that can be plotted on the Managerial Grid:

1.1 **Impoverished Management**   Effective production is unobtainable because people are lazy, apathetic, or indifferent. Sound and mature relationships are difficult to achieve because, human nature being what it is, conflict is inevitable.

1.9 **Country Club Management**   Production is incidental to lack of conflict and good fellowship.

5.5 **Middle of the Road Management**   Push for production but don't go "all out," give some but not all. "Be fair but firm."

9.1 **Task Management**   Men are a commodity just as machines. A manager's responsibility is to plan, direct, and control the work of those subordinate to him.

9.9 **Team Management**   Production is from integration of task and human requirements into a unified system of interplay toward organizational goals.

The value of these and other early conceptions of style by McGregor and Blake and Mouton was to suggest various patterns that were appropriate to various tasks and environments. However, the student of leadership style should note that

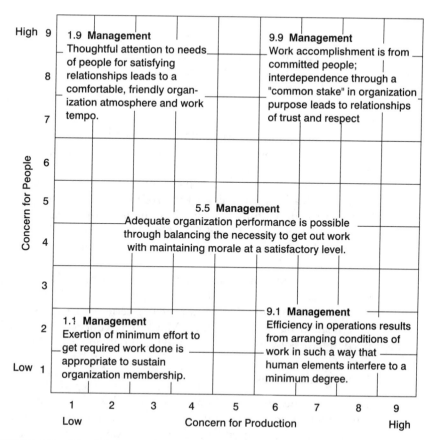

FIGURE 6.2   The Managerial Grid

Source: From *The Managerial Grid,* p. 10, by Robert R. Blake and Jane Mouton. Copyright © 1964 by Gulf Publishing Co., Houston, TX. Reprinted by permission.

both of these models look at style from the leader's position. What is important to understand in this subject area is that style is perceived by the followers, as well as projected by the leaders. To be effective, a leader must successfully transmit a style pattern and have it received in the intended form. Any distortion of that transmission will detract from effective leadership. This point will also be discussed in the sections "Communication in Organizations" and "Group Work."

ROLES AND TASKS

Leadership in curriculum development is not a function of title or appointed position. Titles may legitimize formal authority, but they do not ensure leadership capacity. Leadership is a function of four complex variables:

1. The character of the leader
2. The character of the followers
3. The character of the organization
4. The character of the environment

Leadership in educational organizations is a situational phenomenon. It is determined by the collective perceptions of individuals, is related to group norms, and is influenced by the frequency of interaction among members of the organization. Before leadership can be effective in an open organization such as a school, it must be acknowledged as a group activity.

To some extent, leadership is a product of the leader's vision. The way in which the leader conceives of the group's tasks, and the policies and practices required to successfully achieve those ends, defines leadership. In the words of management specialist Douglas McGregor, "The theoretical assumptions management holds about controlling human resources determine the whole character of the enterprise."[13]

The way in which the leader sees the organization and its needs, when formalized, sets the foundation for a theory of leadership. Without such a theory, leadership behaviors will be little more than a series of activities and projects that have little relationship to one another. Most often, conceptions of leadership are developed in terms of what the leader is to be and do, in terms of roles and tasks.

Leadership Roles

Leadership roles in curriculum are multiple due to the numerous environments in which work is conducted and the levels at which leaders operate. Figure 6.3 shows stereotypical leadership styles appropriate in various environments.

Ronald Havelock and associates have identified nineteen leadership roles that may be applicable to the work of a curriculum worker:[14]

1. **Expert**   Sometimes the consultant is the source of knowledge or skill in an area.
2. **Instructor**   The consultant may take the role of instructor in an area of knowledge.
3. **Trainer**   A trainer goes beyond instruction in that they help people master "do it" behavioral skills in performing actions.
4. **Retriever**   The retriever brings what is needed to the client system.
5. **Referrer**   The referrer sends the client system to a source where it can find what it needs.
6. **Linker**   The linker provides a bridge to parties, or parts of a system, that need to be in contact.
7. **Demonstrator**   The demonstrator shows the client system how something is done, but does not necessarily show him how to do it for himself.
8. **Modeler**   The modeler provides an example of how to do, or be, something by evidencing it in her (the consultant's) own behavior.

1. "TELLS" Leadership
    a. Seeks unquestioning obedience
    b. Sometimes relies on fear, intimidation
    c. Gives orders
    d. Relies heavily on authority
    e. Sets all goals and standards
    f. Makes all decisions without consulting the group

2. "SELLS" Leadership
    a. Work assignments are allotted to workers
    b. Assignments are sometimes arbitrary
    c. Tries to persuade the group to accept assignments
    d. Seldom builds teamwork
    e. Does not motivate worker involvement
    f. Makes decisions without consulting the group

3. "CONSULTS" Leadership
    a. Does not rely on authority
    b. Develops considerable worker loyalty
    c. Does not hesitate to delegate
    d. Will usually explain why a task is to be performed in a certain way
    e. Takes time to inform his group what he thinks may be a solution

4. "JOINS" Leadership
    a. Builds teamwork by group involvement
    b. Accepts suggestions from the work group
    c. Treats each worker as an individual
    d. Helps workers achieve their potential
    e. Uses the decision of the group

5. "DELEGATES" Leadership
    a. Turns the decision-making process over to the group
    b. Accepts all group decisions that fit within accepted parameters
    c. Encourages subordinate participation in many activities
    d. Stimulates creative thinking in employees

FIGURE 6.3 Leadership Styles

Source: From *Supervision: A Guide to Practice*, 4th ed., p. 44, by J. Wiles and J. Bondi, Copyright ©1996 by Merrill-Prentice Hall, Columbus, Ohio. Reprinted by permission.

9. **Advocate**   There are times when a consultant can best facilitate an intention by taking the role of advocate for a goal, value, or strategy.
10. **Confronter**   There are times when the client system needs to be confronted with awareness of a discrepancy.
11. **Counselor**   The role of the counselor generally includes listening, acting as a sounding board, and raising awareness of alternatives. It is a nondirective effort in helping the client think through issues.
12. **Advisor**   The advisor role differs from the counselor role in being more directive about what the client might do and how to do it.
13. **Observer**   The observer comments on the things that exist and how things are being done.
14. **Data collector**   The data collector gathers information about what exists and how things are being done.
15. **Analyzer**   The analyzer interprets the meaning of data found in the system.
16. **Diagnoser**   The diagnoser uses analyses, data, and observations in determining why things happen the way they do in the system.
17. **Designer**   The designer develops action strategies, training programs, and management models for use by the system.
18. **Manager**   The manager takes charge of the development process by ordering events to achieve accountability.
19. **Evaluator**   The evaluator serves to feed back information that will make the system more effective in its task.

These roles, and others, are all legitimate leadership actions given the correct conditions and needs of followers (see Figure 6.4).

Recurring Leadership Tasks

The tasks of curriculum leadership, like roles, are numerous. The exact tasks required to be a leader vary from organization to organization and work situation to work situation. However, some eight generic tasks are found in most curriculum leadership opportunities.

1. **Developing an operating theory**   Leaders must be able to conceptualize tasks and communicate the approach to those tasks to others in the organization. The pattern of task identification and response forms the basis of an operating theory.
2. **Developing organization and a work environment**   Curriculum tasks are often nonpermanent responses to needs. In such cases, the way in which people, resources, and ideas are organized is left to the leader. An important task is to structure an organization and work environment that can respond to those needs.
3. **Setting standards**   Because curriculum problems often involve diverse groups of individuals with different needs and perceptions, an important task for a curriculum leader is to set standards and other expectations that

FIGURE 6.4   Various Styles of Leading Work under Various Conditions

will affect the resolution of problems. Such standards may include work habits, communication procedures, time limitations, or a host of related planning areas.

4. **Using authority to establish an organizational climate**   Persons assigned to leadership positions generally are able to structure organizations by suggesting changes and initiating policies. One of the most important tasks for a curriculum leader is using such authority to estab-

lish a desirable work climate. Such a climate, discussed later in this chapter, is made up of the collective perceptions of persons affected by the structure of the organization.

5. **Establishing effective interpersonal relations**   Because leadership is a product of human exchanges or transactions within organizations, it is essential that interpersonal relationships contribute to the attainment of desired ends. The way in which a curriculum leader interacts with others in the organization can assist in the establishment of a pattern of effective interpersonal relationships.

6. **Planning and initiating action**   The curriculum leader is sometimes the only person with the authority to plan and initiate actions. Deciding when and how to initiate action is a strong leadership activity. Failure to lead planning or initiate action can undermine other leadership functions.

7. **Keeping communication channels open and functioning**   Many times, the curriculum leader is in a unique position of being able to communicate with others in an organization when lateral and horizontal communication is limited for most members. The leader can use his or her position to facilitate the matching of persons who need to communicate with one another. The leader can also make changes in communication patterns, where necessary, to ensure that such communication channels are functioning.

8. **Assessing achievement**   Periodically, every leader must ask, "Are we accomplishing what we intend to achieve in this organization?" The establishment of structure to evaluate and assess progress is a recurring task of leadership. These tasks, in combinations, are used to promote planned change for improving curriculum in schools.

CHANGE AS A FUNCTION OF CURRICULUM IMPROVEMENT

Curriculum improvement is almost always a case of curriculum change. For this reason, persons preparing for positions of leadership in curriculum should have a clear understanding of the change process in educational environments. There are a number of pressing questions in the area of change that need to be addressed. Among these are the following:

☐   What causes a school to change?
☐   Why do innovations nearly always fail in some schools?
☐   Why do some schools never attempt to make changes?
☐   What factors are significant in making a school either a high risk or a low risk for an innovation attempt?
☐   What is the profile of an innovative school?

The answers to such questions as these will not come easily because change in school environments is a highly complex process with an interplay of many multifaceted variables (for a complete set of generalizations about the diffusion of innovations, see Rogers and Shoemaker,[15] Appendix A). Still, a review of existing literature on change as it interacts with educational environments can greatly increase understanding and make curriculum leaders more effective on the job. The study of change in schools, although not new, is being pursued vigorously by researchers.

Part of the difficulty in understanding change in school settings results from the sheer volume of data and the constant nature of change in education. To clarify the topic, several key "lenses" for viewing change are presented here.

Types of Change

Change is not synonymous with innovation. According to Matthew Miles, change is "any alteration in someone or something."[16] An innovation, by contrast, has unique qualities such as novelty or deliberateness. It is the specific application of change that distinguishes an innovation from random changes going on about us at all times. Educators are concerned with change that is purposeful in improving schools.

Warren Bennis presents seven types of change commonly found in formal organizations such as schools:[17]

1. Planned change
2. Indoctrination
3. Coercive change
4. Technocratic change
5. Interactional change
6. Cumulative change
7. Natural change

Models of Change

The literature on change contains numerous models that view the process from a variety of perspectives. Among some of the most interesting to educational planners are those institutional models that reveal how other areas of society approach the concept of planned change. Here are four stereotypic models from other institutions:

1. **Agriculture**   Uses a *change agent* approach by having county agents go into the field to demonstrate new techniques of farming.
2. **Medical**   Uses *action research* in approaching change. The diffusion of medical change proceeds from clinical research to development to dissemination.
3. **Business**   Uses the *incentive approach* of rewards to encourage change. In organizations, sometimes this approach is used to pull persons toward change.
4. **Military**   Uses *authority* to enforce change. This is a pushing strategy.

The emphasis in change models that appears to have captured the greatest concern and attention in education has been the process approach. The tremendous advances that the application of systems concepts has produced in science and technology are now being employed in education with promising results. (See Chapter 5, *Curriculum Management Planning.*)

Kurt Lewin is generally acknowledged to be the intellectual forebearer of process models in change. His three-step change model has become a classic.[18] The process basically involves

1. Unfreezing an old pattern
2. Changing to a new one
3. Refreezing the new pattern

Lewin's model is based on the notion of the opposing forces that create varying amounts of pressure on situations. When forces are equal, the situation does not change. However, by the addition or subtraction of forces, the pressure becomes unequal, and change occurs.

Another popular model is one that conceptualizes the change process in terms of five stages leading to adoption.[19]

1. Awareness
2. Interest
3. Evaluation
4. Trial
5. Adoption

Still another approach to the change process has been offered by R. Lippitt, J. Watson, and B. Wesley in their pioneer work, *The Dynamics of Planned Change.* They focus on the relationship between the change agent and the client system and identify the following seven stages:[20]

1. Development of a need for change
2. Establishment of a change relationship
3. Diagnosis of the client system's problem
4. Examination of goals and alternative routes of action
5. Transformation of intentions into action
6. Generalization and stabilization of change
7. Achievement of a terminal relationship

Strategies of Change

Another area receiving considerable study are the strategies employed to bring about change. Chin has offered a three-part typology for such strategies:[21]

1. A rational approach that would include reading and information gathering
2. A coercive approach where change is forced by power or authority
3. A normative approach where an individual's value code is reconstructed because of new understandings or experiences.

These strategies are interesting to consider. In the first strategy, it is assumed that people are rational and that they will follow their rational self-interests once revealed to them. In education, for instance, teachers would change their classroom behaviors once they studied what research says about teaching. In the second strategy, rationality is not denied, but there is acknowledgment of a organizational influence that may require "push and shove" to achieve directionality. The third strategy, which certainly is the most time consuming, sees social-cultural phenomena in that environment and may use group work extensively to help individuals reconsider their posture on questions of change.

Barriers to Change

The barriers to change that are set forth in the literature are innumerable. Many authors, telescoping particular segments of the process, have identified countless barriers that impede change. Further, such barriers are described with varying amounts of specificity. Most common in the literature are lists of the potential barriers that affect educational change.

Such lists give an overview of the barriers. Here are eight barriers as compiled by W. A. McClelland:[22]

1. Despite rapid social change, forces favoring the status quo in education remain strong as ever.
2. There are no precise goals for educational institutions.
3. There is no established systematic approach in the educational process.
4. Teacher education programs have failed to develop the skills and knowledge needed for innovations.
5. Teachers have failed to develop in themselves the habits of scholarship necessary to stay abreast of the knowledge explosion.
6. Evaluation and revision based on feedback are absent in educational institutions.
7. Many educators are reticent, suspicious, and fearful of change.
8. Complex management and funding problems always cost more than simple divisible problems.

Rogers depicts the barriers in this manner:[23]

1. There is no profit motive for being an innovator in education.
2. There is no corps of change agents in education comparable to extension agents in agriculture.
3. Educational innovations are less clear-cut in their advantage over the existing ideas that they are to replace.
4. Innovation decisions in education may not be an individual matter, and the norms, statuses, and formal structure of the systems affect the process of diffusion.

Even though there are many barriers to change in schools, such resistance may have a functional effect. D. Klein,[24] for instance, notes that resistance

1. Protects the organization against random change, which may be harmful;
2. Protects the system from take-over by vested interests; and
3. May ensure that unanticipated consequences of a change be spelled out and thus possibly avoided.

PROMOTION OF PLANNED CHANGE

One of the first realities that must be acknowledged by a curriculum leader is that change is often a political process. It is this political activity that activates the variables in an educational community. If there were no planning and maneuvering within school districts, there would be no change. According to L. Iannaccone and F. Lutz, " . . . politics is recognized as probably the single most important question in determining the course, present and future, of American education."[25] Rather than being perceived as evil or undemocratic, the use of political influence can be seen as a means of altering the rate of change in school settings. Educators who seek the support of those interest groups that coincide in social intent with the school can legitimately do so in the name of better programs of education for children. Intellectual choices in planning are, inevitably, social choices with political implications.

The second important idea related to change in schools is that resistance to change is not unnatural. Individuals strive to bring order to their world, and most change involves the realignment of roles and relationships. In the words of Warren Bennis:

> Change will be resisted to the degree that the target has little information or knowledge of the change, has little trust in the source of change, and has little influence in controlling the nature and direction of the change.[26]

A third idea about change in school environments, which is supported by case studies, is that change is not an isolated event. Change in any complex organization involves interrelated events.

An awareness of the political dimensions of change, the natural tendency of individuals to resist change, and the awareness of change as a continuing process suggest that desired change is not a haphazard process but one that is the result of a concerted effort to influence the educational environment. Such influence is most effective when the curriculum leader possesses the concept of the change environment and an organizational structure.

While directing a project concerning the analysis of planned change in Florida schools, one of us attempted to develop such a concept in terms of the potential of innovation targets. The result of this effort was a probability chart, shown in Table 6.1, that roughly indicates the degree of readiness for innovation within a school. This construct has proven useful as a way of looking at change in schools.

Curriculum leaders need a structure for promoting planned alternations of the school environment. As Miles has observed:

TABLE 6.1 Educational Innovations Probability Chart

	Higher Risk ◄				► Lower Risk
Source of Innovation	Superimposed from outside	Outside agent brought in	Developed internally with aid	External idea modified	Locally conceived, developed, implemented
Impact of Innovation	Challenges sacrosanct beliefs	Calls for major value shifts	Requires substantial change	Modifies existing values or programs	Does not substantially alter existing values, beliefs, or programs
Official Support	Active opposition by official leaders	Officials on record as opposing	Officials uncommitted	Officials voice support of change	Enthusiastically supported by the official leaders
Planning of Innovation	Completely external	Most planning external	Planning processes balanced	Most of planning done locally	All planning for change done on local site
Means of Adoption	By superiors	By local leaders	By reps	By most of the clients	By group consensus
History of Change	History of failures	No accurate records	Some success with innovation	A history of successful innovations	Known as school where things regularly succeed
Possibility of Revision	No turning back	Final evaluation before committee	Periodic evaluations	Possible to abandon at conclusion	Possible to abort the effort at any time
Role of teachers	Largely bypassed	Minor role	Regular role in implementing	Heavy role in implementation	Primary actor in the classroom effort
Teacher Expectation	Fatalistic	Feel little chance	Willing to give a try	Confident of success	Wildly enthusiastic about chance of success
Work Load Measure	Substantially increased	Heavier but rewarding	Slightly increased	Unchanged	Work load lessened by the innovation
Threat Measure	Definitely threatens some clients	Probably threatening to some	Mild threat resulting from the change	Very remote threat to some	Does not threaten the security or autonomy
Community Factor	Hostile to innovations	Suspicious and uninformed	Indifferent	Ready for a change	Wholeheartedly supports the school

Source: Adapted from *Planning Guidelines for Middle School Education*, p. 13, by Jon Wiles. Copyright © 1976 by Kendall/Hunt Publishing Company, Dubuque, IA. Used by permission.

This review of innovative processes shows clearly that innovative attitudes are not enough. Structures which permit design, adaptation, evaluation, trial, and routinization of innovations are essential. Without them, innovative motivation simply leads to "dithering" quasi-random perturbations of practice.[27]

The long-term goal of any immediate change effort is to construct an institution that becomes capable of updating or renewing itself as the environment changes. What is needed is the complex interweaving of continuity and change. Such a task is the central theme of John Gardner's book, *Self-Renewal*:

Over the centuries the classic question of social reform has been, "How can we cure this or that specific ill?" Now we must ask another kind of question. "How can we design a system that will continuously reform (renew) itself, beginning with presently specifiable ills and moving on to ills that we cannot now foresee?"[28]

LEADING CURRICULUM CHANGE

In schools, owing to the open nature of the organization, curriculum development is basically a process in which organization members interact to produce improved school programs. Although curriculum *planning* can produce philosophy statements, goals, objectives, syllabi, and evaluation guidelines, curriculum *implementation* usually requires face-to-face interaction. Leading curriculum improvement in a human organization such as a school calls for thoughtful and well-planned change; understanding the interpersonal dimension of leadership is essential.

Earlier in this chapter, real leadership was shown to be a transactional process. School leaders must somehow "link" the needs of individuals with the tasks of the organization; while doing so, there is a dependence on those being led. An executive decision is only a moment in the total process of the solution of the problem. It is the final statement of policy that the official leader is asked to administer. The solution begins with a clear definition of the problem, involves analysis of the factors of the situation, is based on procedure formulated by the group, is stated as an official decision, and is implemented by activities agreed on by the group members as their responsibility in carrying out the decision.[29]

With this statement in mind, it is possible to view the dependence of the curriculum leader in each of the basic steps, as shown in Figure 6.5. Because of this dependence and the effect of interaction on the quality of the curriculum development process, curriculum leaders can benefit from an analysis of various interpersonal factors.

Interpersonal relationships in school environments can be thought of as having the following six levels:

FIGURE 6.5 Dependence of the Curriculum Leader

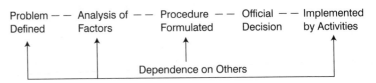

1. **Individual** A personality system that is made up of many parts organized to enable the individual to respond to both internal and external conditions
2. **Dyad** A social unit of two individuals who develop patterns of response to each other as well as response to other levels of the human system
3. **Group** A small social system of individuals with a fairly well-defined purpose, able to respond to itself and to external conditions
4. **Organization** A social unit of individuals with clearly defined and specialized functions requiring a disciplined and systematic relationship among members, able to respond to internal needs and external conditions
5. **Community** A social unit composed of a large number of individuals who form a variety of interacting subparts that are likely to respond more frequently to situations internal to the unit
6. **Society** A social unit including all previous levels interacting, related by some common norms of political, economic, and cultural coordination that together form an observable identity

At each of these levels, the curriculum specialist is interacting to facilitate the development of school programs. Such interaction is carried out through the following standard development functions:

Human Systems	**Functions**	**Interactions**
Individuals	Diagnosing	Perceiving
Dyads	Deciding	Valuing
Groups	Planning	Communicating
Organizations	Managing	Influencing
Communities	Producing	Cooperating
Society	Evaluating	Belonging

Understanding the exact relationship of interaction in curriculum development functions, human systems, and interpersonal relations is aided by a study of communication in organizations, individual personality theory, small group work, and group leadership.

COMMUNICATION IN ORGANIZATIONS

Communication among individuals in organizations is a delicate art requiring, among other things, self-discipline and a cooperative spirit. Spoken English is a complex language full of subtleties. Superimposed on these language patterns is a host of nonverbal clues that can alter the meaning of speech. Add to these dimensions an environmental context, and the result is a communication system that operates at varying levels of effectiveness.

Various social sciences have developed entire languages to describe the intricacies of communication in the American culture. Charles Galloway has provided a model of foci in three such social sciences:[30]

Anthropology	**Sociology**	**Psychology**
Cultural behaviors	Role behaviors	Personal behaviors
Acculturation	Interaction	Personality
Implicit meanings	Empathetic meanings	Inferred meanings

Collectively, social science inquiry in the area of interpersonal communication has added immeasurably to our understanding of this complex and important dimension of curriculum improvement.

In any pattern of communication among humans, there are at least the following nine elements:[31]

1. What the speaker wants to say
2. What the speaker wants to conceal
3. What the speaker reveals without knowing it
4. What the listener wants or expects to hear
5. What the listener's perception of the speaker will let him or her hear
6. What the listener's experiences tell him or her the words mean
7. What the listener wants to conceal
8. What the emotional climate of the situation permits the persons to share
9. What the physical structure of the situation permits the persons to share

Various models have shown communication to be a process of encoding and decoding. A source encodes a message and tries to transmit it to a receiver who tries to receive it and decode the message. Such a transmission between sender and receiver is often distorted by various barriers to communication and by defensive behaviors. J. R. Gibb has defined such communication defense:

> Defensive behavior is defined as that behavior which occurs when an individual perceives a threat or anticipates threat in the group. The person who behaves defensively, even though he gives some attention to the common task, devotes an appreciable portion of his energy to defending himself. Besides talking about the topic, he thinks about how he appears to others, how he can be seen more favorably, how he may win, dominate, impress, or escape punishment, and/or how he may avoid or mitigate a perceived or an anticipated attack.[32]

D. Berlo, in a study of human communication, has identified the following four major predictions of faulty communication that can be used by curriculum leaders to anticipate possible communication breakdown:[33]

1. The amount of competition that messages have
2. The threats to status and ego that are involved
3. The uncertainty and error in what is expected
4. The number of links in the communication chain

Other barriers to effective communication among people might include any of the following:

☐ People use words and symbols that have differing meanings.
☐ People have different perceptions of problems being discussed.
☐ Members of communication groups possess different values.
☐ People bring to discussions varying levels of feeling or affect.
☐ Words are sometimes used to prevent real thinking.
☐ A lack of acceptance of diverse opinion is present in some communication.
☐ Vested interests can interfere with genuine communication.
☐ Feelings of personal insecurity can distort communication.
☐ Tendencies to make premature evaluations are a barrier to communication.
☐ Negative feelings about situations block effective communication.

GROUPS

Group Work

Although relationships exist at the dyad, organizational, community, and societal levels, most curriculum development work proceeds at the group level. For this reason, curriculum leaders need to be particularly attentive to group work as a means of promoting better school programs.

Groups can generally be described as two or more people who possess a common objective. As groups interact in pursuit of an objective, their behavior is affected by a number of variables, such as the background of the group, participation patterns, communication patterns, the cohesiveness of the group, the goals of the group, standards affecting the group, procedures affecting the group, and the atmosphere, or climate, surrounding the group.

Groups perform various tasks that are important to the development of school programs. Among these group tasks are

☐ **Initiating activities**   Suggesting new ideas, defining problems, proposing solutions, reorganizing materials
☐ **Coordinating**   Showing relationships among various ideas or suggestions, pulling ideas together, relating activities of various subgroups
☐ **Summarizing**   Pulling together related data, restating suggestions after discussion
☐ **Testing feasibility**   Examining the practicality or feasibility of ideas, making reevaluation decisions about activities

Group work in educational environments is often ineffective because of various types of nonfunctional behaviors. Leaders should be aware of some of the more common forms of nonfunctional actions:

☐ **Being aggressive**   Showing hostility against the group or some individual, criticizing or blaming others, deflating the status of others
☐ **Blocking**   Interfering with group process by speaking tangentially, citing personal experiences unrelated to the problem, rejecting ideas without consideration

- □ **Competing**   Vying with others to talk most often, produce the best idea, gain favor of the leader
- □ **Special pleading**   Introducing ideas or suggestions that relate to one's own concerns
- □ **Seeking recognition**   Calling attention to oneself by excessive talking, extreme ideas, or unusual behavior.
- □ **Withdrawing**   Being indifferent or passive, daydreaming, doodling, whispering to others, physically leaving the discussion

As a group leader, the curriculum specialist should be able to differentiate between those roles and actions that contribute to group effectiveness and those roles that are basically negative and do not contribute to the effectiveness of the group. Any of the following behaviors by a group member can be thought of as productive and contributing to group effectiveness:

- □ Brings the discussion back to the point
- □ Seeks clarification of meaning when ideas expressed are not clear
- □ Questions and evaluates ideas expressed in objective manner
- □ Challenges reasoning when the soundness of logic is doubtful
- □ Introduces a new way of thinking about topic
- □ Makes a summary of points
- □ Underscores points of agreement or disagreement
- □ Tries to resolve conflict or differences of opinion
- □ Introduces facts or relevant information
- □ Evaluates progress of the group

Roles demonstrated by a group member that can be thought of as negative or nonproductive include the following:

- □ Aggressively expresses disapproval of ideas of others
- □ Attacks the group or the ideas under consideration
- □ Attempts to reintroduce idea after it has been rejected
- □ Tries to assert authority by demanding
- □ Introduces information that is obviously irrelevant
- □ Tries to invoke sympathy by depreciation of self
- □ Uses stereotypes to cover own biases and prejudices
- □ Downgrades the importance of group's role or function

Sensitivity to such roles allows the group leader to analyze the flow of group work and head off potential distraction to group progress.

Leadership of Groups

While working with groups, the curriculum leader does not have to restrict his or her role to that of passive observer. It is possible to encourage greater group productivity actively (see Figure 6.6). In any group discussion, there at least six tasks that the leader must assume to lead the group toward accomplishment of its objectives. These areas are

1. Presenting topic
2. Initiating the discussion
3. Guiding the discussion
4. Controlling the discussion
5. Preventing side-tracking
6. Summarizing the discussion

In presenting the topic to be discussed, the leader should suggest the importance of the problem, place the general purpose of the discussion before the group, suggest a logical pathway for the discussion to follow, and define any ambiguous terms to remove misunderstanding. It is useful, where possible, to relate the current discussion to previous meetings or other convenient reference points.

If a group is to be productive, the individuals in question must first become a group in a psychological sense through acquiring the feeling of group belongingness which can come only from a central purpose which they all accept.

If a group is to be productive, its members must have a common definition of the undertaking in which they are to engage.

If a group is to be productive, it must have a task of some real consequence to perform.

If a group is to be productive, its members must feel that something will actually come of what they are expected to do; said differently, its members must not feel that what they are asked to do is simply busywork.

If a group is to be productive, the dissatisfaction of its members with the aspect of the status quo to which the group's undertaking relates must outweigh in their minds whatever threats to their comfort they perceive in the performance of this undertaking.

If a group is to be productive, its members must not be expected or required to attempt undertakings which are beyond their respective capabilities or which are so easy for the individuals in question to perform that they feel no sense of real accomplishment.

If a group is to be productive, decisions as to work planning, assignment, and scheduling must be made, whenever possible, on a shared basis within the group, and through the method of consensus rather than of majority vote; in instances in which these decisions either have already been made by exterior authority or in which they must be made by the group leader alone, the basis for the decisions made must be clearly explained to all members of the group.

If a group is to be productive, each member of the group must clearly understand what he or she is expected to do and why, accept the role, and feel responsible to the group for its accomplishment.

FIGURE 6.6   Productivity in Group Work

If a group is to be productive, its members must communicate in a common language.

If a group is to be productive, its members must be guided by task-pertinent values which they share in common.

If a group is to be productive, it is usually necessary for its members to be in frequent face-to-face association with one another.

If a group is to be productive, its members must have a common (although not necessarily talked-about) agreement as to their respective statuses within the group.

If a group is to be productive, each of its members must gain a feeling of individual importance from his or her personal contributions in performing the work of the group.

If a group is to be productive, the distribution of credit for its accomplishments must be seen as equitable by its members.

If a group is to be productive, it must keep on the beam and not spend time on inconsequential or irrelevant matters.

If a group is to be productive, the way it goes about its work must be seen by its members as contributing to the fulfillment of their respective issue and social–psychological needs, and, by extension, of those of their dependents (if any) as well.

If a group is to be productive, the status leader must make the actual leadership group-centered, with the leadership role passing freely from member to member.

If a group is to be productive, the task it is to perform must be consistent with the purposes of the other groups to which its members belong.

If a group is to be productive, the satisfactions that its members expect to experience from accomplishing the group's task must outweigh in their minds the satisfactions they gain from their membership in the group *per se*.

FIGURE 6.6   *(Continued)*

In initiating the discussion, the leader provides advanced thinking for the group. Major questions to be answered are identified, and relevant facts and figures are cited. A case in point may be drawn for purposes of illustration. In some instances, it may even be useful purposefully to misstate a position to provoke discussion.

The leader's job in guiding involves keeping the discussion goal-directed, assisting members in expressing themselves through feedback, and providing the transition from one aspect of the discussion to another. In fulfilling this role, the leader may use direct questions, stories, illustrations, or leading questions to maintain the flow of interaction.

In controlling the discussion, the leader is concerned with the pace of progress and the involvement of the participants. Among techniques that can be used to keep discussion moving are purposeful negative statements, drawing contrasts between positions of participants, and regularly calling attention to the time remaining.

The discussion leader in a small group can deal with side-tracking in a number of ways: restating the original question or problems, securing a statement from a reliable group member to head off a rambler, or requesting that side issues be postponed until main issues are settled.

Finally, the leader summarizes the discussion. This involves knowing when to terminate discussion and reviewing the high points that have been addressed.

Three situations, in particular, are troublesome to persons new to leading discussions in small groups: the dead silence, the overtalkative member, and the silent member. Any of these three conditions can sabotage an otherwise fruitful discussion period.

The most anxiety-producing situation is one in which there is a complete absence of participation, resulting in an awkward silence among group members. The natural response in such a situation is to speak to fill the conversational vacuum, but the leader must do just the opposite. Silence in discussions sometimes means that real thinking is occurring, and this assumption must be made by the leader. Another common impulse is to seek out a member of the group and prod him or her for a contribution. Such a tactic will surely contribute to less participation. When the silence period is convincingly unproductive, the leader should try an encouraging remark such as, "There must be some different points of view here." Failing response, the leader should turn to the process involved with a comment such as, "Let's see if we can discover what's blocking us."

Another situation that can ruin a group discussion is an overtalkative member. Such a person, if permitted, will monopolize discussion and produce anxiety among group members. The best strategy in such a situation is to intervene after a respectful period of time with a comment such as, "Perhaps we can hear from other members of the group." In the event that the dominating member still doesn't get the message, the leader can initiate an evaluation of the process and stress that a way must be found to gain input from all members.

A final situation that can be awkward occurs when a member of the group is regularly silent. The leader should recognize that some persons are fearful of being put on the spot and will resent being spotlighted. The leader can, however, observe the silent member and look for signals that he or she is ready to participate. If the member seems to be on the verge of speaking, an encouraging glance or nod may be all that is needed.

In cases where the leader becomes convinced that a member's silence is the result of boredom or withdrawal, it may be useful to confront the member away from other group members with a provocative or challenging question. Whether a member should be forced into a discussion, and whether such an act is productive for the entire group, is a matter of judgment and discretion.

Leaders of small groups should regularly evaluate their own performance following a discussion by asking themselves a series of questions such as the following:

- ☐ Did members contribute to the discussion?
- ☐ Did some people do more talking than others?
- ☐ Are the most talkative persons sitting together? The silent ones?
- ☐ Do members talk mostly to the leader or to each other?
- ☐ Was there evidence of cliques or interest groups in the discussion?

Group leaders can sometimes retard creative thinking by regulating discussions in nonproductive ways. Among the most common errors in this respect are

☐ A preoccupation with order throughout the discussion
☐ Stressing hard evidence or factual information too often
☐ Placing too much emphasis on history or the way things have been done
☐ Using coercive techniques to ensure participation
☐ Suggesting that mistakes are not acceptable

Two useful skills for all small-group leaders are paraphrasing and brainstorming. In paraphrasing, leaders attempt to restate the point of view of another to their satisfaction prior to continuing discussion. This technique is especially useful in argumentative situations and often sets a pattern that is followed by other group members.

In brainstorming, leaders introduce a technique that frees the group discussion from previous barriers to speaking. Here the leaders set ground rules, which include the following: no criticism of others is allowed, the combining of ideas is encouraged, quality ideas are sought, wild ideas are encouraged. In introducing a brainstorming session, the leader hopes to have members "spark" each other and have an idea "hitchhike" upon another. Brainstorming, as a technique, is recommended when discussions continually cover familiar ground, and little or no progress toward a solution to problems is forthcoming.

Finally, leaders of small groups should work to become better listeners. Numerous studies have identified poor listening skills as the biggest block to personal communication. Ralph Nicholas has identified ten steps to better listening:[34]

1. While listening, concentrate on finding areas of interest that are useful to you.
2. Judge the content of what is said rather than the delivery.
3. Postpone early judgment about what is being said. Such a posture will allow you to remain analytical if you favor what is being said or to keep from being distracted by calculating embarrassing questions should you disagree with the speaker's message.
4. Focus on the central ideas proposed by the speaker. What is the central idea? What are the supporting "planks" or statements?
5. Remain flexible in listening. Think of various ways to remember what is being said.
6. Work hard at listening. Try to direct all conscious attention on the presentation being made.
7. Resist distractions in the environment by making adjustments or by greater concentration.
8. Exercise your mind by regularly listening to technical expository material with which you haven't had experience.
9. Keep your mind open to new ideas by being aware of your own biases and limited experiences.
10. Capitalize on thought speed. Since comprehension speed exceeds speaking speed by about 3:1, the listener must work to concentrate. This can be

done by anticipating what is to be said, by making mental summaries, by weighing speaker evidence, and by listening between the lines.

LEADERSHIP APPROACHES FOR CURRICULUM LEADERS

Clearly, educational environments call for special leadership styles and approaches to promote positive curricular change. At the building level, in particular, an interactive and personal approach to leadership is needed. Two comprehensive approaches to leading change that have emerged in the past twenty years—organizational development and climate engineering—are worthy of study. Within organizational development, two theories have developed: systems and motivation.

Organizational Development: Systems

Systems theory, a product of the physical sciences, provides the concept of interdependence in organizations and explains how one part of an organization affects the other parts or whole of the organization. A system is simply a grouping of objects that are treated as a unit. From an educational viewpoint, systems approaches allow leaders to see a school or school district holistically. Relationships, in particular, are clarified:

> [The conceptual skill is] the ability to see the organization as a whole; it includes recognizing how . . . the various functions of the organization depend on one another, and how change in any one part affects all the others. Recognizing these relationships and perceiving the significant elements in any situation, the administrator should then be able to act in a way which advances the overall welfare of the organization.[35]

In school settings, a system might be defined as any set of components organized in a manner that constrains actions toward the accomplishment of a goal. Thus, school programs that are established to educate children are comprised of facilities, materials, funds, teachers, testing, and a host of other contributing variables. The real value of a systems perspective for administrators is as a means of identifying noncontributing conditions or bottlenecks in the flow of activity. Once identified, these systems deficiencies can be targeted for redesign. Systems can also help the leading educator build models of preferred conditions for learning.

Perhaps the high-water mark in the study of organization processes is the concept of *organizational development* (OD), a planned and sustained effort to apply behavioral science for systemic improvement.[36]

The process of organizational development consists of data gathering, organizational diagnosis, and action intervention. The fulfillment of an OD program is, in a real sense, changing the school's way of working.

There are three elements of organization that appear particularly important for curricular changes: (1) the roles various people play, (2) the goals of the department or school, and (3) the operational procedures of the organization being studied.

Organizational development is a people-involving approach to systematic planning. The importance of sharing system goals and control by personnel can hardly be overstressed. Without such sharing, personnel will not be committed to the efficacy of systems function, and it becomes correspondingly difficult to motivate action in accordance with systems needs.

Individuals hold membership in groups when they show somehow that they have taken upon themselves those norms, values, beliefs, and so on, that are most cherished by the group. During OD inquiry, long and strongly held organizational norms concerning such things as decision-making patterns, communications networks, work relationships, interpersonal relations, and attitudes about collaboration are revealed. Organizational development traces the contextual fabric of the organization and discovers and modifies the interlocking programs, roles, norms, and procedures.

Generally, the first stage of OD work involves some form of diagnosis of the situation. Data are gathered by some means (questionnaire, interview, observation) and analyzed to determine those aspects of the organization that seem to warrant some corrective action. The hoped-for outcomes are building an understanding of the situation and gaining a commitment for taking some action.

It is important to realize that there are two kinds of leadership roles that seem important in discussions of curricular reform. The first is intellectual leadership, the leadership that provides insight into what is of worth. The second is political leadership, which offers guidance in how to make things happen.

The second major stage of any OD program will involve goal setting and organization for achieving those goals. Techniques that have proven effective in linking individual and organizational goals are (1) capitalizing of teacher autonomy, (2) the use of democratically formed councils, and (3) the idea of decision making by consensus. The first strategy plays heavily on the professional competence and conscience of the teacher. The second strategy seeks to move the decision-making apparatus closer to the source of information. The third strategy realigns responsibility and, to some extent, authority by allowing teachers to "develop" curriculum.

The third stage in an OD program entails implementing changes and establishing reliable self-correction measures to ensure continued self-renewal.

If the process of self-analysis and goal setting succeeds, the goals—assuming the people have been honest in setting them—act as motivators in their own right. People will support the organizational goals because those goals are a composite of individual goals. Rather than seeing the school as an organization in which they teach, teachers come to see the school as an organizational setting within which they channel their contributive efforts.

The fulfillment of the OD program is, in a real sense, changing the way in which a school works. There are three elements of organization (processes) that appear important for changes: (1) the roles that people play, (2) the goals of the organization, and (3) the operational procedures in place. In effect, OD is a people-involving approach to systemic analysis. Through analysis, it is hoped, the members of the organization will become committed to the efficacy of the systems function.

The other keys to the success of the OD methodology of improving institutional process are the commitments to deal with change over an extended period of time and to use some of the resources of the organization to maintain, rebuild, and expand the structure of the organization. OD technology approaches the goal of a self-renewing school.

Organizational Development: Motivation

Research indicates that the success of any form of social influence depends on altering the ability of others to achieve their goals or satisfy their needs. Leaders in the curriculum development process can have increased success if they keep such research in mind.

To exert influence on the process of program development, the leader must have an understanding of the factors that motivate individuals. The works of two social scientists, Abraham Maslow and Frederick Herzberg, provide insight on motivation and point the way to entry into the transactional process.

Maslow theorized that experienced needs are the primary influences on an individual's behavior. When a particular need emerges, it determines the individual's behavior in terms of motivations, priorities, and actions taken.

Maslow placed all human needs into five need systems. He believed that there is a natural process whereby individuals fulfill needs in an ascending order from primitive to sophisticated, and he, therefore, developed a hierarchical model thought common to all persons. According to this model, people ascend upward toward more complex needs only after successfully fulfilling lower-order needs. The needs are, in order of importance: (1) survival, (2) safety, (3) belonging, (4) status, and (5) self-actualization.

The value of the Maslow model for understanding individual motivation in an organization is that it sensitizes leaders to the complexity of motives and provides a rough analytic tool for estimating the type of motivation appropriate for any individual.

A second major contribution to the understanding of human motivation in organizations has been provided by Frederick Herzberg. Herzberg, following on the work of Maslow and others, stressed that the factors that truly motivate workers are those "growth" experiences that give the worker a sense of personal accomplishment through the challenge of the job itself—in the internal dynamics that the worker experiences in completing a task.

Although it is the job itself that provides satisfaction in work, Herzberg also observed that poor environmental (hygiene) factors can be the source of unhappiness and dissatisfaction in work. In the following list, the Herzberg findings give leadership some variables by which to assess an organization and individual patterns of motivation.[37]

Motivation Factors (Job Content) Satisfiers	Hygiene Factors (Job Environment) Dissatisfiers
Work itself	Company policy and administration
Achievement	Supervision
Recognition	Working conditions
Responsibility	Interpersonal relations
Growth, advancement	Salary

Shown side by side, the Maslow and Herzberg conceptions of motivation provide a leader with a new perspective of follower needs (see Figure 6.7).

FIGURE 6.7 Comparison of Concepts of Motivation

Source: From *Human Relations at Work,* p.37, by K. Davis. Copyright © 1967 by McGraw-Hill, New York. Reprinted by permission.

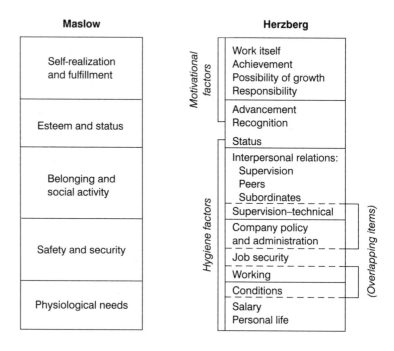

OD approaches school improvement systematically. Another approach—climate engineering—focuses on the individual organization members and their personal motivation. The climate approach culminates fifty years of research on human motivation.

Climate Engineering

The theory behind climate engineering is that if a leader were aware of individual needs, and structured an organization around such needs, "motivation" might be incorporated into the way an organization operated. Specifically, if the leader could selectively apply roles, encourage desired communication patterns, assign tasks, and tailor rewards to the individual needs of the organization members, effective leadership would flourish. It was believed possible for the leader to influence the organization by establishing an environment to control transactions. From these foundations, climate engineering emerged as an approach to leadership.

Research by George Litwin and Robert Stringer shows that the development of a transactional climate can be purposeful activity. In their work, Litwin and Stringer outline a climate theory that consists of the following:

☐ Individuals are attracted to work climates that arouse their dominant needs.
☐ Such on-the-job climates consist of experiences and incentives.
☐ These climates interact with needs to arouse motivation toward need satisfaction.

☐ Climate can mediate between organizational task requirements and individual needs—it is the linkage.

☐ Climates represent the most powerful leverage point available to managers to bring about change.

Leadership can, by its actions, affect the perceptions of individuals in the organization. The collective perceptions of leadership form a climate that influences change in the organization.

In their research, Litwin and Stringer identified nine organizational variables that can be manipulated to influence the climate of an organization.

1. **Structure**   The feelings that employees have about the constraints in the group, how many rules, regulations, procedures there are; is there an emphasis on red tape and going through channels, or is there a loose and informal atmosphere?

2. **Responsibility**   The feeling of being your own boss; not having to double-check all of your decisions; when you have a job to do, knowing that it is your job

3. **Reward**   The feeling of being rewarded for a job well done; emphasizing positive rewards rather than punishments; the perceived fairness of the pay and promotion policies

4. **Risk**   The sense of riskiness and challenge in the job and in the organization; is there an emphasis on taking calculated risks, or is playing it safe the best way to operate?

5. **Warmth**   The feeling of good fellowship that prevails in the work group atmosphere; the emphasis on being well-liked; the prevalence of friendly and informal social groups

6. **Support**   The perceived helpfulness of the managers and other employees in the group; emphasis on mutual support from above and below

7. **Standards**   The perceived importance of implicit and explicit goals and performance standards; the emphasis on doing a good job; the challenge represented in personal and group goals

8. **Conflict**   The feeling that managers and other workers want to hear different opinions; the emphasis placed on getting problems out in the open rather than smoothing them over or ignoring them

9. **Identity**   The feeling that you belong to a company and you are a valuable member of a working team; the importance place on this kind of spirit[38]

Variables such as these allow the leader to make input into the flow of events and influence the perceptions of individuals and groups that make up the organization. To the degree that such input and influence serve organizational members, a successful transaction will be accomplished, and leadership will be strengthened.

Putting the many pieces of leadership theory together, we see that the leader has an active role in curriculum development. A leader must transact, or communicate, with followers in such a way that he or she is recognized as the person with the appropriate skills to help a group satisfy its needs. Most of this transaction is carried out in small-group work. The leader who can analyze individual or small-group needs and highlight those aspects of leadership (goal attainment, warmth, support) that cause him or her to be seen as the leader will be in a position to provide continuing influence. A process of maintaining this leadership, such as organizational development methodology, follows, and the sum of the leader's actions can be considered his or her style of leading.

ISSUES IN CURRICULAR LEADERSHIP

Although there are many leadership styles that are situationally appropriate for bringing about purposeful change to improve schools, some issues exist that may affect these approaches. We do not expect you to gain closure on these questions in the near future, but the issues do illustrate how curriculum development is ultimately a normative experience.

School Mission

Americans differ greatly in their opinions about the purpose of schools. Although specific arguments may revolve around buzzwords such as *basics* or *open education,* the issues underlying these concerns are foundational. Historically, schools in the United States adopted an educational pattern found in Europe in the sixteenth century—a system of education based on the mastery of specific content. By the nineteenth century, a different conception of educating was borrowed from Europe—a child-centered program drawing its rationale from the needs of growing children. Both of these threads of educating have been preserved in the American system and exist in schools of the 1990s.

An important philosophical question underlying the design of school curriculums, however, is whether the intention of the program (the **mission statement)** is to round out the student so that all graduates possess common knowledge and attributes, or whether the schooling experience should accentuate the uniqueness of the individual in an effort to gain the full potential of the student for society. This issue of the school's mission is best seen in the competition between goals of the school—learning competencies and graduation requirements on the one hand, efforts to serve special students and find unique characteristics (gifted, talented, special education) on the other.

Both of these ends are worthy, but a school must be organized in different ways to accomplish these different ends. To encourage sameness and uniformity of the graduate, the school has to employ high degrees of structure so that students experience a near-alike program. To encourage uniqueness, flexibility must be encouraged so that each student could have the freedom to develop to his or her capacity, whatever that capacity is. Arguments over course materials, teaching methods, building designs, and so on, spring from this key difference in the intention of the program. Curriculum leaders need to understand which purposes are seen as dominant to them as educators because they have an unusual degree of control over these variables.

Scope of Responsibility

An issue that separates many curriculum leaders is the scope of their responsibility on the job. Few job descriptions are meant to be comprehensive or restrictive in nature, and the residual dimensions of school leadership provide curriculum specialists with many choices beyond what is identified as their responsibility. Examples of such choices are whether they are obligated to help a teacher who is having personal problems outside of school, whether they are obligated to provide a quality school program for students who are beyond the benefit of the current offerings, and whether they should engineer change in the schools by leading the community toward novel programs and practices.

Exactly what constitutes the job of a curriculum leader, indeed what is meant by the term *curriculum* itself, will be decided by the person filling the position. The definition of what is curriculum will, of course, reflect a larger definition of the purpose of schooling.

Leadership Focus

The curriculum leader, clearly, has significant influence over how educational programs are organized and operate. By the control of task focus, communications, resource allocation, and evaluation, the curriculum leader sets a tone for the organization and channels its activities.

One of the great differences among schools evolves from whether the leader defines his or her leadership as tractive or dynamic in its orientation.

The terms *tractive* and *dynamic* were suggested by Ben Harris to differentiate between a leadership style that preserves and a leadership style that changes an organization. Tractive leaders gear their activities toward continuity, maintenance, and support of existing conditions. Dynamic leaders, by contrast, pursue activities designed to foster change, promoting discontinuity and the substitution of new practices for old.[39]

A balance between reinforcing activities and change-oriented activities is logical, but school environments are characterized by constantly shifting pressures that encourage imbalances and instability. For school leaders to know, then, whether they are attempting to retain an existing pattern of operation or directing these ever-present pressures toward a new pattern of operation is important. Without such vision, leadership may be characterized as random or incongruous.

A corresponding subissue related to tractive or dynamic leadership is the curriculum leader's definition of *professionalism*. Is professionalism the application of skills in operating a school or school district in an optimal fashion (engineer), or is professionalism the act of directing school operations toward an optimal form based on special knowledge (architect)? Each curriculum leader must decide the answers to these questions.

Public Involvement

One of the issues that commonly separates school leaders is whether the public should be fully involved in the operation of schools. Reason would seem to prevail on a case-by-case basis, but the involvement or noninvolvement of citizens actually constitutes an entire strategy for survival of administrators in some cases.

For instance, assessments of need in many districts are conducted to gain information useful in making decisions about school programs. Whether the public should be involved in the gathering and analysis of such information, and whether the public should be involved in the actual decision making resulting from that analysis, are issues. On the one hand, there is the argument that the public sponsors the schools with their tax dollars and entrusts their children to the educational programs of the school. By this argument, involvement in decision making is only natural and almost a right of each interested parent. On the other hand, many curriculum leaders feel that there is no clear consensus on many educational issues and that involvement of the public in decision making serves only to polarize the many publics that support the schools. This position draws an analogy to representative government or speaks of professional judgment when declaring that the school administrator has no real obligation or mandate to involve the public in the daily decision making or operation of the school.

In truth, this issue revolves around the concept of trust and the very democratic principles upon which the nation was founded.

Use of Influence

Perhaps one of the most difficult issues for new curriculum leaders is that of dealing with the use of influence. Most curriculum leaders like to think of public school leadership as a democratic process in which they oversee the many competing forces as professionals. In reality, things are not always as simple.

A curriculum leader is a trained professional who is knowledgeable about the fields of education. Such knowledge should mean that the school administrator has knowledge and skills not possessed by the average citizen. The issue of leadership relating to the use of influence arises when the public makes a poor choice from among limited alternatives and the school administrator knows it. At what point does the curriculum leader step in and share professional knowledge or skills even though this information has not been solicited? When does the sharing of knowledge cross over to become manipulation? An honest leader will acknowledge that even the media (how decisions are made, committees formed, and so on) possess a degree of manipulation.

Obviously, to lead a public institution such as a public school, the leader must have a clear conception of democratic principles and their use. It makes a great deal of difference whether the leader sees himself or herself as a controller of events because of position or simply as one more force in a sea of influencing factors around the school.

Moral Integrity

School leaders, unlike leaders in other institutions, carry a special burden that might be termed *moral integrity*. This extra responsibility stems from the value-laden nature of the schooling enterprise and the precious commodity that is the subject of educational influence. Stated bluntly, the public holds a special expectation for the moral integrity of school leaders.

When compared with business or political leaders, educational leaders clearly have a much narrower range of moral latitude in daily decision making and operational procedures. Business executives, for whatever reason, are permitted great discretion in decision making and their methods of operation: after all, business is business! Politicians, too, are able to rationalize behavior under the banner of expedience or the fact that power corrupts. Even physicians and engineers are able to fall back on "professional judgment" when defending their acts or motivation. School administrators can do none of these things. They must be exemplary in behavior, democratic in procedure, and responsive to the publics from which power is drawn.

The crux of the issue is that the school leader is in the business of human potential. Such potential is, by its complex nature, variable. In educational programming, every act that determines how children are to be nurtured is a value judgment. Curriculum leaders-in-training need to be aware of this and should realize that the special expectations for their behavior reflect the specific expectations for this role.

LEADERSHIP IN THE NEW CENTURY

In the 1990s, educational leaders were forced to lead within the parameters of the restructuring or professionalization movement. Restructuring is an active and participatory process that seeks to enhance leadership in schools, professionalize the teaching profession, and invigorate the learning process for students. Major tenets of restructuring include

- ☐ Recognizing that the school is a unit of collaborative decision making
- ☐ Establishing trust and respect among all parties active in school operations
- ☐ Establishing responsible management practices to meet student needs in the best way

Targets for restructuring efforts may include such curriculum concerns as more effective teaching and learning patterns, more effective leadership patterns, redefined professional roles and responsibilities, and more effective use of school resources. In the 1990s, restructuring also included a significantly increased role for parents in schools (see Figure 6.8).

Along with school officials such as the superintendent and principal, the curriculum leader will transition from a traditional authority figure to a leader-as-manager role based on professional knowledge.

SUMMARY

Leadership is a critical function in curriculum improvement and forms the link between theory and practice. Leadership has many conceptions, and research has focused on three stages: (1) traits of leaders, (2) situations of leadership practice, and (3) transactions between leaders and followers. Entering the new century, lead-

FIGURE 6.8 Four Levels of Parental Involvement in Curriculum

Source: Hilda Wiles, P. K. Yonge Laboratory School, Gainesville, Florida.

Low Interest
1. Sign report cards
2. Provide lunch money
3. Transport child to school

Limited Interest
4. Attend scheduled group parent meetings
5. Attend teacher–parent conferences
6. Assist child with homework
7. Furnish cookies (or other items) for class functions

Teacher-Directed Curriculum
8. Assist child with research at home
9. Serve as resource person to child's class
10. Assist as aid or tutor in classroom
11. Share pupil progress through contract folder
12. Assist with field trips

Parent-Assisted Curriculum
13. Plan learning activities for small groups of students
14. Hold parent-led discussion groups with students
15. Evaluate student progress toward goals according to criteria
16. Parent suggests activities at parent group meetings
17. Serve as junior member of teaching team
18. Help evaluate classroom curriculum according to criteria
19. Extend classroom activities by planning home activities
20. Provide teacher with feedback for instructional improvement

ers will have to possess a wide range of behaviors and apply them to situations in such a manner that they are recognized by the followers.

Being recognized as a leader is a matter of style or combination of behaviors. The classic style model is Theory X and Y leadership; refinements of this model are finding applications in a variety of environments in today's schools. An understanding of change, communication, and group work is essential to promote meaningful change in curriculum work.

Systematic change efforts, such as curriculum management planning and organizational development, are promising to transform the change efforts of curriculum development. Climate engineering and a focus on the motivational needs of individuals in organizations also show promise as tools for promoting meaningful change in schools.

In the new century, new roles of curriculum leadership will be needed. Calls for restructuring of schools will continue with new demands of the workplace brought about by the global economy and increased use of technology.

Those who believe the traditional school setting is inadequate to prepare students for the demands of new century are developing charter schools to provide **alternative school** programs. Tougher standards and tests will require schools to improve both the curriculum and the instructional delivery system. Tractive leadership will not suffice in a climate of increased competition and public scrutiny. Dynamic leadership must be provided by curriculum leaders.

Leaders have faced similar challenges in the past as the United States and other countries prepared students for changes in society. We can learn from the lessons of the past, but we also cannot let the past dictate the future.

SUGGESTED LEARNING ACTIVITIES

1. Develop an operational definition of leadership in curriculum development efforts.
2. Think of a leader that you have known and develop a list of those traits and actions that make up his or her leadership style.
3. Outline specific behaviors identified in this chapter that would allow curriculum leaders to be more effective in transactions.

4. Using Litwin and Stringer's categories, outline a plan for affecting the climate of a school involved in curriculum development.

NOTES

1. J. M. Burns, *Leadership* (New York: Harper & Row, 1978).
2. Ralph M. Stogdill, *Handbook of Leadership* (New York: Free Press, 1974).
3. H. L. Smith and L. M. Kreuger, "A Brief Summary of Literature on Leadership," *Monograph* 9, 4 (Bloomington: Indiana University, 1933), pp. 3–80.
4. F. H. Sanford, *Authoritarianism and Leadership* (Philadelphia: Institute for Research in Human Relations, 1952), p. 66.
5. R. M. Stogdill, "Personal Factors Associated with Leadership: A Survey of the Literature," *The Journal of Psychology* 25 (1948): 64.
6. This approach was popularized in the best-selling book, *I'm O.K., You're O.K.,* by Thomas Harris (New York: Harper & Row, 1967).
7. Kimball Wiles and John Lovell, *Supervision for Better Schools,* 4th ed. (Upper Saddle River, NJ: Prentice Hall, 1975), pp. 65–67.
8. K. Lewin, R. Lippitt, and R. White, "Patterns of Aggressive Behavior in Experimentally Created Social Climates," *Journal of Social Psychology* 10 (1939): 271–99.

9. D. Cartwright and A. Zander, eds., *Group Dynamics: Research and Theory,* 2nd ed. (Evanston, IL: Row, Paterson & Co., 1960).
10. D. Katz and R. Kahn, *The Social Psychology of Organizations* (New York: John Wiley & Sons, Inc., 1966).
11. Douglas McGregor, *The Human Side of Enterprise* (New York: McGraw-Hill, 1960).
12. Robert R. Blake and Jane Mouton, *The Managerial Grid* (Houston, TX: Gulf Publishing Company, 1964).
13. McGregor, *The Human Side of Enterprise,* p. vii.
14. Ronald G. Havelock and Associates, Institute for Social Research, University of Michigan.
15. Everett M. Rogers and F. Floyd Shoemaker, *Communication of Innovations: A Cross-Cultural Approach* (New York: Free Press, 1971), p. xvii.
16. Matthew B. Miles, "Educational Innovation: The Nature of the Problem," *Innovations in Education* (New York: Teachers College Press, 1964), p. 21.
17. Warren G. Bennis, *Changing Organizations* (New York: McGraw-Hill, 1966).

18. Kurt Lewin, *Field Theory in Social Science* (New York: Harper-Torch Books, 1951).

19. H. Lionberger, *Adoption of New Ideas and Practices* (Ames, IA: State University Press, 1961) and E. M. Rogers, *Diffusion of Innovations* (New York: Free Press, 1962).

20. R. Lippitt, J. Watson, and B. Wesley, *The Dynamics of Planned Change* (New York: Harcourt, Brace and World, 1958).

21. W. Bennis, K. Benne, and R. Chin, *The Planning of Change* (New York: Holt, Rinehart & Winston, 1969), pp. 34–35.

22. W. A. McClelland, "The Process of Effecting Change" (Washington, DC: George Washington University Human Resources Office, 1968).

23. E. M. Rogers, *Innovations: Research Design and Field Studies* (Columbus, OH: Research Foundation, Ohio State University, 1965). ED 003120.

24. D. Klein, "Some Notes on the Dynamics of Resistance to Change: The Defender's Role," in G. Watson, ed., *Concepts for Social Change* (Washington, DC: COPED, NTL, 1967).

25. L. Iannaccone and F. Lutz, *Politics, Power, and Policy: The Governing of Local School Districts* (Columbus, OH: Merrill, 1970), p. v.

26. Bennis, Benne, and Chin, *The Planning of Change.*

27. Matthew Miles, *The Development of Innovative Climates in Organizations* (Menlo Park, CA: Stanford Research Institute, 1969), p. 7.

28. J. W. Gardner, *Self-Renewal: The Individual and the Innovative Society* (New York: Harper & Row, 1964).

29. Kimball Wiles, *Supervision for Better Schools,* 3rd ed. (Upper Saddle River, NJ: Prentice Hall, 1967), pp. 39–40.

30. Charles Galloway, speech to the Ohio State Association of Student Teaching, Columbus, OH, October, 1968.

31. Wiles, *Supervision for Better Schools*, p. 53.

32. J. R. Gibb, "Defense Level and Influence Potential in Small Groups," in L. Petrullo and B. M. Bass, eds., *Leadership and Interpersonal Behavior* (New York: Holt, Rinehart & Winston, Inc., 1961), p. 66.

33. D. Berlo, "Avoiding Communication Breakdown," BNA Effective Communication film series.

34. Ralph Nicholas, "Listening Is a Ten-Part Skill," in *Managing Yourself,* compiled by the editors of *Nation's Business.*

35. Robert Katz, "Skills of an Effective Administrator," *Harvard Business Review* (January-February, 1955): 35–36.

36. See Richard Schmuck and Matthew Miles, *Organization Development in Schools* (Palo Alto, CA: National Press Books, 1971).

37. Frederick Herzberg, *Work and the Nature of Man* (Cleveland, OH: World Publishing Company, 1966).

38. George H. Litwin and Robert A. Stringer, Jr., *Motivation and Organizational Climate* (Boston: Division of Research, Harvard University, 1968), pp. 81–82.

39. Ben Harris, *Supervisory Behavior in Education* (Upper Saddle River, NJ: Prentice Hall, 1963), pp. 18–19.

BOOKS TO REVIEW

Beame, James, ed. *Toward A Coherent Curriculum.* Alexandria, VA: ASCD, 1995.

Guskey, Thomas, ed. *Communicating Student Learning.* Alexandria, VA: 1996.

Hanson, E. Mark. *Educational Administration and Organizational Behavior,* 4th ed. Boston: Allyn and Bacon, 1996.

McNeil, John. *Curriculum: A Comprehensive Introduction.* New York: Harper Collins, 1996.

Ornstein, Allan, and Linda Behar, eds. *Contemporary Issues in Curriculum.* Boston: Allyn and Bacon, 1995.

Owens, Robert. *Organizational Behavior in Education,* 5th ed. Boston: Allyn and Bacon, 1996.

Tanner, Daniel, and Laurel Tanner. *Curriculum Development: Theory into Practice,* 3d ed. Upper Saddle River, NJ: Merrill/Prentice Hall, 1995.

PART III

CURRICULUM PRACTICES

chapter 7

ELEMENTARY SCHOOL PROGRAMS AND ISSUES

> The period we're living through has been marked by extraordinary challenges that test our determination, our creativity, and our resources. It is a time of transition not only for education, but for all our society. As we move from the Industrial Age of the 20th Century to the Information Age of the 21st, we keep tripping over remnants of the past, old ideas that we have failed to change.[1]

The elementary school of the first decade of the twenty-first century will represent a dramatic change from the conservatism of the previous three decades. Following the experimentation of the 1960s in open space, nongradedness, **team teaching,** and extended enrichment, the decades of the 1970s, 1980s, and 1990s followed with, "Let's get back to the basics."

Fueled by legislation, national concerns about comparisons of U.S. students with those of other countries, and new demands of American workers in a global economy, "basics" were redefined from minimum skills to higher standards, benchmarks, and a more rigorous curriculum. Although the attention was focused on exit skills for high school students to make sure that they were not deficient in basic literacy and mathematic competency, major changes occurred at the elementary level. By the late 1990s, the elementary curriculum in many school districts included

- ☐ Implementation of national standards in reading, writing, and mathematics
- ☐ The use of performance-based assessments with rubrics
- ☐ **Competency-based instruction**

☐   Academic skills placement tests
☐   State standards and frameworks along with assessment items and bench-
      mark tests
☐   Portfolio assessment systems
☐   Aligning the curriculum through a deliberate curriculum approach that is
      designed to teach **essential learning skills** in a systematic and sequential
      manner. (See the description of the Wiles-Bondi Deliberate Curriculum
      Model later in this chapter.)

In addition, some elementary schools have implemented inclusion programs,
"full-service" schools to cope with large numbers of children from single-parent
and poverty households, and continue to deal with increasing cultural diversity and
mobility of parents. Elementary teachers continue to be "all things to all children."
Characterizing those teachers is the statement shown in Figure 7.1, which was
posted in an elementary teachers' area.

The struggle between those who would narrow the elementary curriculum to
testable areas and those who desire a broader school program continues in many
school districts. With many children attending daycare centers years before they

Plans, writes daily notes, prepares weekly progress reports, distributes fluoride,
collects supermarket receipts for free computers, bundles newspapers, collects
soup labels, writes clinic passes, takes a lunch count, collects money for book
orders, collects money for ticket sales, collects money for after-school movies, collects money for pictures, writes a monies collected form, handles cumulative folders, handles science cards, handles reading and math folders, keeps insert cards
current, computes grades and writes report cards by hand, comes up with a positive comment for each child, creates a science fair project, keeps track of "book it"
and writes pizza slips, escorts children wherever they go, takes attendance, ties
shoes, fastens clothes, wipes noses, evaluates the kids in all areas, files papers,
directs programs, cleans, refers kids for programs (Chapter One, MWA, small
group, ESE), delivers textbooks and keeps track of them, conducts head lice
checks, teaches social skills (burping, nose picking . . .), breaks up fights, takes
place of mom or dad for eight hours a day, watches for signs of abuse, lends lunch
money, creates bulletin-board masterpieces, survives class parties and room mothers, remembers birthdays and other special events, has tremendous bladder control, eats lunch in 27 minutes or less, gives up much free time, counsels parents,
works school fairs, sells candy bars, sings the school song, orders materials, buys
hundreds of girl scout cookies, organizes field trips, teaches many levels in one
subject, deals with the same kiddos for eight hours, prepares honor roll list, locates
appropriate clothing, has bus duty, interns, calls parents, prepares perfect attendance lists, quarterly rewards, finds lost articles, attends PTA meetings, laminates
materials, remediates standardized tests, . . . and, of course, teaches.

FIGURE 7.1   Roles of the Elementary School Teacher

enter elementary school, the socialization function of the early grades (children getting to know adults other than parents and children other than siblings) needs updating. Programs need to be designed to help children cope with disruption of home routine and limited parent contact. According to the last census, over one half of mothers of children under the age of two are in the work force, so this trend will continue. The "Ozzie and Harriet" family of the 1950s no longer exists in America.

Millions of new immigrants have dramatically increased the number of non-English-speaking students in public schools. The elementary school is now serving as the great melting pot of the nation as new languages, customs, and cultures are brought to the school. With the great diversity of student populations in our schools, there are those who favor ability grouping and tracking for the gifted. Ability grouping and tracking most often exclude the minority child, the poor child, and the non-English-speaking child.

Additionally, school districts and state legislatures have begun to explore the concept of school choice in which parents have an opportunity to select public school affiliation. By 1997, most states had considered or enacted choice initiatives.

The idea of choice has an appeal because it seems to be more consistent with our democratic commitment and lends itself to the revitalization of schools. However, there are a number of risks involved in the idea and many questions. For example, will school choice

- ☐ Prove culturally divisive?
- ☐ Provide sufficient common learnings?
- ☐ Increase racial isolation?
- ☐ Increase social class isolation?
- ☐ Result in "skimming" and "dumping"?
- ☐ Yield ability grouping or tracking?
- ☐ Harm nonchoice schools?
- ☐ Harm nonchoosers?
- ☐ Harm poor choosers?
- ☐ Undermine the forging of a public?
- ☐ Give way to an undesirable stress on marketing?
- ☐ Yield indifference and inequity as the best programs become overenrolled?
- ☐ Deny parents an operating base?
- ☐ Compromise professional integrity?

Balancing academics and exploration in early childhood programs is another issue confronting the elementary school. Many teachers of young children are faced with pressures to stress academics at the same time that early childhood specialists urge early childhood programs to be more developmentally appropriate. The goal of developmentally appropriate teaching is to provide instruction suited to the age and cognitive readiness of each child.

Although that concept is not new, schools during the 1970s, 1980s, and 1990s surrendered this principle under pressure to give children a more rigorous academic preparation—pressure fueled in part by the back-to-basics movement and overreliance on testing.

Other issues in elementary education will be discussed later in this chapter. As we prepare for the new century, it is useful to examine the history and purposes of the elementary school and to study the major components of the elementary curriculum.

BASIS OF THE ELEMENTARY SCHOOL CURRICULUM

The modern elementary curriculum has evolved over the past 200 years from a narrow curriculum devoted to the teaching of reading, writing, and arithmetic to a broad program encompassing not only basic skills, but also a variety of learning experiences. Because schools in the United States, as in other countries, are mechanisms for social change, schools often become battlegrounds for diverse groups with conflicting interests. The history of the elementary school during the past several years has been one of continuous change. Schools in the United States, like the nation itself, are in transition. By examining the history of the elementary school, we can see that elementary schools have been responsive to the needs of our expanding and diverse society.

Elementary School History

The establishment of free elementary schools for all children by state legislation was a grand and unique experiment in this country. Free elementary schools became associated with the highest ideals of our citizens.

Unlike most other countries, the United States has no national system of education. Under our Constitution, control of schools has been delegated to the states. Precedents were established early in the history of our country for the exercise of state legislative authority in educational matters. As early as 1642, the colonies were enacting legislation concerning educational matters. The Colonial Assembly of Massachusetts enacted compulsory education laws in 1642 and 1647. The 1647 legislation compelled communities over a certain size to set up grammar schools. That legislation, known as the "Old Deluder Satan" Act, passed by the General Court of the Massachusetts Bay Colony, required towns to establish common schools and grammar schools so men could read the Scriptures and escape the clutches of Satan. The act was not only the first law in America requiring that schools be established, but was also the first example in history requiring that children be provided an education at the expense of the community.

By 1693, legislation was passed allowing selectmen authority to levy school taxes with the consent of the majority of the townspeople. Previously, each town could determine how buildings, salaries, and other matters were handled.

Elementary teachers relied heavily on the *New England Primer,* a book used for more than one hundred years. That book used Bible verses and books to teach reading and number skills. Disciplinary practices also followed religious lines, with flogging and other measures designed to "drive the devil out of children."

In addition to religious purposes, early elementary schools served another purpose—rallying support for the new American political system. James Madison and Thomas Jefferson both spoke out against ignorance and in favor of an educated populace. Elementary schools were established not only for the maintenance of society by inculcating religious doctrine, but also to maintain society by inculcating political doctrines.

As the nation expanded westward with new states admitted to the Union, the elementary school experienced reforms. Many of the reforms were influenced by European examples. Perhaps the person most responsible for building the base for the modern elementary school was the Swiss educational reformer Johann Heinrich Pestalozzi (1746–1827). Pestalozzi viewed child growth and development as organismic (natural) rather than mechanistic. He recognized that the narrow curriculum, consisting mainly of mechanical exercises in reading, was inadequate to prepare children for intelligent citizenship. Through teacher training programs, he helped prepare elementary teachers to provide a variety of learning experiences for children. His ideas were best expressed in his book, *How Gertrude Teaches Her Children.*

In the early 1800s, Prussian educators borrowed many of Pestalozzi's methods to build a national system of education. Horace Mann and other educators of the day visited Prussia and returned to the United States with glowing reports of the Prussian-Pestalozzian system. That system, imitated in this country, included grading students on the basis of ability, better methods of instruction and discipline, setting up a state agency for education, and developing special teacher-training institutions.

Public education became increasingly popular in the first half of the 1800s. The first state board of education was established in Massachusetts in 1837 with Horace Mann as its first secretary. By 1876, the principle of public elementary education had been accepted in all states. The period from 1826 to 1876, known as the *public school revival,* led to a new American conscience in respect of educating children. Legislators were pressured to provide more money for elementary schools, and the curriculum was enriched.

Expansion and Continued Reforms of Elementary Schools

From 1876 to the mid-1930s, the United States became a great industrial nation. As America moved from a simple agricultural society to an industrial power, schools as instruments of society became instruments of change. Elementary enrollments doubled, many new subjects were added to the curricula, and the school day was lengthened. World War I had resulted in demands for new skills on the part of youth, and curriculum change included a back-to-basics movement in 1918 to ensure that all children could read and write. Teacher education is an influence in curriculum change, and because new courses in psychology and methods were introduced in teacher training institutions, the elementary curriculum began to change. By the 1930s, standardized tests were used to determine achievement in school subjects, and individual and group intelligence tests were administered. Efforts were made to differentiate instruction for slow, average, and above-average elementary children.

During the 1920s and 1930s, educational philosophers such as John Dewey had a great influence on the elementary curriculum. Dewey and other "progressive" educators saw schools as agencies of society designed to improve our democratic way of life. Dewey believed that schools should be a reflection of community life, with students studying about the home, neighborhood, and community. By studying what is familiar to them, students become more curious about the disciplines of science, geography, and mathematics. "Learning by doing" is a principle of learning that was central to Dewey's ideas about schools. Active children will learn more. Thus, learning in the elementary school should not include simply rote, mechanistic learning activities, but a variety of creative activities in which students are active participants in the learning process. Dewey maintained that the curricula of the elementary school should build on the interests of students and should represent real life by discussing and continuing the activities with which the child is already familiar at home.

The **progressive education** movement, led by John Dewey, George Counts, Harold Rugg, and others, heavily influenced the elementary curricula until 1957, when *Sputnik* forced a reexamination of the purpose of the elementary school. Critics such as Admiral Rickover and Arthur Bestor censured progressive education as failing to provide students with the necessary skills and knowledge to compete in a scientific world. Congressional acts establishing the National Science Foundation (NSF) and the National Defense Education Act (NDEA) pumped millions of dollars into the development of science and mathematics programs and materials. The elementary curriculum began to reflect a growing emphasis on science and mathematics in student courses such as "Science: A Process Approach" and in-service programs designed to improve teachers' skills in teaching science and mathematics.

The 1960s began an era of innovation in the elementary curriculum. Many of the innovations dealt with organizational changes such as nongradedness, open classrooms, and team teaching. Elementary school buildings were designed to facilitate those organizational changes. As with other innovations involving organizational changes, teachers were not necessarily prepared to cope with such new ideas. Lack of in-services and continued turnover of elementary staffs resulted in growing resistance to nongradedness, open space, and teaming. Moreover, elementary leaders who jumped on bandwagons sometimes confused organizational *means* with *ends*. Although their schools were advertised as "open and nongraded," little change occurred in teaching methods or in curriculum substance. Process had been confused with product, and results of the innovations were disappointing.

Educators in the 1970s and 1980s, for the first time in the history of American education, saw a decline in elementary enrollment. Retrenchment, funding problems, and dissatisfaction with the experimentation of the 1960s led to legislated accountability measures and increased testing programs in the elementary school. Another back-to-basics movement began, with demands for an elementary curriculum emphasizing reading, writing, and arithmetic. By the late 1980s, with enrollment growing for the first time in two decades, the elementary curriculum had expanded to include a variety of learning experiences, but it had narrowed its focus to the basic skills of written and oral communication and mathematics. The shape of the elementary curriculum of the new century has already been determined by radical changes in parenting, new job opportunities for adults, and other societal changes leading to the need for schools to provide a myriad of services that used to be offered by other agencies and institutions.

ORGANIZING THE CURRICULUM

The curriculum of the elementary school is organized around the bases of knowledge, the needs of society, and human learning and development. As discussed in the previous section, early elementary schools were concerned simply with the transmission of knowledge. Later, schools were seen as an instrument of society to foster religious views and the political doctrine of early America. In the first half of the 1900s, elementary schools were seen as serving an emerging industrial society and as an instrument for the improvement of democratic institutions. Human learning and development did not influence the curriculum until the late 1920s and 1930s when psychologists began to introduce educators to research on student learning and child growth and development. Not until the 1960s did major changes in curriculum and in training curriculum leaders result from research studies of learning and development. From the 1960s through the 1990s, many new programs were introduced into the elementary program to accommodate young learners and those learners with special needs. Free public kindergarten programs were implemented for five-year-olds in all states, along with a variety of other programs such as Head Start for disadvantaged young children. Special education programs for elementary students with physical and mental handicaps were greatly expanded and programs for **gifted learners** were made available to more elementary students. Nursery school programs for three- and four-year-olds, extended-day centers for children before and after school, daycare centers, and even prenatal centers are now found in many elementary schools.

Individualizing Instruction in the Elementary Grades

A consistent theme of elementary school learning for years has been that of individualizing instruction to accommodate differences among students. Owing to the complexity of the concept, the term *individualization* is often misunderstood. Individualization has other dimensions than the rate of progress. Among the variables that may be manipulated in **individualized instruction** are

- □ **Materials for Study**   Prescribed or individually chosen; various levels of difficulty and with varying purposes
- □ **Method of Study**   Prescribed or chosen methods of learning
- □ **Pace of Study**   Timed or untimed, structured or fluid
- □ **Sequence of Study**   Ordered or providing the option for personal coverage of material
- □ **Learning Focus**   Factual, skill-based, process, or values
- □ **Place of Learning**   Classroom, school, environment, or optional
- □ **Evaluation of Learning**   Exam-based, product-based, open-ended, or student-evaluated
- □ **Purpose of Learning**   Mastery, understanding, application, or experiential

In most elementary programs, students work with similar materials at about the same pace in the same spaces, and they usually have similar, if not identical, learning criteria for evaluating their progress. Some widespread techniques are used to accommodate differences, however, including grouping, use of materials with differing levels of reading difficulty, and special programs for students at the greatest range from group norms.

Grouping.   Flexibility is the key in any grouping arrangement. The major reason for employing grouping as an instructional technique is to provide more effectively for students' individualized differences. Some common groups found in the elementary school are the following:

- ☐ A *class as a whole* can function as a group. Teachers sometimes have guilt feelings about whole-class activities, but there are occasions when the teacher can address the whole class as a single group. New topic or unit introductions, unit summaries, and activities such as reports, dramatizations, and choral reading may be effectively conducted with the total class.
- ☐ *Reading level groups* formed according to reading achievement levels are commonly found in classrooms. These groups are not static and must accommodate shifts of pupils from group to group as changes in individual achievement occur.
- ☐ *Reading need groups* are formed to assist students in mastering a particular reading skill such as pronouncing a phonic element or finding the main idea in a paragraph.
- ☐ *Interest groups* help students apply reading skills to other language arts and other content areas. Storytelling, recreational reading, writing stories and poems, and dramatization are activities that can be carried out in interest groupings.
- ☐ *Practice or tutorial groups* are often used to allow students to practice oral reading skills, play skill games, and organize peer teaching situations.
- ☐ *Research groups* allow for committee work, group projects, and other research activities. **Learning centers** in the classroom and research areas in the media center are often developed for research groups.
- ☐ *Individualization* allows a student to work as an individual in selecting books and references for learning projects. Developmental programs provide for individual progress through a series of lessons.

Two common terms used in grouping in the elementary school are **heterogeneous** (mixed) and **homogeneous** (like) **groups.** Usually, these two types of groups are used interchangeably during a school day. Teachers who organize skill groups in the classroom are using homogeneous grouping. The key is flexibility. Students are moved from group to group as they achieve required skills. Also, the skill groups are organized only for a portion of the school day. The rest of the day, students are organized into heterogeneous groups where they can interact with students of varying abilities.

Reading Levels.   Another common means of providing for student differences is in providing books of varying degrees of difficulty. Textbook publishers regularly provide grade-specific texts (fourth-grade math, for example) with several "leveled" versions. Teachers use the readability of the text as a means of tailoring instruction to the student.

Readability is the objective measure of the difficulty of a book or article and usually involves the use of a specific formula, with results reported in terms of grade level. Seven such formulas are listed here.

1. **Flesch Reading Ease Score**   Involves checking word length and sentence length (grades 5–12)
2. **Wheeler and Smith—Index Number**   Involves determining sentence length and number of polysyllabic words (grades primary–4)
3. **Cloze Technique**   Can be used to compare the readability of two pieces of material. Measures redundancy (the extent to which words are predictable), whereas standard readability formulas measure the factors of vocabulary and sentence structure. It can be used to determine relative readability of material but cannot predict readability of a new sample. It does not give grade-level designations.
4. **Lorge Grade Placement Score**   Uses average sentence length in words, number of difficult words per 100 words not on the Dale 769-word list, and number of prepositional phrases per 100 words (grades 3—12)
5. **Fry Graph**   Method is based on two factors: average number of syllables per 100 words and average number of sentences per 100 words. Three randomly selected 100-word samples are used.
6. **SMOG Grading Plan**   Involves counting repetition of polysyllabic words (grades 4–12)
7. **Spache Grade Level Score**   Looks at average sentence length and number of words outside of the Dale list of 769 words to give readability level (grades 1–3)

Armed with such assessments, the teacher can provide students with reading materials tailored to their needs and abilities.

Approaches to teaching reading vary according to how the teacher thinks children learn. Table 7.1 outlines seven approaches now found in public schools and cites their advantages and disadvantages.

Whole Language vs. Phonics: A Continuing Debate

During the last decade, debate continued on whether phonics or whole language was the better approach to teach beginning readers. *Phonics,* explicit decoding instruction, is known as basis-skills instruction. Phonics builds on a series of basic steps that introduces emergent readers to such fundamental skills as linking sounds and letters, combining sounds, and recognizing words with similar-letter-sound patterns.

Whole language, as a teaching approach, embraces the theory that children learn to read the way they learn to talk—naturally. The whole-language teaching philosophy builds on a variety of reading and writing activities in which children choose their own books, construct meaning from their own experiences, sound out words in context, and decipher syntactical clues.

TABLE 7.1   Seven Basic Approaches to Teaching Reading

Advantages	Disadvantages
I. Basals	
1. Is comprehensive and systematic	1. Is stereotyped and uncreative
2. Presents reading skills in order	2. Limits students to one reading book
3. Is flexible	3. Has an overabundance of material
4. Has a well-established basic vocabulary	4. Is geared to middle-class whites
5. Is equipped with diagnostic tools	5. Tends to be very expensive
6. Builds themes around familiar situations	6. Depends heavily on visual or sight word methods
7. Gives a well-rounded reading choice	7. Leaves little time for creativity
	8. Facilitates little transfer from skill to functional reading
II. Language Experience	
1. Integrates all listening and speaking skills	1. Has limited materials
2. Utilizes student's own language	2. Does not sequence skills
3. Develops sensitivity to the child's environment	3. Has no concrete evaluation process
4. Can be used with the culturally different	4. Limits word-attack skills
5. Encourages sharing of ideas	
6. Develops confidence in language usage	
7. Develops self-expression	
III. Individualized Approach	
1. Enables the child to select appropriate books	1. Allows for insufficient skill development
2. Gives greater opportunity for children to interact with one another	2. Requires a large amount of record keeping
3. Fosters self-confidence with the child progressing at his or her own rate	3. Requires vast amounts of books and supplementary materials
4. Establishes one-to-one relationships through conferences with the teacher	4. Tends to allow children to limit their own selection
5. Diminishes competition and comparison	5. Makes little provision for readiness
6. Is flexible	6. Allows for no advance preparation for words or concepts
	7. Requires teachers with a wide knowledge of books
IV. Linguistic Approach	
1. Begins with familiar words that are phonetically regular	1. Are many different linguistic approaches

Many researchers today feel that it is not an either/or choice in selecting reading approaches. Studies suggest a balanced approach, combining basic skills and whole language, works best for teaching beginning readers.

Studies by the National Institute of Child Health and Human Development in the mid-1990s suggested that most reading disabilities stem from a deficit in the most basic level of the language system—the phoneme.

About 75 percent to 80 percent of the population will respond to almost any type of teaching method, but others need explicit instruction. Thus, a balanced

TABLE 7.1 *(Continued)*

Advantages	Disadvantages
2. Presents words as wholes	2. Lacks extensive field testing
3. Shows letters as a function by arrangement in the words	3. Has too controlled a vocabulary
4. Develops sentence order early	4. Encourages word-by-word reading
	5. Lacks emphasis on reading for meaning

V. Phonics

Advantages	Disadvantages
1. Develops efficiency in word recognition	1. Tends to isolate speech sounds in an unnatural manner
2. Helps develop independence in word recognition	2. Involves too much repetition; is boring
3. Creates interest because of immediate success for the child	3. Uses the slow process of sounding out words
4. Shows association between print and sounds	4. Are too many exceptions to the rule

VI. Alphabetic Approach

Advantages	Disadvantages
1. Is simpler	1. Lacks clarification regarding techniques and materials
2. Gives opportunity for free expression	2. Makes transition from ITA difficult
3. Engenders enthusiasm to read due to quick success	3. Is very expensive
4. Encourages the learning of words more rapidly	4. Confuses children because they see ITA only at school
	5. Has not been around long enough to know its validity

VII. Programmed Instruction

Advantages	Disadvantages
1. Allows child to proceed at his or her own pace	1. Uses limited research
2. Reinforces student after each step	2. Does not consider limited attention span of student
3. Records student progress	3. Becomes repetitious
4. Is self-instructional	4. Bypasses comprehension because it is difficult to program
5. Helps teacher to understand sequencing	5. Gives little room for child to develop his or her own interests or tastes in reading
	6. Is expensive

instructional approach that combines the best elements of whole language and phonics instruction seems to be the best way to reach the majority of emergent readers.[2]

SELECTION OF CONTENT

Subject content in the elementary school is selected from the basic disciplines of language arts, mathematics, social studies, science, the arts, and health.

Curriculum developers at the national, state, and local levels help to select content. Because we do not have a national system of education, the work of curriculum developers and researchers must fit a variety of learning needs and expectations of students in the 13,000 school districts of this country. Although textbook series and curriculum projects may be designed to accomplish that task, the classroom teacher has the final choice on selection of content. So, although geography may be taught in grade 7 and American history in grade 8 in most school districts, how these courses are taught and which materials and texts are used are decided by the teachers in local school districts. Indeed, the sequence of courses may be altered in some districts to allow the teaching of American history before geography.

Determining Appropriate Elementary School Curriculum Content

Determining what content is appropriate for elementary schoolchildren is not always easy. Testing programs today often dictate the selection of content. "Teaching for the test" has become a common practice in many classrooms.

Another problem facing elementary educators is the changing nature of our society. Divorce, mobility of families, and pressures brought on by the economy have influenced the achievement of elementary students. Testing programs and accountability legislation in many states have resulted in demands to teach more reading, writing, and mathematics.

Language Arts

Language arts includes the communication skills: reading, writing, listening, and speaking. These four modes of learning are interrelated in a developmental sequence. From listening to speaking to reading to writing, children begin to comprehend and use language skills. The reciprocal relationship among all four of the communication areas implies a need for those areas to be taught in a holistic approach.

The reading component of a total language arts program must include development of skills in decoding and comprehension in order to use functional and literary written material. Although reading educators differ on approaches to learning reading, students who fail to master these skills will likely face a lifetime of underachievement.

Reading.   *Reading* is perhaps the most controversial area of the elementary program. Reading is not only an emotional issue, but also a political one in many districts. Reading becomes the concern of parents long before their children enter school. Reading has also become the center of national rage, the focus of numerous research studies, and a federal crusade in the past quarter-century. In recent decades, millions of dollars have been poured into the development of reading programs. There are scores of reading programs that all work, yet we still have millions of nonreaders in our schools. It is debatable whether we are any closer to solving the mysteries of reading. We do know that reading has engaged the time of more teachers and received a larger share of the school dollar than any other subject in the curriculum.

What makes some students find success in reading whereas others find only failure? Some students fail because they deem certain classroom stimuli less important and tend to ignore them; others succeed because they are in tune with the teacher and react positively to instructional stimuli.

Grouping students into high and low groups usually ensures students will be treated differently by teachers. Being in the high group probably ensures the student will be

- ☐ Reading first, when more alert and eager
- ☐ Meeting for a longer time frame
- ☐ Facing a warmer, more receptive teacher, one that smiles, leans toward the children, and makes eye contact more frequently
- ☐ Criticized in a softer, more respectful manner
- ☐ Disciplined with warnings instead of actions
- ☐ Reading approximately three times as much as other reading groups (of which 70 percent will be silent reading) and making more progress
- ☐ Expected to self-correct reading errors. If teacher-corrected, it is at the end of the section, which doesn't disrupt the reader's fluency
- ☐ Asked questions that are comprehension checks and higher-level thinking skills

However, a totally different atmosphere usually exists for the low group, which

- ☐ Meets for less time and later in the day, when they have already begun to tire
- ☐ Reads more orally, which is slow, halting, and labored, therefore reading less and getting further behind
- ☐ Has each error pointed out, as it's made. Errors are made three to five times as often and as often as once every ten words. Less time is allowed for self-correction.
- ☐ Has questions asked that tend to be literal—checking only to see whether children are listening
- ☐ Faces a teacher whose body language is negative—frowns, pursed lips, glares, leaning away, and fidgeting
- ☐ Does silent reading only 30% of the time
- ☐ Is aware that as "lows" they "can't" read and avoid it as much as possible
- ☐ In large groups, are seated furthest from the teacher. These "slow" learners are given less time to respond to questions, have to think faster, thus increasing their chance of failure.[3]

Until teachers see all students as having potential and provide the same stimuli to all students, low and high, reading will continue to be a problem in the elementary school.

Spelling.   Two methods of teaching spelling are found in most elementary schools today. One method, *invented spelling,* involves students writing how they think a word is spelled and checking it later. This method allows students to concentrate on what they are trying to communicate. It also increases the writer's freedom.

The second method, the traditional way, has students memorizing ten to twenty words a week. Students are tested on their spelling rather than on their ability to apply rules to new words. Exercises focus on dictionary use, handwriting, and writing words several times.

New models of spelling in the elementary school suggest that spelling should not be treated as a separate subject, but instead be seen as a total language system involving writing and reading. Learning to spell should be pleasant, natural, and as easy flowing and unconscious an act as learning to speak.

Writing.   *Writing* has again become a center of focus in today's elementary schools. Responding to demands of colleges that students know how to write better, elementary and secondary schools have devoted more time in the day to the teaching of writing skills.

Research on children's writing implies that focus on skill instruction in grammar and spelling may come at the expense of composition. Daily writing, conferences, and the focus of skills in the context of writing appear to be more effective.[4]

Elementary schools are striving to integrate composition and literature into their language arts program and to make remedial and regular language arts programs congruent. The goals of an integrated approach are to

1. Place genuine reading and composing at the center of the language arts curriculum
2. Place skills instruction within rather than before genuine reading and writing
3. Integrate the various components of language arts through content rather than skills
4. Insist that all readers and writers—not just the most able learners—gain equal access to genuine reading and writing[5]

Mathematics

Mathematics is more effective if it is carefully adapted to the developmental characteristics of elementary children. Early in the history of our schools, objectives of mathematics instruction centered on the development of computational skills. By the 1920s and 1930s, objectives shifted to a more practical application of mathematics. Today, mathematics educators are concerned with providing a balanced program in mathematics in which students not only attain computational skills, but also have an understanding of mathematics concepts and reasoning. The rapid increase in the number of microcomputers in elementary schools has resulted in the need for elementary students to perceive and understand structure in mathematics, including concepts, relationships, principles, and modes of mathematical reasoning.

Much of mathematics instruction in the elementary school involves the use of textbooks. A study in 1989 provided an analysis of overlap between textbook content and content taught.[6] Results challenge the popular notion that elementary school teachers' content decisions are dictated by the mathematics textbooks that they use. In each classroom studied, researchers found important differences between the curriculum of the text and the teachers' topic selection, content emphasis, and sequence of instruction.

Use of computers, whole curricular approaches, and interdisciplinary units are giving elementary teachers new instructional options for delivery of content and skills. Practice sheets and end-of-chapter problems are giving way to these new approaches for teaching elementary mathematics.

The 1990s saw a host of efforts to reform curriculum and instruction in mathematics. *Professional Standards for Teaching Mathematics,* published by The National Council of Teachers of Mathematics (NCTM), led the way in redefining elementary mathematics. The standards developed by the NCTM offer detailed images of the mathematics teaching promoted by many reformers in mathematics education.

Approaches in teaching mathematics include cooperative learning, the use of themes and real-life problems, and the use of group grading on cooperative assignments.[7]

Science

Science in the elementary school has also been influenced by the rapid advancements in technology in this country. During the 1960s, there was a reform movement in science to shift the emphasis from the learning of facts in science to an understanding of the processes of science.[8] Recently, there has been an emphasis on the technological applications of science.

Learning scientific concepts, principles, and generalizations allows elementary children to understand better the universe in which they live by enabling them to see orderly arrangement in the natural world and to explain the continual change in the world. A functional competency with the tools of science must also be developed to help students live in a highly technological society.

The *whole approach* to teaching science in the elementary school is the teaching of science with an interdisciplinary scope. In contrast to traditional science instruction, the whole-science approach reinforces the required science curriculum with content from all subject areas in a thematic approach. The integrated approach to teaching science moves science teaching away from lectures and textbooks to a variety of materials and activities. Activities incorporate reading, writing, and mathematics while science concepts are developed. Cooperative learning and a team approach to teaching and learning science are also integral features of the whole-science approach.

In 1990, President Bush stated his goal to "make American students first in the world in mathematics and science achievement by the year 2000." Although no plan of action was presented, elementary schools began to build science programs that nurture conceptional understandings and target scientific attitudes and skills that lead to those understandings.

Table 7.2 illustrates methods of integrating science with other subject areas.

Social Studies

Social studies instruction in the elementary school focuses on the interaction of people with each other and with their natural and human environments. Although

TABLE 7.2 Integration of Science with Other Subject Areas

Reading and Social Studies

Reviewing scientific literature in children's science books, magazines, and reference books. A surprising amount of scientific information is also found in social studies and state studies books.

Map reading

Mathematics

Learning to gather data and record observations

Graphing data such as measurements and recorded data

Language Skills

Note taking

Summarizing

Report writing

Writing

Storytelling

Process writing: Developing poems and stories to communicate how weather has affected students' lives; writing "rap songs" to reinforce learning about proper body care

Artistic Expression

Poster designs

Murals

Models

Critical Thinking Skills

Redesign of the human body

Summarizing information from literature review, experiments, and other observations for report writing

there has been less reform in the social studies area than in the other major areas of the elementary curriculum, educators have recently begun to develop a more relevant program for elementary school students.

Of prime importance today is using social studies in the elementary school to teach critical thinking, develop civic responsibility, build self-concept, and improve human relationships. Children are more open to diversity in the early elementary years than in the later years. Positive self-concepts, important in positively perceiving and judging social interactions, form in the critical early years of schooling. Social studies education that moves beyond the mere acquisition of facts is being developed in many school districts. Citizenship education, in which young children are active participants in examining political feelings—social issues as well as historical and geographical understanding—is forming the basis for social studies education in the elementary school. This approach fits with the instructional practices of cooperative learning and interdisciplinary instruction.[9]

Geography

Efforts have been made in recent years to revitalize the teaching of *geography* in elementary schools. The National Geographic Society contributed $40 million in

1996 to a geography education foundation. The purpose of the foundation was to provide additional training for teachers and to develop classroom materials to increase geography literacy among students.

Health and Physical Education

Health and **developmental physical education** are core components of a complete elementary school curriculum. *Health education* includes learning all aspects of healthful and safe living. Physical education includes adaptive and developmental activities that lead to better coordination and psychomotor skills.

Because the physical being cannot be separated from the mental or social being, health and physical education programs must include activities designed to interrelate all three areas of physical, mental, and social.

The National Association for Sports and Physical Education (NASPE) defines a physically educated person as one who

- ☐ Has the skills necessary to perform a variety of physical activities
- ☐ Participates regularly in physical activity
- ☐ Is physically fit
- ☐ Knows the implications of and the benefits from involvement in physical activities, and
- ☐ Values physical activity and its contributions to a healthful lifestyle[10]

AIDS Education.   Schools have been among key American institutions where the meaning of AIDS has been debated and deciphered. Because AIDS is fatal and linked in people's minds with homosexuality and drug use, it evokes strong opinions and fears. How to protect children and also provide information to them is a growing concern. Schools must accept students who are HIV positive or who have been diagnosed with AIDS, so the need for education of students and parents is crucial. The elementary school represents the first contact of students who have AIDS with others in the classroom and is also the first forum to provide students with an understanding of the disease. Programs are continuing to be developed to assist elementary staffs in implementing AIDS education programs.

The Arts

The *arts* in the elementary school include visual and performing arts. Aesthetic education brings together cognitive, affective, and psychomotor areas of learning and includes experiences in music, fine arts, dance, theater, and other artistic modes of expression.

Until recently, mathematics and language were assumed to be cognitive in nature; the arts, on the other hand, dealt with feelings and emotions and were in the affective domain. Reading, writing, and arithmetic, moreover, were assumed to be essential skills that made information processing possible; the ability to read or to produce in the arts was an end in itself, leading to nothing more than inner satisfaction. Recent research indicates that the basic distinction between intellect and emotion can no longer be rationalized. It is now more clearly understood that our mental activities always involve both intellect and feelings, that we communicate in a rich variety of modes of symbolization, and that each art medium contributes a "language" and experience that adds cognitive data to our functioning brain.

In the push for basic skills in the elementary school, the arts must not be left out of the curriculum. The arts are a necessary part of human experience. Nothing could be more basic.

Holistic Approaches to Curriculum

School curriculum has become fragmented because of budgeting, bureaucratic turfdoms associated with textbook selection, media resources, and accountability aimed at attempting to prove year-to-year performance. Covering the information in a textbook may not relate to objectives in a curriculum or to a school's standardized achievement tests.

Those utilizing holistic approaches to curriculum development are asking the five questions that Tyler posed:

1. What educational purposes are being sought?
2. Is there a range of learning experiences that will facilitate the attainment of the educational purposes?
3. Are the experiences effectively organized and readily available to learners?
4. How well are we determining that the school's purposes are being attained?
5. Are we striving to get wholeness among curricular activities?[11]

DIVERSE NEEDS OF CHILDREN

Children with Attention Deficit Disorder

Attention Deficit Disorder (ADD) is characterized by these symptoms: difficulty remaining seated, calling out without request, interrupting others, and talking excessively. Biochemical abnormalities in the brain are thought to be the cause of ADD. These children are easily distracted, disorganized, lacking in motor skills and have a limited attention span. The majority of ADD children are found in regular classrooms rather than in special programs.[12]

ADD affects 3 to 5 percent of school-age children and occurs six to nine times more with boys than with girls. ADD behaviors continue to be a concern throughout a person's life.

Teachers can aid the ADD child by getting the child organized, giving effective instructions, having consistent discipline, using nonverbal cues, developing the child's self-esteem, and communicating regularly with parents.

Attention Deficit Hyperactivity Disorder (ADHD), as defined by the American Psychiatric Association, is exhibited in a child with eight or more of fourteen systems that reflect difficulties in attention, impulsivity, or motor hyperactivity with the onset before age 17. Self-control strategies are very important in dealing with ADHD, but it is important to first determine whether a child has other behavioral or even cognitive deficits which need to be remediated before self-control strategies are implemented.[13]

Children from Impoverished Families

Poverty still remains a problem in the United States even though President Johnson declared the official War on Poverty in the mid-1960s. Figures in 1997 indicate that the younger the family, the poorer the children. Fifty percent of all U.S. children living in a household headed by a person 25 years of age or younger are poor. If a child lives in a family headed by a woman, chances are better than 50 percent that the child is poor. The U.S. Census Bureau projected that 60 percent of children born in 1996 will live with a single parent. Contrary to popular belief, the majority of poor people live in semi-isolation in towns across the country rather than in the inner cities. Two thirds of Americans that are poor are white.[14]

Children living on the edge of homelessness are usually prevented from finding the stability that makes successful schooling possible. It was estimated in 1997 that 186,000 children were homeless each night.[15]

Foster children and other displaced children often come from poor families. Drug and alcohol abuse by parents has contributed to large numbers of children in juvenile detention centers.[16]

One fourth of mothers receive no prenatal care.[17] Teachers are seeing more learning disabilities as a result of poor health care and drug abuse by mothers. Children who were cocaine babies continue to enter school in large numbers, and their care is adding huge costs to already overburdened school budgets.

Children from Different Cultures

America's newest students speak many languages, practice many religions, come from many different backgrounds, and carry both hopes and frustrations into their new life.[18] The 1990 census figures show large increases in students who speak Spanish as a first language. In Florida, for example, Hispanics were the largest minority group in 1996. The number of Asian students continues to grow in American schools. Providing the melting pot, schools are helping non-English-speaking students by creating a safe and warm learning environment for them. English as a Second Language (ESL) programs have been revised to allow students to learn English and retain their culture. Students are encouraged to express themselves and relate their experiences. Working with parents by giving them make-and-take materials and showing them techniques for playing with their children are also important elements of **bilingual education** programs.

Finding teachers and aides who speak the language of students remains a challenge. Finding qualified instructors who speak Cambodian or Creole (for Haitian students) often frustrates district educators who have large concentrations of those non-English-speaking students.

Several school districts are experimenting with peer tutoring programs in which older students tutor younger students of the same language. "Buddy systems" are also used to pair non-English-speaking students with English-speaking students.

Changes in the world continue to bring fresh young faces into our classrooms. They come from ancient empires, modern cities, remote villages, or refugee camps with one quest—freedom. Figure 7.2 provides information on who these ESL students are.

Children with Disabilities

The period from 1975 to 1995 represented an era of significant progress for students with special needs or disabilities. Public concern resulted in laws guaranteeing access to the curriculum and public dollars to ensure implementation of special programs for these children.

Who is an ESL student?

An ESL* student is an individual

- who was not born in the U.S. and whose native language is not English;
- **or** who comes from a home environment where a language other than English is spoken;
- **or** who is an American Indian or an Alaskan native and who comes from an environment where a language other than English has a significant impact on his or her level of English language proficiency;
- **and** who, for the above reasons, has difficulty listening, speaking, reading, or writing in English, to the extent that he or she is unable to learn successfully in classrooms where English is the language of instruction.

ESL students have learned another language before English and need time to make the transition to a curriculum that uses only English. As students learn more English, the use of the native language is de-emphasized.

ESL students need to develop both communicative skills and cognitive academic skills in English.

Children are not handicapped cognitively by bilingualism; some types of intelligence, such as creativity, may be enhanced by the child's being bilingual.

* English as a Second Language. May also be referred to as LEP (Limited English Proficiency) or ESOL (English for Speakers of Other Languages).

FIGURE 7.2   Who Is an ESL Student?

This Part of ECIA	Replaces These Programs

Chapter 1—Financial Assistance to Meet Special Educational Needs of Disadvantaged Children	ESEA Title I
	    Basic Grants to Local Districts
	    Special Grants
	State-Administered Programs for
	    Migratory Children, Handicapped
	    Children, and Neglected and
	    Delinquent Children
	State Administration

Chapter 2—Consolidation of Federal Programs for Elementary and Secondary Education	

Subchapter A—Basic Skills Development	ESEA Title II—Basic Skills
	    Development (except Part C, Sec.
	    231), Inexpensive Book Distribution
	    Program

Subchapter B—Educational Improvement and Support Services	ESEA Title IV
	Part B—Instructional Materials and
	    School Library Resources
	Part C—Improvement in Local
	    Educational Practices
	Part D—Guidance, Counseling, and
	    Testing
	ESEA Title V—State Leadership
	ESEA Title VI—Emergency School Aid
	Precollege Science Teacher Training*
	    (Sec. 3(a)(1), NSF Act of 1950)
	Teacher Corps (Part A, HEA)
	Teacher Centers (Sec. 532, HEA)

FIGURE 7.3   The Education Consolidation Improvement Act: How Merged Programs Fit into ECIA

*Separate FY 1982; consolidated FY 1983.

Although some 195 federal laws specific to those with disabilities were enacted between 1927 and 1975, the National Advisory Committee on the Handicapped reported in 1975 that only 55 percent of children and youths with handicaps were being served appropriately. Of the 195 acts passed, 61 were passed between March 1970 and November 1975. Public Law 93-380, passed in 1974, was the most important of the laws passed; it extended and amended the Elementary and Secondary Education Act (ESEA) of 1965 and established a national policy on equal educational opportunity. Figure 7.3 notes changes in this original law.

The most far-reaching and significant federal act passed affecting those with handicaps was Public Law 94-142, the Education for All Handicapped Children Act of 1975, which was an amendment to Public Law 93-380. PL 94-142 has been described by many educators as a "Bill of Rights for the Handicapped." This law sets forth specific procedures that school districts must carry out to establish due process for students with disabilities. The most important feature of the law is that all handicapped students between ages 3 and 21 must have available to them a free and appropriate public education. That includes an emphasis on the regular class as the preferred instructional base for all children.

It is the feature of reversing the historical method of referring children with disabilities *out* of regular classes that makes PL 94-142 unique. It also has major implications for classroom teachers and supervisory personnel who implement the act.

The right to education means that children with disabilities are eligible for all programs and activities sponsored by the school. This includes cheerleading, athletics, and other extracurricular activities. Children with disabilities can no longer be excluded from course offerings, most notably, vocational courses.

PL 94-142 also prohibits discriminatory evaluation. Testing and evaluation materials must be selected and administered so as not to be culturally discriminatory. No single test or procedure can be used as the sole criterion for determining educational placement in a program.

Working with children with disabilities requires an individualized instructional plan similar to the plan used for all children in a regular classroom. It requires a substantial amount of diagnostic information about present and past academic and social performance. Finally, it requires teachers and supervisory personnel to project the specific needs of each child with a disability and prescribes special programs to meet those needs.

The **Individual Education Plan (IEP)** provision of PL 94-142, which became practice on October 1, 1977, was really a model for instruction that all good teachers should follow. Collecting diagnostic data, setting goals and objectives, selecting instructional materials, and evaluating student performance are all steps in the instructional process. There are important activities in the instructional process that teachers must consider for students with disabilities.

Mainstreaming has been defined in many ways, most of which center on moving children with disabilities from segregated special education classes into normal classrooms. Since the implementation of special education classes in the United States, segregated classroom environments have been the most popular method of educating these children. Because children were labeled according to the severity of their disabilities and grouped into uniform categories in special classes, they were removed from what educators titled the "mainstream."

PL 94-142 mandates that the most appropriate education for children with disabilities should be the **least restrictive environment.** This means that such students should be integrated into, not segregated from, the normal program of the school. It does *not* mean the wholesale return of all exceptional children in special classes to regular classes.

Mainstreaming means looking at educational needs and creative programs that will help general educators serve children with disabilities in a regular setting. It does not imply that specialists will no longer be needed, but that the specialists and the classroom teachers must be willing to combine efforts and work cooperatively to provide the most appropriate program for all children.

Legal decisions and legislation have made it clear that the rights of all children must be respected in our schools. Unfortunately, legal decisions and legislation won't ensure the development of adequate or appropriate programs. In-service education will be necessary to provide teachers with more specialized skills to deal with specific behavioral and academic problems. Mainstreaming can succeed only with a strong partnership of curriculum specialists, teachers, and supervisory personnel working cooperatively to provide the most appropriate education for all children.

Educating Children with Handicaps in the Regular Classroom. *Special Education* has meant labeling students since federal law established the Education For All Handicapped Children Act. The law requires school districts to identify and label children with special needs, but it has never mandated separate programs. Both federal and state laws have been amended since 1975 to insist on placing special needs students in the "least restrictive environment"—usually in the regular classroom unless their handicaps are severe.

The four most common labels—learning disabled, speech/language impaired, mentally handicapped, and emotionally disturbed—cover 95 percent of all students labeled as disabled. Labels are often confusing because some districts may classify 10 to 15 percent of students as handicapped whereas other districts classify from 1 to 75 percent of their handicapped children as learning disabled.

Labeling also lowers student self-esteem, and moving students out of the regular classroom often limits students' expectation of success.

Mainstreaming students with disabilities, even those with severe disabilities, seems to be a better approach. *Inclusion* is a term used to include teachers of students with disabilities who accompany their students into regular classrooms. The team approach with regular classroom teachers allows the special needs teacher to work in a more integrated instructional pattern.

Two new areas in the education of students with disabilities are (1) the emphasis on preschool identification and services and (2) the transition from school to the world of work. At the preschool level, federal and state mandates require services for very young children. At present, the mandate is age 3, but very shortly it will begin at birth. The idea is that early intervention is best when dealing with handicapping conditions. As these students exit school, much more assistance is being given to them in seeking employment. For many students, vocational goals are identified as early as ninth grade. Many students with disabilities work with job coaches who assist them in functioning at jobs appropriate to their levels of performance. Businesses are encouraged to employ individuals with disabilities while they are still in school and then keep these students employed after graduation. Before this emphasis on transition services, only 25 percent of these students were employed at the end of their schooling. Students ranging from age 3 to 21 are included in these programs. Many students with disabilities have gained employment as a result of recent state and national efforts.

Inclusion: What Does It Mean? *Inclusion* is a term for which few authors can agree on a definition. Some lump inclusion with mainstreaming. Others believe it means keeping all special needs children in the regular classroom while retraining the special staff. Others believe inclusion means *some* children and full inclusion means *all* children. The most common definition of inclusion states that inclusion involves keeping special education students in regular education classrooms and taking support services to the child rather than bringing the child to support services.[19]

A major issue in inclusion has been whether placing severely dysfunctional children in a regular classroom without providing adequate training or support for the teacher puts the other students at risk. Without the training and support, teachers take up much instructional time dealing with distractions, disruptions, and sometimes violence.

Much progress has been made in the 1990s in building successful inclusion programs. When elementary schools have a clear philosophy of inclusion, **mission statements** that include goals for *all* students, and a curriculum that balances the needs of general and special education students, inclusion can be successful.[20]

Gifted Students

It has been estimated that over 2.5 million, or about 6 percent, of all young Americans are endowed with academic, artistic, or social talents far beyond the talents of their peers. These "gifted" children come from all levels of society, all races, and both sexes.

All fifty states have programs for gifted children, but there are still problems of identifying and providing for talented youngsters. For instance, many gifted children cannot be identified by I.Q. tests alone. New yardsticks for identifying gifted children have to be used, including measures of creativity, advanced social skills, and even exceptional physical aptitude such as the kind that marks fine surgeons, watch repairers, or engineers.

As a group, talented and gifted children tend to learn faster and retain more than their peers. A gifted child is also a divergent thinker. All of these characteristics can be unsettling in a class, and sometimes gifted and talented children have been seen as troublemakers. Other gifted children are turned off by boring classes and become alienated from school.

The Federal Office for the Gifted and Talented has adopted a national definition for giftedness, which is as follows:

> Gifted and talented children are those identified by professionally qualified persons who, by virtue of outstanding abilities, are capable of high performance. These are children who require differentiated educational programs in order to realize their contribution to self and society.

Additionally, the Office of Gifted and Talented identified six specific ability areas included in giftedness. These are

1. General intellectual ability
2. Specific academic aptitude

3. Creative or productive thinking
4. Leadership ability
5. Ability in the visual or performing arts
6. Psychomotor ability

The debate over how to educate gifted children often centers on the equity versus excellence issue. Some question whether it is fair to give special treatment to some children and not to others. Some educators have also seen cooperative learning as a threat to gifted children because it holds such students back. Others say cooperative learning works just as well in a homogeneously grouped gifted class because its real strength is bringing out the potential of each child in class.

Tracking, often associated with gifted programs, has come under fire by many educators who see tracking as discriminating against poor children who are most often found in low groups.

The gifted and talented remain a group of students who need special attention whether it be in separate programs or differentiated instruction in a heterogeneous grouping.

The models and research on gifted and talented children have helped provide a sound basis for differentiating instruction and evaluating programs for them.

Differentiating instruction, fostering creativity, allowing for independent study, and encouraging peer learning are all important tasks of teaching. They are especially important for nurturing the diverse aptitudes and abilities of gifted and talented children. Organizational procedures such as cluster grouping, mainstreaming, and part-day grouping have all been used with gifted and talented children.

Other Students with Needs

Between the special education student, who is categorically identified, and the gifted student, who is provided for by a special program, are all other students. Most of these "normal" students have needs, too, particularly during the elementary years. Figure 7.4 provides a checklist of needs for students who are not served by special programs but who may need assistance.

Early Intervention

Prekindergarten programs are designed to smooth the transition from home to school and also from kindergarten to the upper grades. Prekindergarten programs stress cooperative or shared learning experiences. The focus of the curriculum for preschool programs is on developmentally appropriate activities, which includes equal emphasis on physical, cognitive, social, emotional, and creative development. Often, prekindergarten programs use other students as models. Retired teachers, grandparents, and other senior citizens also become involved in such programs.

In many districts, kindergarten is no longer a part-time, play-oriented introduction to school. It is "real" school where children go for the whole day and spend a great deal of their time in academic pursuits.[21] For that reason, many children are failing kindergarten and educators are concerned about a skills-based academic pro-

1. Gross motor and motor flexibility

   _____   incoordination and poor balance

   _____   difficulty with jumping/skipping/hopping (below age 9)

   _____   confusion in games requiring imitation of movements

   _____   poor sense of directionality

   _____   inept in drawing and writing at chalkboard

   _____   inaccuracies in copying at chalkboard

   _____   eyes do not work together

   _____   eyes lose or overshoot target

2. Physical fitness

   _____   tires easily

   _____   lacks strength

3. Auditory acuity, perception, memory/speech

   _____   confuses similar phonetic and phonic elements

   _____   inconsistent pronunciation of words usually pronounced correctly
   by peers

   _____   repeats, but does not comprehend

   _____   forgets oral directions, if more than one or two

4. Visual acuity, perception, memory

   _____   complains that he cannot see blackboard

   _____   says that words move or jump

   _____   facial expression strained

   _____   holds head to one side while reading

5. Hand-eye coordination

   _____   difficulty in tracing/copying/cutting/folding/pasting/coloring at desk

   _____   lack of success with puzzles/yo-yo's/toys involving targets, etc.

6. Language

   _____   has difficulty understanding others

FIGURE 7.4 Checklist for Identifying Students Who May Need Educational Therapy

gram being inappropriate for those students. To hold firm to a developmental approach rather than to step up formal instruction has put additional pressure on kindergarten teachers and elementary principals.

With a focus on early childhood, one cannot forget the term *developmentally appropriate*. The National Association for the Education of Young Children (NAEYC), the nation's largest professional organization of early childhood educa-

_____ has difficulty associating and remembering

_____ has difficulty expressing himself

7. Intellectual functioning

_____ unevenness of intellectual development

_____ learns markedly better through one combination of sensory avenues than another

8. Personality

_____ overreacts to school failures

_____ does not seem to know he has a problem

_____ will not admit he has a problem

9. Academic problems

_____ can't tolerate having his routine disturbed

_____ knows it one time and doesn't the next

_____ writing neat, but slow

_____ writing fast, but sloppy

_____ passes the spelling test, but can't spell functionally

_____ math accurate, but slow

_____ math fast, but inaccurate

_____ reads well orally, but has poor comprehension

_____ does poor oral reading, but comprehends better than would be expected

_____ lacks word attack skills

_____ has conceptual/study skill/organizational problems in content areas

10. Parents

_____ seemingly uninformed about nature of learning problem

_____ seemingly unrealistic toward student's problems

FIGURE 7.4   _(Continued)_

tors, believes one index of the quality of primary education is the extent to which the curriculum and instructional methods are developmentally appropriate for children five through eight years of age.[22]

Other writers point out that cognitive psychology has generally reaffirmed the beliefs of Dewey, Piaget, and Elkind about the construction of meaning and the _constructivist_ view of learning. In the constructivists' view, students are more active agents in their own education. The constructivist approach would also work well with the use of information technology, according to other writers.[23]

Child-Care Programs

Child care, largely the domain of private enterprise in the 1980s, is now being addressed by school districts. Both before- and after-school programs are being implemented across the country for school-age children and, increasingly, preschool-age children. The importance of high-quality, affordable child care is being recognized by policy makers. Legislation requiring higher qualifications for child-care workers, district matching programs with local businesses, tax credits, and minimum salaries for child-care workers are all helping shape child-care programs and services.

Integrated Instructional Systems

Integrated instructional systems (IIS), also commonly known as *integrated learning systems,* are instructional systems that are replacing older computer-assisted instruction (CAI) systems. CAI became associated with dull drill-and-practice activities. Linking computer lessons to accepted standard curriculum provides an integration often missing in CAI programs.

IIS are actually complex integrated hardware/software management systems that give districts the best return on an investment in instructional technology. As with any new program, staff training is a critical factor in the success of IIS. Costs vary for such systems, but hidden costs such as software licensing, updates, and staff salaries (for project managers) can often stretch existing school budgets.

LEARNING STYLES AND SYSTEMS

Learning styles of children have been under study in recent years. Researchers have been studying whether individual differences can result in different concept formation, problem-solving techniques, and shared meanings.

Studies have indicated some children enjoy understanding the big picture before focusing on specifics. Other children enjoy a classroom atmosphere in which personal relationships are important. Still others do best when they verbalize what they learn. For other students, a structured and systematic approach is better suited to their learning.

Elementary teachers who have their own learning and teaching styles can be assured that their students also have individual styles. Effective elementary teachers can assess learning styles and break ineffective learning patterns by adding variety to their teaching activities.

Cooperative Learning

In **cooperative learning,** a technique that gained great favor in the late 1980s and 1990s, children are trained to use one another as resources for learning. Each child plays a specific role in a group such as facilitator, checker, or reporter. Teachers learn to delegate authority to a group of students and to encourage students to engage in a process of **discovery learning.** Cooperative learning requires assignments and curriculum materials that are different from those used in traditional classroom instruction. Tasks and materials that encourage student interaction are most needed in cooperative learning situations. Teachers who are not skilled in the organization and monitoring of small groups need in-service training in cooperative learning.

Grade Level Retention

Two position papers in 1990—*Grade Level Retention: A Failed Procedure,* California State Department, and *Grade Level Retention,* Florida Department of Education—have summarized studies on grade level retention.

Research studies show that there are better approaches to motivating underperforming children than retaining them for a year. Grade level retention (the practice of requiring a student to repeat an entire grade in school) has not been shown to be an effective remedy for students who are not achieving their potential.

When students are held back, they fall behind the students entering the grade in which they are retained. Also, students retained are more likely to drop out of school. Finally, their self-concept is lowered so much that most students are turned off to school.

Unfortunately, most teachers and the general public still believe grade level retention works. New alternatives of grade level retention, such as utilizing a continuous-progress model, intensifying efforts to involve parents in school, and earlier intervention efforts have been proposed as alternatives to failing students.

ORGANIZATION AND GROUPING IN THE ELEMENTARY SCHOOL

Vertical and Horizontal Organizational Patterns

Organizational patterns in elementary schools may include self-contained classrooms, grade level teams, cross-grade teams, a total ungraded structure, or a combination of these patterns. For instance, the primary grades may be **nongraded** while the upper elementary grades are **graded.** Also, teams may operate at certain grade levels while other grade levels are self-contained. Classes may also be self-contained or departmentalized.

There are two basic types of organization groups for instruction: *vertical* and *horizontal.* Vertical organization refers to the movement of students from grade to grade or level to level. Horizontal organization refers to the grouping of students within a grade or level and the assignment of teachers to a grade or level. Self-contained classes and departmentalized classes, with a separate teacher for each discipline, fall within a horizontal organization. Vertical organization may include both graded and nongraded plans.

Two or more teachers may engage in **team teaching,** in which each teacher contributes his or her special competencies while the team is jointly responsible for providing instruction for a group of students. **Interdisciplinary teams** may teach all of the disciplines, or they may have lead teachers in each discipline who take the major responsibility for the teaching of a subject area. Teams may be organized within a grade level or across grade levels. Teams may employ self-contained departmentalized and interdisciplinary instruction during a school year.

Organization and grouping, however, should be flexible. A single pattern of organization or grouping arrangement should not be used in a school. A sound approach is to organize and group according to the needs of students, abilities of teachers, and availability of facilities and resources. No single pattern fits all situations.

Figure 7.5 illustrates an elementary scheduling pattern that includes both a graded and nongraded grouping arrangement. The school is organized into two schools within a school. School A includes grades K through 3; School B, grades 4 through 6. In a **block schedule,** a unit of time is allowed for both graded and non-

School A (K-3)	School B (4-6)	Time
Homeroom *(Nongraded/Reading Level)*	*Homeroom* *(Nongraded/Reading Level)*	
		9:15–9:30
		9:30–9:45
Language Arts	Language Arts	9:45–10:00
(nongraded)	(nongraded)	10:00–10:15
		10:15–10:30
Mathematics		10:30–10:45
(nongraded)	Mathematics	10:45–11:00
	(nongraded)	11:00–11:15
Lunch		11:15–11:30
(nongraded)	Physical Ed.	11:30–11:45
	(nongraded)	11:45–12:00
		12:00–12:15
	Social Studies	12:15–12:30
	(graded)	12:30–12:45
		12:45–1:00
Social Studies	Lunch	1:00–1:15
(graded)	(graded)	1:15–1:30
Science		1:30–1:45
(graded)	Science	1:45–2:00
Physical Ed.	(graded)	2:00–2:15
(graded)		2:15–2:30
Enrichment	Enrichment	2:30–2:45
Program	Program	2:45–3:00
		3:00–3:15

FIGURE 7.5   Schedule with Graded and Nongraded Grouping

Principal
Curriculum Assistant

Steering Committee
2 members of School A
2 members of School B
1 Specialist

Curriculum Committee
Language Arts Chairperson
Math Chairperson
Science Chairperson
Social Studies Chairperson
School A   Specs. Chairperson   *School B*
13 Teachers   Specialists   11 Teachers
1 Chairman   Special Education   1 Chairman
Physical Education
etc.

FIGURE 7.6   Governing Structure of Oakleaf Elementary School

graded courses, thus allowing for time frames for instruction in the discipline to be used. Enrichment classes are taught by all faculty members and are nongraded within School A and School B.

The governance of the school illustrated in Figure 7.6 includes the principal, the curriculum assistant, who also chairs the curriculum committee, and the chairperson of the steering committee. The steering committee consists of the chairperson of School A, chairperson of School B, a representative from the specialists' group (P.E., art, EMR, media, music), and one other teacher from School A and from School B (a total of five members). The chairperson of each school is selected yearly by staff members of that school. The chairperson of the steering committee is also selected by that group on a yearly basis.

INFLUENCE OF THE MIDDLE SCHOOL ON ELEMENTARY CURRICULUM

The growing **middle school** movement in the 1970s and 1980s resulted in curricular and organizational changes in the elementary school. Early in the middle school movement, grades 5 and 6 were taken from the elementary curriculum and combined with grades 7 and 8 of the junior high school or high school. The ninth grade went to the high school. Later, fifth grades were returned to the elementary school in most districts, resulting in a grades K–5, 6–8, 9–12 structure in many districts. By losing the sixth grade, the elementary school was left with two developmental groups: early childhood youth in grades K–3 and late childhood youth in grades 4 and 5. Not having to cope with emerging adolescents in grade six allowed elementary schools to match their curriculum better with the developmental levels of the youth served by the elementary school. Figure 7.7 illustrates the developmental levels and curricular implications for students in elementary, middle, and high schools.

The elementary curriculum in the 1980s and 1990s was affected dramatically by demands brought about by testing and evaluation. Legislators and political groups led the change in insisting that basic skills of reading, writing, and arithmetic be the focus of teaching in the elementary school. Single-series texts in reading, mandated instructional time for reading and mathematics, and **minimum competency testing** at various grade levels have resulted.

The elementary school of the 1990s has been changing to a full-service school with a great variety of programs needed to meet the increasing diversity of the student population.

In looking at the history of the elementary school, we can see how various reform movements have affected the elementary curriculum. Examining lessons from the past, we can see that the elementary curriculum must include many different learning experiences for a variety of learners. A balanced program must be available for all elementary children if the elementary school is to meet the needs of students in the 1990s and beyond. Figure 7.8 lists some organizations that focus on early childhood programs.

Program

Elementary School	Middle School	High School
Introduction to School	Personal Development	Comprehensive
Socialization	Refinement of Skills	Vocational Training
Beginning Skills		College Preparatory
Beginning Learnings	Continued Learnings	In-Depth Learnings
Introduction to Disciplines	Education for Social	
	Competence	Chemistry
Social Studies		Algebra
Science		World History
		American Literature
—		
—	Interdisciplinary Learnings	Career Planning

Organization Developmental Skills

Elementary School	Middle School	High School
K–5	6, 7–8	9–12
	6–8	
K–3 4–5		
Early Late		
Childhood Childhood	Transescence	Adolescence

FIGURE 7.7   Developmental Levels of Students in the Elementary, Middle, and High School

Association for Childhood Education
   International (ACEI)
11141 Georgia Avenue, Suite 200
Wheaton, MD
(301) 942-2443

Association for Supervision and Curriculum
   Development (ASCD)
1250 North Pitt Street
Alexandria, VA
(703) 549-9110

Bank Street College of Education
610 West 112th Street
New York, NY
(212) 663-7200

Children's Defense Fund
122 C Street, N.W.
Washington, DC
(202) 628-8787

ERIC Clearinghouse of Elementary and Early
   Childhood Education
University of Illinois at Urbana-Champaign
805 West Pennsylvania Avenue
Urbana, IL
(217) 333-1386

High/Scope Education Research Foundation
600 North River Street
Ypsilanti, MI
(313) 485-2000

National Association of Elementary School
   Principals (NAESP)
1615 Duke Street
Alexandria, VA
(703) 684-3345

National Association for the Education of
   Young Children (NAEYC)
1834 Connecticut Avenue, N.W.
Washington, DC
(800) 424-2460 or (202) 232-8777

National Association of State Boards of
   Education (NASBE)
701 North Fairfax Street, Suite 340
Alexandria, VA
(703) 684-4000

National State Child Development Institute
1463 Rhode Island Avenue, N.W.
Washington, DC
(202) 387-1281

Southern Association for Children Under Six
   (SACUS)
Box 5403
Brady Station
Little Rock, AR
(501) 666-0353

FIGURE 7.8   Organizations Concerned with Early Childhood Programs

TRENDS IN ELEMENTARY EDUCATION: DETERMINING WHAT WORKS

Year-round schools were seen by proponents as a cost-containment method and better learning environment for elementary students during the period of 1986 to 1996. In 1985, fewer than one half million students were in year-round schools. By 1996, the total had reached 1.8 million students. The number of year-round schools increased 600 percent (from 408 to 2368) from 1986 to 1996. The majority of students in these year-round schools were elementary students. Year-round schools had been established in thirty-nine states by 1996 with most year-round schools in California.

By 1997, the trend had begun to reverse, with over one hundred schools moving back to a traditional calendar. Orange County, Florida (Orlando), phased out all sixty-four of its year-round elementary schools in 1997.

Many schools found little improvement in their scores in year-round schools, and parents complained that they could not coordinate their children's vacation time. Community support has to be present if year-round schools are to succeed, and there is still a debate over how much cost savings really occurs in year-round school operation.

"Back-to-the-basics" is a plea often heard from education critics, yet others plead for schools to move beyond teaching low-level, simplistic objectives. Reformers stress that children need more than the basics to perform today's jobs. It seems the public wants tougher academic standards, yet they feel children can't acquire higher skills unless they have mastered the basics.[24]

Multi-age programs, particularly in the primary grades, became popular in the 1960s and reappeared in the 1990s. Traditional, age/grade-levels schools moved to a multi-age, nongraded structure.

Although proponents point out studies that indicate less student retention, better student achievement, less discipline referrals, and better student achievement in nongraded schools, opponents quickly point out other studies showing just the opposite. Parental support, as in year-round schools, seems to be a critical element in whether such programs last in schools.

Continuous progress programs, team teaching, and multi-year teaching of the same group of students again approach the teaching of elementary students in a climate where uneven development is not viewed as a deficit, but as a normal part of human growth. The teacher or teacher team strives to create a caring, learning community.[25]

Quality assessment practices is a topic that has remained both complicated and controversial. In a country where our culturally diverse population is becoming even more diverse, how do we assess progress of students? Rather than recommending one type of assessment over another, educators are focusing attention on a *set* of assessment practices.[26]

Portfolios, "authentic" assessment, and other terms are now being used by educators to talk about assessing the progress of students. Rather than just relying on standardized test results, teachers are using a variety of practices to assess and report progress of students in the elementary school.

Multicultural education faced strong setbacks in the 1980s and 1990s with conservative voices regularly denouncing the topic. Yet as the nation becomes more diverse and we prepare children to live in the global interdependence society of the next century, we keep revisiting the concept of multiculturalism. In the politically changed arena of today's schools, it is apparent that the topic will remain a controversial one. Technology and its use in the educating of young children remains on the front burner of educational change. In the fall of 1995, the U.S. Department of Education released a national action plan for the use of technology in education. Because technology is such a powerful tool for learning, any kind of comprehensive education reform will be difficult to achieve without utilizing technology to its fullest potential. Quality software, teacher training, and schools equipped with the latest information retrieval systems are necessary to meet the challenge. In 1996, it was estimated by the U.S. Office of Education that only about 10 percent of teachers were proficient users of technology. In an information age, we must understand that the use of technology means much more than using computers.

In concluding this chapter on elementary education, we pose the following curriculum problems that are common and recurrent:

1. With 25 percent of all American families moving each year, how can elementary programs deal with in-migration and out-migration?
2. Elementary children watch up to six hours of television each day. How can teachers compete with the influence of this medium?
3. School consolidations and busing have ended the century-old pattern of the neighborhood school in many communities. How can school identity and school spirit be maintained?
4. With only one family in twelve having a two-parent family in which the mother is home during the day, how can the school gain family support for achievement at school?
5. With fewer new teachers being hired and many staffs "aging in place," how can the school maintain a spirit of growth and an openness to new ideas?
6. Elementary children are coming to school with many new ideas. How can we keep up with finding a remedy for social needs and still carry out the academic function of the elementary school?
7. How can curriculum leaders promote a balanced school experience for learners in the face of accountability laws and policies that focus solely on student achievement of basic skills?

Must we do more for our young children? During the 1990 United Nations World Summit Conference for Children, President Bush joined 34 other presidents, 27 prime ministers, a king, a grand duke, and a cardinal among others to discuss the plight of 150 million children under the age of five suffering from malnutrition, 30 million living in the streets, and 7 million driven from their homes by war and famine. A bold ten-year plan was adopted to improve access to immunizations and education.

In the United States, every 8 seconds of the school day, a child drops out of school. Every 26 seconds, a child runs away from home. Every 47 seconds, a child is abused or neglected. Every 7 minutes, a child is arrested for a drug offense. Every 36 minutes, a child is killed or injured by a gun. Every day, 135,000 children bring guns to school.[27] Yes, we must do more.

SUMMARY

The first decade of the new century will present the elementary school with its greatest challenge ever. Social conditions, and new understandings of human growth and development, require change in both programs and the means of delivery.

In looking at the history of the elementary school, we can see how various forces have caused change and reform throughout our history. Examining those lessons from the past, we can see that the elementary curriculum must include a variety of learning experiences for a diverse population of learners. A balanced program must be available for all elementary students if the elementary school is to serve all learners in the next century.

Elementary educators in the next century will be hard-pressed to keep up with changing conditions that affect the ability of pupils to succeed in school. The goals of this nation, and those of world leaders, are ambitious and present school planners with their greatest challenge ever at this level.

SUGGESTED LEARNING ACTIVITIES

1. Identify the major events in the evolvement of the elementary school in the United States.
2. Analyze the curriculum of your elementary school to determine if there is a **balanced curriculum** available.
3. A group in your community has called for the abolishment of all art and music programs in the elementary school. Prepare a paper defending the inclusion of art and music in elementary curriculum.
4. Develop a schedule for an elementary school that will include provisions for both graded and nongraded classes.
5. Prepare evaluative criteria for a committee charged with developing guidelines for the selection of content in the major areas of language arts, mathematics, science, and social studies.

NOTES

1. Claudia Cohl, "The Future of Education," *Principal* (January, 1996): 22–38.
2. Karen Diegmueller, "The Best of Two Worlds," *Education Week* (March 20, 1996): 32–33.
3. Marjorie A. Wuhrick, "Blue Jays Win! Crows Go Down in Defeat!" *Kappan* (March, 1990): 553–56.
4. Bobbi Fisher, "Moving Beyond Letter of the Week," *Teaching K-8* (January, 1996): 74–76.
5. Jim Henry, "What Is Excellent Writing?" *Instructor* (September, 1995): 39–40.
6. Deborah Ball, "Teacher Learning and the Mathematics Reforms," *Kappan* (March, 1996): 500–508.
7. Maureen Stuart, "Effects of Group Grading on Cooperation and Achievement of Two Fourth-Grade Classes," *The Elementary School Journal* 95, 1 (1994): 11–21.
8. Kathleen Metz, "Reassessment of Developmental Constraints on Children's Science Instruction," *Review of Educational Research* 65, 2 (Summer, 1995): 91–127.
9. Linda Leonard Lamme, "The Literature Based Approach for a Social Studies Curriculum," *Trends and Issues* 8, 1 (Spring, 1996): 7–11.
10. George Graham, "Developmentally Appropriate Physical Education for Children," *Streamlined Seminar*, National Association of Elementary Principals, September, 1991.
11. Ralph Tyler, *Basic Principles of Curriculum and Instruction* (Chicago: University of Chicago Press, 1949), p. 5.
12. John Maag and Robert Reid, "Attention Deficit Hyperactivity Disorder: A Functional Approach to Assessment and Treatment," *Behavioral Disorders* 20, 1 (November, 1994) 5–22.
13. Maag and Reid, "Attention Deficit Hyperactivity Disorder."
14. Harold Hodgkinson, Center for Demographic Studies (Washington, DC: 1997).
15. Hodgkinson, Center for Demographic Studies.
16. Hodgkinson, Center for Demographic Studies.
17. Hodgkinson, Center for Demographic Studies.

18. Carol Ascher, "The Changing Face of Racial Isolation and Desegregation in Urban Schools," *New Schools, New Communities* II, 2 (Winter, 1995): 42–45.
19. R. Smelter and G. Yudeewitz, "Thinking of Inclusion for All Students? Better Think Again," *Kappan* 76, 1 (April, 1996): 35–38.
20. Mary Eums, Becky Holland, and Pat Nichol, "Implementing a Balanced Inclusion Program," *Principal* 75, 4 (March, 1996): 33–34.
21. Gerald W. Bracey, "The Impact of Early Intervention," *Kappan* 7, 4 (March, 1996): 510–11.
22. National Association for the Education of Young Children, *Appropriate Education in the Primary Grades—A Position Statement* (Washington, DC: 1997).
23. Gerald W. Bracey, "Change and Continuity in Elementary Education," *Principal* 75 (January, 1996): 46–50.
24. "At the Crossroads," *American Teacher,* American Federation of Teachers, 80, 5 (February, 1996): 6–7.
25. Don Jeanroy, "The Results of Multiage Grouping," *The School Administrator* (January, 1996): 18–19.
26. Brian Leving, "Quality Assessment Practices in a Diverse Society," *Teaching Exceptional Children* 28, 3 (Spring, 1996): 42–45.
27. Children's Defense Fund, Annual Report, 1997.

BOOKS TO REVIEW

Arcaro, Janice. *Creating Quality in the Classroom.* Delray Beach, FL: St. Lucie Press, 1995.

Barratta, Anthony N., Nancy J. Ellsworth, and Carolyn H. Hedley, eds. *Literacy: A Redefinition.* Hillsdale, NJ: L. Erlbaum Associates, 1994.

Bireley, Marlene. *Crossover Children: A Sourcebook for Helping Children Who Are Gifted and Learning Disabled,* 2nd ed. Reston, VA: Council for Exceptional Children, 1995.

Bireley, Marlene, Judy L. Genshaft, and Constance L. Hollinger, eds. *Serving Gifted and Talented Students: A Resource for School Personnel.* Austin, TX: Pro-Ed, 1995.

Block, Cathy Collins. *Creating a Culturally Enriched Curriculum for Grades K-6.* Boston: Allyn and Bacon, 1995.

Charbonneau, Manon P. *The Integrated Elementary Classroom: A Developmental Model of Education for the 21st Century.* Boston: Allyn and Bacon, 1995.

Collins, Martha D., and Barbara G. Moss, eds. *Literacy Assessment for Today's Schools.* Harrisonburg, VA: College Reading Association, 1996.

Cuffaro, Harriet K. *Experimenting with the World: John Dewey and the Early Childhood Classroom.* New York: Teachers College Press, Teachers College, Columbia University, 1995.

French, Michael P. *Attention Deficit and Reading Instruction.* Bloomington, IN: Phi Delta Kappa Educational Foundation, 1995.

Hohmann, Mary. *Educating Young Children: Active Learning Practices for Preschool and Child Care Programs.* Ypsilanti, MI: High/Scope Press, 1995.

Joyce, Bruce R. *Models of Teaching,* 5th ed. Boston: Allyn and Bacon, 1996.

Levy, Steven. *Starting from Scratch: One Classroom Builds Its Own Curriculum,* Portsmouth, NH: Heinemman, 1996.

Smith, Tom E., ed. *Teaching Students with Special Needs in Inclusive Settings.* Boston: Allyn and Bacon, 1995.

Walling, Donovan, ed. *At the Threshold of the Millennium.* Bloomington, IN: Phi Delta Kappa Educational Foundation, 1995.

chapter 8

MIDDLE SCHOOL PROGRAMS AND ISSUES

After forty years, the middle school is America's longest running innovation. Like its predecessor, the junior high school, the middle school serves as a transitional school between the elementary school and the high school. In this chapter, the middle school will be explored as a preferred model for intermediate education in the century.

The junior high school, originated in 1910, was intended to move the secondary program into the elementary grades. The familiar bulletin *Cardinal Principles of Secondary Education* recommended that a school system be organized into a six-year elementary school and a six-year high school designed to serve pupils twelve to eighteen years of age.[1] The *Bulletin* also suggested that secondary education be divided into two periods, designated the "junior" and "senior" periods. Thus, junior high schools were thought to be a part of the high school, and for fifty years the curriculum of the junior high school tended to parallel that of the high school. Activities such as varsity athletics, marching bands, and even cap-and-gown graduation exercises tended to exert considerable pressures on junior high students. Teacher training institutions also prepared "secondary" teachers for positions in the junior high schools. Most junior high schools were organized with grades 7 through 9.

By 1960, a number of factors led to the emergence of a new school known as the **middle school.** Critics of the junior high school were beginning to try to reform the junior high school in the 1940s and 1950s but could not break the junior high from the high school mold.[2]

Four factors led to the emergence of the middle school. First, the late 1950s and early 1960s were filled with criticisms of American schools, classroom and teacher shortage, double and triple sessions, and soaring tax rates. Books such as *Why Johnny Can't Read* triggered new concerns about the quality of schooling in the United States. The successful launching of *Sputnik* in 1957 led to a new wave of criticism about the curriculum of elementary and secondary schools. *Sputnik* created an obsession with academic achievement, especially in the areas of science, foreign languages, and mathematics. A renewed interest in college preparation led to a call for a four-year high school where specialized courses could remain under the direction of the college preparatory school—the high school. Likewise, the inclusion of grades 5 and 6 in an intermediate school could strengthen instruction by allowing subject area specialists to work with younger students. Many of the first middle schools were organized with grades 5 through 8.

A second factor leading to the emergence of the middle school was the elimination of racial segregation. *The Schoolhouse in the City* stated that the real force behind the middle school movement in the larger cities (New York City, for example) was to eliminate de facto segregation.[3]

A third factor leading to the emergence of the middle school was the increased enrollments of school-age children in the 1950s and 1960s. The shortage of buildings resulted in double and even triple school sessions in some districts. Because older children in high schools were able to cope with overcrowding better than younger students, the ninth grade was moved to the high school to relieve the overcrowded junior high school. The same rationale was used to relieve the elementary school by moving the fifth or sixth grade to the junior high school.

A fourth factor resulting in middle schools was the *bandwagon effect*. Because one middle school received favorable exposure in books and periodicals, some administrators determined that the middle school was "the thing to do."

All of these factors may not have provided a valid reason for middle school organization, but they did provide the right opportunity for reform of the American intermediate school.

Throughout the 1970s and 1980s, junior high schools were converted to a middle school design in record numbers, with the same four factors at play. In the 1990s, a new increase in school-age population caused more conversions to middle schools. By the end of the 1990s, 90 percent of intermediate schools were classified as middle school.

We believe the following reasons, related to providing a more relevant and appropriate program and learning environment for transescent (the period between childhood and adolescence) learners, are easier to justify:

- ☐ To provide a program especially designed for the ten- to fourteen-year-old child going through the unique transescent period of growth and development. Students age 10 to 14 constitute a distinct grouping—physically, socially, and intellectually.

- ☐ To build on the changed elementary school. Historically, the post-*Sputnik* clamor to upgrade schools prepared the way for elementary school personnel to accept the middle school concept. The introduction of the "new" science, the "new" social studies, the "new" mathematics, and the "new" linguistics in elementary schools eroded the sanctity of the self-contained classroom. As part of the reorganization of curriculum that followed *Sputnik,* elementary teachers tended to cultivate a specific content area in the curriculum. This led to a departure from the self-contained classroom toward more sharing of students among teachers.

☐ To counter dissatisfaction with the existing junior high school. The junior high school, in most cases, did not become a transitional school between the elementary and senior high school. Unfortunately, it became a miniature high school with all of the sophisticated activities of the high school. Instruction was often formal and discipline-centered, with insufficient attention given to the student as a person.

☐ To provide much-needed innovations in curriculum and instruction. By creating a new school—the middle school—rather than remodeling the outmoded junior high school, educators provided an atmosphere for implementing those practices long talked about but seldom effected.

FUNCTIONS OF THE MIDDLE SCHOOL

Both in recognition and in numbers, middle schools have become a separate, intermediate institution in America. Cumulative experience, research, and the fact that the middle school "works" have resulted in widespread acceptance of the middle school by children, teachers, administrators, and parents. We define the middle school as a transitional school concerned with the most appropriate program to cope with the personal and educational needs of emerging adolescent learners. The middle school should be an institution that has

1. A unique program adapted to the needs of the pre- and early-adolescent, transescent, student
2. The widest possible range of intellectual, social, and physical experiences
3. Opportunities for exploration and development of fundamental skills needed by all, with allowances for individual learning patterns. An atmosphere of basic respect for individual differences should be maintained.
4. A climate that enables students to develop abilities, find facts, weigh evidence, draw conclusions, determine values, and that keeps their minds open to new facts
5. Staff members who recognize and understand the student's needs, interests, backgrounds, motivations, goals, as well as stresses, strains, frustrations, and fears
6. A smooth educational transition between the elementary school and the high school that allows for the physical and emotional changes of transescence
7. An environment in which the child, not the program, is most important and where the opportunity to succeed is ensured for all students
8. Guidance in the development of mental processes and attitudes needed for constructive citizenship and the development of lifelong competencies and appreciations needed for effective use of leisure

9. Competent instructional personnel who will strive to understand the students whom they serve and who will develop professional competencies that are both unique and applicable to the transescent student
10. Facilities and time to allow students and teachers in opportunity to achieve the goals of the program to their fullest capabilities

Table 8.1 illustrates the unique and transitory nature of the middle school.

The middle school, then, presents a renewed effort to design and implement a program of education that can accommodate the needs of the pre-adolescent population. It is a broadly focused program of education, drawing its philosophy and rationale from the evolving body of knowledge concerned with human growth and development. The middle school represents a systematic effort to organize the schooling experience in a way that will facilitate the maximum growth and development of all learners.

The middle school program consists of arrangements and activities that attempt to tie formal learning directly to the developmental needs of the students who are served. To date, identified **developmental tasks** represent the most promising criteria for curriculum development that will intersect school activity with learner growth and development.

ESTABLISHING AN IDENTITY FOR THE MIDDLE SCHOOL

Education for emerging adolescents has received an intensive reexamination over the past decade. One result has been the verification of a need for a school with a differentiated function for **early adolescents**—ages 10 to 14. That need for a distinct school, unlike the elementary, high, or even the junior high school, is more defensible than ever in light of recent information about growth and development of emerging adolescents. Changing social conditions have also helped to establish the need for a school in the middle with a identity of its own. As middle schools

TABLE 8.1   Schools in the Middle

	Elementary	Middle	High
Teacher–Student Relationship	Parental	Advisor	Random
Teacher Organization	Self-contained	Interdisciplinary team	Department
Curriculum	Skills	Exploration	Depth
Schedule	Self-contained	Block	Periods
Instruction	Teacher-directed	Balance	Student-directed
Student Grouping	Chronological	Multi-age development	Subject
Building Plan	Classroom areas	Team areas	Department areas
Physical Education	Skills and games	Skills and intramurals	Skills and inter-scholastics
Media Center	Classroom groups	Balance	Individual study
Guidance	Diagnostic/ development	Teacher helper	Career-vocational
Teacher Preparation	Child-oriented generalist	Flexible resource	Disciplines specialist

have grown in number and quality, some common elements found in middle schools have contributed to their special identity, such as

☐ Absence of the "little high school" approach
☐ Absence of the "star" system, in which a few special students dominate everything, in favor of an attempt to provide success experience for greater numbers of students
☐ An attempt to use instructional methods more appropriate to this age group; individualized instruction, variable group sizes, multimedia approaches, beginning independent study programs, and inquiry-oriented instruction
☐ Increased opportunity for teacher-student guidance; may include a home base of advisory group program
☐ Increased flexibility in scheduling and student grouping
☐ Some cooperative planning and team teaching
☐ Some interdisciplinary studies, in which teachers from a variety of academic areas provide opportunities for students to see how the areas of knowledge fit together
☐ A wide range of exploratory opportunities, academic and otherwise
☐ Increased opportunity for physical activity and movement and more frequent physical education
☐ Earlier introduction to the areas of organized academic knowledge
☐ Attention to the skills of continued learning, those skills that will permit students to learn better on their own or at higher levels
☐ Accent or increasing the student's ability to be independent, responsible, and self-disciplined
☐ Flexible physical plant facilities
☐ Attention to the personal development of the student; values clarification, group process skills, health and family life education when appropriate, and career education
☐ Teachers trained especially for, and committed to, the education of emerging adolescents

THE MIDDLE SCHOOL STUDENT

The middle school espouses the same goals as did the junior high. Those goals are to provide a transition school between the elementary and the high school and to help students bridge the gap in their development between childhood and adolescence.

Emerging adolescent learners in the middle school represent the most diverse group of students at any organizational level of schooling. As ninth graders moved to the high school and sixth graders came into the middle school, the middle school became a real transitional school with students found at all levels of physical, social, and intellectual maturity. Middle schools, unlike junior high schools that tended to treat all students as adolescents, have attempted to develop programs to help students bridge the gap in development between childhood and adolescence.

Pre- and early adolescents experience dramatic physical, social, emotional, and intellectual changes resulting from maturational changes. More biological changes occur in the bodies and minds of youngsters between the ages of 10 and 14 than at any other period in their lives except the first nine months of their development.

Because the transitional years between childhood and adolescence are marked by distinct changes in the bodies and minds of boys and girls, the success of the middle school depends on teachers and administrators who understand each learner and his or her unique developmental pattern.

Figure 8.1 describes in detail the characteristics of emerging adolescents and the implications for the middle school.

THE MIDDLE SCHOOL TEACHER

The middle school teacher, more than any other factor, holds the key to realization of the type of effective middle school required for emerging adolescents.

The middle school teacher must have all of those characteristics that research indicates are good for teachers of all age groups. However, because of the ages embraced in the middle school, the middle school teacher is responsible for children who are striking in their diversity. What confronts a teacher in the middle school is a rapidly changing group of children in different stages of development.

A number of key competencies have been identified for teachers in the middle school (see Figure 8.2).

MANAGING MIDDLE SCHOOL PROGRAMS

A well-designed middle school features a balanced program focusing on personal development, basic skills for continuous learners, and use of knowledge to foster competence. The curriculum of a middle school thus follows closely the developmental stages represented in the students that it serves.

There has been much progress in recent years in developing new and exciting programs for emerging adolescent learners, yet much still needs to be done. New pressures brought on by the call for a return to basics has narrowed the curriculum of the middle school to the teaching of rote skills and the transmission of knowledge. Exploratory programs, guidance services, and health and physical education programs have been cut back in many schools. Thus, the curriculum area of personal development has been changed in many middle schools. This development forced an imbalance in the middle school program and a return to the more content-centered junior high or imitation high school model in many middle schools. With sixth graders being housed in many middle schools, the result was the thrusting down of a high school program to an even younger group of students. Combined with a six- or seven-period departmentalized organizational model, the lack of emphasis on personal development signals a return to a secondary emphasis in the middle grades. The gains in program development won in the 1960s, 1970s, and 1980s by middle school educators were being washed away in the 1990s in many places by a return to the high school or secondary model, which was easier to schedule and administer. The lessons learned by the failure of the junior high school were lost in the face of doing what was easier and less costly.

Characteristics of Emerging Adolescents	Implications for the Middle School
Physical Development	
Accelerated physical development begins in transescence, marked by increase in weight, height, heart size, lung capacity, and muscular strength. Boys and girls are growing at varying rates. Girls tend to be taller for the first two years and tend to be more physically advanced. Bone growth is faster than muscle development, and the uneven muscle/bone development results in lack of coordination and awkwardness. Bones may lack protection of covering muscles and supporting tendons.	Provide a health and science curriculum that emphasizes self-understanding about body changes. Guidance counselors and community resource persons (e.g., pediatricians) can help students understand what is happening to their bodies.
	Schedule adaptive physical education classes to build physical coordination. Equipment design should help students develop small and large muscles.
In pubescent girls, secondary sex characteristics continue to develop, with breasts enlarging and menstruation beginning.	Intense sports competition; avoid contact sports.
	Schedule sex education classes; health and hygiene seminars.
A wide range of individual differences among students begins to appear. Although the sequential order of development is relatively consistent in each sex, boys tend to lag a year or two behind girls. There are marked individual differences in physical development for boys and girls. The age of greatest variability in physiological development and physical size is about age 13.	Provide opportunities for interaction among students of different ages, but avoid situations where physical development can be compared (e.g., communal showers).
	Emphasize intramural programs rather than interscholastic athletics so that each student may participate regardless of physical development. Where interscholastic sports programs exist, number of games should be limited, with games played in afternoon rather than evening.
Glandular imbalances occur, resulting in acne, allergies, dental and eye defects—some health disturbances are real, and some are imaginary.	Provide regular physical examinations for all middle school students.
Boys and girls display changes in body contour—large nose, protruding ears, long arms—have posture problems, and are self-conscious about their bodies.	Health classes should emphasize exercises for good posture. Students should understand through self-analysis that growth is an individual process and occurs unevenly.
A girdle of fat often appears around the hips and thighs of boys in early puberty. Slight development of tissue under the skin around the nipples occurs briefly, causing anxiety in boys who fear they are developing "the wrong way."	Films and talks by doctors and counselors can help students understand the changes the body goes through during this period. A carefully planned program of sex education developed in collaboration with parents, medical doctors, and community agencies should be developed.

FIGURE 8.1   Development of Emerging Adolescents and Implications for the Middle School

Physical Development *(continued)*	
Students are likely to be disturbed by body changes. Girls especially are likely to be disturbed by the physical changes that accompany sexual maturation.	
Receding chins, cowlicks, dimples, and changes in voice result in possible embarrassment to boys.	Teacher and parental reassurance and understanding are necessary to help students understand that many body changes are temporary in nature.
Boys and girls tend to tire easily but won't admit it.	Advise parents to insist that students get proper rest; overexertion should be discouraged.
Fluctuations in basal metabolism may cause students to be extremely restless at times and listless at others.	Provide an opportunity for daily exercise and a place where students can be children by playing and being noisy for short periods.
	Encourage activities such as special-interest classes and "hands on" exercises. Students should be allowed to move around physically in classes and avoid long periods of passive work.
Boys and girls show ravenous appetites and peculiar tastes; may overtax digestive system with large quantities of improper foods.	Provide snacks to satisfy between-meal hunger as well as nutritional guidance specific to this age group.

Social Development	
Affiliation base broadens from family to peer group. Conflict sometimes results due to splitting of allegiance between peer group and family.	Teachers should work closely with the family to help adults realize that peer pressure is a normal part of the maturation process. Parents should be encouraged to continue to provide love and comfort even though they may feel rejected.
	Teachers should be counselors. Homebase, teacher-adviser house plan arrangements should be encouraged.
Peers become sources for standards and models of behavior. Child's occasional rebellion does not diminish importance of parents for development of values. Emerging adolescents want to make their own choices, but authority still remains primarily with family.	Sponsor school activities that permit students to interact socially with many school personnel. Family studies can help ease parental conflicts. Parental involvement at school should be encouraged, but parents should not be too conspicuous by their presence.

FIGURE 8.1 *(Continued)*

	Encourage co-curriculum activities. For example, an active student government will help students develop guidelines for interpersonal relations and standards of behavior.
Society's mobility has broken ties to peer groups and created anxieties in emerging adolescents.	Promote "family" grouping of students and teachers to provide stability for new students. Interdisciplinary units can be structured to provide interaction among various groups of students. Clubs and special-interest classes should be an integral part of the school day.
Students are confused and frightened by new school settings.	Orientation programs and "buddy systems" can reduce the trauma of moving from an elementary school to a middle school. Family teams can encourage a sense of belonging.
Students show unusual or drastic behavior at times—aggressive, daring, boisterous, argumentative.	Schedule debates, plays, playdays, and other activities to allow students to "show off" in a productive way.
"Puppy love" years emerge, with a show of extreme devotion to a particular boy or girl. However, allegiance may be transferred to a new friend overnight.	Role-playing and guidance exercises can provide the opportunity to act out feelings. Provide opportunities for social interaction between the sexes—parties and games, but not dances in the early grades of the middle school.
Youths feel that the will of the group must prevail and sometimes can be almost cruel to those not in their group. They copy and display fads of extremes in clothes, speech, mannerisms, and handwriting; very susceptible to media advertising.	Set up an active student government so students can develop their own guidelines for dress and behavior. Adults should be encouraged not to react with outrage when extreme dress or mannerisms are displayed.
Boys and girls show strong concern for what is "right" and for social justice; also show concern for those less fortunate.	Foster plans that allow students to engage in service activities, for example, peer teaching, which allow students to help other students. Community projects (e.g., assisting in a senior citizens club or helping in a childcare center) can be planned by students and teachers.
They are influenced by adults—attempt to identify with adults other than their parents.	Flexible teaching patterns should prevail so students can interact with a variety of adults with whom they can identify.

FIGURE 8.1 *(Continued)*

Social Development *(continued)*	
Despite a trend toward heterosexual interests, same-sex affiliation tends to dominate.	Plan large group activities rather than boy-girl events. Intramurals can be scheduled so students can interact with friends of the same or opposite sex.
Students desire direction and regulation but reserve the right to question or reject suggestions of adults.	Provide opportunities for students to accept more responsibility in setting standards for behavior. Students should be helped to establish realistic goals and be assisted in helping realize those goals.

Emotional Development	
Erratic and inconsistent behavior is prevalent. Anxiety and fear contrast with reassuring bravado. Feelings tend to shift between superiority and inferiority. Coping with physical changes, striving for independence from family, becoming a person in his/her own right, and learning a new mode of intellectual functioning are all emotion-laden problems for emerging adolescents. Students have many fears, real and imagined. At no other time in development is he or she likely to encounter such a diverse number of problems simultaneously.	Encourage self-evaluation among students. Design activities that help students play out their emotions. Activity programs should provide opportunities for shy students to be drawn out and loud students to engage in calming activities. Counseling must operate as a part of, rather than an adjunct to, the learning program. Students should be helped to interpret superiority and inferiority feelings. Mature value systems should be encouraged by allowing students to examine options of behavior and to study consequences of various actions.
	Encourage students to assume leadership in group discussions and experience frequent success and recognition for personal efforts and achievements. A general atmosphere of friendliness, relaxation, concern, and group cohesiveness should guide the program.
Chemical and hormone imbalances often trigger emotions that are little understood by the transescent. Students sometimes regress to childlike behavior.	Adults in the middle school should not pressure students to explain their emotions (e.g., crying for no apparent reason). Occasional childlike behavior should not be ridiculed.
	Provide numerous possibilities for releasing emotional stress.
Too-rapid or too-slow physical development is often a source of irritation and concern. Development of secondary sex characteristics may create additional tensions about rate of development.	Provide appropriate sex education and encourage participation of parents and community agencies. Pediatricians, psychologists, and counselors should be called on to assist students in understanding developmental changes.

FIGURE 8.1   *(Continued)*

Emotional Development *(continued)*	
This age group is easily offended and sensitive to criticism of personal shortcomings.	Sarcasm by adults should be avoided. Students should be helped to develop values when solving their problems.
Students tend to exaggerate simple occurrences and believe their problems are unique.	Use sociodrama to enable students to see themselves as others see them. Readings dealing with problems similar to their own can help them see that many problems are not unique.

Intellectual Development	
Students display a wide range of skills and abilities unique to their developmental patterns.	Use a variety of approaches and materials in the teaching-learning process.
Students will range in development from the concrete-manipulatory stage to the ability to deal with abstract concepts. The transescent is intensely curious and growing in mental ability.	Treat students at their own intellectual levels, providing immediate rather than remote goals. All subjects should be individualized. Skill grouping should be flexible.
Middle school learners prefer active over passive learning activities and prefer interaction with peers during learning activities.	Encourage physical movement, with small group discussions, learning centers, and creative dramatics suggested as good activity projects. Provide a program of learning that is exciting and meaningful.
Students are usually very curious and exhibit a strong willingness to learn things they consider useful. They enjoy using skills to solve "real-life" problems.	Organize curricula around real-life concepts (e.g., conflict, competition, peer group influence). Provide activities in formal and informal situations to improve reasoning powers. Studies of the community and the environment are particularly relevant to the age group.
Students often display heightened egocentrism and will argue to convince others or to clarify their own thinking. Independent, critical thinking emerges.	Organized discussions of ideas and feelings in peer groups can facilitate self-understanding. Provide experiences for individuals to express themselves by writing and participating in dramatic productions.
Studies show that brain growth in transescents slows between the ages of 12 and 14.	Learners' cognitive skills should be refined; continued cognitive growth during ages 12 to 14 may not be expected.
	Provide opportunities for enjoyable studies in the arts. Encourage self-expression in all subjects.

FIGURE 8.1 *(Continued)*

Source: From Jon Wiles and Joseph Bondi, *The Essential Middle School,* 2nd ed., pp. 29–34. Copyright ©
1993 by Macmillan Publishing Company. Reprinted by permission.

1. Possesses knowledge of the pre- and early adolescent physical development, which includes knowledge of physical activity needs and the diversity and variety of physical growth rates.
2. Commands knowledge of the pre- and early adolescent intellectual development, with emphasis on the transition from concrete to formal levels of mental development.
3. Has a knowledge of a recognized developmental theory and personality theory which can be used in identifying appropriate learning strategies for the pre- and early adolescent.
4. Understands the socio-emotional development, including the need to adjust to a changing body.
5. Possesses the necessary skills to allow interaction between individual students as well as the opportunity to work in groups of varying sizes.
6. Understands the cultural forces and community relationships, which affect the total school curriculum.
7. Has the ability to organize the curriculum to facilitate the developmental tasks of preadolescence and early adolescence.
8. Understands the transitional nature of grades 3 through 6 as they bridge the gap between the children of the lower elementary grades and late adolescents and early adults of the upper grades.
9. Possesses the skills needed to work with other teachers and school professionals in team teaching situations.
10. Has the ability to plan multidisciplinary lessons or units and teach them personally or with other professionals.
11. Commands a broad academic background, with specialization in at least two allied areas of the curriculum.
12. Possesses the skill to integrate appropriate media and concrete demonstrations into presentations.
13. Is able to develop and conduct learning situations that will promote independent learning and to maximize student choice and responsibility for follow-through.
14. Possesses the knowledge and skills that will allow students to sort information, set priorities, and budget time and energy.
15. Is able to teach problem-solving skills and develop lessons that are inquiry oriented.
16. Has the ability to teach students how to discover knowledge and use both inductive and deductive methods in the discovery of knowledge.
17. Possesses the knowledge and skills necessary to use role-playing simulation, instructional games, and creative dramatics in teaching the content as well as the affective domain in a middle-grade classroom.
18. Commands the knowledge and skill needed to organize and manage a class that allows individuals to learn at a rate commensurate with their ability.
19. Possesses verbal behaviors that will promote student input in a variety to group settings.
20. Is able to write behavioral objectives and design lessons to effectively conclude the objectives.
21. Has the knowledge and skills needed to diagnose strengths and weaknesses, to determine learning levels of individuals, to prescribe courses of action, and to evaluate the outcomes.
22. Has experiences in innovation and possesses the skill to experiment with teaching techniques to find those that are most effective in given situations.
23. Is able to teach the communication skills of reading, writing, and speaking in all subject areas.
24. Commands knowledge of reading techniques that will enable students to

FIGURE 8.2   Selected Teacher Competencies for Middle School Teachers

progress and improve their reading in the subject areas.

25. Possesses the skills needed to diagnose reading problems and provide a remedial program in regular classroom.
26. Has a knowledge of the techniques necessary to promote positive self-concepts and self-reliance.
27. Is able to help students clarify values, consider alternative values, and develop a personal and workable valuing system.
28. Possesses a knowledge of group dynamics and the ability to organize groups that will make decisions and provide their own leadership.
29. Has a knowledge of careers and the ability to help students explore careers.
30. Commands knowledge of several major learning theories and the learning strategies that emanate from the theories.
31. Has a knowledge of how to deal with unusual classroom problems.
32. Possesses skills necessary to effectively manage groups of students in activity settings.
33. Possesses the ability to recognize difficulties that may be emotionally or physically based.
34. Possesses the knowledge and skills needed to effectively manage abusive and deviant behavior.
35. Works with extracurricular activities in the school.
36. Gathers appropriate personal information or students by using questionnaires, interviews, and observation.
37. Provides frequent feedback to students on learning progress.
38. Functions calmly in a high-activity environment.
39. Handles disruptive behavior in a positive and consistent manner.
40. Builds learning experiences for students based on learning skills (reading math)

obtained in elementary grades.

41. Works cooperatively with peers, consultants, resource persons, and paraprofessionals.
42. Exhibits concern for students by listening or empathizing with them.
43. Selects evaluation techniques appropriate to curricular objective in the affective domain.
44. Uses value clarification and other affective teaching techniques to help students develop personal value systems.
45. Provides an informal, flexible classroom environment.
46. Cooperates in curricular planning and revision.
47. Evaluates the teaching situation and selects the grouping techniques most appropriate for the situation: large group instruction (100+ students), small group instruction (15–25 students) or independent study.
48. Uses questioning techniques skillfully to achieve higher-order thinking processes in students.
49. Can move from one type of grouping situation to another smoothly.
50. Functions effectively in various organizational and staffing situations, such as team teaching, differentiated staffing, and multi-age groups.
51. Selects evaluation techniques appropriate to curricular objectives in the psychomotor domain.
52. Establishes positive relationships with the parents and families of students.
53. Works at understanding, accepting, and being accepted by members of the subcultures in the school and the community.
54. Understands the middle school concept and attempts to apply it in the classroom and in the school as a whole.
55. Manages the classroom with a minimum of negative or aversive controls.

FIGURE 8.2 *(Continued)*

56. Uses himself/herself as a tool in promoting the personal growth of students and colleagues.
57. Maintains harmonious and productive relationships with colleagues, administrators, and supervisors.
58. Is aware of the needs, forces, and perceptions that determine his/her personal behavior.

59. Maintains a balance between teacher-directed learning and student-directed learning.
60. Proceeds from a problem-solving framework involving the students in relevant inquiry.
61. Possesses skill in asking questions that encourage student thinking beyond the level of recall.

FIGURE 8.2   *(Continued)*

Source: From J. Wiles and J. Bondi, *The Essential Middle School,* 2nd ed., pp. 55–58. Copyright © 1993 by Macmillan Publishing Company. Reprinted by permission.

The 1980s was a period of great activity in the middle school movement. Organizations such as the Association for Supervision and Curriculum Development (ASCD), local and state leagues of middle schools, the National Middle School Association, National Education Association, the National Association of Secondary School Principals, the National Association of Elementary School Principals, and the National School Boards Association all began presenting conferences, publications, and position papers, advocating the original purposes of the middle school as proposed in the national position document, *The Middle School We Need.*[4] Legislation encouraging middle school development and teacher training was passed in Florida, California, and other states that were active in the early middle school movement. The Carnegie Report, *Turning Points,* was the culmination of an active decade of middle school support.[5]

A milestone in the middle school movement occurred in 1986 with the publication of the best-selling ASCD publication, *Making Middle Schools Work.*[6] That publication addressed the major difficulty in getting middle schools to remain middle schools in program and organization as initially developed. The "shining light" syndrome with middle schools reflected the often-repeated situation in which a new middle school would be developed that would draw hundreds of visitors. That school would be a model for a year or two until the principal left or the staff changed. It would then revert to a junior high school type of program while a new shining light popped up somewhere else.

Seeing the frustration, and recognizing that there was an Achilles heel in the middle school success story throughout the United States, we introduced the Curriculum Management Plan (CMP)★ model for development of middle schools. The CMP model recognized the fact that at the very heart of implementing true middle

---

★The CMP model has been successfully used in the transition to true middle schools in such districts as St. Louis, Denver, Dallas, Orange County (Orlando, FL), Dade County (Miami, FL), Duval County (Jacksonville, FL), Baton Rouge, Long Beach (CA), and hundreds of large and small school districts in the United States. It has also been used by the Kellogg Foundation in developing the model middle school program in Ishpeming, Michigan.

schools is some solid, traditional curriculum development. The Wiles-Bondi CMP model draws from the previous work of Ralph Tyler and Hilda Taba and superimposes management techniques on a widely used accreditation format. Put simply, the CMP introduces regularity into the change process (manages it). Without such logic, the pitfalls for a complex design such as the middle school are multiple. The key to successful implementation of middle school programs remains successful planning.

Middle School Program: Overview

Successful middle schools using the Curriculum Management Plan model develop a design document that outlines program objectives and standards in detail.[7] Each design, or blueprint, is based on an extensive needs assessment outlining academic, social, and physical needs of middle grades students.

Curriculum leaders must not lose sight of the purpose of the middle school. The middle school is a transitional school and must not be an exact replica of the high school or elementary school. The need for balance in the program and organizational flexibility has never been greater. In addition to the normal developmental changes that middle school students are experiencing, social changes have a major impact on the lives of emerging adolescents. Consider the following:

- ☐ The American family is breaking down. For every marriage today, there is a divorce. By the year 2000, 60 percent of children in the middle grades will have spent some time in a single-parent home.
- ☐ More adults moonlight now than at any other time in the history or our country.
- ☐ Only 8 percent of American homes today have the family pattern of a mother at home and father working.
- ☐ Alcoholism increased 800 percent among teenagers in the last ten years. By the end of the ninth grade, 20 percent of adolescents will suffer a serious drinking problem.
- ☐ Forty-three percent of all persons arrested for serious crimes in the United States (rape, murder, robbery) are juveniles, yet juveniles make up only 20 percent of the population.
- ☐ One in two Americans moved during the past five years.
- ☐ One million girls between the ages of 10 and 18 gave birth to illegitimate babies in America last year. One of ten girls will be pregnant before age 18. An estimated 18 million teenage boys and girls are sexually active. AIDS is increasing at a very rapid rate among teenagers.
- ☐ The second leading cause of death among teenagers, after accidents, is suicide. The suicide rate among teenagers doubled in the decade between 1980 and 1990 and continues to increase in the 1990s.
- ☐ It is estimated that pre- and early adolescents spend one third of their waking hours watching television.
- ☐ Seventy-five percent of all advertising is aimed at ten- to eighteen-year-olds.
- ☐ Psychologists regard the lack of a stable home as the biggest contributor to delinquency.

□   The most impressionable age group is that of youngsters twelve to fourteen years of age. It is no accident that the Hitler Youth, Red Guard, and
even our Boy Scouts have age 12 as the starting point.

Dealing with emerging adolescents has become a national priority. In funding
the National Institute of Education (NIE) during the last decade, Congress mandated that the number one priority of NIE be research on emerging adolescent
learners. The *Carnegie Report* on adolescent development in 1989 pointed out the
serious deterioration of health care and the myriad social problems facing preado-
lescents and emerging adolescents. Consider that

□   The middle grades years represent the last chance for students to master
basic skills.
□   The middle grades represent the last time for formal schooling for many
of our youth. Low achievers drop out after the middle grades.
□   The final attitude toward self and others, as well as a lasting attitude
toward learning, is established in the middle grades.
□   Future school success—indeed, future life success—can be predicted for
most students in the middle grades.

Curriculum leaders must take a strong stance to prevent the middle school from
becoming an imitation high school again. There are still many good models of middle
schools and reformed junior high schools that offer promise for curriculum developers desiring to improve middle grades education. (See, for instance, the description for
the significant results of the middle school program in St. Louis, "Miracle on Main
Street—The St. Louis Story."[8]) In addition, the number of articles, texts, and research
studies in the middle school area has grown both in quantity and quality in the last
decade. Organizations such as the National Middle School Association and the Association for Supervision and Curriculum Development have organized numerous conferences and workshops for educators interested in middle school improvement.

Figure 8.3 illustrates the three major program elements needed in the middle
school.

Balance in the Middle School Program

A balanced program needed to serve the diverse group of youngsters found in the
middle grades should include the following:

□   Learning experiences for transescents at their own intellectual levels,
relating to immediate rather then remote academic goals.
□   A wide variety of cognitive learning experiences to account for the full
range of students who are at many different levels of concrete and formal
operations. Learning objectives should be sequenced to allow for the
transition from concrete to formal operations.

I. Personal Development

Guidance—Physical Education—Intramurals—Lifetime Sports—Sex Education—Health Studies—Law Education—Social Services—Drug Education—Special Interest—Clubs—Student Government—Development Groupings—Programs for Students with Special Needs—Mainstreaming—Alternative Programs—Advisory Programs—Intramurals.

II. **Education for Social Competence**	III. **Skills for Continuous Learning**
Basic Studies	Communication
Science	Reading
Social Studies	Writing
Mathematics	Listening
Language Arts	Speaking
Exploratory Studies	Mathematics
Practical Arts	Computation
Home Economics	Comprehension
Industrial Arts	Usage
Business-Distributive	
Education	Observing and Comparing
Fine Arts	
Music	Analyzing
Art	
Foreign Language	Generalizing
Humanities	
Environmental Studies	Organizing
Outdoor Education	
Career Exploration	Evaluating
Consumer Education	
Media Study	

FIGURE 8.3 Program Design for the Essential Middle School

Source: From J. Wiles and J. Bondi, *The Essential Middle School,* p. 84. Copyright © 1986 by Bondi and Associates, Tampa, FL. Reprinted by permission.

- ☐ A diversified curriculum of either exploratory or fundamental, or both, activities resulting in daily successful experiences that will stimulate and nurture intellectual development.
- ☐ Opportunities for the development of problem-solving skills, reflective-thinking processes, and awareness for the order of the student's environment.
- ☐ Cognitive learning experiences so structured that students can progress in an individualized manner. However, within the structure of an individualized learning program, students can interact with one another. Social interaction is not an enemy of individual learning.
- ☐ A curriculum in which all areas are taught to reveal opportunities for further study, to help students learn how to study, and to help them appraise their

own interests and talents. In addition, the middle school should continue the developmental program of basic skills instruction started in the elementary school, with emphasis on both developmental and remedial reading.

☐ A planned sequence of concepts in the general education areas, major emphasis on the interests and skills for continued learning, a balanced program of exploratory experiences and other activities and services for personal development, and appropriate attention to the development of values.

☐ A common program in which areas of learning are combined and integrated to break down artificial and irrelevant divisions of curriculum content. Some previously departmentalized areas of the curriculum should be combined and taught around integrative themes, topics, and experiences. Other areas of the curriculum, particularly those concerned with basic skills that are logical, sequential, and analytical, might best be taught in ungraded or continuous progress programs. Inflexible student scheduling, with its emphasis on departmentalization, should be restructured in the direction of greater flexibility.

☐ Encouragement of personal curiosity, with one learning experience inspiring subsequent activities.

☐ Methods of instruction involving open and individually directed learning experiences. The role of the teacher should be more that of a personal guide and facilitator of learning than of a purveyor of knowledge. Traditional lecture-recitation methods should be minimized.

☐ Grouping criteria that involve not only cognitive, but also physical, social, and emotional criteria.

☐ As much consideration for who the student is and becomes, his or her self-concept, self-responsibility and attitudes toward school and personal happiness, as for how much and what he or she knows.

☐ Experiences in the arts for all transescents to foster aesthetic appreciations and to stimulate creative expression.

☐ Curriculum and teaching methods that reflect cultural, ethnic, and socioeconomic subgroups within the middle school student population.

Advisory Programs

The advisory program helps to bridge the gap between the close, one-to-one relationship of the self-contained elementary school to the less directed, more independent world of the high school. It offers middle school students the best of both worlds. It provides every student with an advisor, a teacher who has a special concern for the student as an individual. Additionally, the program provides instruction that encourages independence and personal growth needed at the high school level.

Finally, an advisor-advisee (A/A) program is designed to help students feel good about themselves and the contributions that they can make to their school, community, and society. An A/A program can serve as a prescriptive antidote for either the unmotivated reluctant learner or the at-risk student, or both, who faces such societal influences as sexual promiscuity, suicide, substance abuse, unsupervised leisure time, and criminal activities.

In the new century, our country will be run by our middle school students of today. Such an awareness is certainly worthy of commitment, consistence, and effort on our part as middle-level educators to help young adolescents become happy, fully functioning citizens of our society. This is our role as advisors and the purpose of an advisory program.

The characteristics of an effective advisory program include the following:

- Advisory should be at a time and place where students feel comfortable and at home.
- Advisory should be in a place where students can foster peer relationships.
- Advisory student numbers should be as low as possible. An *optimum* number of students in one class is twenty.
- A student should ideally begin the day with his or her advisory teacher.
- All information concerning an advisee should be communicated to the advisory teacher.
- The advisory program should have a name which is decided by the teachers, students, administration, and parents of a particular school, district, or county.
- A formal program consisting of a philosophy statement, operating guidelines, and activities should exist and should be formulated by the teachers, administration, parents, and students of a particular school, district, or county.

Physical Education Programs

The physical education program should address both the needs of the individual student and the diversity of the group. Each student should have the opportunity to grow physically, intellectually, socially, and emotionally. Through a broad range of experiences, students should have the opportunity to explore, to develop physical competence, and to view themselves in a positive light.

Traditionally, the grades 6–8 physical education curriculum has been activity centered. It has been organized around games/sports, gymnastics, and dance activities identified as the content of physical education. Units in basketball, volleyball, tumbling, and dance are examples of these activities. Specific skills are taught as they relate to a specific activity. They are means to developing the ability to perform in the activity. The activity has been viewed as the end.

A skill theme curriculum reverses the means-ends relationship. The curriculum is organized around specific skills or groups of skills. The focus is on student outcomes. Activities become means through which the student can practice, refine, and develop competence in the skills. The end is the development of students who are able to use skills in a variety of contexts and situations.

Intramural Programs

Intramural programs are activities that provide for the participation of students in an organized and supervised program. This participation takes place among all students within one school. The program is structured so that all students take part, regardless of their athletic ability or sex. Intramurals strive to offer success for everyone with a great deal of emphasis on fun.

The intramural program serves as an extension of skills and activities previously learned in physical education. Middle school students are offered the opportunity to further develop these skills; to provide recreational activities, physical fitness, mental and emotional health, social contact, group loyalty, success, and to promote a permanent interest in leisure-time activities.

The following are objectives found in most intramural programs:

- To offer a program within the school day to provide fun and enjoyment for all students
- To provide skilled professional leadership through the physical education department for a varied number of activities
- To offer activities that are adapted to the age and skill development of the students and to promote activities that afford wholesome use of leisure time
- To provide opportunities for experience in human relationships, such as cooperation, development of friendships, and acceptance of group responsibility
- To provide the opportunity for development of desirable personality traits, such as perseverance, self-confidence, self-discipline, self-direction, good sportsmanship, courage, and ethical conduct
- To provide recognition to develop group pride, loyalty, and to serve as a means of motivation
- To provide separation of grade levels on intramural days with the intramural program being the only activity at that time
- To provide for participation and cooperation of all teachers and instructional support staff
- To provide an intramural advisory council, who will advise and counsel an intramural director
- To provide funding for adequate staff, facilities, and equipment for a safe environment

Exploratory Programs

The exploratory program offers students in the middle school a chance to explore many areas of interest. Courses taught by specialists include industrial technology, music, art, business, foreign language, agriculture, computer technology, and others. Special interest courses and clubs, taught by all staff members, allow further exploration for middle school students. Media persons and counselors also contribute to exploratory activities.

Special Programs

Special programs such as drug education, sex education, AIDS education, consumer education, and law education are found in many schools. A wide range of community resources, as well as in-house staff, are used for such programs.

Programs for Students with Special Needs

A full range of programs of special needs students, including those for students with physical and mental handicaps, non-English-speaking students, gifted students, and disruptive students are a part of middle school programs. Through processes such as inclusion, mainstreaming, and teaming, students are included in team activities and other school programs.

Inclusion is a philosophy or belief that educational services to students with disabilities should be provided in general education settings, with the same peers, and in neighborhood schools to the extent appropriate for each school. There are many advantages of an inclusion component in the middle school. Most important is that labeling is deemphasized.

Guidance

Guidance is an integral part of the total middle school program. All instructional and special service personnel should be involved in guidance programs.

Guidance counselors serve as leaders of advisory programs and also provide instructional guidance to students along with dealing with specific needs of students.

There has been much progress in the past ten years in developing new and exciting programs for emerging adolescent learners, yet much remains to be done. Whether programs for students in the middle grades are housed in organizational structures called middle schools or are found in upper elementary grades, junior high schools, or secondary schools, the focus of such programs has to be the developmental characteristics of the emerging adolescent learner group itself. Figure 8.4 summarizes the middle school program in a sample philosophy/goal statement.

ORGANIZING FOR INSTRUCTION IN THE MIDDLE SCHOOL

Middle school educators, building on a philosophy and knowledge of the emerging adolescent learner, have structured a broad and relevant program for the varied needs of students found in the middle grades. To facilitate that program, the middle school must be organized to accommodate a flexible approach to instruction. Block schedules, teams of teachers with common planning periods teaching common groups of students, and special activity periods for advisory programs, intramurals, and other activities are essential elements of true middle schools, Inflexible, departmentalized high school organizational structures do not facilitate the broad program needed by middle grade students.

The interdisciplinary team approach to planning and implementing instruction has distinct advantage over a self-contained or departmentalized teaching pattern (see Figure 8.5). Some of these advantages follow:

☐ More than one teacher with the knowledge of scheduling, use of instructional materials, grouping, and instructional methods benefits individual student learning.

The middle school offers a balanced, comprehensive, and success-oriented curriculum.

The middle school is a sensitive, caring, supportive learning environment that will provide those experiences that will assist in making the transition from late childhood to adolescence, thereby helping each individual to bridge the gap between the self-contained structure of the elementary school and the departmental structure of the high school.

The middle school curriculums are more exploratory in nature than the elementary school and less specialized than the high school. Realizing that the uniqueness of individual subject disciplines must be recognized, an emphasis on interdisciplinary curriculum development will be stressed. Curriculum programs should emphasize the natural relationship among academic disciplines that facilitate cohesive learning experiences for middle school students through integrative themes, topics, and units. Interdisciplinary goals should overlap subject area goals and provide for interconnections such as reasoning, logical and critical thought, coping capacities, assuming self-management,

promoting positive personal development, and stimulating career awareness.

The academic program of a middle school emphasizes skills development through science, social studies, reading, mathematics, and language arts courses. A well-defined skills continuum is used as the basic guide in all schools in each area including physical education, health, guidance, and other educational activities. Exploratory opportunities are provided through well-defined and structured club programs, activity programs, and special interest courses, thereby creating opportunities for students to interact socially, to experience democratic living, to explore areas not in the required curriculum, to do independent study and research, to develop and practice responsible behavior, and to experience working with varying age groups.

The middle school curriculum will be a program of planned learning experiences for our students. The three major components for our middle school curriculum are (1) subject content (2) personal development, and (3) essential skills.

FIGURE 8.4   A Sample Philosophy/Goal Statement

□ Curriculums among subject areas can be coordinated so that the students can relate one subject to another; leads to greater breadth of understanding for students, "sees" more relationships.

□ Teachers can better understand individual differences in students when more than one person is making observations and evaluations; can therefore cope with those differences more effectively; discipline problems are more easily handled; guidance for the student is discussed among the team.

□ The team approach enables teachers to contrast a student's behavior and ability from class to class, thereby helping them develop a systematic and consistent approach to helping the child.

□ Closer work with guidance and other specialists is possible.

□ Block scheduling allows the teacher a greater flexibility in grouping to accommodate large- and small-group instruction, remedial work, and independent study.

□ Flexible time schedules can be made more conducive to children's developmental needs at this age level than can rigid departmentalized schedules.

☐ A number of instructors can lend their individual expertise to a given topic simultaneously.

☐ Large blocks of time are available for educational field trips, guest speakers, and so on; at the same time, scheduling is not disrupted. Less teaching time is lost to repetitious film showing.

☐ Teachers can be more aware of what their students are learning in other classes—what assignments, tests, projects are making demands on their time.

☐ Common planning time can lead to more creativity in teaching approaches and consistency in teaching strategies.

☐ Interdisciplinary teaching leads to economy of learning time and transfer among students.

☐ Student leadership is distributed among all of the teams because each team's students are typical of the total school community.

Teams Should

Provide a constructive climate
Focus goals for students
Encourage self-esteem
Set discipline standards
Coordinate activities
Help all students succeed
Build school spirit
Be the parent contact
Raise academic performance
Share work burdens
Set examples for students
Make school fun

Teams Shouldn't

Promote rivalry
Challenge school policy
Be fund raisers
Share negative feelings
Overburden one member
Isolate one member
Take away one's teaching style
Handle severe student problems

Goals for the School Year

Get closer to elective teachers
Meet more often with administrators
Develop interdisciplinary instruction
   patterns
Involve counselors in team activities

Get team bulletin boards
Get more teacher input into team
   formation
Make team leader councils really work

Indicators of a Successful Team

Attendance
Academic achievement
Validating team goals
Getting team bulletin boards
Establishing team-to-team communication

Improved discipline
School/team pride
Funds allocated to team activities
Family atmosphere

FIGURE 8.5 Tasks of Teams in Middle Schools

Source: Dade County, Florida, Workshop by authors, August 30, 1990. This list is the product of brainstorming by approximately 200 team leaders in Dade County schools, August 30, 1990.

□ Students are able to identify themselves with a smaller school within a school; with team representation on student council, they are more closely related to student government.

□ Correlated planning of content and project work is more easily carried out.

□ Parent conferences can be arranged by the guidance counselor for times when all of a student's academic teachers are available.

□ Individual teams may rearrange completely time and period schedules without interference with the overall school program. For example, each team may individually manipulate their block of time to provide periods of various lengths. All students do not move in the hallways at the end of 55 minutes.

□ Field trips can now be planned by teams, and built-in chaperoning is thus provided. Longer times for such trips are now available without disrupting a multiple number of classes.

□ One of the greatest advantages of team teaching is the assistance provided to the beginning teacher.

□ Building use is improved; large and small group space is used as well as regular classrooms.

□ An interdisciplinary team scheduling arrangement promotes the professional growth of the teachers by encouraging the exchange of ideas among the members of their teaching team.

An example of block scheduling to facilitate interdisciplinary teaming is found in Figure 8.6.

Alternative Scheduling Models

Following the high school lead, some middle schools have implemented long blocks of time for students that lengthen class periods to 75 or 90 minutes. Longer periods provide teachers with less students to teach during the school day, cut down on the number of class changes for students thus reducing potential discipline problems, and allow time for more depth of instruction.

Two problems are created for middle school teachers with the longer teaching block—the need to carry out instructional activities and the difficulty in coordinating a common planning time for teachers teaching the same students, a major element of the middle school concept.

There are a number of problems found in longer block schedules, such as the four-by-four block in which students spend 90 minutes in four courses every other day which creates eight subject loads in a school year. Another is the 75-75-3 plan in which a student follows a fairly typical middle school schedule for the first 150 days. Courses end after 75-day terms, and students enroll in specialized courses the last six weeks. The specialized courses can be academically enriching programs or remedial courses to help students master grade level courses.

6th Grade	7th Grade	8th Grade	8:30
Advisory	Advisory	Advisory	← 1 8:50 ← 2

Basics
 	
90*
	Exploratory/
	Physical Education
	90
		Basics
		  English
		  Math
		  Reading
		  Science
		  Social Studies
		
		210	

Exploratory/ Physical Education 90	Basics 60		
	Lunch 30		
Lunch 30	Basics 150		
Basics 120		Lunch 30	12:20 ← 3 12:50
		Exploratory/ Physical Education 90	← 4 2:20
Enrichment and Remediation 40	Enrichment and Remediation 40	Enrichment and Remediation 40	← 5 3:00

FIGURE 8.6   Parts of a Block Schedule

Source: From *The Essential Middle School,* p. 231, by J. Wiles and J. Bondi. Copyright © 1986 by Wiles, Bondi and Associates, Tampa, FL. Reprinted by permission.

In-Service Programs

Because in-service programs for middle school teachers have not been sustained in many schools, and pre-service training has not changed from the old model of training secondary teachers, many teachers prefer the secondary program model and organizational pattern.

To counter that, a much more systematic approach has to be implemented to retool veteran teachers and prepare new teachers for the modern middle school (see Figure 8.7).

Certification Component   (Middle Level Education—Orange County Public Schools Component #20561)

This component will focus on the following topics of study:

1. The middle grades
2. Understanding the middle-grades student
3. Organizing interdisciplinary instruction
4. Curriculum development
5. Developing critical and creative thinking in students
6. Counseling functions of the teacher
7. Developing creative-learning materials
8. Planning and evaluating programs

To meet the requirements of the component, each participant will attend 10 two-hour workshops. The program will consist of 30 hours of instruction in a workshop setting and 30 hours of supervised in-school follow-up activities.

It is anticipated that successful completion of this component plus one year of successful teaching in a middle school will lead to middle school certification for the participants.

Leadership for Team Leaders and Grade Coordinators

This training will focus on group process and communication skills that will enhance the ability of team leaders and grade coordinators to carry out their assigned responsibilities. The participants will receive six hours of skills-based training. All participants will be expected to have successfully completed the Middle Level Education component prior to attending this training.

Overview of the Middle School

An audio-visual presentation giving an overview of middle level education in Orange County public schools. It addresses the planned structure and curriculum of the middle school.

This will be a one-hour activity.

Program of Instruction

An overview of the instructional program of the middle school. This would cover the subject content, areas of personal development, and essential skills. This activity will be one hour of information with opportunity for participants to ask questions.

Middle Level Education for School-Based Administration

The presentation will be modeled on the certification component (OCPS Component #20561—Middle Level Education) with emphasis in those areas of special interest to the school-level administrator. It will consist of 20 hours of instruction with specified activities to be carried out at the school site.

Selected Topics

The training will include topics from the certification that meet special needs of those personnel who deal with the middle school child in other than classroom settings. An example of this would be "Understanding the Middle Grades Student" for school secretaries, custodians, and other classified personnel. This would be a one-hour activity.

FIGURE 8.7   Middle School Training Components

Source: From *The Essential Middle School,* p. 35, by J. Wiles and J. Bondi. Copyright © 1986 by Wiles, Bondi and Associates, Tampa, FL. Reprinted by permission.

The National Education Association in 1985 adopted the *Wiles-Bondi Guide and Plan for Conducting Ten Workshops*. That plan has been modified and is now a part of the Wiles-Bondi **Teachers Training Teachers (TTT)** model[9] that has been used by school districts implementing successful middle school programs. As part of the Curriculum Management Plan (CMP) model, the TTT program focuses on peers (teachers) teaching peers at school sites. Utilizing the Wiles-Bondi training materials[10] (adapted to each school district), a systematic training program can be implemented that includes hands-on and practical materials and activities in workshops. This model eliminates the need for outside consultants who entertain teachers with stories and leave them wondering, "What do I do on Monday?" Since the in-service program is practical and delivered in school settings by teachers, it meets with the approval of middle school teachers. It also fits with the **teacher empowerment** model that dictates that teachers should be in control of their own improvement.

COMPREHENSIVE PLANNING FOR MIDDLE SCHOOLS: A REVIEW

The curriculum of the middle school, with its concern for the special needs of pre- and early adolescents, its comprehensive definition of education, and its promotion of continuity in learning and development, is more than a series of catch phrases and education innovations. The middle school is, in fact, a highly complex plan for educating a special learner. Owing to the complexity of the educational design, successful implementation of the program calls for a significant degree of advanced planning.

The curriculum planning model suggested earlier is necessary if middle schools are to succeed. In assisting in the development of middle schools across America, we have noted that planning often determines the fine line between success and failure. Such planning is necessary at the district, school, and classroom levels. The following district-level planning steps, in sequence, are recommended for the establishment of middle schools.

Analysis

The middle school should arise from need. Ideally, school systems and communities will proceed through value-clarification processes that reveal the logic of the middle school design, and programs will be initiated on what is known about their students. Overcrowding, integration, or building availability are poor reasons for choosing the concept.

An important point in making such an analysis is not to allow the search to be focused only on problems. The analysis should also be projective—what kind of an educational experience do we want for students during this period of development?

Involvement

Preliminary investigations of the middle school should involve all parties with vested interests in intermediate education. A step often taken in planning the middle school is to explore the concept without involving those who will be most directly affected by its activation: students, teachers, parents, and the community. At a superficial level, the elimination of this stage will probably lead to future confrontations over both programs and policy (interscholastic athletics, social events, grading policies, community-based learning). More important from the planning standpoint, however, is the dedication and support that will be needed to put such a program in practice in the first place. The middle school cannot be implemented and maintained unless those involved believe in it.

Of the constituencies just mentioned, particular attention must be given to the community in which in middle school will reside. Unaccustomed to educational jargon and unfamiliar with national trends in educational programs, many citizens may resist the middle school because of misunderstandings about the academic nature of the program and the necessary organizational arrangements. Without a clear understanding of the rational of the program and the reason for these arrangements, community resistance will be high.

Involvement of community members representing all segments of the population in the initial analysis of student needs, in the investigation of the middle school concept, in the drafting of documents, and in the planning of implementation stages will build in a means of communicating with the community at later times.

Commitment

Philosophical commitments to the middle school definition of education should be secured prior to activating the program. This text has repeatedly underscored the necessity of understanding and accepting the middle school's philosophic position on education as a prerequisite for successful implementation of such a program. A lack of understanding of the middle school concept represents the largest potential stumbling block to successful implementation. Without such understanding and a basic philosophic acceptance of the middle school concept, there can be no substantial rationale for practices and programs found in the middle school.

It is important to note that this understanding and acceptance must go beyond school board approval and superintendent acquiescence, although both are consequential. Such an understanding and commitment must be held by the building principal, the involved teachers, and the parents of involved students.

Funding

Appropriate monies must be earmarked for activation of the plan. An observable phenomenon in American education is that finance is the "fuel" of progress. Few major innovations of the past twenty years (middle schools being a notable exception) have really succeeded without substantial financial support.

Although it is not impossible for a building faculty to implement the middle school concept with sheer dedication, two simple facts about middle schools are worth noting: (1) middle schools are a much more complex form of education than traditional programs, and (2) due to this complexity, they require more energy and money to operate.

Every deviation from standardized patterns of education, such as uniform textbooks, the classroom-confined learning experience, and the single-dimension instruction requires effort and expense. As school districts do commit themselves to the middle school concept, a pledge equal to their commitment for financing building conversion, materials acquisition, staff development, and so forth is necessary.

Resources

Resources commensurate with the task must be allocated. One of the common pitfalls in establishing middle schools is to assume that they can operate on the same resource base as traditional intermediate schools. To rely on teacher-made materials exclusively, to overlook a consumable materials budget, to fail to allocate materials to build up the instructional resource center, to make no provision for off-campus experiences is to doom in advance the programs of the middle school. Middle schools, if properly operated, require substantial resources for instruction.

Personnel

There must be an attempt to staff middle schools with dedicated and enthusiastic teachers. There are several appropriate comments to note regarding the selection, training, and use of middle school staff. The middle school will be only as effective as its personnel in succeeding at new roles. With only several colleges in the nation training teachers and staff members exclusively for middle school positions, most teachers and **support personnel** will enter the middle school from other more traditional educational designs. Such persons, regardless of their belief in and allegiance to the middle school philosophy of education, will need special assistance in adjusting to their new roles. Predictably, the middle school staff will need extensive assistance in assuming new roles.

A problem witnessed in many school districts is that middle school teacher behaviors are prone to return to traditional patterns if sufficient support is not maintained. Many middle schools open under the so-called Hawthorne effect (a term coming from the Hawthorne studies in which workers were found to be more productive, regardless of work conditions, if they first received sufficient attention as being special). Because of this, teacher enthusiasm and energy are understandably high in the beginning. However, as program development slows or resource bases erode with the gradual lessening of attention, it is not unusual for old patterns of teacher-pupil interaction and learning to creep in. Such a condition would warn against one short summer treatment for the middle school staff and would call, instead, for long-term, systematic training opportunities.

Detailed Planning

Prior to the development of a middle school, detailed planning is essential. From an administrative/organizational perspective, it is crucial that schools conduct detailed planning to smoothly implement the middle school concept. The past experience of many middle schools suggests that a "broken front" approach to this concept does not work. The middle school concept does not easily emerge because there are prerequisites for implementation. There must be an understanding of objectives; there must be a commitment to this definition of educating; there must be an involvement of those who support the school; there must be money and resources to implement its components; there must be personnel capable and willing to assume the required roles. The time frame for opening a middle school must allow for the magnitude of the process proposed.

Although the amount of preparation time required to open a fully functioning middle school depends on environmental conditions in the community, a minimum period appears to be 18 to 24 months. This estimate is based on several definable steps of planning:

1. Awareness and study phases
2. Educating the community and gaining commitments
3. Budgeting for development
4. Selection of staff, site
5. Construction of a detailed implementation plan
6. Intensive training of staff
7. Development of curriculum
8. Construction or conversion of site
9. Opening of the middle school

In some communities and school districts, it would be possible to accomplish these steps in six months or less because of central office organization and support from the community leaders. The experience of many middle schools, however, suggests that to hasten through steps 2, 6, and 7, or to proceed with step 8 prior to step 7 leads to significant problems later on. Eroding community support, an ill-prepared staff, a superficially constructed curriculum, and a dysfunctional site are all causes of middle school failure.

Evaluating the Middle School

Often missing in the development of middle schools is an evaluation plan that will measure the success of program and organization changes. The following middle school hypotheses, on which middle school evaluations in most school districts today are based, provide areas from which data can be compiled:

- ☐ The middle school will provide a rich program of exploratory courses.
- ☐ There will be fewer and less intense social and psychological problems.
- ☐ Students will develop more adequate self-concepts.
- ☐ Students will become more self-directed learners.
- ☐ Graduates will succeed better in high school.
- ☐ There will be less teacher turnover.
- ☐ Teacher morale will be higher
- ☐ The organization will facilitate better use of individual teacher competencies and skills.

Measures of Evaluation	Measures of Growth
Academic aptitude tests	Aspects of thinking
Reading tests (comprehension and vocabulary)	Work habits and skills
Achievement test in subjects	Reading
Emotional and social adjustment measures	Development of social attitudes
Health assessments	Development of wider interests
Home conditions	Development of appreciations
Pupil questionnaires	Development of social sensitivity
Behavior ratings	Ability to make social adjustments
Interest indexes	Creativeness
Writing sample inventories	Development of personal philosophy
Work habit measures	Physical health
Teacher classroom behavior assessments	Mental health

FIGURE 8.8   Measures of Evaluation

☐   Attendance of students will increase.

☐   Teachers will use a greater variety of media to meet the diverse needs of preadolescent learners.

☐   Patrons (parents, students, teachers) will hold more positive attitudes toward the objectives and procedures.

☐   Student achievement on standardized tests will equal or exceed that of students in conventional schools.

Sample measures of evaluation appropriate for the middle school are offered in Figure 8.8.

THE MIDDLE SCHOOL AS A PART OF THE TOTAL CURRICULUM

As is true of the elementary and high school, the middle school does not stand alone. It must build on the curriculum of the elementary school and, in turn, form a solid educational base for students entering the high school. Although early in the middle school movement, educational leaders fought for a separate identity for the middle school to prevent it from following the path of the junior high school, increasingly, emphasis is being placed on an articulated K–12 curriculum and less on building separate programs for elementary, middle, and high school students. The move toward developing a unified K–12 curriculum is a welcome one. Regardless of housing patterns or grade level organization, students should be viewed as individuals progressing through definite stages of development. An articulated curriculum that accommodates the developmental needs of youngsters is more important than grade organizations of schools. The middle school, however, must be a strong bridge that holds together the total K–12 curriculum.

In concluding this chapter on middle grades education, here are some curriculum problems that are common and recurrent:

1. Absentee rates for students in the intermediate grades are generally higher than those at the elementary and secondary levels. What may be some of the factors causing this condition? How can curriculum leaders address this problem?
2. Because many educators view the high school as a distinctive level of specialized academic preparation, many students are retained at the eighth-grade level. What price do we pay for such retention? What is a reasonable retention rate? What can curriculum personnel do about this problem?
3. Students in the intermediate grades have many interpersonal concerns related to growing up. Yet, the average student-to-counselor ratio for this age group is 1:450. What can be done in the curriculum to address this problem?
4. Declining achievement scores on national tests are a common phenomenon in the intermediate grades. What causes this to happen? What can curriculum teachers do about it?

SUGGESTED LEARNING ACTIVITIES

1. Write a philosophical statement defending the emerging middle school design. Identify the functions of the middle school that are the most important to you.
2. Prepare an oral presentation for parents that would make them aware of the developmental characteristics of middle school students.
3. Identify the ten most important teacher competencies of the selected teacher competencies identified in this chapter. Give reasons why you selected the ones on your list.
4. Develop on outline of an ideal curriculum design for middle school students.
5. Prepare an outline of a district plan for organizing a middle school.

NOTES

1. Commission on the Reorganization of Secondary Education, "Cardinal Principles of Secondary Education," *Bulletin 1918* (Washington, DC: U.S. Dept. of Interior, Bureau of Education, 1918). pp. 12–13.
2. ASCD Commission on Secondary Education, *The Junior High We Need* (Alexandria, VA: Association for Supervision and Curriculum Development, 1961).
3. Education Facilities Laboratories, *The Schoolhouse in the City* (New York: 1966), p. 10.
4. ASCD Working Group on the Emerging Adolescent, Joseph Bondi, ed., *The Middle School We Need* (Washington, DC: Association for Supervision and Curriculum Development, 1960), pp. 11–12.
5. Carnegie Council on Adolescent Development, *Turning Points: Preparing American Youth for the 21st Century* (New York: Carnegie Corporation, 1989).
6. Jon Wiles and Joseph Bondi, *Making Middle Schools Work* (Alexandria, VA: Association for Supervision and Curriculum Development, 1985).
7. Design documents found in Dade County, FL; Duval County, FL; St. Louis, MO; San Bernardino, CA, and other school districts. See also Wiles and Bondi, *Making Middle Schools Work* for Orange County, FL, model.
8. Jon Wiles, Joseph Bondi, and Ron Stodghill, "Miracle on Main Street—The St. Louis Story," *Educational Leadership* (Alexandria, VA:

Association for Supervision and Curriculum Development, November 1982), pp. 52–53.

9. Jon Wiles and Joseph Bondi, *A Guide and Plan for Conducting Ten Workshops with the NEA Middle School Training Program* (Washington, DC: National Education Association, 1985).

10. Wiles, Bondi and Associates, Inc., *Training Materials for Middle School Teachers*—numerous booklets and materials, P.O. Box 16545, Tampa, FL 33687.

BOOKS TO REVIEW

Alexander, W. *Preparing to Teach at the Middle Level.* Columbus, OH: National Middle School Association, 1988.

Beane, J. *A Middle School Curriculum: From Rhetoric to Reality.* Columbus, OH: National Middle School Association, 1990.

Bondi, J., ed. *The Middle School We Need.* Alexandria, VA: Association for Supervision and Curriculum Development, 1975.

Carnegie Council on Adolescent Education. *Turning Points—Preparing American Youth for the 21st Century.* Washington, DC: Carnegie Council on Adolescent Education, 1989.

Cohen, Phillip. "The On-line Classroom: Computer Networks Offer New Resources." *ASCD Update.* Reprinted from *America On-Line*, 36, 10 (1996).

Dunn, R. *Strategies For Educating Diverse Learners.* Fastback 384. Bloomington, IN: Phi Delta Kappa Educational Foundation, 1995.

Elkind, D. *A Sympathetic Understanding of the Child: Birth to Sixteen.* Boston: Allyn and Bacon, 1974.

Gilstrap, R. L., et al. *Improving Instruction In Middle Schools.* Fastback 331. Bloomington, IN: Phi Delta Kappa Educational Foundation, 1994.

Kellough, R. D., N. G. Kellough, and D. L. High. *Middle School Teaching: Methods and Resources.* New York: Macmillan, 1993.

Lounsbury, J., and Donald Claus. *Inside Grade Eight: From Apathy to Excitement.* Reston, VA: National Association of Secondary School Principals, 1990.

National Association of Secondary School Principals. *Assessing Excellence: A Guide for Studying the Middle School.* Reston, VA: National Association of Secondary School Principals, 1988.

National Association of Elementary School Principals. *Effective Teachers: Effective Evaluation in America's Elementary and Middle Schools.* Alexandria, VA: National Association of Secondary School Principals, 1988.

Valentine, J. W., et al. *Leadership in Middle Level Education, Vol. 1: A National Survey of Middle Level Leaders and Schools.* Reston, VA: National Association of Secondary School Principals, 1993.

Wiles, J., and J. Bondi. *The Essential Middle School.* Tampa, FL: Wiles, Bondi and Associates, 1986.

Wiles, J., and J. Bondi. *Making Middle Schools Work.* Alexandria, VA: Association for Supervision and Curriculum Development, 1987.

Willis, Scott. "Untracking in the Middle." *ASCD Update.* Reprinted *America On-Line* 35, 9 (December, 1995).

chapter **9**

SECONDARY SCHOOL PROGRAMS AND ISSUES

The secondary school of today is receiving more attention than at any time since *Sputnik* in the late 1950s. As the exit school for a majority of American youth, the high school is viewed as the "finishing school" and as the means by which American society is renewed. Unfortunately, when the larger society experiences problems such as those plaguing the nation today, the secondary school is expected to find necessary solutions. When scientists, mathematicians, and technical workers are needed for a rapidly emerging high tech/information society, for example, the schools draw criticism because the mathematics and science curriculum is not rigorous enough.

Secondary schools in America are closely wedded to local communities and, therefore, to public opinion. Because schools reflect the weaknesses as well as the strengths of the larger society, they are caught up in the ebb and flow of continual revitalization.

The secondary school of today is not perfect, nor will it ever be in the eyes of society. We can learn from the past, however, and focus on those problems and issues that are important. We can also gain an increased knowledge of how the curriculum of the secondary school is developed and organized. Finally, we can attempt to chart a course for the future of the secondary school so that the secondary school can meet the great expectations that society has for it. In the next sections of this chapter, we shall deal with each of these topics.

HISTORICAL DEVELOPMENT OF THE SECONDARY SCHOOL

Although elementary schools were developed for students at public expense from the mid-1600s, the public secondary school did not become a reality for a majority of American youth until late in the nineteenth century.

From the middle of the eighteenth century until the Civil War period, the principal instrument of secondary education in the United States was the academy. Benjamin Franklin is credited with the establishment of the first academy, the Philadelphia Academy and Charitable School, opened in 1751. The academy achieved great popularity in New England and the Middle Atlantic states. Although the academy was neither wholly private nor wholly public (unlike the Latin grammar school which was highly selective and private), it did not open the door to all youth in need of a secondary education.

In the mid-1800s, leaders in Massachusetts, such as Horace Mann, were successful in obtaining strong support for public schools. The first high school in the United States was founded in Boston in 1821. Known as the English Classical School, the school provided a three-year sequence of English, mathematics, history, and science.

The extension of secondary education in the United States was accomplished by state legislation and later by court cases. Again taking the lead, the Commonwealth of Massachusetts enacted laws that required towns with 500 or more families to establish high schools with a ten-month program. Earlier, Massachusetts had required the establishment of elementary schools in towns of fifty families or more and had reorganized the state's responsibility for the preparation of teachers by establishing, under Horace Mann's leadership, the first state **normal school.** Massachusetts also passed the first compulsory attendance law in 1852. Today, all states compel students to attend school until a certain age, usually sixteen.

As secondary schools emerged in more and more states, from the mid-1850s to the 1870s, there was great debate on whether high schools should be provided at public expense. The high school coexisted for a long time with the academy. With a frontier spirit of increased democracy, more youths were enrolling in high schools. Not until the famous Kalamazoo case in 1874 was the concept of free high school education for all youths firmly established.

The Kalamazoo case resulted when a taxpayer in Kalamazoo, MI, challenged the right of the school board to establish a high school with public funds and to hire a superintendent. In 1874, the Supreme Court of Michigan ruled that a school district was not limited to the support of elementary schools but could establish whatever level of schools it wished as long as the voters were willing to pay the taxes. This historic decision affirmed the idea that secondary education was a legitimate part of the program of public schools.

After the Kalamazoo decision, public secondary schools grew in number. The most popular grade-level organization of schools was the eight-four pattern (eight years of elementary school and four of high school). Later, other patterns emerged, including the popular six-six pattern (six years of elementary school and six years of high school or secondary school). Not until 1910 was the junior high school established, and a three-level organizational system emerged. The popular organizational pattern then became the grades 1–6 elementary school, 7–9 junior high school, and 10–12 high school. For almost fifty years, the elementary-junior high-high school pattern dominated American schools. In the 1960s, a new school emerged—the middle school—which was to force a realignment of grade levels in American schools. Although grade patterns vary in the middle school in many school districts, the most common pattern is the grades 6–8 pattern. In the early 1980s, some large school districts (the St. Louis District, for example), which had ignored the junior high school and were still organized in a grades K–8 elementary and 9–12 high school pattern, organized separate grades 6–8 middle schools.

REFORM MOVEMENTS IN SECONDARY EDUCATION

Although many commissions and reports have called for high school reform in the last two decades, those working in American high schools have never lacked advice on how to improve their school programs.

The tradition of secondary school reform began in the 1890s with a number of committees and commissions organized to examine the high school curriculum, especially its effectiveness in preparing students for college. The Committee of Ten on Secondary Schools, the Committee of Fifteen on Elementary Education, and the Committee on College Entrance Requirements organized in 1893–94, endorsed the idea of pushing high school subjects down into the upper elementary grades (grades 7, 8, and 9).

In 1913, the National Education Association appointed the Commission on the Reorganization of Secondary Education, whose report was five years in the making. Their report in 1918 resulted in the famous seven Cardinal Principles of Education. The report recommended that every subject be reorganized to contribute to the goals expressed in the Cardinal Principles. Most importantly, the commission endorsed the division of secondary education into junior and senior high periods. The commission recommended that vocational courses be introduced into the curriculum and that a comprehensive program be offered to both junior and senior high students.

The pushing down of the high school program into the upper elementary grades continued to be an issue even as school district after school district reorganized to include the junior high school. By the late 1970s, middle schools had all but replaced junior high schools as the dominant intermediate grade school in the United States.

The high school came under strong attack in the late 1950s and early 1960s following *Sputnik*. Although weaknesses in science and mathematics programs were attacked, other areas of the secondary school, such as foreign language instruction, also came under attack. The problem of "why Johnny can't read" was perceived primarily to be a problem for the elementary school.

James Conant and others led a movement in the 1950s to expand the high school curriculum to include both vocational and academic courses for students in a unitary, multipurpose school—the comprehensive high school. Conant and others were finally developing the kind of unitary high school recommended in the

1918 report of the NEA Commission on the Reorganization of Secondary Education. Such a comprehensive school would serve as a prototype of a democracy in which various groups could be federated into a larger whole through the recognition of common interests and ideals. The establishment of cooperative federal-state programs for vocational education in 1917 had resulted in separate specialized vocational schools, and that pattern (modeled after the European system) prevailed until the late 1950s.

The 1970s proved to be a decade in which serious reforms of the American high school were recommended and, in some cases, attempted. Throughout the land, prestigious commissions met to assess the needs of secondary education and to make suggestions for reform. Among those commissions were the following:

- The National Association of Secondary School Principals, whose report *American Youth in the Mid-Seventies* (1972) recommended increased "action learning" programs in the community.
- The President's Science Advisory Committee, whose report *Youth Transition to Adulthood* (1973) advocated the creation of alternative high schools and occupational high schools.
- The Institute for the Development of Education Activities (IDEA), whose report *The Greening of the High School* (1973) called for a new type of institution for modern students, with an emphasis on individual needs and student choice.
- The U.S. Department of Education, HEW, whose report *National Panel on High Schools and Adolescent Education* (1975) recommended decentralization of the comprehensive high school and reduction of the secondary school day by two to four hours.

These observations and recommendations were reflected in a number of innovative secondary schools that emerged and then receded when primary leadership was withdrawn:

- Nova High School (Ft. Lauderdale, FL), an experiment with the application of technology to instructional processes
- Parkway Schools (Philadelphia, PA), an attempt to move learning out into the community—the school without walls
- McGavok High School (Nashville, TN), a truly comprehensive school with a broad range of occupational tracks under one roof and tied closely to business interests in the community
- Melbourne High School (Cocoa Beach, FL), an academic high school with five tracks, including Quest, an advanced placement program in which students could progress to their limits
- Berkeley High Schools (Berkeley, CA), employing the "public schools of choice" concept in which parents and students selected their high school by philosophy and purpose

☐ Adams High School (Portland, OR), an experimental school in which students participated in the governance of the program, thereby learning basic democratic procedures for citizenship.

Typical of the broad goals for education at this period were those advocated by Harold Spears, a long-time advocate of the comprehensive high school (see Figure 9.1). In addition to many special programs, the actual course offerings of high schools grew extensively, as suggested by the English offerings of one high school (Table 9.1).

Around 1974, the picture in secondary education began to change dramatically, and proposals for the expansion of the role of the American high school were no longer heard. Among the major factors causing this reversal were the following:

☐ **Declining Enrollment**   Between 1970 and 1980, secondary enrollment declined by a full 25 percent. This decline, which was projected to last until 1992, meant falling teacher-pupil ratios and an increased cost per pupil in many districts.

1. Learn how to be a good citizen.
2. Learn how to respect and get along with people who think, dress, and act differently.
3. Learn about and try to understand the changes that take place in the world.
4. Develop skills in reading, writing, speaking, and listening.
5. Understand skills and practice democratic ideas and ideals.
6. Learn how to examine and use information.
7. Understand and practice the skills of family living.
8. Learn to respect and get along with people with whom we work and live.
9. Develop skills to enter a specific field of work.
10. Learn how to be a good manager of money, property, and resources.
11. Develop a desire for learning now and in the future.
12. Learn how to use leisure time.
13. Practice and understand the ideas of health and safety.
14. Appreciate culture and beauty in the world.
15. Gain information needed to make job selections.
16. Develop pride in work and a feeling of self-worth.
17. Develop good character and self-respect.
18. Gain a general education.

FIGURE 9.1   The Goals of Education

Source: From a lecture by Harold Spears given at George Peabody College, 1972.

TABLE 9.1   The English Curriculum in One Comprehensive High School

English IX	Practical Communication	Acting I
English X	Science Fiction (Depth)	Acting II
English X (AP)	Science Fiction (Survey)	Films—Communications
English XI (AP)	Speech	Creative Writing I
English XII (AP)	Sports Literature (Depth)	Creative Writing II
Secretarial English I	Sports Literature (Survey)	Film Making
Secretarial English II	Techniques of Research	Folklore
Humanities	Women in Literature	American Literature (Focus)
American Dream	Themes: Modern Life	American Literature (Images)
Your America	Eng. as a Second Lang.	Contemporary Literature
American Novel	Reading—Grade 9	English Literature (Past)
Basic English Skills	Reading—Grade 9	English Literature (Modern)
Directed Reading		Journalism

- ☐ **Inflation**   By 1974, the inflationary effects of the Vietnam War were in full bloom, and taxpayers became painfully aware of the soaring cost of education in a time when the purchasing power of the dollar was shrinking.
- ☐ **Unionization of Teaching Staffs**   Between 1966 and 1977, the number of states recognizing the right of teachers to enter into collective bargaining rose from eleven to thirty. By 1977, 80 percent of all teachers were members of either the NEA (National Education Association) or the AFT (American Federation of Teachers). Because high school teachers tended to be more senior and, therefore, more expensive to the taxpayer, they were often identified with the union movement.
- ☐ **Declining Achievement**   Throughout the 1970s and continuing in the 1990s, there were regular media reports of declining achievement as measured by nationally normed standardized tests such as the Scholastic Aptitude Test (SAT). This was interpreted to mean, in the eyes of the public, that schools were failing.

Between 1975 and 1985, proposals for the expansion of the role of the high school were no longer heard. There were two well-known projects that were largely aimed at improving test scores and academic achievement rather than addressing larger social questions. They were the *Paideia Proposal* (1982), which proposed a twelve-year, single-track academic program with no electives,[1] and the Commission on Excellence which produced the report *A Nation At Risk* in 1983. Other reform efforts after 1983 were aimed at specific problems such as the drop-out rate and mathematics and science achievement rather than with overall school reform.

In the mid-1980s, a book of significance, *A Place Called School,* was written by John Goodlad. In it, Goodlad shared the findings of a research project touching thousands of teachers and pupils, and his report was not glowing. Writing about the secondary school, Goodlad observed:

Usually we saw desks or tables arranged in rows oriented toward the teacher at the front of the room. Instructional amenities, occasionally present in elementary class-rooms, were rarely observed in the secondary classes.[2]

Observing the organization of the standard secondary school, Goodlad observed:

What begins to emerge is a picture not of two kinds of instructional activities in each class appealing to alternative modes of learning, but two curricular divisions in the secondary school. On one side are the more prestigious academic subjects, largely shunning manual activity as a mode of learning. On the other side are the nonacade-mics, generally characterized by the trappings of academic teaching but providing more opportunities to cultivate handedness and often featuring aesthetic qualities.[3]

The power of reputation and the reinforcement of observation by researchers made *A Place Called School* an important book of the 1980s and encouraged further inquiry into secondary school programs. Another author, Ted Sizer in *Horace's Compromise,* the 1984 study of public education, encouraged the push for a higher mission of secondary schools when he wrote:

The best vocational education will be one in general education in the age of the mind.

Sizer led a partnership between Brown University and more than 700 schools called Coalition of Essential Schools to help students use their minds.[4] Sizer's nine principles committed restructured schools in the Coalition not only to get students to use their minds well, but also to apply school goals to every student, allow stu-dents to have the opportunity to discover and construct meaning from their own experiences, and make teaching and learning personalized. Diplomas would be awarded on successful demonstration of mastery and exhibition.

The school reform movement that began in the 1980s continued in the 1990s. The secondary school reform movement was closely tied to the nation's quest for greater economic competitiveness fueled by a global economy and a revolution in the American work place. The industrial age of the first half of the twentieth century was replaced by the technological age, then the high tech age, and, finally at the end of the century, the information age. New jobs stressed brains over brawn. The lunch bucket was replaced by the briefcase and the personal computer. Rather than exit skills of basic reading, writing, and arithmetic, high school graduates were expected to exit with "thinking skills" and the ability to master new knowledge on the job.

In 1994, in a widely circulated report, the Secretary's Commission on Achiev-ing Necessary Skills (SCANS) took a hard look at six goals of *America 2000* and identified five SCANS competencies. In particular, the SCANS report looked at National Goals 3 and 5 which stated:

American students will leave grades four, eight and twelve having demonstrated com-petency in challenging subject matter including English, mathematics, science—and every school in America will ensure that all students use their minds so they will be prepared for responsible citizenship—and employment in our modern society. Goal 3

Every adult American will be literate and will possess the knowledge and skills necessary to compete in a global economy. Goal 5[5]

SCANS originated from the U.S. Department of Labor, but educational implications were paramount. Two conditions were identified as changing young people's entry into the world of work: the globalization of commerce and industry and the explosive growth of technology on the job. Those developments meant schools had to do a better job as well as employers.[6]

SCANS five competencies are outlined in Figure 9.2.

The late 1990s have brought many changes to secondary schools, including new national and state standards, more rigorous academic programs, large blocks of time for instruction, benchmark tests, academic skills placement tests, tech-prep programs that replaced traditional vocational programs, and an increase in numbers of students in advanced placement and international baccalaureate programs. Alternative schooling and alternative schools, including magnet schools, became commonplace in many school districts. Finally, the information highway ran right into many high schools linking even the most remote and smallest schools with information sources, courses never before offered, and a rich variety of learning opportunities. For the first time in a hundred years, the high school had truly begun to change.

Reform has not come easy to the high school; there are still problems and issues.

The push for schools of choice, charter schools, and tuition vouchers raise questions of whether the American public is still committed to a system of general and free public schools. Suggestions by some government and business leaders that secondary education can be offered better by private enterprise are strong evidence that public secondary education does not enjoy the same widespread support that it once had. Curriculum leaders must not let these changes be dictated entirely by those outside of our school systems.

THE CHANGING CURRICULUM OF THE SECONDARY SCHOOL

For the first ninety years of the twentieth century, the high school curriculum remained the same. Basically, the high school consisted of a number of courses that a student must complete to graduate. Credits were given for successful completion of required courses. When a student earned a certain number of credits, he or she would graduate. To ensure that each student received a basic education during the high school years, certain courses and credit hours were required. The number of credit hours required by states varied, but most of the course titles and content were the same. Some states added a proficiency test that students needed to pass to graduate.

In the 1990s, pressures brought on schools by the events discussed in previous sections, and accompanying state and national reports, resulted in a long-awaited curriculum reform movement. Rather than the time-work solutions of more courses or credits and more tests, reforms reflected a concern on what was taught, how it was delivered, and how the curriculum could prepare students for the demands of a high tech workplace and global economy.

Resources: Identifies, organizes, plans, and allocates resources
   A. *Time*—Selects goal-relevant activities, ranks them, allocates time, and prepares and follows schedules
   B. *Money*—Uses or prepares budgets, makes forecasts, keeps records, and makes adjustments to meet objectives
   C. *Material and facilities*—Acquires, stores, allocates, and uses materials or space efficiently
   D. *Human resources*—Assesses skills and distributes work accordingly, evaluates performance and provides feedback

Interpersonal: Works with others
   A. *Participates as member of a team*—Contributes to group effort
   B. *Teaches others new skills*
   C. *Serves clients/customers*—Works to satisfy customers' expectations
   D. *Exercises leadership*—Communicates ideas to justify position, persuades and convinces others, responsibly challenges existing procedures and policies
   E. *Negotiates*—Works toward agreements involving exchange of resources, resolves divergent interests
   F. *Works with diversity*—Works well with men and women from diverse backgrounds

Information: Acquires and uses information
   A. *Acquires and evaluates information*
   B. *Organizes and maintains information*
   C. *Interprets and communicates information*
   D. *Uses computers to process information*

Systems: Understands complex interrelationships
   A. *Understands systems*—Knows how social, organizational, and technological systems work and operates effectively with them
   B. *Monitors and corrects performance*—Distinguishes trends, predicts impacts on system operations, diagnoses deviations in system's performance and corrects malfunctions
   C. *Improves or designs systems*—Suggests modifications to existing systems and develops new or alternative systems to improve performance

Technology: Works with a variety of technologies
   A. *Selects technology*—Chooses procedures, tools, or equipment including computers and related technologies
   B. *Applies technology to task*—Understands overall intent and proper procedures for setup and operation of equipment
   C. *Maintains and troubleshoots equipment*—Prevents, identifies, or solves problems with equipment, including computers and other technologies

FIGURE 9.2   Five Competencies of SCANS

Source: U.S. Dept. of Education, 1993.

Heading the way were groups of educators building national standards in the major school disciplines of mathematics, English, science, and social studies. Other discipline groups followed with standards. Table 9.2 lists a number of those groups.

The term *world class* began to be used to describe new standards. In other words, what would our United States students need to know to compete with the best and brightest graduates from around the world?

In 1995, the American Federation of Teachers (AFT) published a 165-page book entitled, *What Secondary Students Abroad Are Expected To Know* (see Table 9.2). This report offers a comprehensive look at what's expected of average achieving students in France, Germany, and Scotland and includes a profile of each country's education system, including its school-to-work transition program plus lengthy excerpts from the exams given to students at the ninth- or tenth-grade level. A comparative look at the U.S. GED is also included.

Although many countries have national examinations, the United States does not. Only if states agree to impose tests, or standards either for that matter, will any

TABLE 9.2   Sources for Standards and Frameworks

World Class Standards

What Secondary Students Abroad Are Expected to Know, Defining World Class Standards. American Federation of Teachers (AFT), 1995.

Language Arts

Standards for the Assessment of Reading and Writing. Urbana, IL: National Council of Teachers of English, 1994.

NAEP Reading Standards. Washington, DC: National Assessment of Education Progress (NAEP), 1995.

NAEP Writing Standards. Washington, DC: National Assessment of Education Progress (NAEP), 1994.

Reading Standards. Newark, DE: International Reading Association, 1995.

Mathematics

Curriculum and Evaluation Standards for School Mathematics. Reston, VA: National Council of Teachers of Mathematics (NCTM), 1989.

Professional Standards for Teaching Mathematics. Reston, VA: National Council of Teachers of Mathematics (NCTM), 1991.

NAEP Mathematics Standards. Washington, DC: National Assessment of Education Progress (NAEP), 1994.

Social Science

NAEP Social Studies Standards. Washington, DC: National Assessment of Education Progress (NAEP), 1995.

National Content Standards for Civics. Calabasas, CA: Center for Civic Education, 1995.

National Content Standards for Economics. National Council of Economic Education (NCEE), 1995.

National Content Standards for Geography. National Geographic Society, 1994.

National Content Standards for History. National Center for History in the Schools, 1995.

National Content Standards for Social Studies. National Council on Social Studies (NCSS), 1995.

Science

Benchmarks for Science Literacy, Project 2061, American Association for the Advancement of Science (AAAS). New York: Oxford University Press, 1993.

National Science Education Standards, National Research Council. Washington, DC: National Academy Press, 1996.

NAEP Science Standards. Washington, DC: National Association of Education Progress (NAEP), 1995.

Science Performance Standards. New Standards Project, 1995.

*You are encouraged to update development of international, national, and state standards. The Association for Supervision and Curriculum Development (ASCD) in Alexandria, VA, is a prime source for such information.

national standards or tests be implemented. Our Constitution does not impose a national system of education.

Not all educators agree on what "world class standards" are, which lends to even more confusion in the debate on how our students compare with those in other countries. The main comparisons of U.S. and foreign students occur in science and mathematics—the linchpins of a high tech, global economy. However, surveys of business and industry leaders also point to problems in literacy, work ethic, and the ability to solve problems that crop up in any job on a daily basis.

SAT and ACT tests are general aptitude tests which don't measure school performance. Since the U.S. has no national and few state-linked examinations and states just begin spell out what every child should learn in the late 1990s, much still needs to be done to prepare to meet world standards.

With states jealously guarding their rights to determine what is taught, it appears only a natural crisis will precipitate any national approach to education. Americans are wary of the national government using schools as instruments of national policy. Who can forget the Hitler Youth and the Red Guards in the twentieth century?

Examining the content areas, a major shift in curriculum areas took place in the last five years of the twentieth century. New standards encouraged a move away from mastery of low-level, isolated facts to a comprehensive curriculum emphasizing problem solving, integrated tasks, real-life problems, and higher-order thinking processes using portfolios and exhibitions. Assessments of students' work changed to a more authentic assessment. The NCTE Standards for Assessment of Reading and Writing reflects these approaches in its goals:

1. Students must constantly be encouraged about their work in terms of what they can do versus what they cannot do.
2. The primary purpose of assessment of writing is to improve teaching and learning.
3. Students need to realize that they have other audiences besides a teacher for which they can write.
4. Educators need to take into account the outside influences on a student's work when assessing it.
5. Assessment must be fair and equitable, taking into account the diverse ethnic and social groups in the country.
6. The consequences of assessment procedures are important, and each paper that a student writes should have a specific set of criteria to be used in grading it.[7]

Social studies instruction has undergone extensive changes with students having less lecture, more collaborative learning activities, and interactive writing activities that are technology driven. Thematic teaching that integrates social studies with other disciplines has also made social studies instruction more relevant and more interesting.

Mathematics saw a host of inventive curriculum projects in the 1990s. Reformers invested much time and energy in the creation of new mathematics and state curriculum frameworks.[8]

Mathematics context has moved from an almost exclusive focus on computation skills and measurement to a wide variety of activities requiring students to understand the processes and systems of mathematics to problem-solving situations. The Interactive Mathematics Program funded by The National Science Foundation has resulted in programs which integrate traditional mathematics materials with additional topics recommended by the National Council of Teachers of Mathematics (NCTM), such as probability and statistics. It also uses graphing calculator technology to enhance student understanding.

Science, like mathematics, received much attention in the 1990s. New science programs utilizing unifying concepts such as systems and change and application of science rather than accumulation of unrelated facts have replaced traditional programs. The use of themes to demonstrate science's relation to other disciplines and contributions to solving world problems has also been an exciting focus of the new science curriculum of the secondary school.

Other content areas including the arts, physical education, and the extracurricular curriculum have been the focus of national groups as the need for well-rounded youths has never been greater.

Vocational education and the practical arts faced demands for reassessment of their mission in the 1990s. The Carl D. Perkins Vocational Applied Technology Act of 1990 began an approach to use vocational courses to prepare all students for the world of work by integrating academic and vocational education. With the advent of technology in the work place, "tech-prep" became the focus of most secondary schools forcing production types of vocational courses out of the curriculum. Even in agriculture, new technology and the decline of the family farm forced a new approach.

By the late 1990s, the demands of a global economy forced even more drastic changes in vocational education. A high-tech workplace, the need for smarter workers, and the decline of traditional jobs have now blurred the traditional distinction between the academic and vocational curriculum.

The School to Work Opportunities Act of 1994 focused attention on how to help American schools help students make the connection between school and work. As students prepare for a new workplace, that connection must be strengthened.[9]

Magnet and Alternative Schools and Programs

The 1990s saw a rapid increase in the number of choices of school programs for students.

Magnet schools and **magnet programs,** often used as a means of desegregation, were established to offer specialized programs in areas such as the arts, sciences, and technology.

Alternative schools and programs offering new approaches to learning and discipline also have served to break the mold of traditional high school offerings.

Alternative education schools or programs usually offer smaller classes and work-at-your-own-pace incentives for students. Many of the students enrolled in these programs have had trouble conforming to traditional programs and classrooms. Computer software and curriculum packaging have made it possible for students to accelerate completion of courses and time spent in the high school.

Alternative programs usually provide smaller classes, individualized learning, emphasis on improving life skills and a close tie to the community.

Alternative education may take the form of separate schools or separate school programs within traditional schools.

Advance Placement/International Baccalaureate Programs

Advance Placement allows high school students to attain college credit if they pass a national examination in a content area. Many high schools offered such opportunities for students by providing AP courses to prepare students to pass such exams.

Since 1967, the International Baccalaureate (IB) program has uniquely prepared students for further study in colleges and universities both in the United States and around the world.

As the United States attempts to raise the standards of secondary education, the growth of the International Baccalaureate diploma program, which originated in Europe, offers great hope to those who want the United States to have a "world-class" secondary program.

The idea behind this **global education** program is an integrated form of study that offers a broad, liberal approach complemented by the opportunity to study a subject in depth. The IB founders' goal was to help students learn how to learn, how to analyze, and how to reach considered conclusions about people, their languages and literature, ways of society, and the scientific forces of their environment. The birth of the International Baccalaureate Office (IBO) in 1967 started from a concern for students who had attended many schools in the course of their educational experiences. The IBO was created to foster an examination system that could be used and recognized worldwide. After several years of preparation, the first diplomas were issued in 1971.

The IBO operates in four continents, including America, and meets annually in Geneva, Switzerland. The founders of the IB desired a world-class curriculum that would emphasize internal coherence and maintain rigorous integrity. The two-year preparation stresses subjects that cover the many fields of human experience as well as academic pursuits. Almost all of the subjects offered have syllabi for two levels of achievement. The material included on the higher level requires two years of preparation for the examination, assuming five class hours per week, or a minimum of 240 teaching hours. The subsidiary level requires half as much time which may extend over one or two years. During the last two years of secondary school, an IB candidate studies six subjects, three of which must be studied on the higher level and three on the subsidiary. From the courses being offered, the candidate selects one from each of the following areas:

1. **Language A**   Study in the native language includes world literature in translation from at least two other language areas
2. **Language B**   A second language at a level similar to that of Language A, but distinguished by not requiring the same depth and breadth of understanding of cultural and historical contexts

3. **People**   A choice of one of the following courses, using a thematic, comparative, and intellectual approach: history, geography, economics, philosophy, psychology, social anthropology, or business studies
4. **Experimental Sciences**   A choice of one of the following options: biology, chemistry, physics, physical science, or scientific studies
5. **Mathematics**
6. **Electives**   A choice of one of the following: art, music; a classical language; a second language B; an additional option under 3, 4, or 5; computer studies; or special syllabi developed by the IB schools including theater arts.

In addition to these six courses, the candidate takes a course developed for the IB on the philosophy of learning, known as the *Theory of Knowledge*. This course ensures that the students critically reflect on the knowledge and experience acquired. The student also prepares a 4,000- to 5,000-word research paper based on one of the subjects of the IB curriculum. In addition, the student must engage in 150 hours of extracurricular activities in the CAS Program (Creativity, Action, Service).

Assessment procedures include use of written examinations and oral examinations in languages. Grades awarded by the IB examiner are based on a scale of 1 through 7. A minimum of 24 grade points is necessary to be awarded a diploma.

Awareness of the IB program as an educational tool around the world and as a placement device in American colleges and universities is increasing. The comprehensive nature of the program is commendable; its international approach to education is formidable. In this era of expanding global networks and growing need for international understanding, the steady growth of an innovative contribution to world education is an inspiration and invaluable to American secondary education.

Promise of Technology in the Secondary Level

In the schools of the first eight decades of the twentieth century, shop classrooms were developed to train students in the vocational areas. The hands-on classroom of the twenty-first century will be a technology studies laboratory. Students in these classrooms will use computers and critical analysis to solve complex problems in all disciplines—solutions that they can apply to their daily lives.

All students in the secondary school will have word processing skills and will be able to create papers using the libraries of the world.

The tie-in of home and school will allow students to access data, review lessons, and interact with peers well beyond normal school hours. Education as practiced in the high school of the twentieth century will be centered in the home as much or more than in a building called "high school."

Keeping abreast of the latest in technology will require constant evaluation of software and multimedia. The Association for Supervision and Curriculum Development (ASCD) publishes *Only the Best—Annual Guide to Highest-Rated Education Software/Multimedia for PreSchool–Grade Twelve.* Schools and school districts can negotiate site licenses for present and past-year editions directly with ASCD.[10]

The promise of a World Wide Web in the classroom will continue to bring a global audience directly into classrooms. Using the World Wide Web, teachers can develop collaborative projects with international partners, compare data with classes in other parts of the world, share results on their own home pages, and get feedback from the global community on the Internet. Rural or urban schools now will have information that any school may obtain. The World Wide Web makes the virtual classroom a reality.[11]

ORGANIZATIONAL PRACTICES IN THE SECONDARY SCHOOL

The organizational structure of a secondary school is designed to carry out the instructional program. The dominant pattern of organization in most secondary schools is **departmentalization.** Departmentalization operates under the assumption that the disciplinary construct is the purest form of organizing knowledge. The curriculum is organized around separate disciplines that are taught by teachers in a department, such as the mathematics or social studies departments.

Scheduling is fairly simple in a departmentalized school. Courses are taught in uniform lengths of time, for example, 55-minute periods.

For years, most secondary schools have operated under the following assumptions:

1. The appropriate amount of time for learning a subject is the same uniform period of time, 50 to 60 minutes in length, six or seven periods a day, for 36 weeks out of the year.
2. A classroom group size of thirty to thirty-five students is the most appropriate for a wide variety of learning experiences.
3. All learners are capable of mastering the same subject matter in the same length of time. For example, we give everyone the same test on Chapter 5 on Friday. We pass everyone from level one of algebra to level two when June comes.
4. We assume that once a group is formed, the same group composition is equally appropriate for a wide variety of learning activities.
5. We assume that the same classroom is equally appropriate for a wide variety of learning activities. Conference rooms are not provided for teacher-student conferences. Large-group facilities are not provided for mass dissemination of materials. Small-group rooms are unavailable for discussion activities.
6. We assume that all students require the same kind of supervision.
7. We assume that the same teacher is qualified to teach all aspects of his or her subject for one year.

Operating on those assumptions, we have locked students into an educational egg crate with thirty students to a cubicle from 8 A.M. to 3 P.M. five days a week. In short, schools operating under those assumptions have existed more for the convenience of teaching than for the facilitation of learning.

Secondary schools today are attempting to break this lockstep approach to instruction. Rigid class sizes, facilities, and fixed schedules are being challenged. Subject matter is also being organized in terms of more than a single disciplinary instruction. Core or correlation of subjects, interdisciplinary instruction, and fusion (which provides for the merging of related subjects into a new subject) represent alternative patterns of curriculum organization.

The organizational structure in a secondary school must be flexible enough to allow for groups of different size to serve different functions of individualizing instruction. Scheduling in a secondary school should come after it is determined what kind of instrument is desired. For example, if departmentalization and interdisciplinary teaming are desired, then a flexible schedule should be developed to accommodate those goals. Arrangements should be made to accommodate individual teaching, small groups, large groups, and laboratory-study groups.

Teaming and variable grouping can be designed for a secondary school to build on student needs and teacher talents. Interdisciplinary teaming can facilitate the correlation of subject matter. Common groups of students shared by common groups of teachers with **common planning time** is necessary for interdisciplinary teaching to succeed.

Block Scheduling

The 1990s saw a major scheduling innovation implemented in secondary schools—the **block schedule.** As part of the restructuring movement, this scheduling innovation allowed secondary schools to make significant departures from the conventional school organization and practice.

Different schools have had different reasons for considering block scheduling. Common reasons given are (1) to create larger blocks of time for instruction, (2) to permit students to enroll in one or more additional classes during the year, (3) to increase time available for professional development, and (4) for teachers to teach fewer students for longer periods of time, thus getting to know them better.[12] The bottom line, though, in all considerations should be, What is best for students?

If "stand and deliver" did not work in a traditional schedule, it certainly can't in a longer block of time. Reorganizing instruction to include a variety of learning activities, utilizing technology, and greater student participation in their own learning appear to be the greatest challenges of block scheduling.

Figures 9.3, 9.4, 9.5, 9.6, and 9.7 illustrate commonly used block scheduling models.

Figure 9.3 allows eight credits over the school year and 32 possible credits during a four-year high school experience.

Figure 9.4 allows classes to meet every other day for the school year with Fridays being split as "A" week or "B" week. Figure 9.5 is a college-type schedule which features an interim four-week session, thus allowing nine credit hours a year instead of eight.

Figure 9.6 works better with smaller schools. The "skinning" block can be placed anywhere in the school day, and more than one block can be divided. This does reduce the benefit of having just four classes in a day. Figure 9.7 is a trimester model that adds about 45 minutes to the school day and increases each class by about 10 minutes. This model allows for 12 credit opportunities during a year and 48 credits over four years.[13]

FIGURE 9.3 Straight 4 x 4 Block

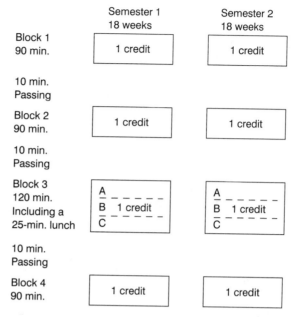

FIGURE 9.4 Rotating A/B Block

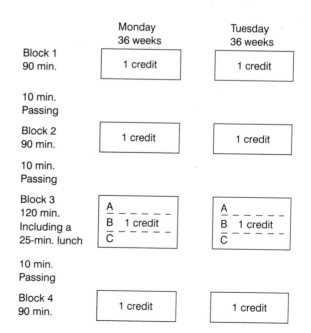

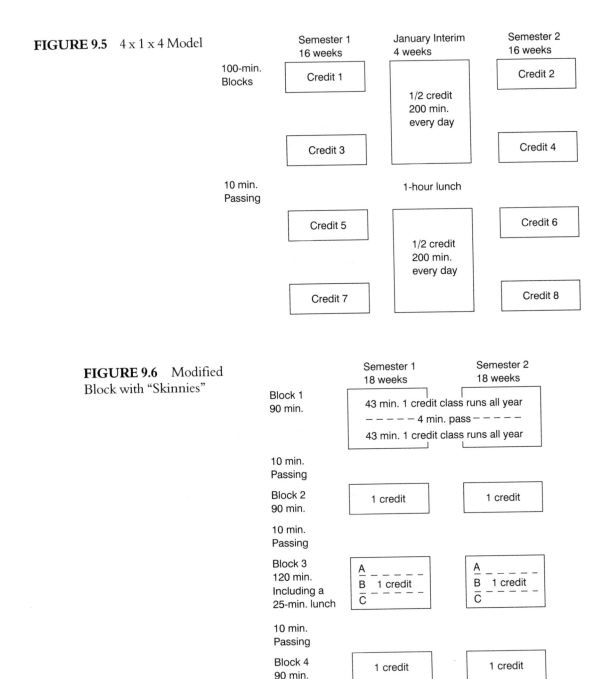

FIGURE 9.5 4 x 1 x 4 Model

	Semester 1 16 weeks	January Interim 4 weeks	Semester 2 16 weeks
100-min. Blocks	Credit 1	1/2 credit 200 min. every day	Credit 2
	Credit 3		Credit 4

10 min. Passing		1-hour lunch	
	Credit 5	1/2 credit 200 min. every day	Credit 6
	Credit 7		Credit 8

FIGURE 9.6 Modified Block with "Skinnies"

	Semester 1 18 weeks	Semester 2 18 weeks
Block 1 90 min.	43 min. 1 credit class runs all year – – – – 4 min. pass – – – – 43 min. 1 credit class runs all year	
10 min. Passing		
Block 2 90 min.	1 credit	1 credit
10 min. Passing		
Block 3 120 min. Including a 25-min. lunch	A B 1 credit C	A B 1 credit C
10 min. Passing		
Block 4 90 min.	1 credit	1 credit

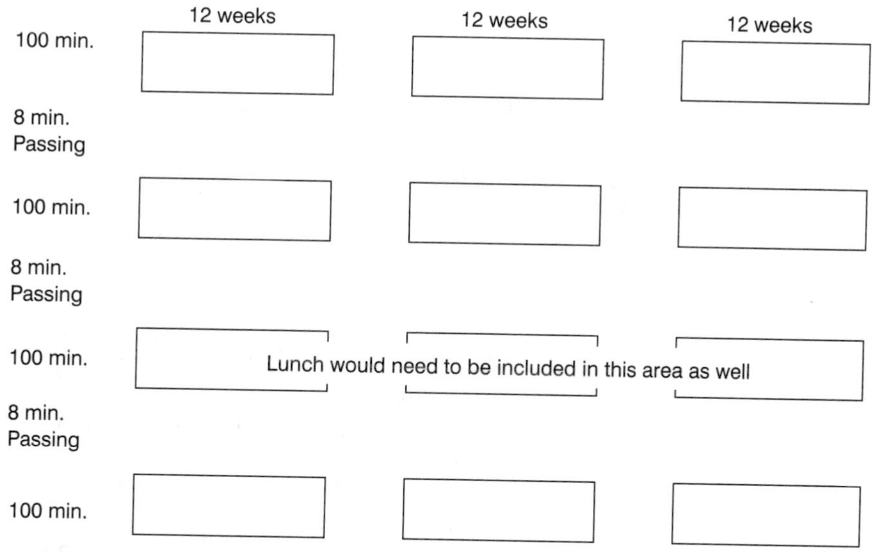

12 weeks	12 weeks	12 weeks

100 min.

8 min.
Passing

100 min.

8 min.
Passing

100 min.   Lunch would need to be included in this area as well

8 min.
Passing

100 min.

FIGURE 9.7 Trimester Model

FUTURE DIRECTIONS OF THE SECONDARY SCHOOL

Many believe that the high school will disappear before it will change to the dynamic school that it should be to shape young people. Today, many districts are experimenting with block scheduling and alternative secondary schools such as magnet schools, academic and performing arts high schools, and charter schools. Also, special schools have been organized for students who have discipline problems. Athletic programs are also coming under increasing review by school officials who fear interscholastic sports have gotten out of hand.

Perhaps the greatest challenge facing the secondary school today is the attempt to establish its real role in American education. In the early years, the secondary school was viewed as an academic school designed to prepare students for college. Later, the high school assumed a greater function—that of preparing students for the immediate work force. Fed by legislation after World War I, vocational programs were organized in school districts to train students who were not going on to higher education. By the 1950s, high schools assumed yet another function, which was to provide a comprehensive curriculum of academic and vocational courses for students under one roof.

By the mid-1980s, the functions of providing students for college and of training for jobs came under attack by numerous groups in the United States. Reeling under pressure to provide better-trained and informed young people for high-tech jobs, colleges and secondary schools increased program requirements for their students. Because many vocational programs are training many young people for jobs that are rapidly becoming obsolete, the supporting public is questioning the value of any vocational programs at the secondary level. Because over one half of our youth do not go on to higher education (of the 65 percent that even graduate), large numbers of our youth may face the future with no marketable skills and be unsuited for college or technical training. Our country can ill afford to write off two thirds of our young people entering society.

Compounding the problem is the increasing number of minority students found in large urban school districts who face language, cultural, family, and economic conditions that prevent them from learning. The experience of compensatory programs does not leave us with great optimism that more money and special programs will make a difference in the achievement of these youngsters.

We know student achievement in secondary schools is higher if

- ☐ There is a high degree of parent involvement
- ☐ There are order and sequence in the curriculum
- ☐ There are high expectations of teachers and the administrative staff
- ☐ Maximum time is spent on instruction time on task
- ☐ There is a strong guidance program and opportunities for tutorial help from peers, parents, and other adults
- ☐ There are structure and discipline existing in the school
- ☐ There are supporting teachers and positive reinforcement from both teachers and support staff

A Changing America and Changing World

To understand the growing interdependence of the world that the secondary education graduate will enter, think about the number of multinational products produced and the military and economic partnerships within and outside the northern hemisphere.

If our world were a village of 1,000 people, it would have

- ☐ 564 Asians
- ☐ 210 Europeans
- ☐ 86 Africans
- ☐ 80 South Americans
- ☐ 60 North Americans

The religious breakdown would be

- ☐ 300 Christians (183 Catholics, 84 Protestants, 33 Eastern Orthodox Christians)
- ☐ 175 Moslems
- ☐ 128 Hindus
- ☐ 55 Buddhists
- ☐ 47 Animists
- ☐ 85 other religions
- ☐ 210 without any religion or atheists

Of these people,

☐   60 would control half the total income
☐   500 would be hungry
☐   600 would live in shanty towns
☐   700 would be illiterate[14]

Of the new workers who come into the workforce between 1990 and 2000, 82 percent will be a combination of female, nonwhite, and immigrant. Table 9.3 illustrates the most rapidly growing occupations.

Minority students are increasing in numbers while the nation's population under age 18 will actually decline between 1990 and 2010. Half of America's children live in only nine states. We will have an estimated 62,644,000 school-age students in the United States in 2010 of whom 32,000,000 will live in our nine largest states. Of those 32,000,000 school-age students, 15 million will be minority. Thirteen states plus Washington, DC, will have more than 40 percent of their students from minority backgrounds. Over 30 percent of all students in 2010 will be minority (see Table 9.4).

The aging of American continues. Over 35 million Americans were identified in the 1996 census as being over 65 years of age. Fifty percent of children born today are first (and probably last) children; in 1950, only 25 percent of infants born were first children, and 75 percent were to families with more than one child.

Poverty continues to plague secondary students. Students who are poor continue to drop out of school in alarming numbers in spite of numerous programs to keep them in school. With new immigrants taking low-paying jobs and many non-skilled jobs going overseas, the need for more education and training is greater than ever. Combined with the increased use of technology in the workplace, the future is indeed bleak for students leaving school early.

TABLE 9.3   Most Rapidly Growing Occupations

Occupation	Percent Growth in Employment 1978–90	Number of New Jobs by 1990
All Occupations	22.5	21,980,000
Data processing machine mechanics	147.6	96,572
Paralegal personnel	132.4	39,310
Computer Systems Analysts	107.8	203,357
Computer operators	87.9	151,100
Office machine and cash register servicers	80.8	40,668
Computer programmers	73.6	153,051
Aero-astronautic engineers	70.4	41,315
Food preparation and service workers, Fast food restaurants	68.8	491,900
Employment interviewers	66.6	35,179
Tax preparers	64.5	19,997

Source: U.S. Department of Labor, *Monthly Labor Review.*

TABLE 9.4   Growth in
Minority Student Population

State	Minority Kids		Total Kids 2010
	1990(%)	2010(%)	
California	46.4	56.9	8,520,000
Texas	47.1	56.9	5,418,000
Florida	46.4	53.4	3,270,000
New York	39.9	52.8	3,862,000
New Jersey	36.6	45.7	1,935,000
Illinois	32.7	41.7	2,684,000
Michigan	22.8	29.2	2,094,000
Ohio	16.7	20.8	2,349,000
Pennsylvania	15.4	18.7	2,260,000

Source: U.S. Bureau of Census, 1996.

The full-service school, offering health care and social programs along with academic programs, may well be the typical school of the future. Subsidized housing and free or reduced transportation for the poor to go to work, along with health and social services centered at school sites, may need to be greatly increased if we are to avoid a permanent underclass of citizens in the United States.

As we enter a truly international era in economic development, America's skills in pluralism will help us, but schools must work to eliminate poverty and develop new approaches to schooling.

The reform efforts of the 1980s and 1990s produced the following:

☐   Threshold exams for kids and teachers, established minimum competence levels, which meant that the child was held back or the teacher did not get hired if their achievement level was too low
☐   More difficult curricula
☐   Choice plans, which assumed that parents would choose the "good" schools for their kids and shut down the "bad" ones
☐   Restructured schools that give the individual school more control over its destiny

Results of such reform included

☐   No increase in high school or college graduation rates
☐   No reduction in youth poverty
☐   City schools that are as segregated for Hispanic students as they were for blacks
☐   No gain in scores of the lowest third
☐   No increase in equity funding, which would provide the resources that would give every child a chance to actually attain the higher standards that some forty states have adopted

In summary, the face of America is changing as it enters a new century. It is likely that the secondary school curriculum will be forced to change as well. Our demographics suggest a growing underclass of citizens who will not have an opportunity to share in America's bounty unless the public school survives and adjusts to changing conditions. The term *at risk,* so popular in the 1990s, threatens to describe the majority of secondary pupils in the first decade of the twenty-first century.

A CLOSING NOTE ON THE SECONDARY SCHOOL

As curriculum persons, we are concerned about the trends of the late 1990s as they relate to the American high school. In the rush to return to the basics, raise achievement scores, and legislate quality control, we seem to have forgotten a purpose for secondary education that underpinned most planning prior to 1955. That purpose for the secondary school is to foster democracy.

Democracy is a word that was used frequently by Dewey, Bode, Kilpatrick, and Rugg. In its context, these leaders spoke of democracy not as a system of government in which supreme power is vested in the people—although they understood these things—but rather as a way of life in which no single group could dominate others on the basis of class distinction, heredity, or privilege. These educators, whom we cherish and whom we quote so often, perceived a danger in our way of life, which pitted social equality against economic competition. If capitalism and competition became dominant, they reasoned, basic human rights might be trampled. Schools, according to Dewey, "were the institution best organized to serve Democracy's cause."

The point that we are making is that we have lost sight of a very important value in recent times—democracy. Education through this century has been the key response to repressive social relations.

The education system, perhaps more than any other contemporary social institution, has become the laboratory in which competing solutions to the problems of personal liberation and social equality are tested and the arena in which social struggles are fought out.

In short, democracy is *the* historic value or social ideal that has given direction to our educational aims. If education in public schools is our primary instrument to shape our destiny as a society, then should not our curriculum be planned with essentials first and refinements second?

What is the future of the secondary school? Perhaps the secondary school is destined to become less of a finishing school and more of a transitional school designed to send students on to higher education or to highly skilled technical jobs in a computer society. Redesigning a static curriculum to accomplish that task will be the greatest challenge facing curriculum workers in the last decade of this century.

SUMMARY

The secondary school today is receiving increased attention. Because it is the exit school for many American youths, the secondary school is expected to find solutions for many of the problems of society by training individuals to make necessary changes to improve society.

Secondary schools have experienced their share of reform movements in education. Tracing the development of the secondary school, one can see where numerous committees and commissions were established to improve the high school curriculum. Many of the reform movements, however, were aimed less at improving the high school than at preparing high school youths for college or specialized jobs needed in society.

Although most secondary schools are organized in a uniform pattern (departmentalization), some secondary schools have tried different scheduling patterns to allow for more flexibility in the instructional program.

The future of the public secondary school is threatened by many forces as we enter the twenty-first century. Educational leaders must begin to give direction to the secondary school. They must not leave decisions about that direction to politicians and special interest groups.

SUGGESTED LEARNING ACTIVITIES

1. Trace the development of the secondary school in the United States.
2. What are the major issues and problems facing secondary schools today? How do they compare with issues and problems found in secondary schools in the past fifty years?
3. The curriculum for the secondary school has often been described as dull and irrelevant. How would you reorganize the present curriculum of the secondary school to fit the needs of a rapidly emerging high-tech society in the United States?
4. Develop a flexible one-block schedule for a medium-size high school that will include provisions for both departmentalization and team instruction.
5. Prepare a paper that will describe the high school found in the first decade of the twenty-first century.

NOTES

1. Mortimer Adler, *The Paideia Proposal* (New York: Macmillan, 1982).
2. John Goodlad, *A Place Called School* (New York: McGraw-Hill, 1984), p. 94.
3. Goodlad, *A Place Called School,* p. 143.
4. Ted Sizer, *Horace's Compromise: The Dilemma of the American High School* (Boston, MA: Houghton-Mifflin, 1984).
5. *America 2000,* U.S. Department of Education, 1989.
6. "What Work Requires of Schools: A SCANS Report for America 2000," U.S. Department of Labor, June, 1991.
7. Maxwell Schauweker, "A Review of Standards of Reading and Writing," *Teaching K–8* (March/April, 1995): 233–34.
8. Deborah L. Ball, "Teacher Learning and the Mathematics Reform—What We Think We Know and What We Need to Learn," *Kappan* 77, 7 (March, 1996): 500–508.
9. Iuan Charner, et al., "Reforms of the School-to-Work Transition—Findings, Implications, and Challenges," *Kappan* 77, 1 (September, 1995): 40–59.
10. Daniel Kinnaman, "ASCD Releases Only the Best," *Learning* 15, 5 (February, 1995): 36.

11. Caroline McCullen, "World Wide Web in the Classroom: The Quintessential Collaboration," *Learning and Leading with Technology* 23, 3 (November, 1995): 7–10.
12. Donald Hackman, "Ten Guidelines for Implementing Block Scheduling," *Educational Leadership,* November, 1995, pp. 24—27.

13. Robert Canady and Michael Rettig, "The Power of Innovative Scheduling," *Educational Leadership,* November, 1995, pp. 4–10.
14. World Development Forum, United Nations, April 1990.

BOOKS TO REVIEW

Anderson, Lorin W., ed. *International Encyclopedia of Teaching and Teacher Education,* 2nd ed. Tarrytown, NY: Pergamon, 1995.

Anderson, Robert Henry. *Nongradedness: Helping It to Happen.* Lancaster, PA: Technomic Publishing Co., 1993.

ASCD Improving Student Achievement Research Panel. *Educating Everybody's Children: Diverse Teaching Strategies for Diverse Learners: What Research and Practice Say About Improving Achievement.* Alexandria, VA: Association for Supervision and Curriculum Development, 1995.

Banks, James A., and Cherry A. Banks, eds. *Handbook of Research on Multicultural Education.* New York: Macmillan Publishing, 1995.

Grossman, Herbert. *Teaching in a Diverse Society.* Boston: Allyn and Bacon, 1995.

McBride, Robert, ed. *Teacher Education Policy: Some Issues Arising from Research and Practice.* Washington, DC: Falmer Press, 1996.

Martin, Eugene G., ed. *Foundations of Technology Education.* New York: Glencoe, 1995.

Sizer, T. R. *Horace's Compromise: The Dilemma of the American High School.* Boston, MA: Houghton-Mifflin, 1984.

Tanner, Daniel, and Laurel Tanner. *Curriculum Development: Theory into Practice,* 3rd ed. Upper Saddle River, NJ: Merrill/Prentice Hall, 1995.

PART IV

CURRICULUM PROSPECTIVES

10 Curriculum Design Alternatives

chapter 10

CURRICULUM DESIGN ALTERNATIVES

It is apparent that the new century will bring substantial alteration to the form and purpose of most public schools.

A combination of economic pressures brought on by a global economy, dissatisfaction with present school programs, continued comparison of U.S. students with the best and brightest students from other countries and dramatic changes in information processing suggests that significant changes will occur in our schools in the first part of the new century. Curriculum development will be at the center of activity as those changes transform our schools into new forms. After two centuries of a traditional model, the new century will see forms of schooling unlike any of the past. Access to knowledge won't just be available from a teacher in a school using a printed text, nor will schools necessarily be run only by those in the public sector. Options for learning will be numerous, and school sites may be one of many places of learning for U.S. students.

In a democratic society, it is expected that differences in opinion will exist about what schools should be doing. After all, the institution called "school" programs millions of Americans daily in thought, behavior, and feeling. Following rising birthrates in the late 1980s, numbers of students in American schools continued to grow in the 1990s, with 1996 seeing an enrollment of 51.7 million students when projections in the 1980s estimated a total of 45 million students by that year. The tax revolts of the 1980s resulted in a slowdown of school construction, thus leading to crowded school buildings in the 1990s. Many districts house students in trailers or portables at school sites. Even establishment of year-round schools hasn't slowed the need for portables in fast-growing districts.

In 1996, the fastest-growing districts were all in the Southeast or West, except for New York City.[1] For instance, in 1996, the districts with the largest enrollment gains were[2]

School District	**Increase**	**Change (%)**
Los Angeles Unified, CA	91,223	16.6
New York City, NY	87,163	9.5
Dade County, FL	86,407	38.9
Broward County, FL	64,118	51.0
Clark County, NV	55,647	62.1
Palm Beach County, FL	51,327	72.5
Gwinnett County, GA	38,263	100.1
Orange County, FL	34,893	44.3
Guilford County, NC	30,214	124.7
Fresno Unified, CA	27,127	55.1

Growing enrollment in the late 1990s seemed to be a constant trend rather than the result of a single baby-boom period.

Over time, the American school seems to have benefitted from a diversity of opinion, and perhaps it is the openness of the system of schooling that protects it from radical change. The case may even by made that, in a rapidly changing world, a highly structured and purposeful institution would become obsolete. We anticipate that the new century will bring a much increased effort by many publics to redirect American education, and curriculum workers should be ready to meet such challenge by being aware of alternatives.

A HISTORY OF CHANGE IN SCHOOLS

In the early years of this century, attempts to introduce changes in our schools came from professional educators who were concerned with broad philosophical issues about the role of education in society. Reform efforts, for the most part, had a philosophical base and evolved slowly over several decades. Only after considerable discussion and experimentation were educational reforms attempted.

Early attempts to reform the American school assumed a somewhat monolithic culture and aimed at developing programs that would serve the entire American society. In the latter half of this century, reform efforts have come more frequently, from more diverse sources, and without clear philosophical bases or records of controlled experimentation.

During the late 1950s and early 1960s, the American society experienced a cultural awakening. The diversity of the society, a pluralistic configuration of many subcultures, was revealed, and the historic pattern of the public school was called into question. If the public school was to serve all members of the society, both the substance and the organization of the institution were open to review.

The frustrations and hopes of the numerous groups of the American public became linked to the schools, which are the social institutions for instilling values. The divergent norms and values of the subcultures suggested new ideas about what schools should be. Some of these ideas and concepts were incorporated by the public schools, but many were not.

Related to these attempts to reform the school, which came primarily from inside the ranks of education, were numerous reformation efforts by external groups. The importance of public education as an influence for social change led industry, foundations, and the federal agencies to introduce changes in the school. The sponsorship of such efforts continues today.

The implications of such trends for curriculum planners are multiple. First, it seems that those responsible for designing school programs should be able to view these forces of change with some degree of perspective. In our opinion, this may be the most important skill required of anyone in curriculum development. Innovations and educational trends need to be seen in terms of some overriding framework and in light of historical precedent. An inability to categorize and order the multitude of curriculum changes found in today's public schools will result in short-range decision criteria and long-term chaos.

Second, it must be recognized that public sophistication concerning curriculum development has grown considerably during the past several decades. Seeing schools as purposeful agents of change has led to the development of many restricting designs with little or no concern for long-term social implications. Such educational focus has also led to the development of some relatively efficient public school programs.

Finally, recent changes in the design of school programs should suggest to curriculum leaders that schools are institutions with numerous possibilities. To be influential in the educational environment, curriculum designers must break away from the familiar and begin to be responsible to the changing needs and values of the society. The clients who support public schools must be given responses that are imaginative.

In the following sections, some of the major curriculum designs in the United States are introduced and discussed.

MAJOR CURRICULUM DESIGNS

There are numerous ways in which the many forms of schooling in the United States might be classified. Each social science perspective would suggest a different set of variables and categorization. Perhaps the most useful existing classification available today is one developed by R. Freeman Butts.[3] In this classification, school forms are separated by function. Six major types of school design, and their rationale, are presented:

1. Conservative liberal arts
2. Educational technology
3. Humanistic
4. Vocational
5. Social reconstruction
6. Deschooling

Conservative Liberal Arts

In the vast majority of the schools in the United States, the pervasive form is one with roots leading back to Hellenistic Greece. This traditional form or design is based on the belief that a human being's unique and distinctive quality is intellect and that the quest for knowledge is the natural fulfillment of such an intellect. In short, the highest purpose in life is to engage in the process of inquiry—to move from ignorance to truth, from confusion to enlightenment.

Historically, this quest for knowledge was seen as a reflection of a world whose laws and physical order were fixed properties. The process of education was concerned simply with the pursuit of objective knowledge for its own sake. A liberal education was suitable to free people who possessed the legal opportunity and means to devote themselves to cultural attainment.

In later times, after scientific revolutions and the loss of a shared culture had diminished the concept of *paideia,* the cultured man, the liberal arts approach to educating became a perspective. Liberal arts was not so much a mastery of subject matter as it was a way of looking at things. The human mind was trained so that the individual might live fully.

As this notion of education was translated into a public education format during the early American experience, such knowing was seen as a means of producing an enlightened citizenry. In the words of R. Freeman Butts:

> . . . the prime purpose of the public schools is to serve the general welfare of a democratic society by assuring the knowledge and understanding necessary to exercise the responsibilities of citizenship are not only made available but are inculcated.[4]

The curriculum of the conservative liberal arts is familiar to most of us as the curriculum we studied in high school and in college. The curriculum was spelled out in a formally declared *permanent studies* or *great books* that included language, mathematics, sciences, history, and foreign languages.[5] Usually dominated by a standard text or set of materials, with a certain amount of time to master units, and leading to formal recognition of learning in a graduation from study, the liberal arts model is familiar to many people. In the last decades, Mortimer Adler's *Paideia Proposal* has served as a guide to this form of learning in public schools.[6]

Educational Technology

Education in the new century will experience a technological "gold rush" atmosphere as very inexpensive and highly reliable products make major inroads to this nation's classrooms and school. Technological instruments and personal systems offer the possibility of significant alterations in the teaching-learning act as we know it. Research, communication, training—all are targets of the proliferation of hardware and systems. Driving this gold rush is the bare fact that schools represent the largest sales market in America. More importantly for planners, such technology also suggests an exit point for the spiraling costs of financing public education.

Most technological designs in this century have focused on process and technique to the exclusion of goals and objectives. An early and nonelectric example can be found in the 1930s when the famous Winnetka Plan used mimeographed assignments to master essential skills. Self-instructive practice exercises were monitored through a diagnostic-practice-remediation format that was a forerunner of much of today's programmed instruction.[7]

Historically, technological designs stressed objectivity, precision, and efficiency. As major proponent B. F. Skinner stated:

> The traditional distinction comes down to this: when we know what we are doing, we are training . . . any behavior that can be specified can be programmed.[8]

Usually, in the past, learner behaviors were described overtly, infrequently lasting beyond the immediate treatment.

In the 1970s, all of the objectivity of the technology of behaviorism began to break down as it was recognized that students were being influenced by unplanned technology. Perhaps the best example of this occurred when millions of elementary students watching the launch of the *Challenger* spacecraft in science class were, instead, treated to a dramatic social studies lesson. Technology is powerful in that it allows the learner new powers!

Technology in the 1990s will be of a different scale than previous decades even though each decade has seen its own miracle technology. Televisions in the 1950s, transistors and computers in the 1960s, video cams and compact discs in the 1970s, and facsimile machines and CD-ROMS in the 1980s, and the personal computer, World Wide Web, and Internet of the 1990s—all have greatly affected learning. However, the new century will be the one of unlimited use of communication of knowledge, and more, with the result that the learner will possess worldwide power from home. Schools, if they are to survive in a viable form, will be hard-pressed to ignore the new technologies, and in some technologically deficient districts, it will be a difficult transition. Technology in the next century may have the power to reform or destroy public education.

In the 1980s and 1990s, the lack of meaningful use of technology depressed its impact on classroom learning. In many districts, there appeared to be little integration of hardware or software in traditional courses, and true visions of how the new technologies could be used were nearly nonexistent. In addition to the computer, schools grappled with interactive television, various electronic networks, interactive cable and satellite-beamed video, CD-ROM technology, and other technological tools.

In the new century, curriculum specialists must do better if they are to maintain control of the programming function. Not only is knowledge of how technology works (literacy) important, but also how technology can be used to improve communication and transmission of knowledge. Five questions should focus this effort to regain control:

1. What are the implications of technology?
2. How can schools receive technology in a meaningful way?

3. What technology is most effective for learning in school?
4. How can we prevent technology from creating an intellectual elite in schools?
5. How can we confront the trend toward home schooling from socially deschooling the learning process?

Curriculum leaders in the next years will play a very large role in defining technological designs by the answers given to these questions. Education in public schools will be redefined by technology, only the form remains to be determined. If educators are not aggressive students of technology, the forces that control the medium will program the curriculum.

Humanistic

A third curriculum design in the United States during the twentieth century has had as its main theme the humanizing of learning. Such designs generally feature student-centered curriculums and instructional patterns and a decentralization of authority and organization.

Humane curriculum designs have deep roots in American education and have taken numerous forms in this century. In such programs, there is a shift in atmosphere toward understanding, compassion, encouragement, and trust. Physical settings usually encourage freedom in the form of student mobility, increased choice of curricular activities, and a learning-by-doing format.

An early example of this design in the United States was the Dalton Plan, which was implemented in the Dalton, MA, schools in the 1920s. The program featured freedom of movement and choice of materials by students, cooperation and interaction of student group life through a **house plan,** and subject matter laboratories in the classrooms.

Another early version of a humanistic curriculum design was the organic method of education developed at the Fairhope, AL, school around 1910. This program held that children are best prepared for adult life by fully experiencing childhood. Children were led naturally into more traditional areas of schooling only after experiencing a curriculum of physical exercise, nature study, music, field geography, storytelling, fundamental conception of numbers, drama, and games. General development, rather than the amount of information, controlled the classification of students.[9]

Contemporary versions of the humanistic design are found in open elementary schools, emerging middle schools, and student-centered programs such as Outward Bound. In such programs, the instruction is humane, personalized, and individualized. Curriculum is geared to the maturational levels of students, and teachers serve as guides to learning rather than authority figures or purveyors of knowledge. The problem-solving process of the instructional format borrows heavily from another humanistic design, the **core curriculum.**

The core curriculum, developed in the 1930s in schools such as the Denver public schools, attempted to present learning from a humane and holistic perspective. The following excerpt from an evaluation report outlines the program objectives:

It is so named because it represents an attack upon those problems which are relatively common to the young people in the school and because it carries the chief responsibility for guidance, for general testing, and for record keeping. It is that part of the total school program which is planned for the development in boys and girls of the ability to solve common problems and of the power to think together and to carry on the democratic process of discussion and group discussions.[10]

Core curriculums used a ten-point plan in organizing for instruction:

1. Continuity of teacher-pupil relationships
2. Greater teacher participation in formulating policies of the program
3. Elimination of barriers to learning experiences through the attack on problems rather than through reliance on the logical organization of subject matter in isolated courses
4. Development of core courses based on student concerns
5. Relating school activities to the community
6. Pupil-teacher planning, emphasizing choice and responsibility
7. Guidance by a teacher who knows the student in an intimate classroom setting
8. Using a wide variety of sources of information
9. Using a wide variety of means of expression—words, art, music
10. Teacher-to-teacher planning

Humanistic designs generally are characterized by highly flexible instructional areas, high degrees of student involvement, and an emphasis on the process of learning as opposed to a product orientation or a *preparation for life* outlook.

Vocational

A fourth curriculum design present in this century has been one concerned with vocation and economic aspects of living. Such programs generally go under either the traditional term *vocational* education, or the broader and newer term, **career education.**

In the early years of this century, vocational programs were perceived as separate from the academic tracks and focused on the non-college-bound student. The curriculum consisted of crafts and labor skills. Such programs were strongest in areas with an industrial or agricultural community. More recently, there have been efforts to connect or combine the vocational and technical areas into a structure called *tech-prep.*

Vocational education programs traditionally studied eight areas: (1) trade and industrial education, (2) business education, (3) agriculture, (4) home economics, (5) marketing education, (6) technical education, (7) technology education, and (8) health education. Vocational curriculum designs either try to integrate academics (interdisciplinary) and use vocational applications to illustrate the utilization of knowledge, or they create new tech-prep alternatives in which students branch off from the precollege curriculum while in high school.[11]

Tech-prep/school-to-work programs emerged from the 1980s and led to a new technical education curriculum for the new college-bound in the 1990s. The Carl Perkins Vocational and Applied Technology Act of 1990 led to over 1,000 tech-prep consortia. All states included tech-prep consortia, and true partnerships were established between secondary and post-secondary schools, between academic and vocational/technical faculty, and between educators and business leaders. The 1994 School to Work Opportunities Act extended the efforts of tech-prep. That act requires business involvement.

Curriculum reform in the late 1990s became a central issue in tech-prep efforts with more attention being given to training teachers in applied learning and implementing applied academic courses. Many districts eliminated traditional vocational or general education programs and required all students to either enroll in a tech-prep program or a precollege program.[12]

Efforts to implement a comprehensive vocational design increased during the past two decades for a number of reasons. First, there has been a growing recognition that the schools were an essential piece of the national economic condition. Welfare, unemployment, large segments of the population without useful skills, and the fact that only 40 to 45 percent of all high school graduates attended college were given as reasons for an increased vocational emphasis in the schools.

Second, the entire relevancy movement of the 1990s revealed a condition of students who are bored and listless in senior high school, resentful of the holding pattern of formal schooling.

Third, vocational/career education has been promoted as a means of assisting minority groups and other disenchanted members of the society in breaking out of the cycle of poverty. Students experiencing such programs can escape the containment of environments and family backgrounds.

Finally, the whole concept of utilitarian education and no-frills curriculums has increased the awareness and demand for vocational designs. There is a growing opinion among the public that insufficient attention has been paid to the hard social reality that everyone must eventually seek gainful employment. Technological and political conditions demand a change in the basic definition of an education.

Proponents of vocational designs in the twentieth century have pictured them as a necessity: a means of serving all students in the public schools, a vehicle for making school useful and relevant, a contributor to the well-being of the American society. More recently, American business has stressed technological and economic education as stimuli to the high school curriculum. Vocational designs are practical, say proponents. Critics of vocational designs, including career education, see them as static conceptions of life in the American society and insufficient preparation for life in an unknown future.

There is little doubt that competing in the new global economy will force an even greater collaboration among business, labor, government, and education (public, private, postsecondary). Long-term industry-education collaboration will focus on staff development/in-service training, curriculum revision, upgrading, instructional materials and equipment, and improving educational management—all central to an effective vocational education delivery system.[13]

Social Reconstruction

A fifth curriculum design found in the United States in this century has as its main theme social reconstruction. The conception of the school as a vehicle for social improvement is not new. Arguments for this type of school were made in the 1930s by members of the social reconstruction wing of the Progressive Education Association. Harold Rugg, for example, spoke of the changes impending in the American society and encouraged the schools to influence social changes. He outlined characteristics of a needed curriculum in the 26th National Society for the Study of the Education Yearbook.

> A curriculum which will not only inform but will constantly have as its ideal the development of an attitude of sympathetic tolerance and critical open-mindedness . . . a curriculum which is constructed on a problem-solving organization providing constant practice in choosing between alternatives, in making decisions, in drawing generalizations . . . a curriculum in which children will be influenced to put their ideas sanely into action.[14]

The social reconstruction designs seek to equip students with tools (skills) for dealing with changes about them. So equipped, the student can meet an unknown future with attitudes and habits of action. In the 1980s and early 1990s, special schools for minority youths illustrated this special kind of intellectual "arming" of the student.

More recently, the American curriculum has seen an increase in the teaching of thinking skills, skills that teach students how to use information. Advocates of the theory of multiple intelligences have focused attention on the idea that the way in which information is treated causes the student to use information in certain ways. In other words, how we teach is how students learn.[15]

Another example of social reconstruction designs is the use of schooling to encourage certain social trends. For example, in the Duval County School district in Jacksonville (FL), magnet programs are offered to encourage voluntary racial integration (see Figure 10.1). Here, the curriculum offerings are multiple and secondary to the primary objective of meeting court-ordered compliance to desegregate under local initiative.

The major assumption of social reconstruction designs is that the future is not fixed, but rather is amenable to modification and improvement. The school, as an institution, cannot remain neutral in a changing world and can influence and direct social change.

Some recent applications of the social reconstruction design have used "futurism" to justify the necessity of social intervention. Since the future will not be like the present, it is necessary to be flexible and develop the ability to make value decisions.

Social reconstruction designs generally combine classroom learning with application in the outer world. Teachers and students are partners in inquiry, and instruction is usually carried on in a problem-solving or inquiry format.

Type of Program	Elementary Grades Pre–K–5		Middle 6–8	Senior 9–12
Academic Enrichment Learning Styles	Fort Caroline Oceanway Ortega	Sabal Palm San Jose Timucuan		
Aviation and Aerospace				Ribault
Business, Finance and Legal Professions			**Matthew Gilbert**	**Wolfson**
Careers	Greenfield		Stilwell	Baldwin
Citizenship	San Mateo West Riverside	Windy Hill		Lee
Communications	Beauclearc Lake Lucina **Norwood**	Ramona Whitehouse	**Eugene Butler**	Englewood
Computers/ Technology	**Bethune** **Central Riverside** Cedar Hills	Pine Estates **Carter G. Woodson**	**Ribault**	Paxon
Foreign Language	John E. Ford	Ruth Upson		
Fundamental	Crystal Springs Hendricks Avenue Holiday Hill	**Lackawanna** **S. P. Livingston** **John Love**		
Gifted and Talented	**R. L. Brown** **R. V. Daniels** **Jacksonville Beach**	**Martin L. King** **Rufus Payne** **Susie Tolbert**	**J. W. Johnson Pre-College Preparatory**	**Stanton College Preparatory**
Government and Public Service/ Community Outreach	Hogan-Spring Glen	Normandy		**Andrew Jackson**
International Studies/ Cultural Diversities	**G. W. Carver** Chimney Lakes Dinsmore	Oak Hill Reynolds Lane		Forrest **Mandarin**
Math/Science/ Pre-Engineering	Lone Star **Moncrief** Louis Sheffield	**Springfield** Stockton	**Kirby-Smith** Mayport Jeb Stuart	**Raines**
Medical Professionals and Health Care			**Darnell-Cookman**	
Modified School Calendar	Crown Point **John E. Ford**	Garden City Loretto		
Montessori	**J. Allen Axson**			
Performing Arts	**Brentwood** Fishweir **Lake Forest**	**Sallye B. Mathis** **Pine Forest**	**Landon**	Douglas Anderson
Physical and Academic Fitness	**S. A. Hull** Thomas Jefferson **Longbranch**	San Pablo Wesconnett **West Jacksonville**	Lake Shore Southside	**Ed White**
Schools for Success	**Sherwood Forest**	Mandarin Oaks		

Note: Bold type indicates magnet schools; nonbold type indicates select schools.

FIGURE 10.1   Social Reconstruction Using Magnet Schools

Source: Duval County Schools, Jacksonville, FL, 1996.

Deschooling

As strange as it sounds, it is possible to design the "deschooling" of public schools. Through purposeful organization, or lack of it, it is possible to deemphasize or disestablish the public school programs and the formality of education by redirecting resources to alternatives. Although early efforts in such designs sought to free the learner from bureaucracy and control by the institution of the school, more recent attempts have attempted to deschool in order to replace public education with economic or political alternatives.

According to its chief spokesperson, Ivan Illich, schools are social tools that actually operate to deprive individuals of an education and real learning. Schools are not the panacea for social ills, but rather are rigid, authoritarian institutions that perpetuate the social order through a number of functions. Illich sees deschooling as an alternative design:

> Will people continue to treat learning as a commodity—a commodity that could be more efficiently produced and consumed by greater numbers of people if new institutional arrangements were established? Or shall we set up only those institutional arrangements that protect the autonomy of the learner—his private initiative to decide what he will learn and his inalienable right to learn what he likes rather than what is useful to somebody else? We must choose between more efficient education of people fit for an increasingly efficient society and a new society in which education ceases to be the task of some special agency.[16]

Problems of institutionalized education revolve around questions of power, leadership, and structure. Schools, by dominating the values and focus of organization, control the leader. Such control is often racist and sexist and is always oppressive. Further, schools are undemocratic in their method of converting knowledge into power.

Opposition to formal schooling and its structure has been a continuous phenomenon of the twentieth century in the United States, but the free school movement of the late 1960s presented the best examples of the deschooling design. Allen Glatthorn outlined the emergence of the free school movement during that period:

> The period of the late sixties, then, was a time ripe for radical change. The curriculum reform movement had run out of steam. The innovations in scheduling and staffing were proving to be only superficial tinkering. And there was acute dissatisfaction with all the public schools. This dissatisfaction was most keenly sensed by militant blacks and by radicals of the New Left. Each of these groups responded by opening their own schools, and these schools were the progenitors of the public alternatives that followed.[17]

Glatthorn identified a number of ways in which free schools and alternative schools attempted to release the individual student from the institutional oppression of the school: travel-learn programs, work and apprenticeship programs, volunteer service, informal study in the community, and affective experiences. Collectively, these curriculum arrangements sought to define education as a personal act.

In the 1990s, new forces entered the deschooling design. There was a significant home schooling movement in America in which parents refused to enroll their students in school and served as a surrogate teacher at home. Although the variety of laws governing this phenomena in the United States precludes any real generalization of motivation and practices, it can be stated that such parents do not support the concept of organized schooling for their children.[18]

A second force that affected public schools in the 1990s was the political push to give parents vouchers and the right to enroll their children in a school of choice. Although the **voucher plan** movement could be seen as a sincere effort to upgrade the public schools, it is probably more about privatizing formal education in America. Using either legislation or incentives, or both, proponents of this educational movement would eliminate foundational funding of public education.[19]

A third force that had an impact on the public schools of the 1990s was the charter school movement. First viewed as a move to privatize public schools by contracting them out to private groups, the movement in the mid-1990s turned to a more inventive approach. Groups both within the public school setting and those outside that setting were encouraged to build innovative school programs using public funds. Even the National Education Association (NEA) joined that movement by developing NEA-run charter schools.[20]

Since charter schools are funded at the same level as public schools and saddled with most of the state and district regulations, many charter schools rely on additional funds from grants from foundations and the private sector. Therefore, building innovative programs with exact dollars that educators use to build traditional programs may not be "as advertised." Private enterprise groups will run schools with deficits for several years with those deficits made up by grants from business foundations. If those same businesses buy into the companies running the schools, they do so with the hope that they can break into the huge education market at a later time. If the state or the national government later provides a "supplement" for private charter schools, those schools can operate at a profit.

Another experiment of the 1970s was performance contracting, in which contractors were paid only for defined increases in test cores. The initial swell of enthusiasm for performance contracting was followed by disappointment in results. Factors such as abuses in testing and the instability of private firms that attempted to make a profit based on delivering instruction which plagued performance contracts may well plague the charter school movement.[21]

The issue is a complex, and whether charter schools supplement or surplant public schools will bear watching.

Efforts to break the monopoly of formal education and deschool learning continue today. They seek to downgrade the importance of accepting the functions of formal schooling and to break the myth of a need for education.

Together, these six curriculum designs outline the diversity of educational programs in the United States during the twentieth century. Curriculum leaders need to be aware that such diversity has always been present in American education and will continue to be present in the future.

Curriculum Design in the Future

Since curriculum leaders are actively concerned with the future so that school programs will genuinely serve learners rather than handicap them, they should be aware of studies that project onrushing forces and events.

Futurism in education is a topic of concern to all educators and has been the subject of numerous commissioned studies and investigations by think tanks such as RAND Incorporated and the Hudson Institute. It is helpful to become familiar with resources such as those presented in the review books suggested at the end of this chapter.

In this chapter, we hope to stimulate thinking about the many possibilities for education that the future might hold and to present the process of curriculum development as the vehicle by which schools might arrive at that unknown future. Following a theme found throughout this book, the future of educational programs is presented in a format that suggests a trend toward greater control in curriculum designs or greater flexibility in educational plans. It is entirely possible, of course, that other intellectual constructs may be more useful in addressing this highly complex topic.

A date of departure for this assessment is 1957, the date of the launch of *Sputnik I.* This event jarred American education into a purposefulness that had been absent in the past and opened fully the idea of using schools as an instrument of national policy. Although the space race of the late 1950s has evaporated in scale to that of "just another federal program," the question of what role the schools should play remains.

Entering the twenty-first century, American education is faced with a bewildering array of alternatives concerning what it might become. The question that must be faced by all leaders in the field of curriculum is the primary question of all educational planning. What is the role of education in our society? Failure to consider this critical question is to abdicate a basic responsibility and decide by indecision.

Specifically, there are some questions that must be considered as we peer into the last years of the twentieth century. Among these are the following:

1. What directions seem to be most promising for the American society to pursue in planning for education?
2. Where and how do professional educators begin to assess educational alternatives?
3. Can the future be influenced by our actions, or is it largely predetermined?
4. Where do we as planners gain the value structure to plan for the future?
5. How can we most effectively involve others in our society in planning for the future?

These questions present a challenge to all who are involved in developing educational programs.

REFORM EFFORTS IN THE TWENTY-FIRST CENTURY

Slightly over one century ago, American education confronted the possibility that education could wear many faces and have many meanings. From an exploration of these ideas, the field of curriculum was born. During the first third of the twentieth century, the competing ideas of traditionalism and progressive thought flourished and found expression in both ideas and programs. The statements of the Commission on the Reorganization of Secondary Education and the schools of the Eight-Year Study probably represent the high-water mark in such explorations of competing ideas. Following this period, sporadic manifestations of traditional and experimental views rose and fell with social forces in our nation.

The real and exciting differences of opinion about what education is and how it should be conducted are far from dormant as we enter the twenty-first century. As the last century evolved to be one in which "process" in curriculum took the forefront, it is our opinion that the twenty-first century may be a time in which the substantive dimension is fully explored. Change is upon us, and the choices for educators which find form in the commitment of valuable and scarce resources are many. We no longer possess the wealth to carry all ideas forward without conviction or commitment to purpose.

Schooling in the twenty-first century will continue to be highly political because the stakes are so high. Schools are the vehicle by which any nation renews itself and programs its youths to carry on values. Schools play a most significant role in determining access to work, providing social equity, and allowing understanding about our system of government and how it works. To control the curriculum is to control the future.

Unlike a century ago, when the philosophic arguments of educators had been reduced to discussions of method and strategy, in the 1990s we have seen a return to a more fundamental and primary argument about purpose in schooling. Should our schools proceed in an orderly fashion, an evolutionary fashion, to guide changes that we face in our society, or must there be an evolutionary alteration in the function and form of schools in America? Margaret Mead, our most famous Anthropologist, saw this as a moral issue:

> Our schools have long been torn between two moralities—the morality of individual success as measured by pecuniary gain in the private competitive system, and the morality of individual success as measured by socially useful work consciously directed to the welfare of the whole community. It is time that education made up its mind as to the kind of America it wants, and sought to educate the young on the basis of the integrated morality.[22]

The philosophical differences of American educators go beyond arguments about subject matter and methods, although there is even little agreement on these topics. In general, traditionalists argue that preparation for the future is primarily a process of preparing the mind through formal discipline, whereas more progressive educators see an immersion in true-life experiences as a superior preparation for a changing world. However, enter the extreme wings of American education and hear their pleas for "control" or lack of control in the educative process. Reform in the 1980s and 1990s has witnessed parallel and unbending prescriptions for reforming schools. The assumptions of these extreme groups are divergent and uncompromising. Issues of "outcomes" or "inclusiveness" speak to different facets of the same system.

As we enter that magical year in which we transition into a new era, and a time of hope, we look for increased competition by those interested in curriculum in schools. Curriculum workers, although sometimes pressed into the role of referee, must acknowledge a basic truth about the field: curriculum is a value-laden area of education. We believe that neutrality, or simply burying professional activity into the development process, may not be possible in the years to come. With the movement to privatize public education may come an opportunity for creative expression in curriculum work. Knowing one's own values, and understanding that schools are about the promotion of values, will help the curriculum worker of the twenty-first century to be effective and maintain a crucial role.

We present, for your consideration, a contrasting set of images of education from the twentieth century that led us to the brink of the twenty-first century. Contemplation of these two apparently incompatible visions of schooling will help you become a thoughtful practitioner in the years to come.

Traditional View of Education

Education is a process of changing the behavior patterns of people. *Ralph Tyler*[23]

The ultimate goal of the educational process is to help human beings become educated persons. Schooling is the preparatory stage: it forms the habit of learning and provides the means for continuing to learn after the schooling process is completed. *Mortimer Adler*[24]

The purpose of public education today is what it always has been: to raise the intellectual level of the American people as a whole. Certain intellectual disciplines are fundamental to the public school curriculum because they are fundamental to modern life. *Arthur Bestor*[25]

Cultural literacy is the network of information that all competent readers possess. It is background information, stored in their minds, that enables them to take up a newspaper, and read it with an adequate level of comprehension.

The failure of schools to create a literate society is sometimes excused on the grounds that the schools have been asked to do too much. There is a pressing need for clarity about our educational priorities.

This author proposes for individuals to agree on the specific items of information that literate people currently share and on the necessity of communicating them in education. *E. Hirsch*[26]

Progressive, Radical, and Post-Modern

Traditional education consists of bodies of information (subjects) and of skills that have been worked out in the past. Progressive education cultivates individuality and acquiring skills to make the most of the opportunities of the present life. *John Dewey*[27]

Capitalism, with its emphasis on individuality and competition, is incompatible with the morals of democracy . . . America is the scene of an irreconcilable conflict between two opposing forces. On the one hand is the democratic tradition inherited from the past; on the other hand is a system of economic arrangements which increasingly partakes of the nature of industrial feudalism. Both of these forces cannot survive; one or the other must give way. Unless the democratic tradition is able to organize a successful attack on the economic system, its complete destruction is inevitable. *George Counts*[28]

Reconstructionism evolved based on the premise that social change is inevitable. Since it is inevitable, social change is best when it is directed as opposed to the result of natural drift. While many social groups are eager to direct social change, teachers should be the architects of the new social order as they are the most dedicated to democratic values, knowledgeable about social trends, and occupy the most strategic position to elicit change. *W. B. Stanley*[29]

I believe a new sense of educational order will emerge, as well as a new relation between teachers and students, culminating in a new concept of curriculum. The linear, sequential, easily quantifiable ordering system dominating education today could easily give way to a more complex, pluralistic, unpredictable system or network. Such a complex network, like life itself, would always be in transition, in process. *William Doll, Jr.*[30]

We should develop a system where students have the opportunity to experience the meanings of creating, love, knowing, and organizing; the components needed for the future. *Louise Berman*[31]

Schools should be disestablished because they have a polarizing effect on society. Deschooling means an end to submission to an obligatory curriculum.
    A primary alteration in the present educational system would entail the abolishment of the definition of school as an age-specific, instructor-related defined curriculum process that is mandatory for all for a specified period of time . . . we are taught in school that valuable learning is the result of attendance; that the value of learning increases with the amount of input; and that this value can be measured, and documented by grades and certificates. *Ivan Illich*[32]

Curriculum is not neutral knowledge. The knowledge included in textbooks is the result of political, economic, and cultural activities, battles, and compromises . . . separation between education and politics is a myth.
    The language of learning tends to be apolitical and ahistorical, thus hiding the complex political and economic resources that lies behind a considerable amount of curriculum organization and selection.
    The study of educational knowledge is a study of ideology, the investigation of what is considered legitimate knowledge by specific groups and classes and specified institutions in specified historical moments . . . it is based on a de-integrative strategy which attempts to disenfranchise groups considered to be outside the mainstream (e.g., African Americans). *Michael Apple*[33]

The educational system perpetuates the class structure. Education should be viewed as reproducing inequality by legitimizing the allocation of individuals to economic positions on the basis of ostensibly objective merit. *S. Bowles and H. Gintis*[34]

Education is that terrain where power and politics are given fundamental expression, since it is where meaning, desire, language, and values engage and respond to the deeper beliefs about the very nature of what it means to be human.
    Education represents a struggle for meaning and power. For the dominating class it becomes a political and social act that perpetuates a "culture of silence" among the masses and functions for the purpose of domestication . . . in the context of oppressive

societies, education is dehumanizing and mechanistic and imparts the transference of knowledge. Schools have served as the mechanism for maintaining social control.

The poor, voluntarily or involuntarily, knowingly or unknowingly, have been led by the rich and powerful to define themselves as naturally ignorant and inferior. Their minds have been invaded. They see reality with the outlook of the invaders rather than their own . . . and the more they mimic the invaders, the more stable the dominant position of the latter becomes . . . as long as the poor perceive themselves to be powerless, they will remain so. *Paulo Freire*[35]

Curriculum, by its very nature, is a social and historical construction that links knowledge and power in very specific ways. Curriculum, along with its representative courses, is never value-free or objective. Its function is to name and privilege particular histories and experiences. In its current dominant form, it does so in such a way as to marginalize or silence the voices of subordinate groups.

There is no agreed upon meaning for the term postmodern. It is certainly a rejection of grand narratives and any form of totalizing thought. It embraces diversity and locality. It creates a world where individuals must make their own way, where knowledge is constantly changing, and where meaning can no longer be anchored in history. *Henry Giroux*[36]

More advanced technology has hit the schools at about the same time as have ideas for school restructuring. *Howard Mehlinger*[37]

Radical educational theory has brought to focus several relevant issues for the future: a) the political nature of schooling and the influence of the dominant culture b) the potential for schools to serve as resistance to the dominant order and c) the power of teachers to impact change. *P. G. Altbach*[38]

SUMMARY

Throughout this century, divergent opinions about education have led to efforts to reform the American public school. Because these efforts continue today, curriculum leaders should be aware of the multiple curriculum designs in existence and be open to new thinking about how schools and educational programs are organized.

Six designs have been prominent in the American experience: educational conservatism, technological designs, humanistic designs, vocational designs, social reconstruction designs, and deschooling designs. Such diversity has unquestionably enriched the programs of the American public school. The future holds multiple possibilities for education in the United States. Curriculum development is the vehicle by which schools will approach the unknown future in planning education.

Studies of the future reveal that we have experienced enormous changes in the American society during the last quarter of the twentieth century. It is probable that the rate and scale of change in our society will continue in the twenty-first century.

Planning for the future of education is made difficult by impermanence in our society, by cultural lag in educational institutions, and by the inefficiency of traditional linear projections of the future. Educational futurists have responded to these conditions by using projection and prediction techniques to attempt to attract schools to preferred futures.

There are numerous conceptions of what education should be like in the future. Some educators favor decentralized programs focused on the individual or specific publics in the American society. Others favor highly centralized programs that serve the state. School districts throughout the United States have responded to these options during the past twenty-five years by pursuing diverse and multiple ends for education.

The exact nature of educational programs in the United States in the first decades of the twenty-first century will be heavily influenced by the thoughts and work of curriculum specialists. The challenge to all curriculum workers is to think about the meaning of education in our society and present viable alternatives to the sponsoring public.

SUGGESTED LEARNING ACTIVITIES

1. State in three sentences or fewer what you believe to be the purpose of formal education in the United States.
2. Try to brainstorm likely changes in our society during the coming decade. How will such changes affect public school education? Which of your identified changes will have the greatest impact on educational planning?
3. Develop a list of ways in which the public schools might incorporate future thinking into their daily operations. How might curriculum specialists in public schools become more aware of alternatives in education?
4. Describe the purposes of tech-prep/school-to-work programs.
5. Compare at least two reform movements of the past with two recent reform movements (e.g., performance contracting of the 1970s vs. charter schools of the 1990s).

NOTES

1. U.S. Department of Education—National Center for Educational Statistics, 1996.
2. U.S. Dept. of Education, National Center of Education Statistics, 1997.
3. R. Freeman Butts, "Assault on a Great Idea," *The Nation* (April 30, 1973): 553–60.
4. Butts, "Assault on a Great Idea."
5. Robert M. Hutchins, *The Restoration of Learning* (New York: Knopf, 1955).
6. Mortimer Adler, *The Paideia Proposal* (New York: Macmillan, 1982).
7. J. Wayne Wrightstone, *Appraisal of Experimental Schools* (New York: Bureau of Publications, Teachers College, Columbia University, 1936).
8. B. F. Skinner, *Beyond Freedom and Dignity* (New York: Knopf, 1971), p. 169.
9. John and Evelyn Dewey, *Schools of Tomorrow* (New York: Dutton and Company, 1915).
10. The Progressive Education Association, *Thirty Schools Tell Their Story*, Vol. 5 (New York: Harper and Brothers, 1943), p. 166.
11. Norman Grubb, "The New Vocationalism: What It Is, What It Can Be," *Kappan* 77, 8 (April, 1996): 528–34.
12. Maurice Dulton, "Tech Prep/School-to-Work: Career Paths for All," *NASSD Bulletin*, January, 1996, pp. 61–63.
13. Donald M. Clark, "Industry-Education Collaboration That Works," *Youth Record*, January, 1996, pp. 60–63.
14. Harold Rugg, *The Foundation and Techniques of Curriculum Making*, 26th Yearbook (Bloom-

ington, IN: National Society for the Study of Education, 1927), pp. 7–8.

15. Howard Garner, "Reflections on Multiple Intelligences: Myths and Messages," *Kappan* 77, 3 (November, 1995): 201–209.

16. Ivan Illich, "After Deschooling, What?" in Alan Gartner et al., eds., *After Deschooling, What?* (New York: Perennial Library, 1973), p. 1.

17. Allen A. Glatthorn, *Alternatives in Education: Schools and Programs* (New York: Dodd, Mead, and Company, 1975), pp. 117–36.

18. Mary Moynatian, "Parents Opt for Home Schooling," *L. I. Business,* January, 1995, p. 28.

19. James Goenner, "Charter Schools: The Revitalization of Public Education," *Kappan* 78, 1 (September, 1996): 32–36.

20. Anne Lewis, "Public Schools, Choice, and Reform," *Kappan* 77, 3 (December, 1995): 267–58.

21. Carol Ascher, "Performance Contracting: A Forgotten Experiment in School Privatization," *Kappan* 77, 9 (May, 1996): 615–21.

22. Margaret Mead, *The School in American Culture (The Inglis Lecture, 1950)* (Cambridge, MA: Harvard University, Press, 1951), p. 236.

23. Ralph Tyler, *Basic Principles of Curriculum and Instruction* (Chicago: University of Chicago Press, 1949), p. 5.

24. Mortimer Adler, *The Paideia Proposal: An Educational Manifesto* (New York: Macmillan, 1982), p. 10.

25. Arthur Bestor, *The Restoration of Learning* (New York: Alfred A. Knopf, 1936), pp. 48–49.

26. E. D. Hirsch, *Cultural Literacy: What Every American Needs to Know* (Boston: Houghton-Mifflin, 1987), pp. 2, 26.

27. John Dewey, *Experience and Education* (New York: The Macmillan Company, 1938).

28. George Counts, *Dare the Schools Create A New Social Order?* (New York: Day Company, 1932), p. 45.

29. W. B. Stanley, *Curriculum for Utopia* (Albany: State University of New York Press, 1992).

30. William Doll, Jr., *A Post-Modern Perspective of Curriculum* (New York: Teachers College Press, 1993.

31. Louise Berman, *New Priorities in the Curriculum* (Columbus, OH: Charles Merrill, 1968.

32. Ivan Illich, *Deschooling Society* (New York: Harper, 1970), pp. 38, 108, 112.

33. Michael Apple, *Ideology and Curriculum* (New York: Routledge, 1990), pp. 29, 45. *Official Knowledge: Democratic Education in a Conservative Age* (New York: Routledge, 1993), pp. 4, 46.

34. S. Bowles and H. Gintis, *Schooling in Capitalist America* (New York: Bantam Books, 1976).

35. Paulo Freire, *The Politics of Education* (South Hadley, MA: Bergin and Garvey, 1985), pp. 9, 116. *Pedagogy of the Oppressed* (New York: Continuum, 1993), p. 33.

36. Stanley Aronowitz and Henry Giroux, *Postmodern Education* (Minneapolis: University of Minnesota Press, 1991), p. 96.

37. Howard Mehlinger, "School Reform in an Information Age," *Phi Delta Kappan,* February, 1996, p. 402.

38. P. G. Altbach, et al. *Textbooks in American Society* (Albany: State University of New York Press, 1991).

BOOKS TO REVIEW

Cruickshank, Donald. *Preparing America's Teachers.* Bloomington, IN: Phi Delta Kappa, 1996.

Guskev, Thomas, ed. *Communicating Student Learning.* Alexandria, VA: ASCD, 1996.

Johnson, Jean, et al. *Assignment Incomplete: The Unfinished Business of Education Reform.* New York: Public Agenda Foundation, 1995.

Medler, Alex, and Joe Nathan. *Charter-Schools—What Are They Up To?* Denver: Education Commission of the States, 1995.

Oldenquist, Andrew. *Can Democracy Be Taught?* Bloomington, IN: Phi Delta Kappa, 1996.

Pinar, William. *Understanding Curriculum: An Introduction to the Study of Historical and Contemporary Curriculum Discourses.* New York: P. Lang, 1995.

Tanner, Daniel, and Laurel Tanner. *Curriculum Development: Theory into Practice,* 3d ed. Upper Saddle River, NJ: Merrill/Prentice Hall, 1995.

Wishnietsky, Dan. *Brooks Global Studies Extended Year-Magnet School.* Bloomington, IN: Phi Delta Kappa, 1996.

APPENDIXES

appendix A

TRAINING PARADIGM FOR CURRICULUM DEVELOPERS

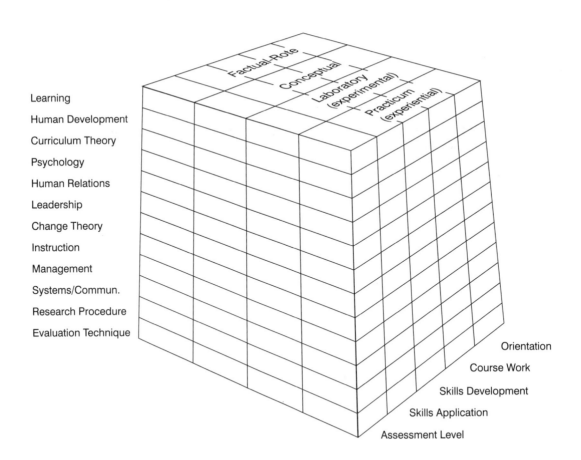

appendix B

PARTIAL LISTING OF ORGANIZATIONS AND ASSOCIATIONS AFFECTING AMERICAN EDUCATION

Citizens' Organizations
Council for Basic Education
725 15th Street, NW
Washington, DC 20005

National Coalition for Children
6542 Hitt Street
McLean, VA 22101

National Congress of Parents and Teachers
1715 25th Street
Rock Island, IL 61201

Educationally Related Organizations and Associations
American Association for Higher Education
One DuPont Circle, NW
Washington, DC 20036

American Association of School Administrators
1800 North Moore Street
Arlington, VA 22209

American Council on Education
One Dupont Circle, NW
Washington, DC 20036

American Educational Research Association
1230 17th Street, NW
Washington, DC 20036

American Vocational Association, Inc.
1510 H Street, NW
Washington, DC 20005

Association for Supervision and Curriculum Development (ASCD)
125 N. West Street
Washington, DC 20006

Children's Television Workshop
One Lincoln Plaza
New York, NY 10023

College Entrance Examination Board
888 7th Avenue
New York, NY 10019

Council for American Private Education
1625 I Street, NW
Washington, DC

Council of Chief State School Officers
1201 16th Street, NW
Washington, DC 20036

International Reading Association
800 Barksdale Road
Newark, DE

Joint Council on Economic Education
1212 Avenue of the Americas
New York, NY 10036

National Art Education Association
1916 Association Drive
Reston, VA 22091

National Association for Education of Young Children
1834 Connecticut Avenue
Washington, DC

National Association of Elementary School Principals
1801 North Moore Street
Arlington, VA 22209

National Association for Public Continuing Adult
Education
1201 16th Street, NW
Washington, DC 20036

National Association of Secondary School Principals
1904 Association Drive
Reston, VA 22091

National Council of Teachers of English
1111 Kenyon Road
Urbana, IL 61801

National Council of Teachers of Mathematics
1906 Association Drive
Reston, VA 22091

National Education Association
1201 16th Street, NW
Washington, DC 20036

National Middle School Association
P.O. Box 968
Fairborn, OH 45324

National School Boards Association
800 State National Bank Plaza
Evanston, IL 60204

National Science Teachers Association
1742 Connecticut Avenue, NW
Washington, DC 20009

Ethnic and Minority Organizations

Bilingual Education Service Center
500 South Dwyer
Arlington Heights, IL 60005

National Council of Negro Women, Inc.
1346 Connecticut Avenue, NW
Washington, DC 20036

National Indian Education Association
3036 University Avenue, SE
Minneapolis, MN 55419

National Organization for Women (NOW)
1401 New York Avenue, NW
Suite 800
Washington, DC 20005

General Associations

Committee for Economic Development
477 Madison Avenue
New York, NY 10022

National Association of Manufacturers Economic
Development Department
1776 F Street, NW
Washington, DC 20006

National Urban League
500 E. 62nd St.
New York, NY 10021

Labor Organizations

American Federation of Teachers
555 New Jersey Avenue NW
Washington, DC 20001

Publishers

American Association of Publishers
One Park Avenue
New York, NY 10016

Association of Media Producers
1221 Avenue of the Americas
New York, NY 10020

Federal Bodies

House of Representatives
Capitol Building
Washington, DC 20001

National Institute of Education
555 New Jersey Avenue, NW
Washington, DC 20208

National Science Foundation
1800 G Street, NW
Washington, DC 20550

Office of Education
Office of the Assistant Secretary
Room 3153
400 Maryland Avenue, SW
Washington, DC 20202

U.S. Senate
Capitol Building
Washington, DC 20001

appendix C

INTERNET SITES: CURRICULUM RELATED

ASCD Web: http://www.ascd.org/index

Alphabetical Index of ASCD Book Titles:
http://www.ascd.org/market/resources/books/list

Education Law Institute: http://www.fplc.edu/ediconf

International Association for Evaluation of Educational Achievement (IEA):
http://uttou2.to.utwente.nl/

Public Service Curriculum Exchange: http://cases.pubaf.washington.edu/0c:/ps.html/

GNN Education Center Home Page: http://gnn.com/gnn/meta/edu/index.html

GLOSSARY

ability grouping Organizing pupils into homogeneous groups according to intellectual ability for instruction.

academic freedom The right of instructors to decide the materials, methods, and content of instruction within legal and ethical parameters.

accountability Holding schools and teachers responsible for what students learn.

accreditation Recognition given to an educational institution that has met accepted standards applied to it by an outside agency.

achievement test Standardized test designed to measure how much has been learned from a particular subject.

affective domain Attitudinal and emotional areas of learning, such as values and feelings.

aligned A term used to indicate a school curriculum is matched with state and national standards as well as with state and national tests.

alternative education Instructional programs that modify traditional approaches in one or more of the following areas: setting, structure, scheduling, instructional materials, curriculum development, and assessment.

alternative school A school—public or private—that provides alternatives to the regular public school.

anecdotal record A narrative accounting of students' academic and social-emotional behaviors.

attribution training Training that deals with the role of the individual's explanation for his or her own successes or failures.

balanced curriculum Incorporates all three areas: essential learning skills, subject content, and personal development.

behavioral approach An approach that focuses on observable behaviors instead of on internal events such as thinking and emotions.

behavioral objective Precise statement of what the learner must do to demonstrate mastery at the end of a prescribed learning task.

bilingual education Educational programs in which both English-speaking and non-English-speaking students participate in a bicultural curriculum using both languages.

block scheduling The reorganization of the daily or annual school schedule to allow students and teachers to have larger, more concentrated segments of time each day, week, or grading period on each subject. *See also* modular scheduling.

career education Instructional activities designed to provide students with the knowledge and skill necessary for selecting a vocation as well as for making decisions regarding educational and training options.

categorical aid Financial aid to local school districts from state or federal agencies for specific, limited purposes only.

certification   The licensure of personnel through prescribed programs of training and education.

cognition   Process of logical thinking.

cognitive domain   In Bloom's Taxonomy, memory and reasoning objectives.

cognitive learning   Academic learning of subject matter.

common planning time   A scheduling procedure that allows teachers to share the same period for instructional planning. The provision of common planning times facilitates collaborative efforts between teachers.

competency   The demonstrated ability to perform specified acts at a particular level of skill or accuracy.

competency-based instruction   Instructional programming that measures learning through the demonstration of predetermined outcomes. Mastery is assessed through an evaluation of the process as well as the product.

conditioning   Reinforcing learning through repetitive response.

cooperative learning   Two or more students working together on a learning task.

continued learning   Refers to skills used in all disciplines, e.g., reading, writing, research skills.

core (fused) curriculum   Integration of two or more subjects; for example, English and social studies. Problem and theme orientations often serve as the integrating design. *See also* interdisciplinary program.

crisis intervention center   A resource room within a school that contains special materials and equipment as well as a specially trained teacher. These rooms are designed to be used for a brief period of time (one hour—one week) when a general education teacher is unable to provide adequate attention to a student in need of more intensive services. Counseling may be provided.

criterion-referenced evaluation   Evaluation that measures success by the attainment of established levels of performance. Individual success is based wholly on the performance of the individual without regard to the performance of others.

criterion-referenced test   Measures of performance compared to predetermined standards or objectives.

cultural diversity   The existence of several different cultures within a group encouraging each group to keep its individual qualities within the larger society.

cultural pluralism   Cultural diversity; the existence of many different cultures within a group; encouraging different cultures to maintain their distinctive qualities within the larger society.

culture   The capacity for constantly expanding the range and accuracy of one's perception of meanings. An attempt to prepare human beings to add continuously to the meaning of their experiences.

curriculum   The total experiences planned for a school or students.

curriculum alignment   Matching learning activities with desired outcomes, or matching what is taught to what is tested.

curriculum compacting   Content development and delivery models that abbreviate the amount of time to cover a topic without compromising the depth and breadth of material taught.

curriculum guide   A written statement of objectives, content, and activities to be used with a particular subject at specified grade levels; usually produced by state departments of education or local education agencies.

curriculum management planning   A systematic method of planning for change (Wiles-Bondi Curriculum Management Plan Model).

deductive learning   Instructional materials and activities that allow students to discover the specific attributes of a concept through an exploration that moves from the general to the particular.

departmentalization   The division of instructional staff, resources, and classes by academic disciplines; service delivery models such as separate general and special education programming; or some other arbitrary structure for compartmentalization.

developmental physical education   Instruction based on the physical development of the individual preadolescent learner, as opposed to a team sports approach.

developmental tasks   Social, physical, maturational tasks regularly encountered by all individuals in our society as they progress from childhood to adolescence.

discovery learning   A type of inquiry, emphasized especially in individualized instruction, in which a student moves through his or her own activities toward new learnings, usually expressed in generalizations and principles; typically involves inductive approaches. *See also* inductive learning.

early adolescence   Stage of human development generally between age 10 and 14 when individuals begin to reach puberty.

educational goals   A statement of expectations for students or a school program.

environmental approach   An approach to learning that is concerned with the restructuring of the learning environment or the students' perceptions so they may be free to develop.

epistemology   A branch of philosophy that examines (a) how knowledge is gained, (b) how much can be known, and (c) what justification there is for what is known.

essential learning skills   Basic skills, such as reading, listening, and speaking that are introduced in the elementary school and reinforced in the middle and high school.

essentialism   A philosophy rooted in idealism and realism that began in the l930s as a reaction to progressivism. Reading, writing, and arithmetic are the focus in elementary schools. English, mathematics, science, history, and foreign language comprise the secondary curriculum. Essentialism is subject centered like perennialism, but maintains a contemporary orientation. The arts and vocational education are rejected.

exploration   Regularly scheduled curriculum experiences designed to help students discover and/or examine learnings related to their changing needs, aptitudes, and interests. Often referred to as the *wheel* or *miniclasses. See also* minicourses.

extinction   Conditioning learning by withdrawing reinforcement.

feedback   Evidence from student responses and reactions that indicates the degree of success being encountered in lesson objectives. Teachers seek feedback by way of discussion, student questions, written exercises, and test returns.

flexible scheduling   Provisions in scheduling allowing for variance in length of time, order, or rotation of classes.

formal operations   The last state in Piaget's theory of cognitive development characterized by an ability to manipulate concepts abstractly and apply logical methods in the solution of complex

problems. Children are not generally expected to exhibit these abilities before 11 to 15 years of age.

formative evaluation   A method of assessment that occurs before or during instruction to (a) guide teacher planning or (b) identify students' needs.

gifted learner   The term most frequently applied to those with exceptional intellectual ability, but may also refer to learners with outstanding ability in athletics, leadership, music, creativity, and so forth.

global education   Instructional strategies and curriculum frameworks that include multiple, diverse, and international resources through the use of technology.

goal displacement   Inadvertently letting the attainment of the goal replace the purpose for having the goal.

goals, educational   Desired learning outcomes stated for a group of students and requiring from several weeks to several years to attain.

graded school system   A division of schools into groups of students according to the curriculum or the ages of pupils as in the six elementary grades.

heterogeneous grouping   Student grouping that does not divide learners on the basis of ability or academic achievement.

homogeneous grouping   Student grouping that divides learners on the basis of specific levels of ability, achievement, or interest. Sometimes referred to as *tracking*.

house plan   Type of organization in which the school is divided into units ("houses"), with each having an identity and containing the various grades and, in large part, its own faculty. The purpose of a house plan is to achieve decentralization (closer student–faculty relationships) and easier and more flexible team-teaching arrangements.

identification   A defense mechanism in which we identify a part of ourselves with another person.

imitation   A process where students learn by modeling the behavior of others.

innovation   New instructional strategy, organizational design, building modification from which improved learning results are anticipated.

in-service education   Continuing education for teachers who are actually teaching, or who are in service.

independent study   Work performed by students without the direct supervision of the teacher to develop self-study skills and to expand and deepen interests.

individualized education plan (IEP) The mechanism through which a handicapped child's special needs are identified; goals, objectives, and services are outlined; and methods for evaluating progress are delineated.

individualized instruction Instruction that focuses on the interests, needs, and achievements of individual learners.

inductive learning Instructional materials and activities designed to assist students in the acquisition of knowledge through the master of specific subskills that lead to more general concepts and processes.

innovations New instructional strategies, organizational designs, building rearrangements, equipment utilizations, or materials from which improved learning results are anticipated.

integration of disciplines The organization of objectives under an interdisciplinary topic that allows students to utilize skills and knowledge from more than one content area within a given instructional activity or unit of study.

interdisciplinary program Instruction that integrates and combines subject matter ordinarily taught separately into a single organizational structure.

interdisciplinary team Combination of teachers from different subject areas who plan and conduct coordinated lessons in those areas for particular groups of pupils. Common planning time, flexible scheduling, and cooperation and communication among team teachers is essential to interdisciplinary teaming.

interscholastic program Athletic activities or events whose primary purpose is to foster competition between school and school districts. Participation usually is limited to students with exceptional athletic ability.

intramural (intrascholastic) program Athletic activities or events held during the school day, or shortly thereafter, whose primary purpose is to encourage all students to participate regardless of athletic ability.

learning A change of behavior as a result of experience.

learning center Usually a large multimedia area designed to influence learning and teaching styles and to foster independent study. Also called a *learning station.*

least restrictive environment The program best suited to meet a handicapped child's special needs while remaining as close as possible to the regular educational program.

magnet program A specialized school program usually designed to draw minority students to schools that historically have been racially segregated. School-based programs are developed around a common theme, discipline, theory, or philosophy. Performing arts, mathematics, and medical fields are representative of the curriculum and instructional components on which magnet programs have been built.

mainstreaming A plan by which exceptional children receive special education in the regular classroom as much of the time as possible.

metacognition Process by which individuals examine their own thinking processes.

middle school A school in between elementary and high school, housed separately, ideally in a building designed for its purpose, and covering usually three of the middle school years, beginning with grade 5 or 6.

minicourses Special-interest (enrichment) activities of short duration that provide learning opportunities based on student interest, faculty expertise, and community involvement. Also called *exploratory courses, short-interest-centered courses,* or *electives.*

minimum competency testing Exit-level tests designed to ascertain whether students have achieved basic levels of performance in such areas as reading, writing, and computation.

mission statement A statement of the goals or intent of a school.

model A written or drawn description used to improve the understanding.

modeling Demonstrating a behavior, lesson, or teaching style.

modular scheduling The division of the school day into modules, typically fifteen or twenty minutes long, with the number of modules used for various activities and experiences flexibly arranged.

multicultural education Educational goals and methods that teach students the value of cultural diversity.

need-structured approach   A learning theory which is concerned with the needs and drives of students and seeks to use such natural motivational energy to promote learning.

nongraded school   A type of school organization in which grade lines are eliminated for a sequence of two or more years.

nonverbal communication   The act of transmitting and/or receiving messages through any means not having to do with oral or written language, such as eye contact, facial expressions, or body language.

norm-referenced grading   A student's performance is evaluated by comparing it to the performance of others.

normal learning curve   The expected progress of the average student in a class.

normal school   Historically, the first American institution devoted exclusively to teacher training.

paraprofessional   A person employed by a school, program, or district to assist a certified professional and extend the services provided to the students. The paraprofessional may have entry-level training but is not a fully licensed educator or therapist.

performance objective   Targeted outcome measures for evaluating the learning of particular process-based skills and knowledge.

personal development   Designed to foster intellectual, social, emotional, and moral growth of students through such programs as adviser/advisee, developmental physical education, and minicourses.

portfolio, learner's   A diversified combination of samples of a student's quantitative and qualitative work.

process-pattern learning   Learning design that focuses on each student's experience rather than on a predetermined body of information.

progressive education   An educational philosophy emphasizing democracy, the importance of creative and meaningful activity, the real needs of students, and the relationship between school and community.

readiness   The point at which a student is intellectually, physically, or socially able to learn a concept or exhibit a particular behavior.

reinforcement   Strengthening behavior through supportive action.

restructuring   Changing a school's entire program and procedure as opposed to changing only one part of the curriculum.

scaffolding   Providing a context for student learning, such as an outline or question stem (Vygotsky).

schema theory   In cognitive learning, large basic units for organizing information. Schemata serve as guides describing what to expect in a given situation.

scope   The parameters of learning; for example, a subject-matter discipline sets its own scope, often by grade level.

self-contained classroom   A form of classroom organization in which the same teacher conducts all or nearly all of the instruction in all or most subjects in the same classroom for all or most of the school day.

semantic mapping   Organizing meanings in language.

sequence   The organization of an area of study. Frequently the organization is chronological, moving from simple to complex. Some sequences are spiraled, using structure, themes, or concept development as guidelines. A few schools use persistent life situations to shape sequence.

social competence   The ability to interact positively with persons and groups.

special learning center   A designated area of a classroom, media center, or some other setting on the school campus with materials and activities designed to (a) enrich the existing educational program or (b) provide students with additional drill and practice in a targeted skill.

staff development   Body of activities designed to improve the proficiencies of the educator-practitioner.

subject content   A type of curriculum that stresses the mastery of subject matter, with all other outcomes considered subsidiary. Also called *subject-matter curriculum*. See also homogeneous grouping.

support personnel   Ancillary personnel such as guidance, media, custodial, clerical, and social services persons who help facilitate the instructional program.

teacher empowerment   Policies and procedures that enlarge the scope of decisions that educators are allowed to make individually as well as in collaboration with others. Curriculum, instructional materials, budget, scheduling, and pupil assignments in particular classes are a few of the areas that practitioners are increasingly called upon to address.

team teaching   A plan by which several teachers, organized into a team with a leader, provide the instruction for a larger group of children than would usually be found in a self-contained classroom.

tracking   The method of grouping students according to their ability level in homogeneous classes or learning experiences.

TTT (Teachers Training Teachers)   In-service process by which teachers receive instruction from peers, usually at the school level.

transfer   In learning, shaping the student to a predetermined form by connecting behavior with response.

unified arts   Would include all nonacademic subjects such as the fine arts, vocational education, and physical education.

unified studies   Also known as integrated or interdisciplinary studies. Combines subjects around themes or problems.

unstructured time   Periods of time during the school day that have not been designated for a specific purpose and that present students with less supervision. The time between finishing lunch and the bell to return to the classroom is an example of unstructured time.

voucher plan   Governmental funding programs that allow students and their parents to select among options for schooling by providing predetermined tuition allotments that can be applied to private or public institutions.

work-study program   Collaborative efforts between the school and community-based employers that allow students to earn course credit for time spent working. Students attend school for a designated number of periods per day and work a predetermined number of hours per week. Grades for work in the community are assigned based on the number of hours worked and the evaluation of the employer.

AUTHOR INDEX

SUBJECT INDEX

ISBN 0-13-262098-7

90000